The Sikhs of the Punjab
Revised Edition

In a revised edition of his original book, J. S. Grewal brings the history of
the Sikhs, from its beginnings in the time of Guru Nanak, the founder of
Sikhism, right up to the present day. Against the background of the history
of the Punjab, the volume surveys the changing pattern of human
settlements in the region until the fifteenth century and the emergence of
the Punjabi language as the basis of regional articulation. Subsequent
chapters explore the life and beliefs of Guru Nanak, the development of
his ideas by his successors and the growth of his following. The book
offers a comprehensive statement on one of the largest and most important
communities in India today

J. S. GREWAL is Director of the Institute of Punjab Studies in
Chandigarh. He has written extensively on India, the Punjab, and the
Sikhs. His books on Sikh history include *Guru Nanak in History* (1969),
Sikh Ideology, Polity and Social Order (1996), *Historical Perspectives on
Sikh Identity* (1997) and *Contesting Interpretations of the Sikh Tradition*
(1998).

THE NEW CAMBRIDGE HISTORY OF INDIA

General editor GORDON JOHNSON
President of Wolfson College, and Director, Centre of South Asian Studies,
University of Cambridge

Associate editors C. A. BAYLY
Vere Harmsworth Professor of Imperial and Naval History, University of Cambridge,
and Fellow of St Catharine's College

and JOHN F. RICHARDS
Professor of History, Duke University

Although the original *Cambridge History of India*, published between 1922 and 1937, did much to formulate a chronology for Indian history and describe the administrative structures of government in India, it has inevitably been overtaken by the mass of new research published over the past fifty years.

Designed to take full account of recent scholarship and changing conceptions of South Asia's historical development, *The New Cambridge History of India* will be published as a series of short, self-contained volumes, each dealing with a separate theme and written by a single person. Within an overall four-part structure, thirty-one complementary volumes in uniform format will be published. As before, each will conclude with a substantial bibliographical essay designed to lead non-specialists further into the literature.

The four parts planned are as follows:

I The Mughals and Their Contemporaries

II Indian states and the Transition to Colonialism

III The Indian Empire and the Beginnings of Modern Society

IV The Evolution of Contemporary South Asia

*A list of individual titles in preparation will be found
at the end of the volume.*

THE NEW CAMBRIDGE HISTORY OF INDIA

II.3

The Sikhs of the Punjab

Revised Edition

J. S. GREWAL

CAMBRIDGE
UNIVERSITY PRESS

† Available in paperback
PUBLISHED BY THE PRESS SYNDICATE OF THE UNIVERSITY OF CAMBRIDGE
The Pitt Building, Trumpington Street, Cambridge CB2 1RP, United Kingdom

CAMBRIDGE UNIVERSITY PRESS
The Edinburgh Building, Cambridge, CB2 2RU, UK   http://www.cup.cam.ac.uk
40 West 20th Street, New York, NY 10011-4211, USA   http://www.cup.org
10 Stamford Road, Oakleigh, Melbourne 3166, Australia

First published 1990

Reprinted 1994, 1998
First paperback edition 1998

Typeset in Sabon [CE]

British Library cataloguing in publication data
Grewal J. S.
The Sikhs of the Punjab. – (The New Cambridge History of India: II:3)
1. India (Republic). Sikhs, history
I. Title
954′.00882946

Library of Congress cataloguing in publication data
Grewal, J. S.
The Sikhs of the Punjab/J. S. Grewal.
p.   cm. – (The New Cambridge history of India: II.3)
Includes bibliographical references.
ISBN 0 521 26884 2
1. Sikhs–History
2. Punjab (India)–History.
I. Title.
II. Series.
DS436.N47 1987 pt. 2. vol. 3
[DS485.P3]
954′.5′0882946–dc20
89–17348
CIP

ISBN 0 521 26884 2 hardback
ISBN 0 521 63764 3 paperback

Transferred to digital printing 2003

For
Reeta, Aneeta, Harinder, Ravinder
Tara, Sharan, Ranbir and Manek

CONTENTS

MAPS

GENERAL EDITOR'S PREFACE

The New Cambridge History of India covers the period from the beginning of the sixteenth century. In some respects it marks a radical change in the style of Cambridge Histories, but in others the editors feel that they are working firmly within an established academic tradition.

During the summer of 1896, F.W. Maitland and Lord Acton between them evolved the idea for a comprehensive modern history. By the end of the year the Syndics of the University Press had committed themselves to the *Cambridge Modern History*, and Lord Acton had been put in charge of it. It was hoped that publication would begin in 1899 and be completed by 1904, but the first volume in fact came out in 1902 and the last in 1910, with additional volumes of tables and maps in 1911 and 1912.

The *History* was a great success, and it was followed by a whole series of distinctive Cambridge Histories covering English Literature, the Ancient World, India, British Foreign Policy, Economic History, Medieval History, the British Empire, Africa, China and Latin America; and even now other new series are being prepared. Indeed, the various Histories have given the Press notable strength in the publication of general reference books in the arts and social sciences.

What has made the Cambridge Histories so distinctive is that they have never been simply dictionaries or encyclopaedias. The Histories have, in H.A.L. Fisher's words, always been 'written by an army of specialists concentrating the latest results of special study'. Yet as Acton agreed with the Syndics in 1896, they have not been mere compilations of existing material but original works. Undoubtedly many of the Histories are uneven in quality, some have become out of date very rapidly, but their virtue has been that they have consistently done more than simply record an existing state of knowledge: they have tended to focus interest on research and they have provided a massive stimulus to further work. This has made their publication doubly worthwhile and has distinguished them intellectually from other sorts of reference book. The Editors of the *New Cambridge History of India* have acknowledged this in their work.

The original *Cambridge History of India* was published between 1922 and 1937. It was planned in six volumes, but of these, Volume 2 dealing with the period between the first century A.D. and the Muslim invasion of India never appeared. Some of the material is still of value, but in many respects it is now out of date. The last fifty years have seen a great deal of new research on India, and a striking feature of recent work has been to cast doubt on the validity of the quite arbitrary chronological and categorical way in which Indian history has been conventionally divided.

The Editors decided that it would not be academically desirable to prepare a new *History of India* using the traditional format. The selective nature of research on Indian history over the last half-century would doom such a project from the start and the whole of Indian history could not be covered in an even or comprehensive manner. They concluded that the best scheme would be to have a History divided into four overlapping chronological volumes, each containing about eight short books on individual themes or subjects. Although in extent the work will therefore be equivalent to a dozen massive tomes of the traditional sort, in form the *New Cambridge History of India* will appear as a shelf full of separate but complementary parts. Accordingly, the main divisions are between I *The Mughals and their Contemporaries*, II *Indian States and the Transition to Colonialism*, III *The Indian Empire and the Beginnings of Modern Society*, and IV *The Evolution of Contemporary South Asia*.

Just as the books within these volumes are complementary so too do they intersect with each other, both thematically and chronologically. As the books appear they are intended to give a view of the subject as it now stands and to act as a stimulus to further research. We do not expect the *New Cambridge History of India* to be the last word on the subject but an essential voice in the continuing discourse about it.

PREFACE

Writing his *History of the Sikhs* in the 1960s Khushwant Singh looked upon J. D. Cunningham as his predecessor whose work, written over a century earlier, had become a classic. Khushwant Singh himself has written with 'power and passion' under 'masterly restraint'. That the present volume takes into account the research on Sikh history during the past two decades may be regarded as its major claim upon the reader's attention. It touches upon religious, social, political, economic, cultural and demographic developments over the entire span of Sikh history.

Within the broad context of Indian history, Sikh history falls into four well-marked periods: from its beginning with the mission of Guru Nanak to the death of Guru Gobind Singh in 1708; from the rise of Banda Bahadur to the annexation of the Punjab by the British in 1849; the near century of colonial rule up to 1947; and the four decades of Independence. During the past century historians of the Sikhs have concentrated on the first two periods. Interest in the colonial period goes back only to the 1960s. The movement for a Punjabi-speaking state and the crisis culminating in the Operation Bluestar in June 1984 have induced many a writer to take interest in the history of the Sikhs in independent India. This broad pattern of historiography is reflected in the treatment of Sikh history in the present volume: generalizations yield more and more place to factual though analytical narrative as we pass from one period to another in an attempt to identify change.

For an invitation to pursue a subject which had been my major occupation for two decades, I am thankful to the Syndics of the Cambridge University Press; I am equally thankful to the editors of *The New Cambridge History of India* for leaving me all the freedom I needed to write this volume.

I am indebted to many scholars and institutions for help, but I would like to mention specifically Professor Indu Banga and Professor W. H. McLeod among the scholars, and the Nehru Memorial Museum and Library, New Delhi, the Indian Council of Historical Research, New Delhi, Guru Nanak Dev University, Amritsar, and the Indian Institute

of Advanced Study, Shimla, among the institutions. Dr Veena Sachdeva, Dr Radha Sharma and Dr Harish Sharma have helped me the
most from amongst my colleagues and research students. I am thankful
to Jaswant Singh and T. K. Majumdar for secretarial help, and to O. P.
Sarna for cartographic assistance. N. K. Maini has helped me in
checking the proofs and in preparing the index.

My wife, Harjinder, gave me all the care and affection I needed for
completing this study through the 1980s.

P.S.

Since the publication of this book in 1990, the publishers have found
its sales satisfactory enough to bring out a paperback edition. The
author has taken the opportunity to bring its Epilogue up to 1997, to
add to its Chronology events from 1849 onwards, to replace its maps
for better cartographic representation, to update the Bibliographical
Essay, and to make necessary 'corrections' in the text, footnotes and
the Index.

GLOSSARY

'adālatī	a touring justice under Sikh rule.
akālī	a staunch follower of Guru Gobind Singh; in the early nineteenth century equated with the Nihang; in the twentieth century, initially a volunteer to take over Sikh temples and afterwards a member of the Shiromani Akali Dal.
akhand-pāṭh	'unbroken reading'; an uninterrupted reading of the entire Ādi Granth performed by a team of readers.
akhāṛa	arena; a temple or monastery of the Udāsīs.
a'lā mālik	a 'superior owner', entitled to a certain share in the produce from land; also called *ta'alluqdār* or *biswedār*.
'āmil	a revenue collector; interchangeable with *kārdār* as the administrator of a *ta'alluqa* under Sikh rule.
ardās	the Sikh prayer.
ardāsia	literally, one who offers *ardās*; a person employed by Sikh rulers and *jāgīrdārs* for this purpose.
auliyā	plural of *walī*, a favourite or friend of God; saints.
avtār	'descent'; incarnation of a deity, usually Vishnu.
bairāgī	a renunciant, usually a Vaishnavite.
bandh	to stop work as a mark of protest; a method of agitation; a strike.
bāṇī	speech; the utterances of the Gurus and *bhaktas* recorded in the Ādi Granth; the amplified form *gurbāṇī* or *bhagat-baṇi* is commonly used.
bār	the upland between two river valleys in the Punjab plains.

bemukh	'without face'; one who has turned away from the Guru.
bhāi	'brother'; a Sikh formally connected with religious affairs; an epithet of respect.
bhandār	store; a storehouse; a place for the preparation and distribution of food in religious institutions.
bhandārī	one who looks after a *bhandār*.
bhāt	a popular bard who also kept genealogies of important families.
bhog	conclusion of the reading of the Ādi Granth, followed generally by singing of hymns and always by an *ardās*.
bigha	a measure of land generally considered equal to 20 *biswās* or 2 *kanāls*; also one-half of a *ghumāon*; the actual size varied from region to region
bīmā	insurance.
bīrādār	a local representative of the Nirankārī Guru.
biswedār	'the holder of a twentieth part'; a person entitled to a certain share in the produce from land; also called *a'lā mālik* or *ta'alluqdār*.
chaṇḍī-pāṭh	a ceremony observed by the Nāmdhārīs in which Guru Gobind Singh's composition on the Goddess Chaṇḍi was recited over a fire kept burning; also called *hom*.
chaudharī	the hereditary headman of a group of villages for collecting revenues on behalf of the government.
chelā	a disciple.
daftar-i-mu'allā	the exalted office; a term used for the central secretariat of Maharaja Ranjit Singh.
dal khālsā	a term used for the combined forces of the Sikhs during the eighteenth century.
dām	a small coin, equal to one-fortieth of a silver rupee in the Mughal times; equated in due course with *paisa*.

deoḍhī	entrance hall; royal residence; the royal court.
deoḍhīdār	the keeper of the royal residence in the time of Maharaja Ranjit Singh.
derā	camp; encampment; a unit in the army of Maharaja Ranjit Singh and his successors; the place of a religious personage.
dhāḍī	a minstrel; among the Sikhs, a musician who used to sing in praise of the Sikh Gurus and recount the heroic deeds of the Sikhs.
dhaṛā	a factional group.
dharma	the appropriate moral and religious obligations attached to any particular section in Hindu society; duty, moral obligation; a righteous cause.
dharm-yudh	war in the cause of religion; a righteous war.
dīwān	the keeper of a treasury; the head of the finance department; an honorofic given to Hindu nobles by Maharaja Ranjit Singh and his successors.
doāb	an area lying between two rivers.
farmān	a royal order.
faujdār	one who keeps troops; a military officer under the Mughals whose duty in peace time was to maintain law and order and to assist civil authorities; the office survived into the early nineteenth century in the Punjab.
ghadar	'revolt'; revolution.
ghurcharha	literally a horse-rider; a traditional horseman in the kingdom of Lahore.
ghorcharhā-i-khās	a special cavalry raised by Maharaja Ranjit Singh to act as royal body-guards.
giānī	one who possesses knowledge (*giān*); among the Sikhs, a person well-versed in the scriptures.
granthī	a professional reader of the Granth; the functionary in charge of a *gurdwāra*.
gurbāṇī	'the utterance of the Guru'.
gurdwāra	'the door of the Guru'; a Sikh temple, generally also the centre of social activity.

gurmatā	a decision arrived at by a congregation of Sikhs, generally in the presence of the Granth Sahib.
gurmukhī	a script adopted by the first successor of Guru Nanak for recording his compositions and used subsequently by the Sikhs for writing Punjabi.
gursikh	a true Sikh of the Guru.
guru	preceptor; religious teacher; an epithet used for the founder of Sikhism and each of his nine successors, and also for the Granth Sahib and the Panth.
harmandir	'the temple of God'; the central Sikh shrine in Amritsar commonly known as the Golden Temple.
haumai	self-centredness.
havan	offering an oblation with fire.
holī	an important spring festival observed by sprinkling coloured powder or water on one another.
hukmnāma	'a written order'; used generally for the letters of the Sikh Gurus to their followers.
huṇḍī	a bill of exchange.
ijāra	an arrangement in which a certain source of income was placed in the charge of a person on the condition of his paying a certain stipulated sum to the state.
jāgīr	an assignment of land revenue in lieu of salary.
jāgīrdār	the holder of a *jāgīr*; an assignee.
jathā	a group, a band; used particularly for Akali volunteers during their agitations.
jathedār	the leader of a *jathā*; a leader-organizer of the Shiromani Akali Dal.
jhīwar	a water-carrier by caste.
jihād	'endeavour'; a crusade; a holy war.
jogī	from *yogī*, or one who practises *yoga*; a person belonging to any of the twelve orders of the followers of Gorakhnāth.
julāhā	a weaver by caste.
kachchī	unripe; spurious; false.
kalāl	a brewer or distiller by caste.

kaliyuga	the fourth and last of the cosmic ages; the age of degeneracy.
kampū-i-muʻallā	the exalted camp: a term used for the standing army of Maharaja Ranjit Singh.
kanpāṭā	'split-ear'; a follower of Gorakhnāth who wears rings in pierced ears.
kārdār	an agent; an official; generally used for the administrator at the *taʻalluqa* (or *pargana*) level under Sikh rule.
karhā-prasād	sacramental food dispensed in *gurdwāras*.
kārkhāna	a work house, a manufactory; generally maintained by rulers and members of the ruling class.
kesh	in Sikh literature, refers to uncut hair.
khālisa	lands from which revenues were collected directly by the state in contrast to land alienated in *jāgīr*, *dharmarth*, *inʻām* or any other kind of alienation.
khālsā	the Sikh brotherhood instituted by Guru Gobind Singh; used for an individual as well as for the collective body.
khande-kī-pauhl	the ceremony introduced by Guru Gobind Singh, in which a double-edged sword was used for preparing the water known as *amrit* to be drunk by the person baptized.
khānqah	a hospice; the establishment of a Sūfī Shaikh.
khatrī	from Kshatriya; an important caste in the Punjab.
khutba	a sermon, address; pronouncement made in Friday mosques regarding the ruler of the day.
kīkar	*babūl*, a hardy and thorny tree in the Punjab.
kirpān	a sword.
kīrtan	the singing of hymns from the sacred scriptures of the Sikhs; hence *kīrtan darbār* for an elaborate performance.
kotwāl	the official in charge of a fort; used generally for the city official meant to keep law and order.
laṇḍā	a script used by shopkeepers in the Punjab.

langar	the kitchen attached to a *gurdwāra* from which food is served to all regardless of caste or creed; a community meal.
lāvān	stanzas composed by Guru Ram Das for the solemnization of marriage.
madad-i-ma'āsh	literally, aid for subsistence; most commonly used in the Mughal times for land revenue alienated in favour of a religious personage or institution.
madrassa	a place where teaching is imparted; generally of high learning.
mahal	a revenue sub-division usually corresponding with *pargana*; also applied to a source of revenue.
mahzar	an attestation signed by a number of persons.
maktab	a place where books are taught; generally used for a school.
manmukh	self-oriented; one who follows his own impulses rather than the guidance of the Guru.
mansab	literally office, position of rank; indicating under the Mughals the status, obligations and remuneration of its holder in the official hierarchy.
mansabdār	the holder of a rank in the system evolved by the Mughal emperor Akbar and his successors; hence, the *mansabdārī* system.
maṛhī	a small structure raised over a spot of cremation.
masand	a representative appointed by the Guru to look after the affairs of a local congregation of Sikhs, or a number of such congregations.
mastāna	an intoxicated person; used for a Nāmdhārī who was so deeply affected by the singing of hymns that he behaved like an intoxicated person, shouting and moving in frenzy. It was because of such *mastānas* that the Nāmdhārīs were given the label *kūkā* (from *kūk* or shout) by others.
maṭh	a monastery; a religious establishment.

mātrās	religious writings of the Udāsīs.
mazār	a mausoleum; the tomb of a Sūfī Shaikh.
mīṇā	a derogatory epithet used for Prithi Chand, the elder brother of Guru Arjan, and also for his successors and their followers.
misl	a combination of Sikh leaders in the eighteenth century for the purpose of defence and for the occupation of territories.
morchā	an embrasure; an entrenchment for besieging a fort; used metaphorically by the Akalis for their non-violent agitations.
muftī	an expounder of the law in Islam.
muhtasib	the superintendent of police, who examined weights, measures and provisions, and prevented drinking and gambling.
munsif	from *insāf* (justice), one who gives justice, a judicial officer; a judge; an arbitrator.
muqaddam	the headman of a village or a part thereof.
nadar	from the Persian *nazr*, 'sight'; grace.
nāī	a barber by caste.
nawāb	plural of *nāib*, a vicegerent; a title used generally for provincial governors under the Mughals; used also for some rulers who succeeded them.
nāzim	an administrator; the governor of a province.
nindak	detractor; used for the opponents of the Gurus.
nizāmat	the office of *nāzim* (governor) under the Mughals; the territory under a *nāzim*; also used for lower officials and smaller units of administration in later times.
panchāyat	a local assembly of the representatives of a caste or brotherhood; used for the representatives of the soldiers in the army of Lahore in the 1840s; *panch* for an individual member.
parchār	propagation of ideas, particularly of one's faith.
pargana	the first administrative unit in a province under the Mughals; remained in use in the Punjab till the mid nineteenth century and became synonymous with *ta'alluqa*.

pāṭhshāla	an elementary school, especially for simple arithmetic and book-keeping.
paṭwārī	the village accountant.
pauṛī	stanza in a *vār*.
pothī	volume, tome.
qānūngo	a hereditary keeper of the revenue records at the *pargana* or the *ta'alluqa* level.
qāzī	the judicial officer who administered Islamic law; the office survived into the early nineteenth century in the Punjab.
rabābī	one who plays on the *rabāb*, a kind of violin with three strings.
rāgī	a singer, particularly of the verses in the Sikh scriptures.
ra'īs	a socially eminent and affluent person.
rākhī	literally 'protection'; a transitional arrangement signifying essentially the Sikh chief's claim to a part of the produce from land in return for protection afforded against all other claimants.
rām-līlā	the folk drama on the life of Rama as the incarnation of Vishnu.
rehat	the code of conduct for the Khālsā.
rehatia	'one who conforms to *rehat*'; used actually for a category of low-caste Sikhs.
sādh	a person devoted to religious pursuits; a mendicant; a recluse.
sādh-sangat	an association of *sādhs* or pious persons; used for a Sikh congregation.
sangat	assembly, religious congregation; a congregation of Sikhs; the collective body of Sikhs at one place.
sanyāsī	a renunciant, generally a Shaivite.
saropā	literally 'head and foot'; a robe of honour; a token of honour.
sarovar	a pool, a tank.
sarrāf	a money-changer; a jeweller.
satī	voluntary burning of a widow on her husband's funeral pyre.

sat-sangat	true association or assembly; used for a Sikh congregation.
savayya	a poetical stanza in a particular metre with a particular rhyme scheme.
sehajdhārī	a Sikh who is not baptized as a Khālsā and does not observe the Khālsā code of discipline; a non-Khālsā Sikh.
shahīdī jathā	a band of martyrs in non-violent agitation; the first band was organized in connection with the Rikabganj Gurdwara agitation in 1920.
sharādh	rite commemorating deceased forbears.
sharī'at	the Islamic law.
shiqdār	a person appointed by the king under Afghan rule to look after the civil and military administration of a territory.
shivālā	a temple dedicated to Shiva.
shūdar	the Punjabi form of *shudra*.
shuddhī	'purification'; a ceremony conducted by the Arya Samaj to induct or restore to Hindu society those outside its bounds.
silsilah	a line, a chain; a Sūfī order.
sītalā	the goddess of small pox.
smādh	a memorial raised on a place of cremation, generally for persons prominent in one sphere or another.
sūba	a province or the primary division of an empire; used also for the representative of Baba Ram Singh as an abbreviated form of *sūbedār* or governor.
sūfīs	the mystics of Islam.
sūtak	the period of 'impurity' for a woman after she has given birth to a child; supposed to be eleven days for a Brahman, thirteen for a Khatrī, seventeen for a Vaish and thirty days for a *shūdar*.
ta'alluqa	synonymous with *pargana* under the Sikh rule (see *pargana*).

ta'alluqdār	a person entitled to a share in the produce from land; also called *a'lā mālik* or *biswedār*.
tablīgh	propagation of Islam.
tarkhān	a carpenter by caste.
tat-khālsā	the staunch Khālsā; used for the Khālsā of Guru Gobind Singh who opposed Banda Bahadur and his followers in the early eighteenth century, and also for the Singh reformers of the early twentieth century.
ta'ziya	the annual mourning of the death of Hasan and Husain, the sons of the Caliph Ali, observed by the Shī'as by taking out the representations of their shrines in a procession.
thākurdwāra	a temple dedicated to Vishnu or one of His incarnations.
thānadār	the commandant of a garrison or a fort.
udāsī	a renunciant belonging to an order tracing its origin to Guru Nanak through his son Sri Chand and not through Guru Angad and his successors.
'ulamā	the plural of *'ālim*, a person who possesses knowledge; used generally for the learned in Islamic theology and law.
vaish	the Punjabi form of Vaishya, one of the four castes of the *varṇa* order.
vār	a literary genre, generally used for heroic poetry; Guru Nanak used it for his religious compositions; the most famous *vārs* in Sikh literature were composed by Bhai Gurdas in the early seventeenth century in praise of the Sikh Gurus and their teachings.
varṇa	literally, colour; used for the ideal norm of the four-caste social order.
walī	singular of *auliyā*; used for a Sūfī who has attained to the highest spiritual state of subsistence in God.
wazīfa	a stipend.
wazīr	the first or the prime minister, next in power and importance to the king.

zabt	a method of assessment per unit area, based on measurement; applied commonly to perishable and superior crops under Sikh rule.
zakāt	charity for fellow Muslims institutionalized as a tax collected by the state.
zamīndār	literally the holder of land; applied alike to the intermediary who collected revenue on behalf of the state and to a vassal chief as well as to a peasant proprietor.
zimmī	the non-Muslims who paid poll-tax (*jizya*) to a Muslim ruler to ensure protection of their life and property.

INTRODUCTION

I

For every twenty Sikhs in the Punjab there are no more than four in the rest of India and not more than one in the rest of the world; among those who live outside, there are not many who do not have their roots in the Punjab.

The literal meaning of the Persian term *panj-āb* is 'five-waters'. It was meant to signify the land of five rivers. But it was not meant to be taken literally. When it became current in the reign of Akbar in the late sixteenth century, it was synonymous with the province of Lahore and, therefore, actually smaller than the area lying between the rivers Indus and Satlej. The British Punjab, however, embraced the entire plain between the Jamuna and the Indus. This region had a geographical entity of its own. Its southern boundary was marked by a desert in historical times. The Himalayas stood in its north even before the Punjab plains emerged as a geological entity.

As a geographical region, the Punjab was probably wetter in prehistoric times, but there has been little climatic change during the Christian era. The rains of July and August mark the end of the extreme heat of May and June, and the return of the spring in March and April marks the end of the extreme cold of December and January. The most temperate weeks come in February-March and October-November. The rivers have changed course from time to time. The river Sarswati, which either fell directly into the Arabian Sea or joined the Indus during the second millennium before Christ, is now marked by the stream called Ghaggar and its dry bed. This was a major change.

Minor changes in the courses of the rivers of the Punjab are also known to have taken place even during the past five hundred years. Consequently, the inter-fluvial area between any two rivers (*doāb*) has not remained the same. The names given to the *doāb*s by Akbar have found general acceptance: the Bist Jalandhar Doab between the Beas and the Satlej, the Bari Doab between the Beas and the Ravi, the Rachna Doab between the Ravi and the Chenab, the Chaj Doab

Map 1 The land of the Five Rivers

between the Chenab and the Jhelum and the Sindh Sagar Doab
between the Jhelum and the Indus.

In the third millennium before Christ the Punjab formed a part of
the civilization called the Indus Culture when its cities and towns were
located close to the rivers, particularly in their lower courses. The city
of Harappa which flourished as a major urban centre for about 500
years was situated then on the left bank of the river Ravi, about a
hundred miles lower than Lahore at present. The site of the prehistoric
Ropar is still very close to the river Satlej. The villages which supported
the towns and cities were also in or close to river valleys, and not in the
upland (*bār*) between the rivers.

Though the cities and large towns of the Indus Culture began to
decline in the second millennium before Christ, the broad pattern of

human settlements persisted till about 1000 B.C. Thereafter, a slow but sure movement up the river valleys, and into the lower Himalayas, was made possible largely by the use of iron implements. Heavier rainfall among the mountain ranges then became an asset. The new cities like Taxila, Sialkot and Jalandhar as well as Lahore were among other things an index of this northward movement. A large number of villages grew up in the upperparts of the *doābs*. The balance in favour of the northern parts was tilted further by the introduction of artificial irrigation by wells with the Persian wheel, particularly after the Turkish conquest of the Punjab at the beginning of the eleventh century. The number and the size of towns began to increase in the upper portions of the *doābs* in the thirteenth century. This trend was accentuated further during the Mughal period.

The change in the broad pattern of human settlements in the Punjab was a result of political as well as technological changes. At the time of the Aryan influx into India in the second millennium before Christ, the Indus Culture was in decline. Agricultural economy was revived when the nomadic Aryans established small republics and monarchies nearly all over the Punjab. At the time of Alexander's invasion during the fourth century before Christ the kingdom of Ambhi was situated in the upper Sindh Sagar Doab, and King Puru (Poros) was ruling over a kingdom in the adjoining Chaj Doab. These areas had earlier remained peripheral to the Indus Culture. Soon after Alexander's return the Punjab became an integral part of the vast Mauryan empire which stretched from Bengal to Afghanistan under Ashoka. Taxila was linked by a highway with the imperial capital Pataliputra in Bihar. Itself a cosmopolitan centre of art and learning, Taxila served as an important centre of trade with Iran and the Mediterranean world.

For nearly a thousand years after the fall of the Mauryan empire, the Punjab remained politically isolated from the Ganges plains. In the second century before Christ, the Greek king Menander, known to Buddhist monks as Milinda, ruled over the western *doābs* of the Punjab; Greek coins bear testimony to Greek influence over the whole of the Punjab before the intrusion of the Shakas or the Scythians. In the first century before Christ, the Kushanas under Kanishka established a large empire which covered the whole of the Punjab but extended more towards Central Asia. The successors of Kanishka submitted to the Sassanian emperor Ardashir in the early third century after Christ. In the fifth century the Huns established their power in the Punjab; their king Tormana carried his arms beyond the Jamuna, but his successor Mihirakula was pushed back into the Punjab first and then into Kashmir. In the seventh century Harsha ruled over the eastern Punjab up to the river Beas, while the upper portions of the remaining *doābs* were subjugated by the rulers of Kashmir and the lower portions were covered by a Kingdom known as Takka. Before the advent of the Ghaznavid Turks, the Hindu Shahi rulers were dominant in the Punjab proper and the Satlej-Jamuna Divide was under the Tomar Rajputs.

From the eleventh century the Punjab became once again a part of large empires when Mahmud of Ghazni annexed it to his dominions in Afghanistan and Central Asia. His successors ruled over the land of the five rivers for over 150 years without extending their territory much beyond the river Ghaggar. The last of them was ousted from Lahore by the new rulers of Afghanistan, the Ghurids, before the end of the twelfth century. The Turkish Generals of the Ghurids conquered nearly the whole of northern India, and three Turkish dynasties ruled over the Sultanate of Delhi during the thirteenth century. During the fourteenth century, much of the Punjab was a part of the large empire established by the Khalji Turks and maintained by the Tughluqs. The western *doābs*, however, had come under the influence of the Mongol successors of Chingiz Khan before Timur, the acknowledged ancestor of the Mughal emperors, invaded India towards the end of the fourteenth century. The Sayyid rulers came into power at Delhi during the early fifteenth century and tried to extend their influence over the Punjab, but without much success. This position was inherited by the Afghan ruler Bahlol Lodhi in the late fifteenth century. Under his successors, Sikandar and Ibrahim, the Afghan governor of the Punjab extended his influence up to the river Jhelum. Meanwhile, Babur had occupied Afghanistan as a successor of Timur, and was keen to expand his dominions in the direction of India. He occupied the Punjab in the early 1520s before he defeated Ibrahim Lodhi in the battle of Panipat in 1526. For over two centuries then, the Punjab was to remain an integral part of the Mughal empire in India.

Political changes affected *inter multa alia* the character of population in the Punjab. The dominant tribes of the region during the fifteenth and sixteenth centuries were an important legacy of political changes. Many a Baloch and Pathan clan was dominant in the area which became the Multan province of the Mughal empire. The Kharal and Sial tribes were dominant in the lower portions of the Bari and Rachna Doabs. The Gakkhars, Awans and the Janjuas were dominant in the upper Sindh Sagar Doab. Many Rajput clans held lands along the Shivaliks and the border along Rajasthan. However, the most numerous of the agricultural tribes were the Jats. They had come from Sindh and Rajasthan along the river valleys, moving up, displacing the Gujjars and the Rajputs to occupy culturable lands. Before the end of the sixteenth century they were more numerous than any other agricultural tribe between the rivers Jhelum and Jamuna. However, it was still possible to trace the remnants of the original inhabitants of the Indus Culture, not only in the unprivileged *shudras* but also in the dark-skinned among the Brahmans who belonged to the privileged castes. Most of the Brahmans, however, and nearly all the mercantile Khatrīs and Aroras were the decendants of the Aryans who were represented among the artisans too.

The ethnic plurality in the Punjab was matched by the variety in its cultural tradition. The Vedic Aryans interacted with the people of the Indus Culture not only to produce the prototype of the social system based on caste but also to evolve new systems of religious belief and practice, combining the simple worship of their nature-gods with the well-developed cults of the Indus people. This was most evident in the cult of the Goddess. Due partly to the patronage of non-Aryan rulers, Buddhism dominated the religious life of the Punjab for several centuries before its decline became irretrievable in the seventh century. The forms of religious belief and practice referred to as Shaiva and Vaishnava were surely becoming popular much before the Turkish invasions of the Punjab. A variety of Islamic religious beliefs and practices were introduced in the Punjab during the centuries of Turko-Afghan rule. To the scriptural authority of the Vedas and the Puranas was added the authority of the Quran. To Sanskrit in Devanagri script were added Arabic and Persian in slightly different scripts of their own. In the past, however, Greek and Kharoshthi scripts too were known in the Punjab, and so was Brahmi which was used by the Prakrit writers.

Neither Sanskrit nor Arabic or Persian, however, was the language understood or spoken by the mass of the people in the Punjab. Just as they used Laṇḍā or Tākrī script for their simple accounts, they used the regional dialects in their daily intercourse. These dialects had begun to emerge clearly between the fall of the kingdom of Harsha in the seventh century and the rise of the Sultanate of Delhi in the thirteenth. The great poet Amir Khusrau referred to Lāhaurī as the spoken language of the people of the Lahore region, later to be called Punjabi. At this time, Shaikh Fariduddin Chishti of Pakpattan was using another major dialect of Punjabi, namely Multani, as the medium of his literary expression. Those who wished to address themselves to the mass of the people naturally preferred to use their language. The bards and minstrels (*dhāḍīs*) entertained the common people with tales of love and war in their own dialects, developing in the process a rich tradition of oral literature in Punjabi.

II

The history of the Sikhs in the Punjab can be traced to the late fifteenth century. The founder of Sikhism, Guru Nanak, was born in the Rachna Doab in April, 1469, when Bahlol Lodhi was ruling at Delhi and Tatar Khan Lodhi was governing the province of Lahore on his behalf. Guru Nanak's father, Kalu, was a Khatrī, a high caste among the Punjabi Hindus but the subcaste Bedi to which he belonged was rather unimportant among the Khatrī subcastes. Kalu was residing in a village called Rai Bhoi dī Talwandi in which the most prominent resident was a Muslim, popularly known as Rai Bular. Like many of his contemporary Khatrīs, Kalu had learnt Persian to be able to serve as a *paṭwārī*. He wanted to educate his son well enough to find a place in life. Guru Nanak appears from his compositions to be a well-educated person. He could have been self-schooled. But probably he did learn all that the village teachers of accounts and Persian had to teach.

As a young man Nanak was married to Sulakhni, daughter of Mula, a Khatrī of the newly founded town of Batala who had come there from his village, Pakho dī Randhawi, on the left bank of the river Ravi. Mula belonged to the subcaste Chona which was less important than even the subcaste Bedi. As a married young man Nanak was expected sooner rather than later to earn a living for himself. But there was not much in the village for a precocious young man in terms of a profession. Sometime before or after 1490, search for employment took him across the Bari Doab to Sultanpur in the Bist Jalandhar Doab.

Sultanpur at this time was the seat of an important *shiqdār*, Daulat Khan Lodhi, who was later to become the governor of Lahore. It was a flourishing town on the route from Delhi to Lahore. Its populace

6

consisted of Hindus and Muslims, following diverse professions. It is difficult to imagine that there was no one in Sultanpur to expound or to administer Islamic law, or that there was no one to represent Islamic mysticism. It is safe to assume that there were Khatrī shopkeepers and traders, Brahman priests and astrologers. There were many who served Daulat Khan in the administration of the territory under his jurisdiction. There were *qānūngos* to assist the administrator in the assessment and collection of land revenue. Indeed, there was an official storehouse (*modīkhāna*) for the revenues collected in kind. One of its employees was Jai Ram, an Uppal Khatrī, who was married to Guru Nanak's sister, Nanki. On his request and surety Guru Nanak was given employment in the *modīkhāna* of Daulat Khan.

For about a decade Guru Nanak performed his duties well, living as a householder in Sultanpur. His two sons, Sri Chand and Lakhmi Chand, were born there. But neither his service to Daulat Khan Lodhi nor his attention to his family was the most important aspect of his life at Sultanpur. He was in search of something more valuable, the purpose of human life. Possibly, he had met wandering ascetics (*sādhs*) in or near Rai Bhoi dī Talwandi. In Sultanpur he could meet the representatives of both Hinduism and Islam. Religious discussions between Hindus and Muslims were not uncommon in the fifteenth-century Punjab. Guru Nanak meditated on the mysteries of life and reflected on views expressed by others on some of the fundamental questions of life. His search for truth ended in a sense of divine calling. This marked the end of his stay in Sultanpur around 1500.

During the first quarter of the sixteenth century Guru Nanak undertook long journeys in and outside the Indian subcontinent. In one of his verses there is a reference to towns and cities he visited in all 'the nine regions of the earth' (*nau-khand*). There is hardly any doubt that he visited the important centres of Hindu and Muslim pilgrimage. He debated with the protagonists of nearly all systems of religious belief and practice in contemporary India. He kept his eyes and ears open. Even a cursory reading of his compositions is enough to realize that there was hardly anything that he missed, in politics or government, in society or religion, or in nature. His followers came to believe that he had undertaken these journeys for 'the redemption of the world'. At the end of his journey the sole purpose of his life was to deliver his message of salvation to all.

Sometime before or after the age of fifty-five Guru Nanak finally settled down at a place he named Kartarpur on the right bank of the Ravi. During the Kartarpur years he seldom moved, not out of the Punjab anyway. He visited Achal, near Batala, which was an important centre of the Gorakhnāthī *jogīs* in those days. He also visited Pakpattan and Multan where the descendant–successors of Shaikh Fariduddin and Shaikh Bahauddin Zakariya were still holding discourses on the *sūfī* way of life. Guru Nanak gave 'instruction' (*sikhyā*) to all who visited Kartarpur for nearly a decade and a half before he died in September, 1539. It is difficult to estimate the number of his followers in his lifetime. It is clear, however, that the great majority of them belonged to the Punjab.

The followers of Guru Nanak came to be known as Sikhs, from the Sanskrit *shishya* or disciple. Their number began to increase under his successors. Within a century of his death they were found in many cities of the Mughal empire as well as in the villages and towns of the Punjab. For nearly two centuries however, they remained confined to the Punjab as a result of the political struggle of the Khalsa instituted by Guru Gobind Singh at the end of the seventeenth century. Under colonial rule, once again, they began to move out, to other parts of the country and to other continents. This outmigration gained greater pace after 1947 when India became independent. The partition of the Punjab at the same time concentrated the Sikhs in about a dozen districts of the Indian Punjab. Thus, though it is possible to see a Sikh in every state of the Indian Union and in almost every country of the world, the great majority of the Sikhs reside in the Punjab, their 'homeland'.

CHAPTER 1

THE TURKO-AFGHAN RULE

I

Babur's invading army in the eyes of Guru Nanak was a 'marriage-party of sin'. Not even the ladies of the nobles were spared dishonour. With heads once of luxuriant tresses and partings adorned with red, they suffered now the shears of brutality; their throats were filled with choking dust; they wandered forlorn, away from the places that had sheltered them. No longer were there the sports of the nobles themselves, and gone were their horses and stables, their trumpets and clarions, their scarlet tunics and sword belts, their mansions and palaces, and their seraglios with soft beds and 'beautiful women whose sight banished sleep'. Rocklike buildings were razed to the ground and princes were trampled into dust. 'It is Babur who rules in their place now'.[1]

Guru Nanak's sharp response to Babur's invasions underlines the most important political development during his life, the transition from Afghan to Mughal rule in the Punjab and in northern India. The first fifty years of Guru Nanak's life had been marked by a period of peace in the Punjab. At the time of his birth in 1469 the Punjab was a part of the Sultanate of Delhi under Bahlol Lodhi. The major conquest of Bahlol and his successors was that of the Sharqi kingdom of Jaunpur. Their battles for minor political or territorial gains were fought in Rajasthan. There were only a few insignificant revolts in the Punjab during a period of about seventy years. Rehabilitation and resettlement of the countryside and the foundation of new towns like Bahlolpur and Batala can be seen as the reflection of a long spell of peace in the Punjab.

More important than wars and battles were the administrative arrangements made by the Turko-Afghan rulers which had a more lasting effect on the lives of the people. The Lodhi Sultans, like their

---

[1] These verses occur in the compositions of Guru Nanak referred to as *Bābur-vāni* or the 'utterances concerning Babur': *Adi Granth* (hereafter *AG*), 360, 417–18, 722–23.

9

predecessors, acknowledged the fictional authority of the Abbasid Caliphs by styling themselves as their deputies (*nāib-i-amīr al-mūminīn*). This convention symbolized the cherished unity of an Islamic world that was actually divided into a large number of states. More important was the informal authority of the articulate members of the Sunni Muslim community to whose religious sentiments the Sultans could appeal in situations of weakness or stress. Only Sikandar Lodhi (1469–1517) felt the need to destroy temples in war and peace. Significantly, he also prohibited the annual procession of the spear of the legendary Muslim martyr Masud Salar and forbade Muslim women to visit the mausoleums (*mazārs*) of Muslim saints. He yielded to the pressure of the *'ulamā* in allowing the execution of a Brahman who had maintained the equal veracity of his own faith with Islam. All these measures, like his wars and battles, related to the eastern parts of his dominions. Sikandar was not a full-blooded Afghan: his mother was the daughter of a Hindu goldsmith. As a political expediency he tried to make up for the deficiency in racial purity by a strong dose of Sunni orthodoxy.

Sikandar's interest in judicial reform too was partly a reflection of his 'religious orthodoxy'. Tribal and caste *panchāyats* in villages and towns, local administrators, provincial governors and the *wazīr* performed judicial duties; the Sultan continued to consult the expounders of the Islamic law (*sharī'at*). The most important result of Sikandar's interest in the administration of justice was the establishment of the *qāzi's* court in a number of towns. With or without the assistance of the expounder (*muftī*), the *qāzis* administered the *sharī'at* in all those towns and cities which contained a considerable proportion of Muslim population. The *qāzi's* court was open to non-Muslims as well for matters relating to property and secular contracts.[2]

The state patronage under the Lodhi Sultans, as under their predecessors, was virtually confined to the learned Muslims (*'ulamā*) and *sūfī shaikhs* who received stipends in cash (*wazīfa*) or revenue-free lands (*madad-i-ma'āsh*) for the maintenance of mosques and *khānqahs*. To grant entire villages as *madad-i-ma'āsh* was not uncommon. Such patronage was extended to the genuine or supposed descendants of the Prophet, and to the members of the tribe to which he belonged.

[2] For documentry evidence and its discussion, J. S. Grewal, *In the By-Lanes of History: Some Persian Documents from a Punjab Town*, Indian Institute of Advanced Study, Simla, 1975.

By contrast, the non-Muslim subjects of the Lodhi Sultans and their predecessors suffered some disabilities. They were supposed to pay the tax called *jizya* as the price of their protection by the state. The Muslims were supposed to pay the tax called *zakāt*, but for religious merit. In some parts of the Lodhi Sultanate, the Hindus had also to pay a pilgrimage tax.[3]

Acknowledgment of the Sultan's political supremacy enabled non-Muslim chiefs to retain administrative control of their territories on certain conditions which made them an integral part of the polity of the Sultanate. In the territories directly held by the Sultans, however, the political and administrative power was almost exclusively the prerogative of Muslims. By far the most dominant among them were the Afghan tribal leaders and individuals of eminence. They were the real co-sharers of power with the Sultan. Notwithstanding occasional transfers, they tended to regard their territories (*sarkār*) consisting of several small units (*parganas*) as hereditary possessions.[4]

In the revenue administration of the Lodhi Sultanate, particularly on the middle and lower rungs, Hindu participation was very considerable. Brahmans and Khatrīs in the Punjab were encouraged to learn Persian. They were associated with account-keeping, some of them rising to become *dīwāns* of the provincial governors. The local administrators often employed Hindu accountants and worked with the assistance of Hindu *qānūngos* familiar with local customs, castes and clans. Many a *chaudharī* of the *pargana*, or the part of a *pargana*, who assisted the Afghan administrator in the collection of revenue was Hindu. In all the non-Muslim villages the village headmen (*muqaddam*) were Hindu and so were many of the village accountants (*paṭwārīs*) even in Muslim villages. The association of the Hindus with Afghan administration made them important collaborators at the subordinate levels. Their loyalty to the rulers outweighed their concern for the common mass of the subject people, whether Hindu or Muslim.[5] There was no effective check on the exploitation of the peasantry by the intermediaries at various levels.

---

[3] Guru Nanak's reference to the customary tax on gods and their temples is suggestive of pilgrimage tax: *AG*, 1191.

[4] The term generally used for the Afghan administrator was *shiqdār* and his jurisdiction varied from a few *parganas* to a small province.

[5] Guru Nanak brackets all administrators irrespective of their religious affiliation when he refers to their oppression.

II

In imitation of the Lodhi Sultans, the Khāns and Maliks of the realm, the titled nobility, lived a life of luxury and ostentation. They had their own armies, palace-like mansions, harems, dancing girls and concubines, slaves, musicians and boon companions. Those who could not afford all the luxuries of the privileged nobles could find consolation in dancing girls and prostitutes. The brothel was a socially recognized institution. The Khāns and Maliks expressed their piety in raising mosques, patronizing the ʿulamā, and paying homage to holy men.

The ʿulamā formed an important section of the middling class. Apart from their role in the administration of justice, they tried to guard the shariʿat through public congregations and the traditional system of education. Schools and colleges were attached to small or large mosques in towns and cities. The major subjects of higher education were interpretation of the Quran (tafsīr), tradition with regard to the sayings and actions of the Prophet (hadīs), and jurisprudence (fiqh). As the recognized guardians of the traditional socio-religious order, the ʿulamā constituted the most conservative element in the Muslim community. More popular, however, were the sūfī shaikhs who were venerated by all sections of the Muslim community except the die-hards among the ʿulamā. The descendants of shaikhs and pīrs, known as shaikhzādas and pīrzādas were held in great respect, and many of them were not lacking in material means. Equally respectable were the sayyids whose social status was well recognized by the Afghans. There was hardly a sayyid family which did not enjoy state patronage.

The middling class in the Muslim community was not confined to the religious or racial luminaries. There were scholars, soldiers, clerks, traders, shopkeepers, physicians, scientists and men of letters. The Muslim community did not consist only of the nobility and the middling classes. There were artisans and craftsmen: masons, blacksmiths, dyers, weavers, leather-workers, shoe-makers, oil-pressers, water-carriers and the like. Furthermore, the slave was an important article of trade in the market, and the institution of slavery was an integral part of Muslim society in India as elsewhere in the world. Slaves did not make up a significant part of the agricultural labour force and the great days of the 'official slave', who served in civil and military capacities and who could thereby enter the ruling class, were over; but male and female slaves were found in plenty in affluent Muslim homes for domestic work or concubinage.[6]

This differentiated Muslim population in the Punjab during the late fifteenth and early sixteenth century consisted of both foreign and native elements. The land of the five rivers had remained under Turkish and Afghan rule for nearly five centuries. Muslim soldiers, administrators, scholars, men of letters, and learned and pious men had adopted the Punjab as their home. More numerous, however, were the native Punjabis who had accepted the faith of the rulers. In a long process of conversion, enslavement of men, women and children as a measure of war played a considerable role; and so did the institution of slavery even during the times of peace. An equally important part was played by the *sūfī shaikhs*, particularly in the countryside. The majority of the foreign Muslims lived in cities and towns but the number of Indian Muslims even in urban centres was probably larger, consisting partly of the middling classes but largely of artisans, craftsmen and slaves. On the whole, the proportion of Muslims in the total population of all the major towns and cities of the Punjab was quite considerable, and it was larger than the proportion of Muslims in the total population of the countryside. The majority of native Muslims in the countryside were to be found in the Sindh Sagar and Chaj Doabs and in the lower parts of the Rachna and Bari Doabs. Ethnically, they belonged to Afghan, Baloch, Rajput, Jat and Gujjar clans.

The cities and towns of the Punjab, as elsewhere in northern India, served as the centres not only of administration but also of Muslim culture. Known for their learned men were the cities like Lahore and Multan and the towns like Tulamba, Ajodhan, Jalandhar, Sultanpur, Sarhind, Thanesar, Panipat, Samana and Narnaul. Learned men of local repute were to be found in all the towns. Altogether, they cultivated not only 'religious sciences' but also secular sciences like medicine, astronomy and mathematics. There were men of letters too in the cities and towns. The Persian classics like the *Gulistān*, *Būstān* and the *Sikandarnāmā* were regarded as an essential part of a liberal education. Literacy, however, was confined to a very small proportion of the population.

Those who wished to address themselves to the common people started making use of the indigenous languages. Malik Muhammad Jaisi remarked in one of his own works in Hindi that the *sūfīs* had

[6] *The Encyclopaedia of Islam*, London, 1965, Vol. 2, 1079.

always adopted the language of the people among whom they lived and worked; he specifically mentioned Hindi and Punjabi. Indeed, Shaikh Fariduddin Shakarganj, popularly known as Baba Farid, composed verses in Punjabi during the early thirteenth century for his message to reach the people of the Punjab. His verses were quoted by his disciples and successors when they addressed other people. The ground was thus prepared for Punjabi to become a literary language. There was an oral tradition of heroic and love poetry in Punjabi. The *sūfīs* lent a certain degree of respectability to the folk tradition by contributing religious poetry.

III

All Muslims formally subscribed to the belief that there was no god but Allah and Muhammad was His messenger (*rasūl*). However, sectarian division had appeared among Muslims even before the advent of the Turks into the Punjab. Imported by the immigrant Muslims, ideological differences were perpetuated also by those who came under their influence in India. It is easy to identify three old sects: the Sunni, the Shia and the Ismaili. A parallel interpretation of Islam was cherished, advocated and developed by the *sūfīs*, the mystics of Islam, from the very beginning of the Turkish conquest of the Punjab. In the late fifteenth century a new movement, known as the Mahdavi movement, arose in northern India. Of all these sectarian and religious groups the most important were the Sunnis and the *sūfīs*. The Lodhi rulers professed to subscribe to Sunni Islam, like all their predecessors and like the majority of their Muslim subjects. But profession of Sunni Islam and veneration for the *sūfīs* were not mutually exclusive. The Lodhi rulers and the Afghan nobles had no difficulty in reconciling their 'orthodoxy' to their regard for the *sūfī shaikhs*.

The Sunni *'ulamā* accepted and popularized the theology formulated by al-Ashari in the tenth century.[7] In this theology, Allah's uniqueness and His absolute transcendence over His creation was emphasized, and so was His majesty and power. Allah is the lord of the universe. He raised up heavens without visible supports. Not a leaf falls but He knows it. If all the trees of the earth were pens and all the seven seas

[7] For a good presentation of Islam in India on the basis of contemporary evidence, Peter Hardy, 'Islam in Medieval India', *Sources of Indian Tradition* (ed. W. M. Theodore de Bary), Columbia University Press, New York, 1958, 371–435.

were ink, the praise of Allah could not be exhausted. His is the command (*hukm*), and unto Him all shall be brought back.'He sends men astray and He places them on the straight path. His is the final judgment. Allah is hard towards His enemies but He is essentially just and righteous. He is omnipotent and inscrutable but He is merciful. 'Praise be to Allah, the lord of the worlds, the beneficent, the merciful'. The Sunnis believed that Muhammad as the messenger of Allah was the last of the prophets; the Quran was literally the speech of Allah. They believed in angels, the day of judgment, paradise and hell. They professed equal respect for all the first four Caliphs but with a sneaking sympathy for Ali and his martyr sons Hasan and Husain.

The supreme aim of life for the Sunnis was to earn sufficient religious merit to enter paradise. The path to paradise was well paved by right conduct and worship coupled with right belief. There were four practices which insured piety; five daily prayers (*salāt*), daily fast (*rozah*) during the month of Ramzān, pilgrimage to Mecca (*hajj*), and charity to brother Muslims (*zakāt*). All these observances were rather external, devoid of religious emotion. Just as Sunni theology tended to be formal, Sunni piety tended to be ritualistic. Both were nonetheless valued by the orthodox. Furthermore, the collection of *zakāt* was supposed to be the duty of the state. Only a few could afford to go to Mecca for pilgrimage. The one who did, and thereby became a *hājī*, was treated with respect bordering on veneration. What was left open to the majority of the people were the daily prayers and the fast in Ramzān.

The Shias recognized the authority of the Quran as the revealed word of Allah and they subscribed to the finality of Muhammad's prophethood. But they rejected the first three Caliphs and regarded Ali as the true successor of the Prophet and, therefore, the first Imam. The twelfth Imam, Muhammad al-Mahdi, disappeared from the world and he was expected to reappear to restore righteousness and justice. The authority of the Imam tended to overshadow the other beliefs of the Shias. The martyrdom of Husain, in the Shia belief, had paved the way to paradise for all Shias. Based on this belief was the great importance attached to the *ta'ziya* for the annual commemoration of his death. The Shias condemned the first three Caliphs as a logical corollary of their belief in the exclusive legitimacy of Ali to be the successor of the Prophet. Because of their considered view that they should conceal their true identity it was not easy to distinguish them from the Sunnis.

But the Sunnis felt their presence in almost all the cities and large towns of the Punjab.

The Ismailis believed in Allah as the only God, in Muhammad as His prophet, and in the Quran as His revelation. But they did not believe that prophethood had ended with Muhammad. They believed in fact that divine light had passed on to the Imams through Muhammad, the first Imam being the Caliph Ali. According to them the seventh Imam, Muhammad ibn Ismail, had disappeared and he was to reappear on the Last Day. His vicegerents were nonetheless important; they alone could interpret the Quran because of its esoteric meaning. In the eyes of some believers they were the incarnation of God. The laws of the *shari'at* were not meant for them. The number of Ismailis in the Punjab was negligible.

The Mahdavi movement had virtually no impact in the Punjab. Sayyid Muhammad of Jaunpur proclaimed himself to be the Mahdi expected more or less vaguely by all: the Ismailis, the Shias and the Sunnis. He was opposed by the *'ulamā*, but he was patronized by Sultan Husain of Jaunpur (1458-1479). Obliged to leave the kingdom of Jaunpur later, he found shelter in Gujarat under Sultan Mahmud. He did not dabble in politics, but he was prepared to treat the non-Mahdavis as *harbīs* who should be obliged to pay *jizya* like the protected people (*zimmīs*) in Muslim states. He claimed to be the restorer of the pristine purity of Islam, interpreting the Quran according to his lights. He also claimed to be the last of the *walīs*, which indicated his intimate connection with the *sūfīs*. Some of his beliefs and practices had indeed a close resemblance with those of the *sūfīs*.

More and more people were coming under the influence of the *sūfīs*.[8] Their importance is reflected in the increasing recognition given to them by the Persian chroniclers from the thirteenth to the sixteenth century, much of whose information was gathered from the works of the disciples of the *shaikhs*, like the *Siyar al-Auliyā* and the *Siyar al-'Ārifīn* written between 1350 and 1550. The *sūfī* orders (*silsilahs*) proliferated in India as in the rest of the Islamic world. If anything, the influence of the *sūfīs* in the Punjab was more pervasive than elsewhere in the country. Lahore was known as the abode of many *shaikhs* since the time of Ali al-Hujwiri, the author of the *Kashf al-Mahjūb*, who

---

[8] Much has been written on the *sūfīs* in general but very little specifically on their ideas and practices in India on the basis of literature produced in India. For a brief but comprehensive discussion, J. S. Grewal, *Guru Nanak in History*, Panjab University, Chandigarh, 1979, 71–103.

settled in Lahore during the rule of the Ghaznavids to be venerated by successive generations as Data Ganj Bakhsh (the bestower of treasures). Multan was similarly a seat of many *shaikhs*, besides the famous Bahauddin Zakariya. The *khānqah* of Shaikh Farid at Pakpattan remained an eminent centre from the thirteenth to the sixteenth century. His successor in the early sixteenth century, Shaikh Ibrahim was known as the 'Second Farid' (*farīd-i-sānī*). There were *sūfīs* in Hansi, Thanesar and Narnaul. The town of Panipat was associated with Shaikh Sharfuddin, popularly known as Bu Ali Qalandar. Lesser luminaries adorned other towns and pockets of the countryside.

There is a wide range of ideas in *sūfī* literature produced in India and abroad. In it are found contradictory positions, and there are differences of emphasis and detail. But there is much that is common and rather basic. There was a general tendency to find support for theosophy in some of the verses of the Quran. 'Allah is the light of the heavens and the earth'; 'Everything will perish save His countenance'; 'He loveth them and they love Him'; 'We verily created man and We know what his soul whispereth to him, and We are nearer to him than his jugular vein'; 'Adore, and draw thou nigh.' These, and some other similar verses, held a crucial significance for the *sūfīs*. To verses from the Quran were added some 'sayings' of the Prophet.

However, the most fundamental source of their theosophy was the mystical experience of the *sūfīs* themselves. This experience consisted essentially of a kind of union with God. The pleasures of paradise are nothing compared to the everlasting ecstasy of this union. The torment of hell is nothing compared to the torture of separation from God. The basis of unification lies in the omnipresence of God: 'everything is He' and 'He is in everything'. The *sūfīs* underlined God's immanence. For them the relationship between God and man was that of love, and this mutual relationship eventually led to unification. It was for man to strive and for God to give. The path to unification was marked by 'stages' and 'states' corresponding to each other, the former attained through human effort and the latter through God's grace. Man had to die to his human self (*fanā*) before he could subsist in God (*baqā*). Unification was also explained by what may be called the theory of light (*nūr*). The human heart or soul was comparable to a mirror in which the divine light could be seen reflected.

The *shaikh* as a guide (*pīr*) who showed the path to his disciple (*murīd*) held a crucial position both in theory and practice. The prophets (*nabīs*) are sinless; the saints (*walīs*) are protected from sin. The miracle of the prophet (*mu'jiza*) found a parallel in the miracle of the saint (*karāmat*). The command of the *shaikh* is like the command of the prophet. In the worship of the *pīr* lies the worship of God. The formal disciples of the *shaikh*, from their initiation to the attainment of the goal, need his guidance.

In contemporary literature the stages between the state of ungeneration and the state of subsistence in God (*baqā*) vary in number and sequence.In Indian *sūfī* literature great emphasis is laid on repentance (*taubah*), renunciation (*tark*) and satisfaction with whatever is ordained by God (*razā*). The first implied realization of heedlessness; the second involved abandoning pleasures and earthly desires; and the third meant an eager acceptance of God's decree. One of the most important practices of the *sūfīs* was 'remembrance of God' (*zikr*). To repeat the name of Allah alone was preferable to 'There is no god but Allah' because the latter involved 'negation' whereas in 'Allah' there is complete affirmation. Throughout the Islamic world the *shaikhs* thought of *samā'* or *qawwālī* as good for spiritual progress. Shaikh Bakhtyār Kākī of Delhi died while listening to a Persian couplet during an audition: 'They who are killed by the dagger of submission to God receive every moment a fresh life from Him.' The verses which affected Shaikh Nizamuddin were recited by people for a long time after the audition. The practice of audition was never discarded by the *shaikhs* in India despite opposition from the *'ulamā*.

The *sūfī* path (*tarīqat*) was not only different from the path of the *sharī'at*, it was also more difficult to pursue. The practice of *zikr* did not replace the five daily prayers; it went beyond. Instead of fasting only in the month of Ramzān, the *sūfīs* advocated much fasting throughout the year. Charity to brother Muslims was restricted to a certain share in the idea of *zakāt*; the *sūfīs* placed no limits on charity: one could give away all one possessed. The Chishti *sūfīs* did not see much merit in the pilgrimage to Mecca; the time spent in *hajj* could be more fruitfully utilized nearer home with the *pīr*. On the whole, the *sūfīs* thought that their path began where the path of the *sharī'at* ended. Abu Hanifa and al-Shafi, the great masters of Muslim Law, had nothing to teach of love.

The system of *sūfī* beliefs and practices can be appreciated only in terms of a parallel interpretation of Islam. Indeed, the *sūfīs* believed

18

that they were the true representatives of Islam. The essence of *sūfī* ethics for Shaikh Nizamuddin consisted in not doing unto others what one did not wish for oneself. Not to injure others, by word or deed, is recommended again and again. The *sūfīs* were inclined to extend the benefit of spiritual merit to the lowest castes and to women. They favoured manumission of slaves and humane treatment of the subject people. They were more tolerant of the non-Muslims, and they were prepared as much to learn from them as to teach them. They attributed the relative ineffectiveness of Islam as a religious force in India to the lack of ethical superiority in the Muslims themselves.

I V

The Arab and Persian writers referred to the Indian subcontinent as Sindh-wa-Hind and to the peoples of the subcontinent as 'Hindus'. This in turn gave the name Hindustan to the county of the 'Hindus', that is Indians. One result of Muslim migration to India, and of conversion of Indians to the faith of Islam, was that the non-Muslim Indians came to be equated with Hindus. A secular identity was thus turned into a religious identity. In due course, not only the Muslim writers but also the non-Muslims of northern India started referring to themselves as 'Hindu' in the sense of non-Muslim Indians.

In the Punjab, as in other parts of the Lodhi Sultanate, the number of Hindus was larger than the number of Muslims, but their proportion in the total population was smaller in the Punjab than elsewhere, particularly in the western and southern parts of the land of the five rivers. Hindus lived in towns and cities as well as in the countryside. Even in towns founded by Turkish or Afghan administrators the proportion of Hindus was very considerable. They were indispensable for the economic life of the urban centres. However, they were predominant in the countryside, except in those areas where a whole tribe or a clan had accepted Islam, as in the Sindh Sagar Doab and in the southern parts of the Chaj, Rachna and Bari Doabs.

The character of Hindu population had undergone a sea change during the five centuries of Turko-Afghan rule. The Rajput ruling classes had widely been dislodged from power. Some had migrated to the neighbouring hills or deserts and some others had accepted Islam. Their remnants among the Hindus were found in the intermediary *zamīndārs* called Rāis. They held *zamīndārīs* as *chaudharīs* and *muqaddams* in a large number of *parganas*, particularly along the Shivaliks. Their control over the vital politics of the Punjab had declined. In a few pockets, however, they enjoyed local power under the aegis of the Lodhi Sultans. Some of them accepted Islam during the late fifteenth and the early sixteenth century.

The loss of Rajput sovereignty meant also the loss of traditional patronage to Brahmans. A few Brahmans found favour with the Afghan nobles for their knowledge of astrology, but as a class they had to look for new patrons. They acted as family priests to perform various rites and ceremonies; they looked after the temples and taught in *pāṭhshālas*; they expounded scriptures to a humbler but more numerous class of patrons; and they cultivated religious and secular sciences. However, not all the Brahmans of the Punjab belonged to the priestly or the learned classes. Many of them had taken to non-priestly professions like trade and money-lending, agriculture or even petty service. Nevertheless, their influence in the towns as well as the countryside was strong though subtle, pervasive though unobtrusive. They were easily the most conservative element among the Hindus, the counterpart in a sense of the *'ulamā* but without the patronage of the state. They were extremely meticulous about observing rites and ceremonies, whether personal, social or religious. In the sphere of religion, however, theirs was not the only voice among the Hindus of the Punjab.

In the social sphere they were less important than the Khatrīs at least in towns and cities. Besides participation in the civil administration of the Lodhis, the Khatrīs of the Punjab had taken to trade and banking. As *sāhūkārs* and merchants they made large profits and invested their earnings in landed property in urban centres. They had probably gained much from the tremendous development of commerce during the fourteenth century and retained some of this advantage during the fifteenth. But the Khatrīs as a class were not reluctant to take to shopkeeping and money-lending even in the countryside. They felt proud of their old Kshatriya lineage, and they were certainly older than the Rajputs, but they showed a remarkable sense of adaptability to the changing historical situation. In trade and shopkeeping, however, they were not alone. The Aroras in the western *doābs* of the Punjab and the Banias in the Satlej-Jamuna Divide were equally important.

In the countryside there was a preponderance of Jats, besides the Rajputs, particularly in the upper Rachna and Bari Doabs, the Bist

Jalandhar Doab and the Satlej-Jamuna Divide. They had been moving up the river valleys during the previous four or five centuries, encouraged by artificial irrigation made possible by the Persian wheel, to take up agriculture. Divided into a large number of clans, they had their *chaudharīs* and *muqaddams*, many of whom were important as intermediaries between the cultivators and the rulers. The bulk of the Jats were ordinary cultivators. Some of the Jat clans, entirely or partially, had accepted Islam, while some of the Gujjars (originally a pastoral group) who were taking up cultivation by the fifteenth century were still clinging to their non-Muslim beliefs and practices.

The cultivators of land needed the services of several categories of people in the village. They needed the carpenter, the leather-worker, the potter and the agricultural labourer for cultivation. They needed the services of many others for their social life, like the *jhīwar* and the *nāī*, who performed more than one service. There were several other categories, but their number varied from village to village. One village could have a few weavers, and another one or two goldsmiths; one village could have a few shoe-makers, and another could have a few oil-pressers. Similarly, a brewer, a *bhāt*, a singer, a dyer or a tailor could be found in some villages. Some Chandāls or untouchables also lived in most of the villages. In the towns and cities too there were artisans and craftsmen of various categories, and there were menials and untouchables.

The Hindus of the Punjab during the late fifteenth century did not fit into the four-caste *varṇa* order. This was not a new development. In the eleventh century, Alberuni had observed that there were four *varṇas* among the Hindus: the Brahman, the Kshatriya, the Vaishya and the Shudra. He also observed that there were a number of subcastes in each *varṇa*. Below these four *varṇas* there were several professional and crafts groups, like the shoe-maker, the weaver, the washerman, the basket-maker, the fisherman, the boatman, the hunter and the juggler. This was not all: there were the Chandāls and the like who were outside the pale of society. By the fifteenth century, strictly speaking, there were no Kshatriyas in the Punjab. Their role had been taken over by the new rulers. The Brahman was no longer the most important or the most honoured caste, and the Brahmans as a class performed duties which were never dreamt of in the *varṇa* concept. There was a similar ambiguity about the Vaishyas and the Shudras. Nevertheless, the *varṇa* order was cherished as the ideal norm. The gulf between the ideal norm and the social reality had become much wider under the Turko-Afghan rule than ever before. The Rajputs, the Khatrīs and the Brahmans were nonetheless proud of their lineage, regarding themselves as socially superior to the rest of the Hindu population.

Though without state patronage now, some of the traditional 'sciences' were cultivated by the Brahmans and Khatrīs. The study of the Vedas, the Upanishads and the Puranas was an important part of Hindu learning. Some scholars were familiar with the six philosophical systems. Some branches of knowledge cultivated by the Khatrīs as well as the Brahmans were mathematics, astronomy, medicine, grammar and prosody. There was some interest in jurisprudence, architecture and music, and also in astrology, palmistry and magic. Almost all scholars were to be found in cities and towns. The traders and shop-keepers learnt account-keeping and a good proportion of them were literate. Some Khatrīs and Brahmans learned Persian for its use in administrative service.

Among the Rajputs, Khatrīs and the Brahmans, women were respected as daughters, wives and mothers, but their position was clearly subordinate to that of men. Their best virtues are an eloquent witness to their subordination. A childless widow was expected to burn herself on the funeral pyre of her deceased husband to become a satī, and satīs were held in great esteem after self-immolation. She who did not immolate herself was 'ill-treated' for the rest of her life. In no case was a widow supposed to remarry. All these practices were related to the ideal of conjugal fidelity. But for men there was no bar; the idea of reciprocity was preposterous, not only for self-immolation but also in terms of monogamy. The ideal of chastity dictated the practice of child-marriage, but this practice was not confined to the upper castes and it was prevalent in northern India before its conquest by the Turks.

Much before the advent of the Turks the peoples of India had come to subscribe to the concept of the four cosmic ages: the satyuga, the treta, the duapar and the kaliyuga. By the time this idea became current, the first three ages had already passed and people were passing through the last, the worst of the four. Much of the evil around could be explained in terms of the kaliyuga, but 'evil' was defined differently in different historical situations. In the eleventh century, as Alberuni tells us, the kaliyuga was associated, among other things, with the loss of the Brahman's dignity, the rebellion of the small against the great, the abolition of the four *varṇas*, proliferation of religions and sects, destruction of temples and oppression by the rulers.

V

All non-Muslim Indians were not 'Hindu' as the term is used today. There were pockets of Tantric Buddhism in the Punjab hills. In the plains, there were Jain monks with a lay following among traders and shop-keepers of many a town in the Punjab. The wandering monks (*yatīs*) were rather small in number but they were obtrusive because of their peculiar appearance. They were known for their ascetical living and their meticulousness about non-injury to living beings, both visible and invisible. They were unpopular because of their atheistical system of beliefs.

What is now called 'Hinduism' was represented by Shaiva, Vaishnava and Shakta beliefs and practices. Temples dedicated to Shiva as the supreme deity were looked after by Shaiva Brahmans who also cultivated Shaiva literature, the Agamas and Puranas. There were Shaiva monks too, generally known as *sanyāsīs*. They were known for their hard penance and austerity. They belonged to several different orders, traditionally considered to be ten, because of which they were also known as Dasnāmīs. They generally wore ochre-coloured garments, though some of them went naked and others of them carried tiger's or panther's skin over their shoulders. Almost all of them wore ash marks on their foreheads, known as *tilak*. Some used three horizontal lines, representing Shiva's trident, or his third eye. Some others used two horizontal lines with a dot as the phalic emblem of Shiva. The *sanyāsīs* wandered from place to place, but they also founded establishments called *maṭhs*. The head of the establishment could be nominated by the predecessor or elected by his fellow disciples.

Turning to Vaishnavism in the Punjab we notice that the Vaishnava texts *par excellence* were known to Alberuni in the eleventh century: the *Bhagavadgītā*, the *Bhagavata Purana* and the *Vishnu Purana*. Temples dedicated to Vishnu as the supreme deity, as Lakshmi-Narayan or one of his incarnations, were looked after by Vaishnava Brahmans. The ascetics among the Vaishnavas were generally known as *bairāgīs*. They recognized merit in ceremonial ritual and pilgrimage to sacred places. Veneration for the cow and the Brahman they shared

23

with many other Hindus. They advocated total abstention from meat and liquor. The bulk of the Vaishnavas appear to have belonged to the trading communities in cities and towns.

The Shaktas worshipped the Goddess in her various forms, giving primacy to the active principle or the cosmic force (*shakti*) which sustains the universe and the various manifestations of gods. Worship of the Goddess was of two kinds, generally referred to as 'the *cultus* of the right hand' and 'the *cultus* of the left hand'. Animal sacrifice in honour of Durga or Kali, or any other terrible form of the Great Goddess, was an essential element of the *cultus* of the right. Otherwise, the right-handers observed the general usages of the Shaivas. The left-handers performed 'black rites' which, in theory, were meant only for the adept, and which involved wine (*madya*), fish (*matsya*), flesh (*mānsa*), parched grain (*mudra*) and coition (*maithuna*). The purpose of this ritual was to attain to a state of complete identification with Shakti and Shiva. The practice of this rite was secretive and limited but it made the left-handers (*vāmachārīs*) extremely disreputable in the eyes of the majority of the people.

This brief account of the major forms of Muslim and Hindu religious beliefs and practices does not take into account a large mass of the common people and their 'popular religion' which bordered on animism and fetishism. Godlings of nature, of disease, malevolent spirits, animal worship, heroic godlings, worship of ancestors, totems and fetishes made a conspicuous appearance in this popular religion. It was not a new thing. It had been there for many centuries; it was older in fact than all formal theologies and theosophies. This popular religion had survived partly in spite of the 'higher' religions and partly because of them.

Within Shaivism a new movement arose probably after the Ghaznavid conquest of the Punjab. In this movement, initiated by Gorakhnāth, Haṭhyoga was adapted to a theological system with Shiva as the supreme deity. The protagonists and the followers of this movement came to be known as Gorakhnāthī *jogīs* or simply as *jogīs* (from *yogī*). They figure frequently in Indian *sūfī* literature, and by the fifteenth century they had come to enjoy great influence in the Punjab. The Tilla of Gorakhnāth in the Sindh Sagar Doab remained their premier establishment, but *jogī* centres (*maṭhs*) were established at other places also. By the early sixteenth century there were twelve different sections known as *bhekh-bāra*. The adept among the disciples were allowed to wear ear-rings (*mudrā*), and they were known as *kanpātā* (ear-torn). They were also allowed to use the epithet *nāth* (master) with their names. The *jogīs* greeted one another with the epithet *ādes*, and they kept with them a blowing horn (*singī*). An important feature of their monastic centres was a continuous fire (*dhūṇī*). Their centres were well organized, maintaining a common kitchen (*bhandār*) for all the permanent and temporary inmates.

The psycho-physical techniques of the *jogīs* were meant to attain to liberation-in-life (*jīwan-muktī*), a state of everlasting bliss (*sahaj*). It was also a state of great power, because the *jogī* then became a *siddha*, possessing supernatural powers. He could become tiny or huge, light or heavy, and obtain everything at will; he could walk on water or fly in the air; he could assume any shape or form he liked. The *jogīs* were believed to be capable of prolonging their life by practising suspension of breath (*habs-i-dam*, in Persian). They were associated with alchemy, possessing the knowledge of turning base metals or even ash into gold. They were associated with herbal medicine too. Altogether, they inspired both fear and respect among the common people. They rejected ritualism and metaphysical speculation. In accepting disciples they disregarded the differences of caste. But they regarded woman as 'the tigress of the night', a great temptation and, therefore, a great danger in the *jogī's* path.

As in Shaivism so in Vaishnavism arose a new movement known as the *bhaktī* movement. The idea of *bhaktī* or devotion to God was centuries old. The path of *bhaktī* came to be regarded as a valid path for salvation, like the path of knowledge (*jnāna* or *giān*) and the path of correct observance of ritual (*karma*). Ramanuja in the south in the eleventh-twelfth century made a significant contribution to the *bhaktī* movement by giving primacy to the path of *bhaktī*. In the thirteenth and fourteenth centuries two further steps were taken: Vaishnava *bhaktī* began to be addressed to the human incarnations of Vishnu, that is Rama and Krishna, and it began to be claimed that *bhaktī* was the only path to salvation. The consorts of Rama and Krishna, namely Sita and Radha, were also associated with them; the images of Sita-and-Rama and of Radha-and-Krishna were installed in temples dedicated to them.

The cult of Rama *bhaktī* was popularized by Ramanand in northern India during the fourteenth and fifteenth centuries. His disciples established centres (*maths*) at many places. The Ramanandi *bairāgīs* derived much strength from these establishments. Food was provided in these centres not only to the inmates but also to the visitors. An integral part of these establishments were *pāthshālas* for teaching and *goshālas* for cows. The daily round of worship was well established. The cult of Krishna was popularized in the north during the late fifteenth and the early sixteenth century by Chaitanya in Bengal and Orissa and by Vallabhacharya in Uttar Pradesh, Rajasthan and Gujarat. Chaitanya cultivated the emotional side of Krishna *bhaktī* through *kirtanas* or devotional poetry sung with musical instruments and in ecstatic dance. Vallabha developed the ceremonial side of Krishna *bhaktī* in temples where the daily round of his activities were ceremonialized from the early morning when the Lord awoke till he went to bed at night for sleep. Vaishnava *bhaktī* was meant primarily for the upper or middling castes, though its protagonists made some use of the language of the people and they were more indulgent towards the lower castes.

VI

For a really lower-class movement we have to look to the Sants of northern India.[9] They discarded the idea of incarnation and the practice of image-worship in temples. In fact they did not address their devotion to Vishnu. Nevertheless they were deeply influenced by the Vaishnava *bhaktī* movement. Almost equally important, however, was the influence of the *sufis* and the *jogīs*. The most outstanding figure of the Sant movement was Kabir, but he was by no means alone. In Benares itself, where Kabir pursued the profession of a weaver (*julāhā*), there was Ravidas who plied his trade as a cobbler (*chamār*). What is true of Kabir is more or less true of Ravidas.

Kabir denounced much of the religious belief and practice of his times. The *mullā* and the *pandit*, the guardians of Muslim and Hindu orthodoxy, were 'pots of the same clay'; the paths that they advocated only led astray. The Hindu and Muslim revelational scriptures, the Vedas and the Quran, were discarded along with their custodians. Kabir does not believe in Vishnu. All his ten incarnations (*avatārs*), including Rama and Krishna, are a part of the *māyā* which is constantly

---

[9] For the Sant tradition in northern India and its significance, W. H. McLeod, *Guru Nanak and the Sikh Religion*, Oxford University Press, 1968, 151–58, 189–90; J. S. Grewal, *Guru Nanak in History*, 125–30.

subject to annihilation. In unambiguous and uncompromising terms Kabir denounced worship of images in temples, purificatory bathings, ritual fasts and pilgrimage to places regarded sacred. His God, neither Hari nor Allah (but one may call Him Hari or Allah) does not reside in the east or in the west; He resides in the heart of man. This, and some other ideas reveal his affinity with the *sūfis*. 'When I was, Hari was not; now Hari is, and I am no more.' What led to God was the path of love 'cutting as the edge of the sword'. Separation (*viraha*) involves torment in which the lover bleeds silently in the depths of his soul, he suffers many deaths every day. This torment is nevertheless a divine favour, a mark of God's grace. Love involves sacrifice of self, and metaphorically of life. Kabir's *bhaktī* is an ardent quest in which he is completely involved at the peril of his life.

Kabir's familiarity with the beliefs and practices of the *jogīs* is equally evident from his compositions. The ideas of *jīwan-muktā* (liberated-in-life), *sahaja-samādhī* (the state of unison with the divinity) and *shabad* (the Word) are given great prominence in his verses. Occasionally, he refers to God as 'the true guide' (*satgurū*). Ideas from three major sources were integrated by Kabir in a system which came to possess the originality of a new whole. His ineffable God is both immanent and transcendant, and to Him alone Kabir offers his love and devotion. Far from being a disciple of Ramanand, as it is generally but wrongly believed, Kabir discovered and delineated a new path which for want of a better term is still called *bhaktī*.

The social situation in the Punjab in particular and in northern India in general during the late fifteenth and the early sixteenth centuries was marked by a great change due to circumstances brought about by the Turko-Afghan rule in the sphere of politics and administration, urban and rural economy, and the sphere of religious and secular culture. The continuities, however, remained as important as the changes. Sensitive individuals responded to the changed situation according to their lights and moral fervour. Their social background and social position were equally relevant for the nature and character of their response. Social change was accompanied by social tension of various kinds. These tensions were probably the strongest in the Punjab. This might explain at least partly the distinctive response of Guru Nanak to the social situation in which he lived and moved.

CHAPTER 2

FOUNDATION OF THE SIKH PANTH

A rigorous analysis of the compositions of Guru Nanak reveals that there is hardly anything in contemporary politics, society or religion that he finds commendable. Yet the age of Guru Nanak was not fundamentally or even radically different from the previous or the following few centuries. Much of his denunciation, therefore, can be understood in terms of his moral fervour. For a rational conceptualization of his position it may be suggested that the entire social order had lost its legitimacy in the eyes of Guru Nanak because it had lost its support from the prevalent religious ideologies: it was neither 'Hindu' nor 'Muslim'. A new religious ideology was needed to become the basis of a new social order. At one stage in his life Guru Nanak came to believe that he had discovered a new ideology and he was looking at the contemporary situation from the standpoint of this new ideology. His denunciation of contemporary practices and beliefs is only an inverted statement of his positive ideals.

I

Guru Nanak was thoroughly familiar with the politico-administrative arrangements made by the Afghan rulers, particularly in the Punjab. This familiarity, reflected in the use of his metaphors, is a measure of his preoccupation with this vital aspect of the social situation. Moreover, there is direct denunciation of contemporary rule. The rulers are unjust; they discriminate against their non-Muslim subjects by extorting *jizya* and pilgrimage tax. The ruling class is oppressing the cultivators and the common people. The *rājās* prey like lions and the *muqaddams* eat like dogs; they fall upon the *raʿiyat* day and night. Notwithstanding the association of non-Muslims with the administration at subordinate levels, contemporary rule is occasionally equated with 'Muslim' rule:[1]

> The Primeval Being is now called Allah; the turn of the *shaikhs* has come.

[1] *AG*, 1191, 470.

In fact, the Turko-Afghan rule is seen as a mark of the *kaliyuga*:[2]

> The *kaliyuga* is a knife; the *rājās* are butchers; *dharma* is fast vanishing; in the dark night of falsehood the moon of truth nowhere seems to rise.

The rulers did justice when their palms were greased but not in the name of God.[3] They live and die in ignorance of the lord; singed by their own pride, they would burn like the forest reed in a wild fire.[4]

Guru Nanak exhorted people to turn to God, the true king, the king of kings. His service alone is true service. He who finds a place with the true king does not have to look towards an earthly potentate. In a trice He can degrade the high and the mighty and raise the low to rulership. He protects the righteous against brute force; many a time has He cast down the wicked and exalted the righteous.

II

The compositions of Guru Nanak reveal his familiarity as much with the socio-economic life of his times as with the politico-administrative arrangements. It was his conviction that the entire universe is suffused with divine light and all creation is His creation. The only source of light in all human beings is the divine light; God alone is the bestower of life upon all living beings. Caste distinctions and social differentiation did not harmonize with this conviction. God has no 'caste'; He gives no consideration to caste. None should be regarded high (*uttam*) on the basis of his birth or caste; and none should be regarded low (*nich*). Against the Brahmans and the Khatrīs, Guru Nanak identifies himself with the lower castes and the untouchables:[5]

> Be there the lowest among the low, or even the lower, Nanak is with them.

The pride of the Brahman and the Khatrī is totally misplaced. Many a Brahman eats bread provided by the rulers, reads their books and adopts their dress in public, taxing the cow and the Brahman, and yet he tries to maintain ritual purity in private. Many a Khatrī has adopted the language of the rulers, and their manners. They are a part of the oppressive establishment.

The social reality did not conform to the ideal norm of the *varṇa* order. Consequently, the actual role of the 'high castes' did not

---

[2] *AG*, 145, 1288.　　[3] *AG*, 63.　　[4] *AG*, 350.　　[5] *AG*, 15.

conform to the role conceived for them. A true Brahman should attain to salvation through his conduct and worship. A true Khatrī should be a hero in martial action. These were no longer the roles of the Brahmans and Khatrīs; there was nothing commendable in their conduct. Conversely, those who follow the true path are the true Brahmans and those who fight bravely in action are the true Khatrīs. Degeneration was not peculiar to the Brahman and the Khatrī. It was general. There are millions of fools fallen in the depths of utter darkness; there are millions of thieves subsisting on the earnings of others; there are millions of murderers, sinners and slanderers; and there are millions of the false and the wicked. The chariot of *kaliyuga* is made of passion and driven by falsehood. Guru Nanak invites people to come out of the shells of their castes as individuals to tread the path of truth; he encourages the lowest of the low to feel confident of his spiritual regeneration. Do good deeds and think of yourself as low; think of everyone else as high because 'there is none who is low (*nīch*)'.[6]

The idea of equality and the universality of spiritual opportunity are the obverse and the reverse of the same socio-religious coin. The *shudra* and the untouchable are placed at par with the Brahman and the Khatrī. The woman is placed at par with the man. The differences of caste and sex, and similarly the differences of country and creed, are set aside as irrelevant for salvation.

III

As may be expected, Guru Nanak was interested in all the major forms of contemporary religious belief and practice, whether 'Hindu' or 'Muslim'. He knows what the '*ulamā* and the *shaikhs* stand for; he knows what the *pandit* and the *jogī* represent; he is also familiar with the Jain monks and the practices of those who worship Krishna and Rama. Thus, he is in a position to react to some of the new as well as the traditional systems of belief and practice. Except for '*sants*', he finds nothing commendable in the contemporary systems.

Guru Nanak is hard on the Jain monks. They have discarded the occupations of their parents and their families weep for them; they sit together, each covered with a cloth, as if in condolence; their hair is plucked by pluckers whose hands are smeared with ash; they always

[6] *AG*, 62.

30

remain filthy; they walk in a single file, with cups tied to their waists and threads on their heads; they go about despised by the people. If the pluckheads do not wash, let there be seven handfuls of dust on their heads. They wore no *tilak* mark and observed no Brahmanical rites; they were not allowed to go to the sacred places of pilgrimage, and the Brahmans did not eat their food.[7] But for their atheism, Guru Nanak might not have taken any notice of them. They commanded little social influence.

Guru Nanak's attitude towards the traditional Hindu deities and scriptures is intimately linked up with his attitude towards the *pandit*. God created Brahma, Vishnu and Mahesh; Shiva–Shakti is God's creation too. Thus, none of the Hindu deities could be equated with the Supreme Being. In fact, everything known to myth, legend and history was the creation of Guru Nanak's God. The human incarnations of Hindu deities, like Krishna, could add nothing to God's greatness. Even if the Vedas were revealed by Brahma, it hardly made them a 'revealed' scripture for Guru Nanak. The position of the Puranas, Smritis and Shastras was even weaker. Without direct denunciation or categorical rejection, the attitude of Guru Nanak has in-built rejection of the traditional authority of the Hindu scriptures. To read them, or to hear them read, in a language understood only by a handful of people, was at best useless.

With the rejection of Hindu deities and scriptures went the repudiation of traditional modes of worship and religious practices. There was no merit in pilgrimage to the sixty-eight sacred places, not even to the *sangam* at Prayag where the Ganges and the Jamuna mingled with a third invisible stream. There was no merit in the worship of images:[8]

> The gods and goddesses whom you worship and to whom you pray, what can they give? You wash them yourselves; left to themselves, they will sink in the water.

Ritual reading of scriptures is a waste of time. The performance of *hom* is equally useless. Ritual charities are of no use either.

The protagonists of such beliefs and practices, the *pandits*, naturally come in for denunciation. 'Can you advise me O learned Pandit how to find the Master?' This rhetorical question implies that the *pandit* does not know. Nor does he care. It is not his primary concern. He does not believe that the 'truth is within him'. He doles out externalities. He is a

---

[7] *AG*, 149–50.   [8] *AG*, 637.

'broker' in false practices. He does it in mundane self-interest. With his intrinsic interest in worldly occupations, his pretence of knowledge increases the inner dirt which keeps on multiplying. He is like the spider that weaves its web all the time, living and dying upside down. The sacred thread of the *pandit*, the sacred mark on his forehead, his spotless *dhotī* and his rosary are useless without a genuine faith. Notwithstanding his eristic wrangling, he does not know that he does not know.[9]

Guru Nanak gives as much attention to the *jogī* as to the *pandit*, and he is equally familiar with the beliefs and practices of both. Guru Nanak has no appreciation for the *jogī* aspiration to gain supranatural powers:[10]

> Were I to don fire, build a house of snow and eat iron; were I to drink all miseries like water; were I to drive the earth as a steed; were I to lightly weigh the skies in a balance; were I to become so large as to be contained nowhere; to lead everyone by the nose; were I to have the power to do all this and get it done by others – all this will be futile.

Guru Nanak does not appreciate the *jogī* assumption that one can attain to salvation by psycho-physical or chemico-physical means. Nor does he appreciate their idea of renunciation (*udās*):[11]

> *Jog* does not lie in the cloak, nor in the staff, nor in smearing the body with ash; it does not consist in the ear-ring, nor in shaving of the hair, nor in blowing the horn; it is obtained by living pure amidst the impurities of attachment.

Constant devotion to God is real *sahaj-samādh*; absorption in the *shabad* or the *guru* is real meditation (*tārī*); the Name is the real nectar (*mahāras*). Far from appreciating the *jogī*, Guru Nanak asks the *jogī* to adopt his own values.

The few references to the worshippers of Krishna and Rama in the compositions of Guru Nanak indicate only his disapproval of their practices. Once the idea of incarnation is rejected it becomes impossible to treat Rama and Krishna as deities. Any worship addressed to them, therefore, becomes misplaced. With reference to *rām-līlā* and *kīrtanas*, and patronage of plays with quasi-religious themes, Guru Nanak makes his attitude clear:[12]

---

[9] *AG*, 56, 221, 355, 358, 413, 432, 470, 471–72, 635, 1171, 1256, 1290.　　[10] *AG*, 147.
[11] *AG*, 17.　　[12] *AG*, 349–50.

The disciples play and the *gurūs* dance; they shake their feet and they roll their heads; dust arises and falls on their heads; people are amused, they laugh and they return home; the performers beat time perfectly for bread and the dancers dash themselves to the ground. They sing of Gopīs and of Kānh; they sing of Sītā and of Rām.

The dancers are likened to the spinning wheel, the oil-press, the potter's wheel, the churning stave and the top. They fail to realize that the whole universe is a cosmic dance praising the Creator. The patrons of musical dances or dance-dramas ignorantly think of their charity as an act of religious merit:[13]

> The *giānīs* dance and play on musical instruments and they don costumes to sing loudly of battles and heroes.

Guru Nanak's attitude towards the *'ulamā* and the *shaikhs* is similar to his attitude towards the *pandit* and the *jogī*. Just as there were thousands of Brahmas, Vishnus and Shivas created by God, there were millions of Muhammads. The Quran and the other Semitic scriptures were a sign of God's glory but none of them was a scripture 'revealed' by God. The mere fact of subscribing to the faith of Muhammad ensured nothing, neither paradise nor salvation. Such a presumption refuted an essential attribute of Allah Himself: He is inscrutable. God's grace cannot be taken for granted:[14]

> Allah does not consult anyone when he makes or unmakes, or when he gives or takes away; He alone knows His *qudrat*; He alone is the doer. He watches everyone and bestows His grace on whomsoever He wills.

Mere talk does not lead to paradise; salvation lies in right conduct:[15]

> If you add spices to unlawfully earned food, it does not become lawful. Falsehood begets only falsehood.

While addressing the Muslims Guru Nanak shows his preference for the path of the *sūfīs* over that of the *'ulamā*. The Musalmans praise the *sharī'at* and they read and ponder, but God's true servants 'become His slaves to see His Face'. They who wish to become true Musalmans should 'first adopt the path of the Auliyā, treating renunciation as the file that removes the rust' of the human soul. They who wish to become true Musalmans should 'accept God's decree most willingly,

---

[13] *AG*, 468–69.   [14] *AG*, 53.   [15] *AG*, 141.

believe in Him as the true Creator and efface themselves'. Only then might they receive His grace.[16]

This relative appreciation of the *sūfī* path does not mean, however, that Guru Nanak gave the *sūfīs* his unqualified approval. A true *darvīsh* abandons everything, including his 'self', to meet the Creator, placing complete trust in Him. But many a *shaikh* subsisted on revenue-free land granted by the rulers. Presuming to be sure of his own place of honour with God, the *shaikh* gave assurance to others as well, and distributed 'caps' among them to authorize them to guide still others. He is likened to a mouse which itself is too big to enter the hole and yet ties a winnowing basket to its tail.[17] Considering their earthly pursuits, Guru Nanak reminds the *shaikhs* of their own belief that God alone is everlasting. The earth and the heavens shall perish; only He, the only One, remains for ever.[18]

Guru Nanak's basic attitude towards Islam and Hinduism is explicitly stated in the line:[19]

> Neither the *Veda* nor the *Kateb* know the mystery.

In the same way the *qāzī*, the *pandit* and the *jogī* are bracketed:[20]

> The *qāzī* utters lies and eats what is unclean; the *brahman* takes life and then goes off to bathe ceremoniously; the blind *jogī* does not know the way; all three are desolated.

IV

God, for Guru Nanak, is the eternally unchanging Formless One. He has no material sign; He is inscrutable; He is beyond the reach of human intellect. He is boundless, beyond time, beyond seeing, infinite, unsearchable, beyond description, eternally constant, unborn, self-existent and wholly apart from creation. God created the universe as and when He wished. Consequently, he came to acquire attributes which become the means of understanding Him. He is the creator, the sustainer and the destroyer of the universe.

> He, the One, is Himself Brahmā, Vishnu and Shiva, and He Himself performs all.[21]

---

[16] *AG*, 465–66, 140–41.   [17] *AG*, 1286.   [18] *AG*, 64.   [19] *AG*, 1021.
[20] *AG*, 662, 951.   [21] *AG*, 1908.

He is the only One; there is no second; there is no partner. God possesses unqualified power and absolute authority. He can oblige the carnivorous beasts and birds to eat grass, and He can feed the grass-eaters on meat; He can turn flowing rivers into sand-dunes, and He can create fathomless waters in place of deserts; He can confer rule upon an ant, and He can reduce whole armies to dust.[22]

God is omnipresent and immanent as well as omnipotent and transcendant.

> Within all there is light and it is
> Thy light which is in all.[23]

It is His light that shines in the creation; His light is in everything and in everyone. Wherever you look there is He; He is everywhere, and there is no other. He is not far, He is near; He is not far. He fills the earth and the heavens, and the space in between; He fills all the three worlds. He is the tablet and the pen and the writing. The ocean is in the drop, and the drop is in the ocean. He is the speech, the speaker and the listener. All is He. He is 'within' and He is 'without'. God is as well in the microcosm as He is in the macrocosm.

For entering into a meaningful relationship with God it is necessary to understand 'divine self-expression', that is how He stands revealed in His creation, and to see the implications of that understanding. Guru Nanak is emphatic about recognizing the Truth (sachch). God's creation is real but it is not everlasting. God alone is eternal. To attribute all creation to God is to recognize the Truth. Men become 'true' only when they lodge the Truth in their hearts and act in accordance with the Truth. Equally important is the appropriation of the Name (nām) and the Word (shabad), the object and the medium of communication. Through the Name one gets recognition from others; without the Name there can be no honour. There is no fulfilment without the Name. In the Name is real power, the authority of the diwān, the might of the army, and the sovereignty of the Sultan. The treasure of excellence is obtained by meditating on the Word. Having no form, colour or material sign, God is revealed through the Word. The Name and the Word are the revelation of the divine preceptor (gurū). The Truth is recognized through the divine preceptor's instruction. Without the True Guru one wanders through the cycle of death

---

[22] AG, 144.   [23] AG, 13, 663.

and rebirth. Without the True Guru one wanders in the darkness of ignorance. Only the True Guru bestows the Name without which there is no purpose in human life; 'one comes and goes like a crow in an abandoned house'. The recognition of divine order (*hukm, bhāṇa, razā*) is equally essential. The divine order is an all-embracing principle that accounts for everything: the creation of all forms, high or low status, misery and happiness, bliss and transmigratory chain. All are subject to divine order; none is beyond its operation. Everything in the universe points to the intelligent working of the divine order. It reveals God as the only doer. Man should recognize the divine order and submit himself to it. The divine order is a manifestation of God's omnipotence.

The rigour of God's omnipotence is supported yet softened by His grace (*nadar, kirpa, karam, prasād, mihr, dayā, bakhsīs, tars*). It is through the True Guru's *prasād* that ignorance is obliterated and the light of the Truth is perceived. One receives the Truth through God's *karam*. The gift of the Name is received through God's *nadar*. Through His grace comes the recognition of the divine order. One 'sees' only what He 'shows'. There is a point beyond which human understanding cannot proceed and there, it is the bestowing or withholding of God's grace that decides the issue of salvation. Guru Nanak's idea of God's grace repudiates all presumption to liberation by human effort alone.

Nevertheless, though human effort is not sufficient, it is absolutely necessary. Discarding heedlessness man is to remember God, which implies not a mere repetition of His name but meditation on the nature of God and His attributes. Consequently, the remembrance of God comes to embrace thought, word and deed. Loving devotion and dedication to God is true *bhaktī* without which there is no salvation. Man should love God as the *chakvī* loves the Sun, as the *chātrik* loves the rain or as the fish loves water (so much so that it dies without water). Bracketed with *bhaktī* is *bhai* or *bhau*, that is awe, so that the term *bhai-bhaktī* is many a time used as one idea. Indeed, they alone can offer *bhaktī* who have *bhai* lodged in their hearts. God's awe is the remedy for the fear of death. He who lodges God's fear in his heart becomes fearless. But fear catches hold of those who are not afraid of God.

In contrast to the 'truth' of God, His creation is 'false' and, therefore, a snare. So long as man remains attached to the creation he suffers from the misery of *dubidhā*, misery arising from dual affiliation:[24]

> If you worship the attendant you will never see the Master.

Attachment to earthly things is bound to shut out the Truth.[25]

> The love of gold and silver, women and fragrant scents, horses, couches, and dwellings, sweets and meats – these are all lusts of the flesh. Where in the heart can there be room for the Name?

But the multiformed *māyā* allures man to itself, thanks to his lust, covetousness, attachment to earthly things, anger and pride. These five adversaries of man are difficult to subdue. But there can be no compromise, because there can be no conciliation between man's affiliation to *māyā* and his affiliation to God.

One of the five adversaries of man, namely pride, becomes much more formidable in the form of self-centredness (*haumai*). In fact, pride springs from this self-centredness. Man attributes things to himself rather than to God, in opposition to the Truth and the divine order. *Haumai* is thus opposed to God as the only omnipotent reality; it is a subtle psychological barrier between man and God. It is a disease that only the recognition of the divine order and the understanding of the Word can cure. To die to 'self' is to prepare the ground for life everlasting. The life of the self-willed man (*manmukh*), who vainly attributes things to himself, is like that of spurious sesame which is left desolate in the field.

Psychological detachment from *māyā* and eradication of *haumai* enable man to perceive God in the microcosm, just as his understanding enables him to perceive God in the macrocosm. Yearning for a union with God increases the pangs of separation:[26]

> I cannot live for a moment without the Beloved;
> I cannot have a wink of sleep without meeting Him.

Supplication is made in devout humility:[27]

> My sins are as numerous as the drops of water in the ocean.
> Through your mercy O Lord! even stones can cross the waters.

If man's sins are countless, God's bounty is boundless. In His kindness God leads the devotee on the path towards Him:[28]

---

[24] *AG*, 229, 75.   [25] *AG*, 15.   [26] *AG*, 1274.   [27] *AG*, 156.
[28] *AG*, 931.

He who is immersed in His love day and night sees Him immanent
in the three worlds, and throughout all time. He becomes like Him
whom he knows. He becomes wholly pure, his body is sanctified,
and God dwells in his heart as his only love. Within him is the
Word; he is blended in the True One.

In the process of man's union with God, an important experience is
visamād, the awe-inspiring vision of God's greatness and the feeling of
ecstasy resulting from it. The emotion of wonder engendered by the
overwhelming greatness of God leads to refined and intense meditation
which purges man of his *haumai*. It leads to an intense adoration too,
and the best praises of God appear to be inadequate. This too is His gift
to man. He shows the way; He leads to union.

The ever-widening *visamād* leads to higher and yet higher levels of
understanding and experience. Recognizing the law of cause and effect
in the moral as well as the physical world, man realizes the justice of
God. In His court stand revealed the true and the false. Man's wider
understanding of the nature of God becomes a source of joy. Consequently, he puts in greater exertion, and his acts conform to his
increasing understanding. As the reward of his devotion, he ascends to
the Realm of Truth, the dwelling place of the Formless One, in which
there is perfect harmony with His *hukm*. The transmigratory process
ends with the state of union with God, a state of consummate joy and
perfect peace.

In Guru Nanak's conception of the path to salvation 'the law of
karma' is set aside and a new context is provided for right conduct. He
does make use of the current notion to emphasize the need for good
acts. 'Do not blame others; you receive the reward or retribution for
what you yourself do.' The 'law of *karma*' is invoked also to explain
the differences of birth; immediately, however, the grace of God is
invoked for explaining the attainment to salvation. In any case, the 'law
of *karma*' is not independent of God's *hukm*. The subordination of
karma to the *hukm* is not without significance. Paradoxically, submission to God's *hukm* becomes a means to release from the 'law of
karma'. The chain of *karma* obviously cannot bind God; rather His
grace breaks the chain of *karma*. Human acts acquire fresh importance
in this context:[29]

---

[29] *AG*, 579, 1110.

The words man speaks shall be taken into account; the food he eats shall be taken into account; his movements shall be taken into account; what he sees and hears shall be taken into account. Indeed, every breath he draws shall be taken into account.

Loving devotion to God becomes a good act. In fact all those deeds which enable men to tread the path shown by Guru Nanak become 'true' acts, and those deeds which hinder men on that path are 'false' acts. Thus, right conduct is closely connected with Guru Nanak's idea of right belief and right worship. Foremost in right conduct was honest living and charity based on that:[30]

He who eats what he has earned by his own labour and gives some to others – Nanak, he it is who knows the true way.

V

By the time Babur established his rule in northern India, Guru Nanak had fully formulated his system of inter-related ideas and corresponding practices. True to his convictions, he attributed all his understanding and all his experience to God. On His authority, therefore, he was saying what he was saying and doing what he was doing. He regarded himself as God's herald (*tabal-bāz*) to proclaim His Truth:[31]

I was a minstrel (*dhāḍī*) without an occupation, but God gave me an occupation. He ordered me to sing His praises. He called the *dhāḍī* to His abode of Truth, and gave him the robe of 'true praise and adoration'. The true nectar of the Name has been sent as food. They are happy who taste it to the full in accordance with the Guru's instruction. The *dhāḍī* openly proclaims the glory of the Word. By adoring the Truth, Nanak has found the Perfect One.

During the last fifteen years of his life Guru Nanak settled down at Kartarpur, a place founded by him then on the right bank of the river Ravi, represented by the present Dera Baba Nanak on the left bank. Concerned seriously with showing to others the path he had discovered for himself, he acted as a guide. Disciples gathered around him as an acknowledged preceptor. The work of these years proved to be the most influential in terms of its legacy for the future. He imparted regular instruction to his disciples and exhorted the visitors as well to discard trust in external forms and in status based on caste or wealth, to

[30] *AG*, 1245.   [31] *AG*, 150.

cultivate inner devotion and a truly religious attitude by recognizing the greatness of God and reflecting upon His revelation. A regular discipline was evolved for the adoration of God. The early hours of the morning were devoted to meditation. All the disciples and visitors joined Guru Nanak in singing the praises of God in the evening as in the morning. There is a good deal of emphasis in the compositions of Guru Nanak upon 'true association' or association with the true devotees of God. This ideal found concrete expression in corporate worship at Kartarpur. The disciples and the visitors ate communal meals, for which the believers in the new faith made contribution in cash, kind or service.

It is difficult to estimate the number or the social background of the followers of Guru Nanak. There is no doubt, however, that Khatrīs were rather numerous among his followers. His successor-to-be was only one of them. They were petty traders, shop-keepers, agents of merchants, itinerant salesmen. It is equally certain that cultivators were among the followers of Guru Nanak, and most of them were Jats. Then there were some artisans and craftsmen, bond-servants and slaves. The followers came from towns and the countryside. Most of them belonged to the lower classes, and all of them were house-holders. Among themselves they thought they were all equal. 'We are not high, or low, or the middling; we have taken refuge in God, and we are His people.'[32]

The most important aspect of the mode of worship adopted by Guru Nanak for himself and his followers was the use of his own compositions for this purpose. This was a logical corollary of his rejection of scriptural authority and the scriptures of contemporary religions. Some of his definitive utterances were used for liturgical purposes. The later importance given to his *Japujī* and to his *So-dar* appears to have been a continuation of Guru Nanak's own practice. It is likely that these, and many other compositions, were recorded in writing by Guru Nanak himself. This aspect of his work became the basis of vital developments under his successors.

Guru Nanak lived at Kartarpur as a house-holder, with his wife and his two sons. This fact carried a great significance for the future. In the compositions of Guru Nanak there are verses which can be interpreted as supporting renunciation (*udās*), and Guru Nanak himself had travelled widely, leaving his family behind. His decision to return to

[32] *AG*, 504.

the life of a house-holder, therefore, was important. It demonstrated his basic ideal that true renunciation consisted in living pure amidst the impurities of attachment. The followers of Guru Nanak at Kartarpur and elsewhere pursued honest occupations for livelihood. They demonstrated thus how to combine piety with worldly activity. A disciplined worldliness was the hallmark of this new community.

Before his death at Kartarpur in 1539 Guru Nanak chose his successor from amongst his followers, setting aside the claims of his sons. Nomination of a successor from amongst one's own disciples was not a new thing; it was known to many an ascetical order of the times. But the nomination of Lehna by Guru Nanak was regarded as unique because Lehna was installed in his office by Guru Nanak himself. His name too was changed from Lehna to Angad, making him 'a limb' of the founder. This nomination was important not merely because it enabled Guru Nanak to ensure the continuation of his work but also because it served as the basis of the idea that the positions of the Guru and the disciple were interchangeable. Closely linked with this was the idea that there was no difference between the founder and the successor; they represented one and the same light. By the time Guru Nanak breathed his last the nucleus of a new social group had come into existence with an acknowledged Guru to guide its social and religious life according to a pattern set by the founder and in the light of ideas expounded by him.

CHAPTER 3

EVOLUTION OF THE SIKH PANTH
(1539–1606)

By the beginning of the seventeenth century the socio-religious community of Guru Nanak's followers became 'a state within the state'. Each of his first four successors made his own distinctive contribution, working within the ideological and institutional parameters adumbrated by him. We have to study their own compositions closely to perceive the slow but sure development of the Sikh Panth in terms of numbers, composition, material resources, social institutions and a multi-dimensional transmutation of ideas in a creative response to changing situations. To listen to those who were closely connected with them is equally rewarding. The context for this development was provided by the politico-administrative arrangements evolved by Akbar, giving peace and prosperity to a vast empire. The position of the Sikh Panth at the end of his reign may be seen as the culmination of a peaceful evolution of nearly three-quarters of a century. This evolutionary phase came dramatically to a grave end with the martyrdom of Guru Arjan in the very first year of Jahangir's reign.

I

Babur ruled over the territory he conquered from Bhera to Bihar for only four years till his death in 1530. His son and successor, Nasiruddin Humayun, temporarily added Malwa and Gujarat to the dominions inherited from Babur. The Afghan resurgence under the leadership of the Sur Afghan Sher Khan obliged Humayun to abandon the Mughal territory in India in 1540. Sher Shah Sur and his successors ruled over northern India for fifteen years before Humayun staged a successful return in 1555. He died a year later. It was left for his son and successor, Jalaluddin Muhammad Akbar, to conquer territories from Kabul and Qandahar in the west to the Bay of Bengal in the east, from Kashmir in the north to across the Narbada in the south, and to introduce changes of great significance during his rule of nearly half a century till his death in 1605.

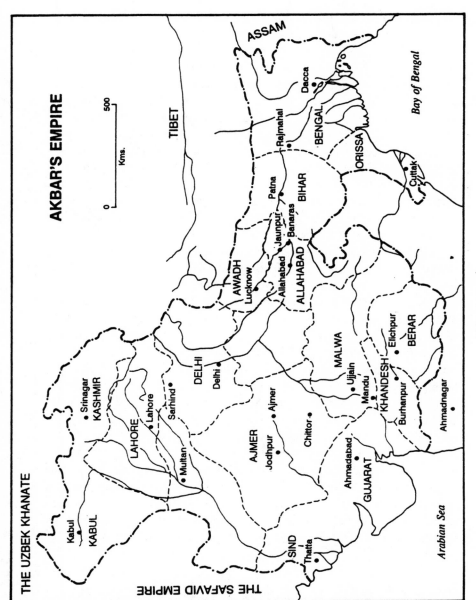

AKBAR'S EMPIRE

THE UZBEK KHANATE

THE SAFAVID EMPIRE

TIBET

ASSAM

Kms.

0   500

KABUL

Kabul •

KASHMIR

Srinagar •

LAHORE

Lahore •

Multan •

Serhind •

DELHI

Delhi •

SIND

Thatta •

AJMER

Jodhpur •

Ajmer •

Chittor •

GUJARAT

Ahmadabad •

MALWA

Ujjain •

Mandu •

KHANDESH

Burhanpur •

BERAR

Elichpur •

Ahmadnagar •

AWADH

Lucknow •

ALLAHABAD

Allahabad •

Jaunpur •

Banaras •

Patna •

BIHAR

Rajmahal •

BENGAL

Decca •

ORISSA

Cuttak •

Bay of Bengal

Arabian Sea

2 Akbar's empire

Akbar adopted several measures which modified the character of the state. He made an extensive and effective use of suzerain–vassal polity in which the administrative control of a territory was left in the hands of its chief under the political control of the suzerain on certain well-stipulated conditions, especially the payment of annual tribute and the supply of contingents for imperial service. There were hundreds of chiefs in Akbar's empire who retained their territories on the conditions of vassalage; the extent of their territories was by no means negligible. Akbar tried to induct the willing vassal chiefs into the *mansabdārī* system. Many a vassal chief received high rank to serve the empire with zeal.[1] The bulk of the chiefs were Hindu, and Akbar's attitude towards them was an important plank of his general policy. He abolished the discriminatory *jizya* and the pilgrimage tax. He remitted the tax on cows and discouraged cow-slaughter. He showed respect for native customs by participating in the celebration of Dusehra and Diwālī. He showed interest in traditional learning and literature by getting Sanskrit works translated into Persian. He extended state patronage to non-Muslim institutions and individuals of known merit by giving them revenue-free lands (*madad-i-ma'āsh*).[2]

Akbar had a rare genius for organization. For all practical purposes he dispensed with the office of the all-powerful minister known as the *wazīr* or the *vakīl*, and distributed the work of the government among four ministers of more or less equal importance to deal with the finances of the state, its army and justice and the royal household. This arrangement imparted stability and efficiency to the government at the centre and, together with some other measures, increased the control of the emperor over the administration of the different parts of the empire. Akbar divided his empire into a small number of rather large provinces. His province was also qualitatively different from the primary divisions of the earlier empires. Each province had three types of territory: vassal territory attached to the province, lands given in *jāgīr* to the servants of the state, and the *khālisa* lands from which revenue was collected directly for the emperor. In the last decade of the sixteenth century the *dīwān* in the province was made independent of the governor to look after the revenue administration under the control

---

[1] For vassal chiefs under Akbar, Ahsan Raza Khan, *Chieftains in the Mughal Empire During the Reign of Akbar*, Indian Institute of Advanced Study, Simla, 1977.

[2] For a discussion of Akbar's *madad-i-ma'āsh* grants to non-Muslims, B. N. Goswamy and J. S. Grewal, *The Mughals and the Jogis of Jakhbar*, Indian Institute of Advanced Study, Simla, 1967.

of the *dīwān* at the centre. Besides the permanent local officials, full-fledged officials of the imperial administration were appointed to help and control the *jāgīrdārs*. The *zabtī* system, which implied the collection of land-revenue in cash according to rates for a unit area under cultivation, was introduced on a large scale. Even from villages not brought under the system of measurement (*zabt*), the revenue was generally collected in cash.

Akbar's conquests, his concessions and measures on conciliation resulted in peace and security in his vast dominions, particularly during the second half of his reign. This peace and security became an important condition for the growth of prosperity. Extension of agriculture was an important objective of Akbar's revenue policy, and there are clear indications that more and more land was brought under cultivation during the late sixteenth century. 'Cash crops' were sown for the market, and agricultural produce was used for manufactures. Akbar introduced standardization in weights, measures and currency with the Ilāhī *gaz*, Akbarī *man* and the silver rupees as the standard. Two small coins were widely current for small transactions in villages and towns: one was the *paisa*, one-fortieth of the rupee; the other was the *anna*, equal to four *paisa*. To encourage trade, Akbar abolished many internal imposts. Routes were protected for caravans and trade became a pretty safe proposition.

Akbar's reign was marked by a revival of trade on a large scale. Bankers' drafts or bills of exchange (*hundīs*) were widely used for the purpose of trade. An organized system of insurance also protected trade interests. River traffic was well developed, and large or small boats were manufactured at many places, besides ship-building for coastal and sea trade. There were several mercantile communities to handle trade. Their distribution over large areas was an asset for commercial transactions. The increase in the size and number of urban centres in the dominions of Akbar during the late sixteenth century was an indication of an increase in the volume of trade and manufactures as well as an increase in agricultural production. On the whole, in the late sixteenth century northern India presented a historical situation which was markedly different from that of the late fifteenth or even of the early sixteenth century.

The province of Lahore was among the advanced provinces of Akbar's empire in terms of agriculture, manufactures and trade, with Lahore as one of the largest cities of the Mughal empire, which also meant that it was one of the largest cities of the world around 1600. Expansion of cultivation in the Punjab had started under Afghan rule. When Babur crossed the river Jhelum he curiously noticed the Persian wheel which, later, he found in use for irrigation in the regions of Lahore and Dipalpur. It extended in fact to the Sarhind region. Akbar's court historian Abul Fazl observed that most of the province of Lahore was irrigated by wells with Persian wheels. This artificial means of irrigation enabled the landholders of the province to grow high quality or cash crops. Akbar's long presence in Lahore during the fourth decade of his reign added to the importance of the province. Well-known for its rock-salt, the province was known also for its exports of textiles, sugar candy of high quality, boats, shawls and carpets. Lahore was on the trade route from Delhi to Kabul, while Multan was on the route to Qandahar, and both these cities were linked with the ports of the Arabian Sea through riverain traffic. The economic development of the Punjab provided good opportunities for enterprising traders and cultivators. The Khatrīs and Jats of the province of Lahore were surely not unenterprising. In the empire of Akbar they tried to make the best of the opportunities offered by peace and prosperity.

Akbar's reign was covered by the pontificates of three of the first four successors of Guru Nanak. These three were Guru Amar Das, Guru Ram Das and Guru Arjan.[3] The first successor of Guru Nanak was Guru Angad, a Khatrī of the Trehan subcaste who was a petty trader and a devotee of the Goddess before he came under the influence of Guru Nanak. Guru Amar Das too was a Khatrī but of the Bhalla subcaste, and he was a Vaishnava before he became a disciple of Guru Angad; he too was a petty trader in a village near the present-day Amritsar. Guru Ram Das was a Khatrī of the Sodhi subcaste, and he came under the influence of Guru Amar Das as a young hawker. Guru Ram Das nominated one of his own three sons, namely Guru Arjan, as his successor. Henceforth, Guruship was to remain in the Sodhi family of Guru Ram Das. All the Gurus, thus, were Khatrīs with a rural background. The subcastes to which they belonged were not among the important Khatrī subcastes, not even the Bedi subcaste to which the founder of the Sikh Panth belonged. Their social position was rather low among the Khatrīs.

[3] For the successors of Guru Nanak see appendix 1.

II

Guru Angad's pontificate was an extension of Guru Nanak's work, but with significant shifts of emphasis. He shows a thorough grasp of the compositions of Guru Nanak. To preserve these compositions for posterity he adopted a new script called Gurmukhī which has served this purpose ever since its adoption by Guru Angad. His own compositions consist of short verses (*shaloks*), only a little over sixty and the longest having only twelve lines. These are composed significantly under the name 'Nānak', implying thereby that there was no difference between the compositions of the successor and the founder. This practice was followed by others to underline the idea of unity between the founder and the successors.

In the compositions of Guru Angad the unity, omnipotence, omnipresence, omniscience and immanence of God are taken for granted, and so are the divine order (*hukm, razā, farmān*) and grace (*nadar, kirpā, prasād*). The disease of self-centredness (*haumai*) keeps man entangled in the net of transmigration. Devotion is to be addressed voluntarily with love and dedication to the only God, in trust and fear, remembering Him in misery and comfort. The head that does not bow to Him is better cut off. One should be ready to die in His way.[4]

There are references to the divine preceptor, but more significant are the references to Nanak as the Guru. The connotation of the statements with a bearing on the Guru begins to change. 'The Guru has the key to salvation'; 'There is utter darkness without the Guru.'[5] Such statements are as much applicable to Guru Nanak as to the divine preceptor. Similarly, the Word and the Name get equated with the sacred compositions (*bāṇī*) of Guru Nanak. There is only one true *shabad*, the nectar-like *bāṇī* of Guru Nanak.[6] The Gurmukh (God-oriented) gets equated with the followers of Guru Nanak, and by implication with the followers of Guru Angad.[7]

Guru Angad had to establish a new centre. The law of the state could be invoked by the legal heirs of Guru Nanak to claim Kartarpur as a matter of right. But Guru Angad voluntarily moved to Khadur (in the Amritsar district), leaving Kartarpur in the hands of Sri Chand and Lakhmi Chand, the sons of Guru Nanak. Sri Chand built in fact a structure over the spot where Guru Nanak was cremated, and refused

---

[4] AG, 83, 88, 138, 463, 787, 788, 954, 1238, 1239.   [5] AG, 145, 146, 463, 1237.
[6] AG, 466, 469, 787, 1283.   [7] AG, 138, 463, 1288.

to recognize Guru Angad as the Guru. Some people were taken in by his claim to Guruship. The followers of Guru Angad were not thus the only followers of Guru Nanak. In the compositions of Guru Angad the presence of the 'others' is assumed. He invokes the principle of nomination against any other kind of claim to be the successor of Guru Nanak. 'What kind of a gift is this that one gives to oneself? The true gift is that which is received by serving the Master to his satisfaction.'[8] His faithful followers 'need no instruction' for they have been 'given instruction by Guru Nanak'.[9] The blind are not those who have no eyes; the blind are those who fail to recognize the Master even when they have eyes.[10]

Guru Angad established a community kitchen (langar) at Khadur where his followers and visitors used to meet for congregational worship. His wife, known as Mother Khīvī, took special interest in the community kitchen, and it was not uncommon to serve sweet pudding of rice boiled in milk, a sign perhaps of the ability of the Sikhs to bring substantial offerings.[11] Guru Angad refers to the early morning meditation and daily worship practised by his followers. Their spiritual state is reflected in the brightness of their faces; the grace of the sarrāf (God) has in fact gilded their entire frames.[12] The metaphors from trade in Guru Angad's compositions underline the importance of the Khatrī component of his followers, but there were certainly others. An ironsmith (lohār) and a barber (nāī) were among his eminent followers.[13] New followers were initiated in addition to the old disciples of Guru Nanak. To look after the needs of the congregation Guru Angad had to appoint a store-keeper (bhandārī) and a master-cook (rasoiyā).[14]

Guru Angad shows a deep regard for his followers. 'Nānak' is the slave of those who recognize the only true shabad; they are like God to him. 'Nānak' is the slave of those who recognize the unity of God and the secret of His Divinity; they are like God to him.[15] Only those who have turned to the Guru know that in the outside world of kaliyuga the king is really a pauper and the learned pandit is really a fool.[16] The 'Gurmukh' thus stands distinguished from the rest of his contemporaries. One such Gurmukh had served Guru Angad with devotion

---

[8] AG, 474.   [9] AG, 150.   [10] AG, 954.   [11] AG, 966–67.
[12] AG, 146.
[13] Varān Bhāī Gurdās (ed. Giani Hazara Singh), Wazir-i-Hind Press, Amritsar, 1962, vār 11, pauṛī 14.
[14] Ibid., vār 11, pauṛī 15.   [15] AG, 469.   [16] AG, 1288.

since 1540. In 1552, Guru Angad nominated him as the successor-Guru.

III

Guru Amar Das had to leave Khadur because it was claimed by Dasu and Datu, the sons of Guru Angad, as their inheritance. They set themselves up as Guru Angad's spiritual heirs. Guru Amar Das founded a new centre a few miles away on the right bank of the river Beas, on the route from Lahore to Delhi, which developed into a township known as Goindwal. His community kitchen in Goindwal came to be known for the plenty of its fine flour and clarified butter, which may be taken as an indication of the growing prosperity of his centre.[17]

In his compositions Guru Amar Das underlines the importance of true association (sat-sangat), that of his followers who came to the abode of the Guru (gurdwāra) for singing the shabad of the Guru and to listen to the bāṇī sung by the minstrels appointed by the Guru for this purpose. This true association of 'brothers-in-faith' and 'friends-in-faith' is a source of 'understanding'; it opens the door to salvation. Access to the sangat is a gift of the Guru. He who fails to turn to the Guru and to recognize the shabad is self-oriented (manmukh). There are detractors (nindak) too, and there are deserters who have turned away (bemukh). The Guru does not regard anyone as his enemy, and his Sikhs are safe under the protection of the all-powerful God. Their enemies do not know that He is the only true king; His worshippers cannot come to any harm at the hands of the agents of the earthly kings. There are indications, thus, that the opponents of the Guru were seeking help from the local administrators. Opposition to the Guru may be taken as a measure of his increasing success in propagating his faith.[18]

The compositions of Guru Amar Das read like annotations to the compositions of Guru Nanak. There is hardly an important idea of Guru Nanak which does not find a similar expression in the compositions of Guru Amar Das. Figuring frequently in his compositions is God in His attributeless state, His revelation through the Word, the

---

[17] AG, 967.
[18] AG, 26, 28, 29, 30, 31, 33, 35, 37–38, 65, 67–68, 114, 115, 120, 129, 233, 364, 425, 427, 516, 517, 586, 587, 590, 601, 638, 643, 645, 849, 854, 909, 912, 1046, 1249, 1258, 1259, 1260, 1276, 1334, 1415, 1416, 1417.

49

divine order, the divine preceptor, His grace, His transcendence and immanence, the *māyā* and *haumai* and the true path of *bhaktī*. However, there are significant shifts of emphasis and connotation. Every cosmic age (*yuga*) had its appropriate faith (*dharma*); the present age (*kaliyuga*) has the Name.[19] There is no *guru* but the true Guru. Those who do not serve the true Guru remain in misery throughout the four cosmic ages.[20] One should do as the Guru says, and conform to his wishes (*bhāṇā*).[21] The *bāṇī* of the true Guru is true. The *bāṇī* of the Guru is the sweet nectar of immortality. 'Gurmukh *bāṇī* is Brahm.' *Bāṇī* is God.[22]

All compositions other than the *bāṇī* of the true Guru are unripe (*kachchī*). They who recite or pronounce unripe compositions are themselves unripe; they who listen to unripe compositions remain unripe; what is conveyed by unripe compositions is unripe.[23] Guru Amar Das prepared two volumes of true *bāṇī*, consisting mostly of the compositions of Guru Nanak, Guru Angad and Guru Amar Das himself. Included in these two volumes was the *bāṇī* of *sants* and *bhaktas* like Kabir and Namdev.[24] Guru Amar Das refers to Namdev, the calico-printer, and Kabir, the weaver, who attained to the state of salvation with the grace of the perfect Guru; they recognized the divine *shabad* and got rid of *haumai* and the restrictions of caste; now their *bāṇī* is sung by both gods and men.[25] Guru Amar Das found rather kindred spirits in Kabir and Namdev and collected their compositions to be incorporated in the volumes containing the *bāṇī* of the Gurus. There was a professional scribe among his followers; there was also an eminent singer of the sacred *bāṇī*.[26]

The number of Sikhs increased considerably in the time of Guru Amar Das. Instead of a few individuals here and there in the country-side, some villages came to have a large number of Sikhs. For the propagation of his faith he visited Kurukshetra and some of the sacred places on the Jamuna and the Ganges.[27] It is not unlikely that some of the Khatrī followers of Guru Amar Das had started their trading activity outside the province of Lahore. In any case, new bonds were

---

[19] *AG*, 229, 797, 880.   [20] *AG*, 519.

[21] *AG*, 37, 665, 757, 905, 943, 1015, 1248.

[22] *AG*, 39, 246, 515.   [23] *AG*, 920; for *sachchī* (authentic) *bāṇī*, by contrast, 968.

[24] W. H. McLeod, *The Evolution of the Sikh Community*, Oxford University Press, 1975, 61.

[25] *AG*, 67, 555, 1380.   [26] Bhai Gurdas, *vār* 11, *pauṛī* 16.

[27] Stated by Guru Ram Das: *AG*, 2116.

needed for the growing community of followers. Guru Amar Das constructed a well at Goindwal, with eighty-four steps to reach the water for bathing, which became sacred for the Sikhs. In a sense, the first pilgrimage centre for the Sikhs was established at Goindwal. The Baisākhī and the Diwālī became festival days for the Sikhs who visited Goindwal. Guru Amar Das introduced distinctly Sikh ceremonies for the occasions of death, birth and marriage, asking the Sikhs not to cry and lament in their hour of loss and not to forget the divine source of supreme happiness in their hour of earthly bliss.[28] Guru Amar Das spoke against self-immolation, female infanticide and the consumption of liquor.[29] The first injunction was perhaps meant for his Khatrī followers; the second and the third, for the Jat cultivators of the countryside.

Guru Amar Das upheld the principle of nomination. 'God Himself is the Guru and He Himself is the disciple (chela).'[30] This could be applied to Guru Nanak and Guru Angad as well. In any case, it is a part of the divine order that the Guru can raise another to the status of the Guru.[31] As his own successor, Guru Amar Das chose his son-in-law, Bhai Jetha, as Guru Ram Das. Thinking of the likely opposition from his sons, Mohan and Mohri, Guru Amar Das decided to found a new centre. The site was chosen and work was started on digging a pool when Guru Amar Das died in 1574.

IV

Guru Ram Das got a tank (sarovar) dug where we find it today in the city of Amritsar. From the very beginning it was meant to be a sacred tank. The pure water of this 'divine pool' removes dust and dirt from the bodies of those who bathe here, and their bodies become pure.[32] All sins are removed from those to whom the Guru gives the gift of bathing in this pool filled with 'the nectar of immortality' (amritsar).[33] Indeed, Amritsar was the name given to this tank in the beginning; it came to be extended to the city much later. A township started growing around the tank and it was appropriately called Ramdaspur or the town of Guru Ram Das. Besides the followers of the Guru, other

---

[28] In the compositions of Guru Arjan there are references to the recitation of *Anand* at the birth of his son Hargobind: *AG*, 396.

[29] *AG*, 554, 787, 1413.   [30] *AG*, 797.   [31] *AG*, 490.   [32] *AG*, 774.

[33] *AG*, 732, 774.

traders, shopkeepers, artisans and craftsmen were encouraged to live in the town.

The founding of a town and the excavation of a large tank is indicative of the resources mobilized by Guru Ram Das. The Sikhs were expected to make contributions in cash, kind and service. In the compositions of Guru Ram Das there is a good deal of insistence on the merit of offerings to the Guru. 'Give your wealth and riches to him who enables you to meet the Friend.'[34] The followers are asked to send corn and cloth. All their wishes are fulfilled who serve the Guru with devotion. Whatever they wish, all they wish for, is given: true faith, earthly riches, pleasures and salvation (*dharma, artha, kāma, moksha*). There are indications in the compositions of Guru Ram Das that he authorized some of his Sikhs to act as his representatives and to collect offerings from those Sikhs who could not come personally to the Guru.[35]

In the compositions of Guru Ram Das, the food, dress and possessions of those who have appropriated the name are sanctified. They who entertain the Sikhs, their houses and mansions are sanctified. The caparisoned horses which the Sikhs ride are sanctified.[36] They who have God's name on their lips, their actions and affairs are sanctified. They who bring offerings to the Guru, acquire the true merit of charity. The low caste also figure prominently in the compositions of Guru Ram Das. While Khatrīs and Brahmans were ignored by God, Namdev was drawn close. There were other low-caste devotees of God who attained to salvation through their devotion, like Kabir, Jaidev, Tarlochan, Ravidas, Dhanna and Sen.[37] Appreciation for the low-caste Sants and Bhaktas may be treated as an indication of the presence of the low caste among the Sikhs. Guru Ram Das is aware of the presence of the cultivators among the Sikhs. He feels concerned about drought and gratified about timely rainfall; he is also aware of the wells with the Persian wheel to irrigate the fields.'[38] Then there were shopkeepers, petty traders, artisans and craftsmen among the Sikhs, besides the wealthy merchants and traders. The community was never much short of women, but in the compositions of Guru Ram Das their presence is as palpable as that of men.

There are some other important dimensions of the compositions of

---

[34] *AG*, 301, 443, 588, 719, 853, 1264.   [35] *AG*, 301, 303, 307, 443, 588, 590.
[36] *AG*, 648, 1246.
[37] *AG*, 733, 799, 835, 976, 995.   [38] *AG*, 304, 368, 1250, 1318, 1329.

Guru Ram Das. The importance of the Guru is increasing with the increasing number and prosperity of the Sikhs. He provides the common bond. He is the father and the mother; he is the friend and the relation. He is the honour of those who possess no honour on their own.[39] Equally important is the *bāṇī* of the Guru (*gurbāṇī*). It is the embodiment of truth; there is no other true *bāṇī*.[40] The Sikh of the Guru (*gursikh*) is like the Guru himself; the true Guru dwells in them. They meditate on God day and night: 'I am their slave.'[41] To meet a *gursikh* is the sign of God's grace. The *sangat* becomes the collective body of the Sikhs in the compositions of Guru Ram Das. The *sangat* of the Guru is dear to God.[42] Guru Ram Das composed *lāvān* for the solemnization of Sikh marriage, and *ghoriān* to be sung on days preceding the day of marriage.[43] He contributed even more to the Sikh awareness of a distinct identity by separating them clearly from 'the others' in his compositions. The 'noseless' *manmukh* stands dishonoured; he is a 'nameless' bastard born to a prostitute.[44]

The distinctive identity of the Sikhs is underlined by Guru Ram Das partly because of the dissension among the professed followers of Guru Nanak. There are deserters who have turned away from the Guru (*bemukh*), the 'black-faced' thieves of God. They are misled by the detractors (*nindak*) of the Guru who are envious of his success and his wealth. They try to imitate the Guru, but what they say is 'unripe'.[45] Guru Ram Das upholds the principle of nomination to castigate his opponents. They do not realize that the treasure of *bhakti* had been bestowed upon the true devotees of God from the very beginning; they stood cursed by Guru Nanak and by Guru Angad; the third Guru thought that they possessed no power to harm; the fourth Guru forgave the detractors and their associates. But the detractors persist in their folly and suffer ignominy. They seek the support of local administrators and *chaudharīs*. This combination presented a threat which Guru Ram Das could not fail to notice.[46]

Guru Ram Das advises his followers not to retaliate, but to leave things to God. The *dīwāns* of God, the Sikhs, need not be afraid of the earthly *dīwāns*, the administrators of the empire.[47] All the emperors and *kings*, *khāns* and *amīrs* and *shiqdārs* are subject to the power of

---

[39] *AG*, 167.   [40] *AG*, 304.   [41] *AG*, 305–06, 493, 1263.
[42] *AG*, 446, 1197, 1297.
[43] *AG*, 575, 576, 774.   [44] *AG*, 837.   [45] *AG*, 304, 1250.
[46] *AG*, 303, 306, 307, 316, 366, 651, 733, 850, 853–54.
[47] *AG*, 591.

God and they do what He wills for them.[48] Since the Sikhs belong to the 'faction' of God they need not fear an earthly faction (*dhaṛā*).[49] Guru Ram Das invokes myth and legend to reassure the Sikhs that God is their protector. He is also keen to underline that he is the only legitimate successor of the world-preceptor (*jagat-gurū*), Guru Nanak.[50] Before his death in 1581, Guru Ram Das chose his youngest son, Arjan, as the successor-Guru. The principle of nomination was upheld, but it was restricted to the family of Guru Ram Das.

V

If the idea of Guru Ram Das was to enable his successor to have legal claims over Ramdaspur as one of his heirs, and thereby to enable him to remain in control of the headquarters, it was eminently successful. Guru Arjan was the first successor of Guru Nanak who succeeded to the missionary centre of his immediate predecessor. However, the other legal heirs could claim a share in the property. Guru Arjan's eldest brother, Prithi Chand, approached the local administrators probably to claim the position of his father but he had to be content with a share in the income from Ramdaspur. Guru Arjan was only eighteen years old at the time of his nomination, and he had no son. Prithi Chand bided his time, remaining unreconciled to the Guruship of his younger brother. After the birth of Guru Arjan's son Hargobind in 1595, Prithi Chand's hostility was sharpened but he did not openly defy the Guru. Nevertheless, Guru Arjan had to face covert enmity from within the family.

There were other detractors too. Guru Arjan refers to them rather frequently in his compositions. They are generally foiled in their attempt to harm the Guru's interests. If one of them submitted an affidavit signed by a number of persons (*mahzar*) to the *qāzī* against the Guru, it turned out to be false and the author of this falsehood met an ignominious end.[51] If another tried to poison the child Hargobind, he was himself killed.[52] An inveterate enemy of Guru Arjan was one Sulhi; he got axed to death before his evil intentions got clothed in action.[53] The faces of the detractors were 'blackened' when they made a representation against the Guru to a high dignitary of the state who

[48] *AG*, 851.   [49] *AG*, 366.   [50] *AG*, 733.   [51] *AG*, 199.
[52] *AG*, 1137–38.
[53] *AG*, 825.

found their charges baseless and allowed the Guru to return home safe.[54] It is possible that Akbar's attitude towards Guru Arjan had a sheltering effect. On his return from Lahore after a long stay, Akbar met the Guru at Goindwal in November, 1598. Two weeks later, he decreased the rate of revenue in the province to bring it down to what it was before his long stay in Lahore.[55]

To cope with the feeling of insecurity, arising particularly from the hostility of the Guru's opponents and detractors, Guru Arjan exhorted his followers to cultivate profound faith and trust in God. He who remembers God gets rid of fear. The *shabad* of the Guru acts like a protective garrison all around. The 'wealth of God' is the antidote for anxiety. The Name makes one fearless. They who take refuge in God have nothing to fear.[56] Indeed, God is given new attributes; He is free from anxiety (*achinta*); He is the remover of misery (*dukh-bhanjan*); and, above all, He is the annihilator of the enemy (*satr-dahan*).[57] With God lodged in one's heart, not only was the fear of insecurity removed but also the day-to-day actions of the Sikhs were sanctified. One could attain to salvation while laughing and playing, and eating and dressing.[58]

The *bāni* of the Guru was like a shower of rain for those who were thirsty in spirit. Guru Arjan composed more than any of his predecessors, particularly the short lyrical pieces (*shabads*) which could be easily memorized. He found 'priceless gems' and an 'inexhaustible treasure' in what had been preserved by his predecessors.[59] To the two volumes compiled by Guru Amar Das were added the compositions of Guru Ram Das and Guru Arjan himself, besides the compositions of a few more Bhaktas. A book was compiled in 1604, marked by an unusually systematic arrangement and a complex but generally consistent pattern of division and subdivision.[60] That book is now known as the Ādi Granth, the old book, to distinguish it from the later Dasam Granth, the book of the tenth Guru; it is more popularly referred to as Granth Sahib as a mark of respect, and as Guru Granth Sahib to indicate that it enjoys the status of the Guru. Already for Guru

[54] *AG*, 826–27.
[55] Sujan Rai, 'Khulāsat ut-Tawārīkh' (late seventeenth century) in Ganda Singh (ed.), *Mākhiz-i-Tawārīkh-i-Sikhān*, 59.
[56] *AG*, 42, 43, 107, 131–32, 211, 240, 261, 262, 281, 285, 286, 287, 289, 292, 371, 674, 823, 1145.
[57] *AG*, 502, 503, 1157.   [58] *AG*, 212, 522.   [59] *AG*, 185.
[60] W. H. McLeod, *The Evolution of the Sikh Community*, 70–73.

Arjan, it was no ordinary compilation: it was 'the abode of God.'[61]

By this time the tank of Guru Ram Das had been enlarged, and paved and walled with burnt bricks. He felt gratified that the construction work was completed without any hindrance as if God Himself was amidst the Sikhs when they were working. The tank looked beautiful, like the earth around, and water flowed into it like nectar.[62] Once the work was completed, all anxieties were gone. They who bathe in the tank earn salvation for their families as well.[63] In the midst of the tank a temple dedicated to God (*harmandir*) had been constructed for singing His praises. It was truly a happy conjunction when the 'everlasting foundation' of the temple was laid with God's grace. Now the Sikhs can blissfully sing the praises of God all the twenty-four hours of the day; the *bāṇī* of the Guru is now recited and sung here day and night.[64]

The town of Guru Ram Das continued to flourish under Guru Arjan. For him, there was no other place like the beautiful and thickly populated Ramdaspur, founded by God Himself. In this everlasting city of the Guru, the Name is the source of happiness, and all wishes are fulfilled. The Sikhs, who are like brothers and sons to the Guru feel pleased with the beauty of the town, a standing monument to God's grace. The rule of Rama (*rām-rāj*) prevails in Ramdaspur, due to the grace of the Guru. No *jizya* is levied, nor any fine; there is no collector of taxes.[65] The administrative control of the town was in the hands of Guru Arjan. In the context and the framework of the Mughal empire, Ramdaspur was an autonomous town.

Guru Arjan founded Tarn Taran and Sri Hargobindpur in the Bari Doab and Kartarpur in the Bist Jalandhar Doab. This can be taken as an indication of the growing number of Sikhs, particularly in the countryside. But this is only one indication. Guru Arjan feels gratified that the greatness of Guru Nanak has been revealed to the entire world. Sikhs come to the Guru from all the four corners of the world.[66] The Name has proved to be the salvation of all the four *varṇas*: the Khatri, the Brahman, the Shūdar and the Vaish.[67] There is no doubt that the number of Sikhs increased considerably in the Punjab during the pontificate of Guru Arjan. There were many Sikhs in Lahore. Similarly, Sultanpur Lodhi was known as a great centre of Sikhism. There

---

[61] *AG*, 1226.   [62] *AG*, 781.   [63] *AG*, 174, 1362.   [64] *AG*, 820–21.
[65] *AG*, 430, 620, 781, 817, 1002.
[66] *AG*, 43, 611, 724, 801, 811, 819, 1100, 1139, 1141, 1217, 1364, 1429.
[67] *AG*, 1001.

were Sikhs in the smaller towns like Patti Haibatpur, and there were Sikhs in many villages. There were certainly some Brahmans among the Sikhs and some of the out-caste. The trading communities, the cultivators, the artisans and craftsmen were well represented. Among the trading communities, there was a clear preponderance of the Khatrīs; and among the cultivators, that of the Jats. There was one Mian Jamal among the eminent Sikhs who remained present with the Guru.[68] Furthermore, the Sikhs were not confined to the Punjab. There were Sikhs in Kashmir and Kabul, and in Delhi and Agra. It is most likely indeed that Sikhs could be found now in all the provinces of Akbar's empire.[69] Guru Arjan had to appoint a number of representatives authorized to look after the affairs of the local *sangats* at various places, not only outside the Punjab but also in the Punjab. Once a year, the authorized representatives brought offerings to the Guru, collected from the Sikhs under their supervision, together with some of the Sikhs themselves to have an audience with the Guru.

The Guru was at the centre of the whole organization. In the compositions of Guru Arjan he is the true king, the king of kings, for his Sikhs who deemed it a great boon to sit with him even for a moment. His court was the most high. He was the source of all gifts. His sight removed all sins. His instruction led to salvation. His service was always well rewarded. The Sikh was expected to remember the Guru all the time. Indeed, the Guru is God (*pār-brahm*). 'Do not be misled by his human form; the Guru is the veritable God (*niranjan*).'[70] Guru Arjan, like his predecessors, carried an aura of divinity for his Sikhs.

VI

Over a dozen professional composers (*bhāts*) have sung the praises of the Gurus in one *vār* and over 120 *savayyās* are preserved in the Granth compiled by Guru Arjan.[71] They refer to the congregational worship,

---

[68] This is one of the few explicit references to Muslims accepting the Sikh faith though in the seventeenth-century *janamsākhīs* Mardana and even Daulat Khan Lodhi are treated as the followers of Guru Nanak.

[69] Bhai Gurdas, *vār* 11, *pauṛī* 22–31.   [70] *AG*, 1476.

[71] Sahib Singh (ed.), *Stīk Satta Balwand dī Vār*, Amritsar 1949; *Sadd Stīk*, Amritsar, 1958. For the *Savayyās, Adi Granth* 1389–1409.

the community kitchen, the increasing number of the Sikhs, and the centres of pilgrimage at Goindwal and Ramdaspur. They admire the combination of religious faith and social commitment (*jog* and *rāj*) in the mission of the Gurus. They underline the importance of the Name and the *shabad*; they refer to the *bāṇī* of the Gurus as an alternative to the Vedas and the Quran. The divine sanction for the *bhaktī* and the truth proclaimed by Guru Nanak is emphasized, and it is also suggested that his path possesses an exclusive validity and efficacy during the present cosmic age (*kaliyuga*). The divinity of the Guru is underlined, and so is his grace. One is redeemed by seeing him. He is the destroyer of fear. By serving the Guru and remembering him, all one's wishes are fulfilled.

The uniqueness of the Guru is brought out by the *bhāts* in unambiguous terms. Guru Nanak is the preceptor of the world (*jagat-gurū*); his mission is universal redemption. The unique status of Guru Nanak and his successors is brought out by invoking myth, legend and history. The thirty-three crores of gods and goddesses sing their praises. What they are doing in *kaliyuga* was done by Rama in the *treta* and by Krishna in the *duapur*. The saints like Kabir, Ravidas, Namdev, Jaidev, Tarlochan and Beni sing the praises of the Guru. The greatest emphasis of the *bhāts* is on the unity of Guruship. The direct line of succession is repeated from Guru Nanak to Guru Arjan, through Guru Angad, Guru Amar Das and Guru Ram Das, underlining the exclusive validity of nomination by the reigning Guru. The same divine light shone through all of them. It is explicitly pointed out that Guru Arjan is as much a successor of Guru Nanak as the others. The fact that he is a son of Guru Ram Das makes no difference to the legitimacy of nomination. One vital idea which is put forth in the *vār* of Balwand and Satta is that Guru Nanak installed Angad as the Guru during his lifetime and bowed to him; the position of the Guru and the disciple (*chela*) was thus reversed. That is how Guru Nanak makes 'the water run upstream'. The metaphors used by the *bhāts* in connection with the Gurus are also significant: the true king, his rule, throne, umbrella, flywhisk, canopy, crown, court, armies, for instance. Many of the *bhāts* refer to slanderers, their opposition to the Gurus and their discomfiture. The *bhāts* show a thorough familiarity with the teachings of the Gurus but they were not formal Sikhs, which makes their ideas all the more important. In any case, all these ideas are expressed even more crisply and emphatically by Bhai Gurdas who is often referred to as the 'St Paul of Sikhism'.[72]

VII

At the death of Akbar in 1605, the Sikhs were living in many cities of the Mughal empire, with a clear concentration in the towns and the villages of the province of Lahore. Accredited representatives (*masands*) of the Guru looked after the distant congregations (*sangats*) and brought their offerings to Ramdaspur (Amritsar) at least once in a year. Included among the Sikhs were members of the trading communities of merchants and shopkeepers, and of the producing communities of cultivators and craftsmen. Themselves self-reliant, they provided the economic backbone for the organization evolved by the Gurus to enable them to undertake large projects without financial dependence on outside agencies.

The religious ideology of Guru Nanak was reinforced by his successors in a manner that added new dimensions without minimizing the importance of his basic ideas. With reference to the nomination of Angad as the Guru in the lifetime of Guru Nanak, the successors were brought into equal prominence with the founder; the idea of the unity of Guruship was adumbrated and upheld; the office of the Guru became more important than the person of the Guru; and his decisions became as legitimate as the decisions of the founder. Thus, the pontificates of the successors became an extension of the mission of the founder, and the work of his successors became an extension of his work. With reference to the reversal of the position of the disciple with the Guru, the individual Sikh was given great consideration by the Guru, and the collective body of the congregation (*sangat*) was given even greater importance. With reference to the *shabad* as the medium of divine revelation, and the *bāṇī* of Guru Nanak as a part of that revelation, the compositions of the Gurus were brought into parallel prominence with the Guru. Though neither an incarnation of God nor His prophet, the Guru was so near allied to Him that his followers regarded him as the *locus* of divinity.

---

[72] Bhai Gurdas Bhalla was closely related to Guru Amar Das and associated himself with Guru Ram Das, Guru Arjan and Guru Hargobind. He served as the scribe when Guru Arjan compiled the Granth. For his basic ideas, J. S. Grewal, *Guru Nanak in History*, Panjab University, Chandigarh, 1979, 295–302.

59

The religious ideology of the Sikhs, which informed their attitudes to life, was embodied in the Granth compiled by Guru Arjan. The Sikhs were now becoming more and more conscious that their scripture was tangibly distinct from the Veda and the Quran. Incorporating the ideas contained in the compositions of *sants*, *bhaktas* and *sūfīs*, which had the greatest affinity with the ideas of the Gurus themselves, the Sikh scripture thus contained ideas becoming current in much of the Indian subcontinent. Composed in a language that was easily understood by common people over a large part of northern India, it was written out in a script that was easily the simplest of all the scripts known to India. It became the only authentic source of the characteristically Sikh ideas which were distinct from much in the contemporary systems of religious belief and practice. Copies could be made of the entire Granth, or a significant selection could be made, for use in distant places. To listen to *gurbāṇī*, in any case, was to hear the voice of the Guru himself.

The distinctive Sikh identity, based initially on religious ideology, was reinforced by the adoption of distinctly Sikh ceremonies on the occasions of birth, marriage and death. The Sikhs were free to maintain the old horizontal links of castes and sub-castes for matrimonial purposes but there was nothing in the teachings of the Guru that could be invoked in support of such links. The ideal of equality was openly demonstrated in the institutions of congregational worship and community meals. Ramdaspur (Amritsar) as the place of pilgrimage was open to all Sikhs from far and near, and large crowds used to come for the festivals of Baisākhī and Diwālī. The bi-annual convergence of Sikh pilgrims to the autonomous town of Guru Ram Das gave them a feeling of spiritual elation; it gave them also a sense of belonging to a large brotherhood.

The Sikh Panth was a state within the Mughal empire at the death of Akbar, but a state that had its opponents and enemies whose presence was continuously felt by the successors of Guru Nanak. The enemies were becoming more numerous, and their intrigues were on the increase. If the law of the state enabled some of them to approach the administrators with plausible claims over the property and wealth of the Gurus, the cupidity of the administrators induced them to entertain those claims. Akbar's catholicity could protect the Gurus and their followers against open violence but it could not obviate the nefarious designs of their enemies. The removal of a protecting umbrella could increase the heat of hostility for the Guru and his followers.

The withdrawal of symbolic protection came rather suddenly and in such a form that to call it harsh or hostile would be an understatement. Within eight months of Akbar's death in October, 1605, Guru Arjan died the death of a martyr at the end of May, 1606, tortured by the new emperor's underlings at Lahore.

CHAPTER 4

TRANSFORMATION OF THE SIKH PANTH (1606–1708)

During the seventeenth century five Gurus succeeded Guru Arjan. His son, Guru Hargobind was succeeded by a grandson, Guru Har Rai. The younger son of Guru Har Rai, Guru Har Krishan was succeeded by a grand uncle, Guru Tegh Bahadur, the youngest son of Guru Hargobind. Guru Gobind Singh, who succeeded his father Guru Tegh Bahadur in 1675, abolished personal Guruship before his death in 1708.[1]

Interference by the Mughal emperors Jahangir, Shah Jahan and Aurangzeb in the affairs of the Sikh Panth was an important feature of this period. We have already referred to the martyrdom of Guru Arjan at the beginning of Jahangir's rule. A few years later, Jahangir ordered the detention of Guru Hargobind in the fort of Gwalior which was generally used for detaining political prisoners. In the reign of Shah Jahan the Mughal administrators of the Punjab came into armed conflict with Guru Hargobind. Aurangzeb took an active interest in the issue of succession, passed orders for the execution of Guru Tegh Bahadur, and at one time ordered total extirpation of Guru Gobind Singh and his family. State interference was, thus, a serious matter.

State interference encouraged dissent within the Sikh Panth and accentuated disunity. Prithi Chand, significantly, put forth his claim to be the successor of Guru Arjan after his martyrdom, becoming thus a rival of Guru Hargobind. Dhir Mal, a grandson of Guru Hargobind, preferred to remain in the good books of the emperors and chose to have his own centre in the province of Lahore rather than succeeding to the office of Guru Hargobind at his headquarters in a vassal principality. Ram Rai, the elder brother of Guru Har Krishan, chose to become a protégé of Aurangzeb.[2]

Apart from rival claimants from the Sodhi family of Guru Ram Das, there were the Udāsīs who traced their origin to Guru Nanak through his son Sri Chand; they were renunciant recluses rather than householders. Then there were the followers of Hindal, who did not show

---

[1] For the successors of Guru Nanak after Guru Arjan see appendix 1.
[2] For the descendants of Guru Ram Das see appendix 2.

much veneration even for the founder of Sikhism; they were trying to hijack the Sikh movement. In this situation the *masands* became lukewarm or indifferent to the nominated Gurus, or actually changed sides. There was one attitude which all the dissidents and detractors shared: they were all what may be called 'pro-establishment'.

As a result of the combination of these circumstances the successors of Guru Arjan shifted the theatre of their activities to the east of the river Satlej, giving new cradle lands to the Sikh movement. Furthermore, the places now regarded as the most historic outside the land of the five rivers were associated with the last Guru: Patna in Bihar, Anandpur and Muktsar in the Punjab, and Nanded in Maharashtra. The transformation of the Sikh Panth, which began in the time of Guru Hargobind reached its culmination under Guru Gobind Singh in response to external interference and internal disunity.

I

Nuruddin Jahangir, the son and successor of Akbar, states in his *Memoirs* that he called for Guru Arjan on account of the charge brought against him that he had put a saffron mark on the forehead of the rebel Prince Khusrau as a token of his blessings.[3] As a prince, Jahangir had heard about the 'shop' which had done brisk business for three or four generations before Guru Arjan started luring ignorant Muslims as well as foolish Hindus to purchase 'falsehood'.[4] Many a time it had occurred to Jahangir that either this shop of falsehood should be closed or Guru Arjan should be brought into the fold of Islam. He ordered Guru Arjan to be put to death, his mansions and his family to be entrusted to Murtaza Khan and his property to be confiscated.[5]

In the Sikh tradition, however, there is hardly any reference to Jahangir's order of capital punishment. Bhai Gurdas admires the incredible equanimity of Guru Arjan under unbearable torture, but he says nothing more. In the *Bachittar Nātak*, composed in the last decade of the seventeenth century, there is a reference to the martyrdom of

---

[3] It was a common practice with Guru Arjan to place his hand on the forehead of a visitor. This could be easily exaggerated into putting of a saffron mark on Khusrau's forehead by the opponents of the Guru.

[4] Guru Arjan's followers did include at least a few former Muslims.

[5] Persian text of the *Memoirs* printed in *Mākhiz-i-Tawārikh-i-Sikhān* (ed. Ganda Singh), Sikh History, Amritsar, 1949, 20–22.

Guru Tegh Bahadur, but nothing about the martyrdom of Guru Arjan. In the late eighteenth century, it was believed that Jahangir imposed a fine of 200,000 rupees which Guru Arjan refused to pay and he was tortured. Already in the 1640s the author of the *Dabistān-i-Mazāhab* had stated that Jahangir imposed a heavy fine on Guru Arjan which he was not in a position to pay, and consequently he was tortured in hot weather and he died.[6] It was generally believed that the person responsible for torturing Guru Arjan was the *dīwān* of Lahore. All this evidence suggests that the capital punishment was commuted into heavy fine. It is nevertheless certain that Jahangir was strongly prejudiced against Guru Arjan partly because of the vast size of his 'shop' which offered its 'wares' to all, irrespective of their caste or creed.

The action of the state authorities was a stunning blow to the followers of Guru Arjan. Whether it was due to the intrigues of the slanderers of the Guru, or the enmity of some local administrator, or the autocratic prejudice of the emperor, the injustice was patent enough. Guru Hargobind reacted to the event in proportion to the enormity of the injustice. He girded two swords, as the Sikh tradition puts it, one symbolizing his spiritual authority and the other his temporal power. He encouraged his followers in martial activity. The Jat component of his followers needed only a little persuasion. Guru Hargobind added two new features to Ramdaspur. Opposite the Harmandir he constructed a high platform which came to be known as Akāl Takht, 'the immortal throne'. Here the Guru held a kind of court to conduct temporal business. He also constructed a fort called Lohgarh for the purpose of defence.

A clear departure from the practices of his predecessors made Guru Hargobind conspicuous in the eyes of the administrators and on their representation Jahangir ordered his detention in the fort of Gwalior. Before long, however, counter-representations were made on behalf of Guru Hargobind and he was released. The emperor appears eventually to have felt satisfied with the justification given by the Guru for his interests and activities. Guru Hargobind was left free to pursue them for the rest of Jahangir's reign.[7]

The slanderers of the Guru, his opponents, criticized him for his martial activities, with the implication that he was not a true Guru. After the martyrdom of Guru Arjan, his elder brother Prithi Chand

[6] (*Dabistan-i-Mazahib*) *Mākhiz-i-Tawārīkh-i-Sikhān*, 35–37.   [7] *Ibid.*, 38.

put forth his claim to be the successor of Guru Arjan. After Prithi Chand's death his son Miharban claimed to be the seventh Guru. Some of the Sikhs who could not appreciate the measures adopted by Guru Hargobind were influenced by the propaganda of these rival claimants popularly known as *mīṇās*. Bhai Gurdas in his *vārs* refers to the plank of these propagandists. In contrast to the former Gurus, they say, the present Guru does not stay long at any one place; he was sent into imprisonment by the emperor; he roams the land without fear; he keeps dogs and goes out hunting; he does not compose *bāṇī*, nor does he listen to it or sing it; and he gives preference to scoundrels over his devoted servants. Bhai Gurdas asserts, however, that Guru Hargobind is bearing an unbearable burden and the true Sikhs are devoted to him.[8] He justifies the new measures of Guru Hargobind with the argument that an orchard needs the protective hedge of the hardy and thorny *kīkar* trees.[9] In other words, the Panth of Guru Nanak needed physical force for its protection.

Guru Hargobind's interest in hunting brought him into conflict with the Mughal administrators of the province of Lahore in the reign of Shah Jahan who had ascended the throne after Jahangir's death in 1627. Under imperial orders a Mughal commandant attacked Ramdaspur but he was repulsed. Nevertheless, Guru Hargobind abandoned Ramdaspur and went to Kartarpur in the Bist Jalandhar Doab. There too he was attacked by the Mughal forces. Two Mughal commandants were killed in the battle and the Guru was victorious.[10] He was convinced, however, that Mughal authorities would not leave him alone. He decided to leave the province of Lahore, to go into the territory of a Rajput vassal of the Mughal empire. The place he chose was Kiratpur in the small principality of Hindur (Nalagarh), protected not by the physical barrier of the Shivaliks so much as by the political barrier between the imperial and the vassal territory.

For eight or nine years Guru Hargobind lived at Kiratpur before he died in the first week of March, 1644. He maintained his stables, his horsemen and his matchlockmen at Kiratpur. He did not abandon martial exercises, but there were no battles to fight. In his personal correspondence he used the epithet 'Nānak' for himself, indicating clearly that he regarded himself as one with the founder of the Sikh

---

[8] Bhai Gurdas, *Vārān Bhāi Gurdās* (ed. Giani Hazara Singh), Wazir-i-Hind Press, Amritsar, 1962 (reprint), *vār* 26, *pauṛī* 24.
[9] *Ibid., pauṛī* 25. [10] (*Dabistān-i-Mazāhib*) *Mākhiz-i-Tawārīkh-i-Sikhān*, 39.

Panth and his successors. The ideas and beliefs which are attributed to him by the author of the *Dabistān-i-Mazāhib* indicate that there was no change in the religious ideology of Guru Hargobind.[11] He had numerous followers in Ujjain, Burhanpur, Lucknow, Prayag, Jaunpur, Patna, Raj Mahal and Dacca.[12] Like his eminent followers in the Punjab, they too were mostly Khatrīs. Among his important *masands*, however, there were many Jats, and agriculture was one of the two most important professions of the Sikhs. The Guru's dependence on the *masands* had increased, and some of them had started appointing their own deputies or agents for the collection of offerings as well as for initiating others to the Sikh faith. On the day of the Baisākhī they brought the offerings to the Guru. Some of the *masands* did not have their own source of income; they lived on a part of the collections made.[13]

With Guru Hargobind's absence from the plains, the field was left open to his opponents or rival claimants. Ramdaspur was taken over by Miharban, son of Prithi Chand, who wrote his own *bāṇī* as 'Nānak' and claimed to be the seventh Guru. He composed a *janamsākhī* of Guru Nanak to buttress his claims.[14] His son Harji, succeeded to his position at Ramdaspur in the 1640s as the eighth 'Nānak'. It may not be too much to presume that some of the followers of Guru Arjan went over to the *miṇās*. Guru Hargobind's own grandson, Dhir Mal, son of Gurditta who predeceased the Guru in the late 1630s, was not interested in succeeding to his position at Kiratpur. With the original copy of the scripture prepared by Bhai Gurdas under the instruction of Guru Arjan, Dhir Mal moved to Kartarpur in the early 1640s.[15] He was given revenue-free land at Kartarpur by the emperor Shah Jahan.[16] Dhir Mal did not merely leave his grandfather; he also abandoned his anti-establishment stance. The hostility of the Mughal state was impinging upon the Sikh Panth in more than one way to affect its character. As the spokesman of Guru Hargobind, Bhai Gurdas pro-

---

[11] *Ibid.*, 40–41.   [12] *Bhai Gurdas, vār* 11, *pauṛīs* 30–31.
[13] (*Dabistān-i-Mazāhib*) *Mākhiz-i-Tawārikh-i-Sikhān*, 35.
[14] The *janamsākhī* attributed to Miharban was edited by Kirpal Singh and published by the Sikh History Research Department of Khalsa College, Amritsar in 1962 as the *Janam Sakhī Shri Guru Nanak Dev Jī.*
[15] The descendants of Dhir Mal at Kartarpur are still in possession of the original Granth: W. H. McLeod, *The Evolution of the Sikh Community*, Oxford University Press, 1975, 61–62, 74.
[16] The text of an imperial order issued by Shah Jahan in 1643 is given in *Mākhiz-i-Tawārikh-i-Sikhān*, 51–52.

jects him sharply as the only legitimate successor of Guru Nanak and condemns the slanderers in general and the *miṇās* in particular in loud and clear terms. His emphatic 'orthodoxy' was partly a result of the growing dissent.[17]

Guru Hargobind nominated Har Rai, the younger brother of Dhir Mal, as the successor-Guru in 1644. Guru Har Rai was only fourteen years old at this time and he died in 1661 at the young age of a little over thirty. His pontificate of about seventeen years was rather uneventful. Soon after his accession he moved to Thapal in the territory of Sirmur (Nahan) temporarily, not to embroil himself in an armed conflict between the chief of Hindur (Nalagarh) and the Mughal commandants who invaded his territories.[18] He continued to maintain the retainers raised by Guru Hargobind, and his *masands* apparently held their own in competition with Dhir Mal at Kartarpur and Harji at Ramdaspur in the Bari Doab. A change in this situation came after Aurangzeb ascended the Mughal throne in 1658, defeating his elder brother Dara Shikoh in two battles.

II

The reign of Aurangzeb from 1658 to 1707 was marked by some important changes, making the context of the late seventeenth century rather different from that of the late sixteenth century when Akbar was on the throne. In the first half of his reign Aurangzeb adopted an aggressive social and political policy. He destroyed some important Hindu temples even in times of peace. In the early 1670s he ordered that all grants of revenue-free land given to non-Muslims should be resumed. That this order was immediately implemented in the Punjab is evident from the resumption of the *madad-i-ma'āsh* grant of the *jogīs* of Jakhbar near Pathankot in the fifteenth year of Aurangzeb's reign.[19] In 1679 the emperor re-imposed the *jizya* after more than a century of its abolition by Akbar. That this order too was implemented in the Punjab is evident from a document laying down the amount of *jizya* to be collected from all the three classes of assessees in a village.[20]

[17] For a brief analysis of the *vārs* of Bhai Gurdas, J. S. Grewal, 'Religious Literature and Secular History', *Proceedings Indian History Congress*, Amritsar, 1985, 273–84.

[18] (*Dabistān-i-Mazāhib*) *Mākhiz-i-Tawārīkh-i-Sikhān*, 45.

[19] B. N. Goswamy and J. S. Grewal, *The Mughals and the Jogis of Jakhbar*, Indian Institute of Advanced study, Simla, 1967, Documents 9, 12.

[20] Irfan Habib, *Agrarian System of Mughal India (1526–1707)*, Asia Publishing House, Bombay, 1963, 119–20.

Even during the first half of Aurangzeb's reign there were uprisings against his authority. In 1669 the Jat *zamīndār* of Talpat near Mathura rose in revolt with the support of nearly 20,000 peasants. In 1672, the Satnāmīs rose in revolt in the *pargana* of Narnaul, about 120 kilometres from Delhi. There were some other revolts in northern India, including the Punjab, but of much smaller magnitude. In the south, a new sovereign state was established by Shivaji in the teeth of opposition from the Mughal commanders and partly at the cost of the Mughal empire. After a long struggle he declared himself to be a sovereign ruler in 1674 and died as a sovereign ruler in 1680. Despite his tremendous exertion Aurangzeb failed to subvert the kingdom founded by Shivaji. In the process, the Mughals brought down the rulers of Bijapur and Golkonda. Bijapur was annexed to the Mughal empire in 1686, and Golkonda in 1687. Two years later the emperor was able to capture and kill Shivaji's son Shambuji. But the struggle for independence was kept up by the Maratha leaders under the nominal rule of Raja Ram, another son of Shivaji. When Aurangzeb died in 1707, Maratha horsemen were hovering around the imperial camp at Ahmadnagar.

Aurangzeb's long stay in the Deccan, from 1682 to 1707, affected the general administration of the Mughal empire as adversely as his wars affected its finances. It became increasingly difficult to assign adequately remunerative lands in *jāgīr* to the *mansabdārs*. There ensued in due course a scramble for *jāgīrs*, and the *mansabdārs* tended to align with one or another of the most powerful nobles in self-interest. The beginning of factional alignment was one serious result of the crisis in the *jāgīrdārī* system. Another was the exploitation of the peasantry by the *jāgīrdārs*. So long as the prospect of getting a good *jāgīr* was there, the *jāgīrdārs'* attitude was not affected by the transfer of his *jāgīr*. But in the absence of such a prospect he tried to extract as much as he could without caring for the future of the land or its cultivators. This tendency was accentuated by a relative regression in agricultural production. Exploitation of the peasantry led to unrest among the peasants.

In the province of Lahore during the reign of Aurangzeb, both agriculture and trade received an appreciable setback. In the reign of Jahangir and Shah Jahan expansion of agriculture is evident from the creation of new *parganas* and the emergence of new towns. The most important canal for irrigation in the province was dug in the reign of Shah Jahan, namely the Shah Nahr which irrigated thousands of acres in the upper Bari Doab. There was a large increase in the revenues of the province during the early seventeenth century. It amounted to nearly 68 per cent, from about 66,000,000 of *dāms* in 1595–1596 to about 100,000,000 *dāms* in 1656.[21] In the reign of Aurangzeb the revenue figures went down to less than 90,000,000 *dāms*. Seen in conjunction with the rise in prices, which enhanced the revenue figures, this decrease in the revenue meant a considerable decline in agricultural production. There is evidence also for a setback to commerce in the Punjab. Since trade was intimately connected with agricultural production, both suffered together. However, the countryside suffered more, and in the countryside the cultivators suffered the most.[22]

III

Aurangzeb's aggressive policy is reflected in his attitude towards the successors of Guru Hargobind. On the rumoured support of Guru Har Rai to Dara Shikoh during his flight to the Punjab, Aurangzeb called him to his court. Guru Har Rai sent his elder son, Ram Rai. The emperor kept him as a hostage in Delhi. Guru Har Rai chose his younger son, Har Krishan, as his successor. Aurangzeb summoned Guru Har Krishan also to Delhi. He continued to patronize Ram Rai and eventually granted revenue-free land to him in the present Dehra Dun in Uttar Pradesh. Guru Har Krishan died of smallpox in Delhi in 1664 after indicating that his 'grandfather' (*bābā*) Tegh Bahadur, the youngest son of Guru Hargobind, was his successor.

Tegh Bahadur had left Kiratpur after the death of Guru Hargobind in 1644 and settled in Bakala, the parental village of his mother in the upper Bari Doab. He started his career as the eighth successor of Guru Nanak at Bakala. However, the opposition from his nephew, Dhir Mal, at Kartarpur across the river Beas, and from his other nephew, Harji, at Ramdaspur, obliged him to leave the Bari Doab, and go to Kiratpur. There too he was not a welcome guest for his brother Suraj Mal. During the very first year of his pontificate therefore, Guru Tegh

---

[21] A small coin in Persia, the copper *dām* in Akbar's empire was the fortieth of a silver rupee; it came generally to be known as *paisa* and its value in the seventeenth century was merely a theoretical fraction of the rupee.

[22] For a decline in trade in the Punjab during the seventeenth century see Chetan Singh, *Region and Empire: Punjab in the Seventeenth Century*, Oxford University Press, Delhi 1991, 270–85.

Bahadur had to look for a new centre. He chose a place called Makhowal, only a few miles from Kiratpur but in the territory of the chief of Kahlur (Bilaspur). By accepting his nomination as the Guru, Tegh Bahadur gave an affront to Aurangzeb who had presumed to arbitrate in the matter of succession. Had Guru Tegh Bahadur stayed on in Makhowal, Aurangzeb might have ignored the affront.

Before the end of 1665, however, Guru Tegh Bahadur left Makhowal to establish contact with some of the Sikh centres (sangats) in the Mughal provinces of the Gangetic plain. Before long, he was taken to Delhi by one Alam Khan Rohila under imperial orders. On the intercession of Kanwar Ram Singh, son of Mirza Raja Jai Singh of Mewar, he was released from detention in December. From Delhi, Guru Tegh Bahadur went to Agra, from Agra then to Prayag (Allahabad), Benares, Sahsaram and Patna. At all these places there were old Sikh sangats. He left his family at Patna to be looked after by the local Sikhs before he moved on to Monghir. There he heard the news of the birth of his first and only son at Patna on December 22, 1666. From Monghir, Guru Tegh Bahadur moved to Dacca where Raja Ram Singh joined him early in 1668. He accompanied the Raja on his expedition into Assam. In March, 1670, Guru Tegh Bahadur moved back towards the Punjab, through Patna and Delhi, and reached Makhowal in April, 1671.

In the first five or six years of his pontificate Guru Tegh Bahadur travelled more than any of his predecessors after Guru Nanak. If his idea was to reassure the far-flung congregations (sangats) of the Guru's concern for them, he was amply successful. From his extant letters (hukmnāmas) to the congregations at Patna and Benares it is evident that the Sikhs of those regions served Guru Tegh Bahadur with veneration. They looked after his favourite horse, Sri Dhar; they celebrated the birth of his son Gobind Das with a lot of fanfare;[23] they lodged his family in a spacious mansion; they sent costly articles for his camp; they sent cloth, fine turbans and cash to him; they went to see him in large numbers at the time of the Diwālī. In one of his letters he talks of the entire sangat of the province of Allahabad; in another, he asks the masands of the province of Bihar to bring the sangats along when they were to bring their offerings to the Guru.[24] There is hardly

[23] Though the historians generally refer to the young Gobind as Gobind Rai, in the hukmnāmas of Guru Tegh Bahadur he is referred to as Gobind Das.

[24] Ganda Singh (ed.), Hukmnāmey (Pbi), Punjabi University, Patiala, 1965, Nos. 8–25.

any doubt that the Khatrī traders of the Gangetic plains formed an important constituency for Guru Tegh Bahadur.

According to the Persian chronicler Khafi Khan, when Aurangzeb came to know that the Sikhs had built temples in all towns and populous places in the empire and that the agents of their Guru collected offerings from the multitude of his followers to be scrupulously forwarded to him, he ordered the deputies of the Guru to be driven out of the temples.[25] The temples were to be demolished. According to the author of the Ma'āsir-i-'Ālamgīrī, Aurangzeb had issued a general order in 1669 that all the schools and temples of the non-Muslims should be demolished. In the town called Buriya in the sarkār of Sarhind the Sikh temple was demolished by the local administrator in accordance with the imperial orders, and a mosque was built in its place. The mosque was in turn demolished by the Sikhs and Aurangzeb felt annoyed with the qāzī and the muhtasib of the place.[26] This incident reveals the tensions created by the imperial orders.

In the compositions of Guru Tegh Bahadur under the name 'Nānak', which form now a part of the Granth Sahib, there is a clear indication that he regarded his situation as very grave. They bear witness to the truths enunciated by Guru Nanak and his successors and the conformity of Guru Tegh Bahadur to their religious ideology. Nevertheless there is a new dimension, a new note of urgency, and a sense of intense concern. Life is short; it hastens away; but it provides opportunity for those who would take it. Participation without entanglement is the ideal, which can be realized only through conquest of fear. The idea is not altogether new, but the insistence is. The Sikhs are asked to acknowledge him alone as truly wise who is not afraid of others and who inspires no fear in others. Himself prepared for the worst possible eventualities, Guru Tegh Bahadur wanted others also to face life with courage. His compositions reveal him as a prophet of reassurance in a trying situation.[27]

In 1673 Guru Tegh Bahadur moved out of Makhowal to impart his message of reassurance to peasants and zamīndārs in the province of Delhi. He moved from village to village in most of the districts now

[25] *Muntakhab al-Lubāb*, quoted, Indubhushan Banerjee, *Evolution of the Khalsa*, Calcutta, 1980, II, 59.
[26] The text of the imperial order issued by Aurangzeb is given in *Mākhiz-i-Tawārīkh-i-Sikhān*, 73.
[27] J. S. Grewal, 'The Prophet of Assurance', *From Guru Nanak to Maharaja Ranjit Singh*, Guru Nanak Dev University, Amritsar, 1982 (2nd edn), 64–70.

covered by the states of Punjab and Haryana. There was a good response to this missionary work of about two years. The news-writers of the Mughal empire were bound to send reports of this response, and Aurangzeb was not likely to ignore this. Guru Tegh Bahadur was making a public demonstration of his convictions at a time when the emperor was bent upon discouraging such demonstrations. Whereas the emperor could use the power of the state in support of his policy, the Guru could rely on moral courage inherited from a long line of illustrious predecessors to defend the claims of conscience.

A deputation of Brahmans met Guru Tegh Bahadur at Makhowal in May, 1675, with a woeful tale of religious persecution in the valley of Kashmir by its Mughal governor. After a deep reflection on the situation, Guru Tegh Bahadur decided to court martyrdom to uphold his beliefs. In July, 1675, he nominated his young son Gobind Das as the successor-Guru and moved out of Makhowal. He was arrested soon after he entered the Mughal territory in the *pargana* of Ropar and kept in custody for nearly four months in the *sarkār* of Sarhind before he was taken to Delhi in November, 1675. In Delhi, he was asked to perform a miracle as the proof of his nearness to God. He refuted the idea that occult powers were a proof of one's nearness to God.[28] As a logical corollary of his 'failure' to perform a miracle he was asked to accept Islam. Three of his companions were put to death in his presence to impress upon him the consequence of a refusal. Guru Tegh Bahadur refused to accept Islam, and he was beheaded in Chandni Chauk, the main market-square close to the Red Fort, on the 11th of November 1675.

Guru Tegh Bahadur's unique sacrifice in the cause not only of his own faith but also in the cause of freedom of conscience in general was admired by his son and successor. Metaphorically, he protected the sacred thread (*janjū*) and the sacred mark (*tilak*) of the men of faith. The world was 'enwrapped in mourning' at his departure.[29] The grief was great and the sorrow was deep, but there was also some resentment. A Sikh in Agra threw two bricks at Aurangzeb in October, 1676, when he was returning from the *jāmi' masjid*. The

[28] The Sikh Gurus, reinforcing the attitude of Guru Nanak, believed in the possibility of miracles but regarded the power to perform miracles as irrelevant for one's spiritual status and beneath the concerns of a devotee of God.

[29] *Shabdarth Dasam Granth Sahib* (ed. Taran Singh), Punjabi University, Patiala, 1973, I, 70.

unfortunate assailant was handed over to the *kotwāl*, presumably for execution.[30]

IV

The first decade of Guru Gobind Singh's pontificate was rather uneventful. Growing into manhood, he received literary and religious education, and also training in the use of arms. He was particularly fond of hunting wild boar. He inspired his young companions and followers to take interest in martial activity. There were some old Sikhs too who remembered the days of Guru Hargobind. The annual visits of the Sikhs at the time of the Baisākhī and the Diwālī swelled the numbers at Makhowal which gave the appearance of an armed camp. The young chief of Kahlur (Bilaspur), Bhim Chand, did not relish this development, regarding it as a threat to the integrity of his territories. He insisted on a formal acknowledgment by Guru Gobind Singh that he was subject to the authority of the chief. The situation was becoming more and more tense when, in 1685, the chief of Sirmur (Nahan) invited Guru Gobind Singh to his principality.

Guru Gobind Singh accepted the invitation of the chief of Sirmur and settled down at Paunta on the right bank of the river Jamuna. This place was on the border of Sirmur, adjoining the territory of Garhwal, and there was a long-standing dispute between the chiefs of Sirmur and Garhwal over the border territories. This unenviable position induced Guru Gobind Singh not only to build a fortress at Paunta but also to raise an efficient fighting force from amongst his followers and kinsmen. Before long they were put to a severe test when the chief of Garhwal invaded the territory of Sirmur in 1688 with a number of hill chiefs as his allies, and with the help of some mercenary commanders. Guru Gobind Singh moved out of Paunta to give them battle at a place called Bhangani. The mercenary commanders Hayat Khan and Najabat Khan were killed in the battle and Bhikhan Khan was unhorsed. The most valiant fighter on the side of the enemy, Hari Chand, died on the field. The Guru lost his cousin Sango Shah, one of the five sons of Guru Hargobind's daughter, besides a good number of

---

[30] *Ma'āsir-i-'Ālamgīrī* (Pbi, ed. Fauja Singh), Punjabi University, Patiala, 1977, 135.

his followers. But the losses of the enemy were much heavier and they lost the battle.[31]

Guru Gobind Singh's victory at Bhangani proclaimed the fact that he was more powerful than any single chief in the hills. He had good resources in men, bows and arrows, javelins, swords, maces and horses. But he had no intention of embroiling himself any further in the affairs of a chief who had tricked him into unreciprocated support. He left Paunta and returned to Makhowal in 1689 to found Anandpur in its vicinity. The new township was built with better defences. The men who had not fought in the battle at Bhangani were not allowed to reside in Anandpur. Those who had fought well were rewarded and patronized.

Guru Gobind Singh was building up his strength when a few years later Bhim Chand, the chief of Kahlur, sought his help against the Mughal *faujdārs* of the hills. Bhim Chand was heading the hill chiefs who had refused to pay tribute, and the Mughal *faujdār* of Jammu had sent a force against the rebels. The commandant of this force was supported by the loyal vassals. Guru Gobind Singh participated in the battle at Nadaun which ended in Bhim Chand's victory. But soon after the battle the rebel chief patched up his quarrel with the Mughal *faujdār* and agreed to pay tribute. Guru Gobind Singh expressed his disapproval of his submission by plundering a village in his territory. Returning then to Anandpur he picked up the old threads.

The concourse at Anandpur became so conspicuous that towards the end of 1693 the news-writer of Sarhind was constrained to report of the gathering crowds. Aurangzeb was now in the Deccan, vainly chasing the Maratha rebels. He ordered the *faujdārs* to ensure that no crowds gathered at Anandpur.[32] A Mughal force was sent to Anandpur with the intention of a night attack. But Guru Gobind Singh was awakened by his guards in time to prepare for defence. The young commander of the Mughal force was disheartened to hear the unexpected din of preparation for battle and left the environs of Anandpur without a fight. Another expedition was sent against the Guru. But, by then, some of the hill chiefs had become rebellious. The Mughal commander, Husain Khan, though supported by some hill chiefs, was defeated and

---

[31] The battle is described in the 'Bachittar Nātak': *Shabdarth Dasam Granth Sahib*, 77–79; for an English translation, Indubhushan Banerjee, *Evolution of the Khalsa*, Vol. 2, 179–82.

[32] (*Akhbārāt-i-Darbār-i-Muʿallā*) Chetan Singh, *Region and Empire*, 274 and n 129.

killed by the rebel chiefs. A small contingent sent by Guru Gobind Singh was supporting them. The leader of this contingent died fighting, together with seven of his horsemen. Another Mughal force was sent under a Rajput commandant, Jujhar Singh. He too was defeated and killed by the rebel chiefs. Thus, the campaign against Guru Gobind Singh was diverted into a campaign against the rebel hill chiefs. When Aurangzeb sent his son to the Punjab in 1696, he chastised the rebel chiefs and their supporters. Guru Gobind Singh remained safe at Anandpur.[33]

During all these years Guru Gobind Singh was in contact with the Sikh *sangats* in the country. His extant letters (*hukmnāmas*) to some of these reveal the nature of his interests. The *sangats* of 'the east' (Dacca, Chittagong, Sondeep and Sylhet) were asked to send offerings collected on various accounts, including fine quality cloth, swords and matchlocks, a war elephant, besides gold and cash. The Sikhs were asked to come personally at the time of the Baisākhī and the Diwālī. Some of them were asked to come with batches of foot-soldiers and horsemen. It is interesting to find the bulk of the *hukmnāmās* addressed to *sangats* outside the Punjab and to *sangats* on the east of the Satlej.[34]

There was indeed a shift in the constituency of the successors of Guru Arjan. It was partly a result of dissent within Sikhism. The successors of Guru Nanak had experienced opposition from rival claimants from the very beginning. In the early seventeenth century, when Guru Hargobind came into armed conflict with the Mughal authorities and felt obliged to leave Ramdaspur, the rival claimants became more effective. In terms of followers, the *doābs* of the Punjab were virtually lost to the successors of Guru Hargobind. The erosion of their influence is reflected among other things in the *janamsākhī* literature of the seventeenth century.[35] This form of literature was used for missionary work by the 'orthodox' followers of Guru Nanak to underline his uniqueness and to uphold the unity of Guruship on the principle of nomination. The rival claimants were quick to realize the importance of this form. The successors of Prithi Chand composed a *janamsākhī* to promote their own sectarian purpose. The Udāsīs tried

[33] 'Bachittar Nātak', *Shabdarth Dasam Granth Sahib*, 80–91; for English version, Indubhushan Banerjee, *Evolution of the Khalsa*, Vol. 2, 182–89.

[34] Ganda Singh (ed.), *Hukmnāmey* (Pbi) Nos. 33–65.

[35] W. H. McLeod, *Early Sikh Tradition*, Clarendon Press, Oxford, 1980; for a brief discussion, W. H. McLeod, *The Evolution of the Sikh Community*, 20–36.

to minimize the importance of all the successors of Guru Nanak and the followers of Hindal tried to undermine the position of Guru Nanak himself. The *janamsākhīs* they produced bear testimony to their partial success.

V

Faced with threat from outside and dissension within the Sikh Panth, Guru Gobind Singh thought long and deeply about his own position as the successor of Guru Nanak. Turning to the Dasam Granth, or the Book of the Tenth Master, we find that all that is there in this compilation was not written by the Tenth Master. But there is much that was, and more that was approved by him. A careful analysis of this evidence reveals that Guru Gobind Singh believed in the supersession of all faiths by the faith enunciated by Guru Nanak; he subscribed to the idea of the unity of Guruship from Guru Nanak to Guru Tegh Bahadur; and he regarded himself as their only true successor. Like Guru Nanak, he believed in one God, the creator, the sustainer and the destroyer of the universe. He also believed that God exalts the pious and destroys the wicked. In the universal struggle between the forces of good and evil, God intervened from time to time to restore the balance in favour of the forces of good.

It is in this context that Guru Gobind Singh's interest in the 'incarnations' of God acquires meaning and significance. His interest in the Goddess and in Rama and Krishna springs from his preoccupation with the meaning of his own mission. What was common to these crucial figures of the old Shaktas in the hills and the new Vaishnavas of the plains was the use of physical force made by the 'instruments' of God in favour of the good. The use of physical force in defence of the good was sanctified by God:[36]

> Having created Durga, O God, You destroyed the demons. From You alone did Rama receive his power to slay Rawana with his arrows. From you alone did Krishna receive his power to seize Kansa by the hair and to dash him on the ground.

Guru Gobind Singh believed that he too was a chosen instrument of God. This providential role he was to fulfil in his own way as the successor of Guru Nanak. In terms of his historical situation, his

---

[36] Kala Singh Bedi (ed.), *Vār Srī Bhagautī Jī Kī*, New Delhi, 1966, 104–5.

problem was to defend the claims of conscience against external interference. Guru Tegh Bahadur had given one answer to this problem. Guru Gobind Singh proposed to give another. His aim was to obviate external interference with the use of physical force. For the fulfilment of this purpose he had to set his own house in order, that is, the Panth founded by Guru Nanak.

On the Baisākhī of 1699, when there was a large gathering at Anandpur, Guru Gobind Singh proclaimed that henceforth all Sikhs would be his Khālsā. The term Khālsā was used by that time for the Sikhs initiated into the Sikh faith by the Gurus themselves and not by the *masands*. The far-reaching implication of this declaration was that all those who were not directly linked with him were not Sikhs either. This proclamation removed the mediacy of the *masands*. It also meant that the followers of the dissidents were not to be treated as true Sikhs. In fact the Khālsā were instructed not to have any connection with the *masands* and their followers (*masandīs*); the Khālsā were similarly instructed not to have any connection with the followers of Ram Rai, Dhir Mal and Prithi Chand.[37]   Direct link of the Khālsā with the Guru was symbolized by a new baptismal ceremony introduced by Guru Gobind Singh. This was the chastening baptism of the double-edged sword (*khande kī pauhl*) which obliged the initiate to keep the hair unshorn, to wear arms and to bear the epithet 'Singh' with their names. Any five Singhs could initiate others to the new order. These indeed were very vital measures. The principle of unity and equality was re-introduced in the Sikh Panth. Given the vested interests of the *masands* and the dissidents, and even of the high-caste Sikhs of Guru Gobind Singh, this principle introduced an element of internal tussle between those who accepted the new order and those who did not. Furthermore, since in their outward appearance the baptized Singhs stood distinguished from their contemporaries, their socio-religious identity became more distinctly pronounced than that of the earlier Sikhs. Indeed, as a contemporary writer puts it, the Khālsā stood distinguished from the rest of the world.[38] The local Khālsā *sangats* assumed collectively the position relinquished by the *masands*. The Khālsā *sangats* now represented the Guru. Their decisions were

[37] Senapat, *Srī Gursobha* (ed. Ganda Singh), Punjabi University, Patiala, 1980, 22; For dissent in Sikhism, J. S. Grewal, 'The Dissidents', *From Guru Nanak to Maharaja Ranjit Singh* (2nd edn), 50–63.
[38] J. S. Grewal and S. S. Bal, *Guru Gobind Singh (A Biographical Study)*, Panjab University, Chandigarh, 1967, 121.

binding on the individual members of the *sangat*. Guru Gobind Singh declared the Khālsā to be the heir of everything he possessed, because he himself owed everything to them.[39] In the common consecration of their lives to God, the baptized Singhs and the Guru became one.

VI

The immediate result of the measures of Guru Gobind Singh was to invite the outside interference which the Singhs were meant to withstand. The increasing number of armed Singhs at Anandpur, particularly at the time of the Diwālī and the Baisākhī, presented a grave threat to the neighbouring hill chiefs. Bhim Chand did not take long to notice their presence with apprehension. No single chief, however, was able to confront them. Bhim Chand formed an alliance with some other chiefs of the hills and attacked Anandpur. They found it difficult to dislodge Guru Gobind Singh and decided to approach the Mughal *faujdārs* for help. The combined forces of the Mughal *faujdārs* and the hill chiefs, coupled with the suggestion of an honourable peace, induced Guru Gobind Singh to cross the river Satlej into the territory of a friendly chief, and the Mughal troops went back. Bhim Chand, however, was rash enough to attack the Guru but only to suffer defeat. His men fled from the field of battle 'as the arrow flies from a stretched bow'.[40] Guru Gobind Singh rode back to Anandpur in triumph.

The success of Guru Gobind Singh encouraged more and more of the Singhs to come to Anandpur. Their increasing numbers created the problem of supplies. It became necesssary for them to raid the neighbouring villages for food and forage. The hill chiefs could not close their eyes to this new development. But they felt helpless. Ultimately they decided to approach Aurangzeb for protection as his vassals. Imperial and vassal forces were mobilized against Guru Gobind Singh and a siege was laid to Anandpur. A long blockade and promise of safe conduct induced the Singhs to agree to evacuate the fortresses, and Guru Gobind Singh left Anandpur towards the end of 1704 against his better judgment. While crossing a flooded stream near Ropar he was attacked by the Mughal troops. His wife, Mata Sundri,

---

[39] Guru Gobind Singh's feeling for the Khālsā is well rendered into English by Harbans Singh: *Guru Gobind Singh*, Sterling Publishers, New Delhi, 1979, 47.
[40] Senapat, *Srī Gursobha* (ed. Ganda Singh), 63.

and his mother, Màta Gujri, and his two youngest sons were separated from him in the mêlée. He crossed the stream and stopped at a village called Chamkaur. He was pursued and attacked. All his followers and his two eldest sons fell fighting at Chamkaur. Meanwhile, Mata Sundri was escorted to Delhi by a devoted follower, but Mata Gujri and the two youngest sons fell into the hands of Wazir Khan, the Mughal *faujdār* of Sarhind. He put the young boys to death.

Guru Gobind Singh was able to establish contact with the Khālsā in the present districts of Faridkot and Bhatinda, and he was able to repulse an attack from Wazir Khan at a place called Khidrana (Muktsar). Aurangzeb came to know of these developments in the Punjab and he thought of conciliating Guru Gobind Singh. When the Guru wrote a spirited letter (*zafarnāma*) in response, justifying his position on moral grounds and indicting the emperor with perfidy, Aurangzeb sent special messengers with orders for Mun'im Khan, the governor of Lahore, to conciliate the Guru at all costs and to persuade him to meet the emperor personally in the Deccan.[41] Guru Gobind Singh refused the help offered by the Lahore governor, but he decided to meet Aurangzeb. On his way to the Deccan he was in Rajasthan when he heard the news of the emperor's death. Aurangzeb had died in February, 1707.

Guru Gobind Singh met the new emperor, Bahadur Shah, at Agra in the summer of 1707. He was well received and encouraged to hope that he would get Anandpur back. Bahadur Shah went to Rajasthan, and from Rahjasthan to the Deccan to fight for the throne with his brother Kam Bakhsh. Guru Gobind Singh remained close to the imperial camp for nearly a year, hoping that the issue could be resolved any time. Bahadur Shah, not yet in a position to offend either the Guru or the hill chiefs, went on postponing the decision to restore the *status quo ante*. When the imperial camp halted near Nanded on the banks of the river Godavari, Guru Gobind Singh decided to stay behind. A few days later he was stabbed and badly wounded by an Afghan connected with either Wazir Khan or an imperial officer.[42] On October 7, 1708, Guru Gobind Singh breathed his last.

---

[41] J. S. Grewal, 'The Zafarnama', *From Guru Nanak to Maharaja Ranjit Singh*, 85-93.

[42] J. S. Grewal, 'Guru Gobind Singh and Bahadur Shah', *ibid.*, 94-99; in the *Akhbārāt-i-Darbār-i-Mu'alla* the name of the Afghan given is Jamshid Khan and it is added that his son was given a robe by way of condolence by the emperor: *Mākhiz-i-Tawārīkh-i-Sikhān*, 83.

VII

Guru Gobind Singh did not nominate any individual as his successor. For nearly a century now the Sikhs had been nurtured in the belief that Guruship was confined to the family of Guru Ram Das. This is explicitly stated not only in the *Bachittar Nātak* towards the end of the seventeenth century but also at the beginning in the *vārs* of Bhai Gurdas.[43] At the time of Guru Gobind Singh's death, however, there was none in the three generations of the surviving Sodhis who could be considered for taking up this grave responsibility. More important than this was the process by which Guruship had been gradually impersonalized, bringing the *bāṇī* and the *sangat* into parallel prominence with the personal Guru. The decision taken by Guru Gobind Singh did not abolish Guruship itself but personal Guruship. The position of the Guru was henceforth given to the Khālsā and to *shabad-bāṇī* as a logical development from Guru Nanak's decision to nominate a disciple as the Guru during his lifetime and his equation of the Shabad with the Guru. As a further logical development, the decision of Guru Gobind Singh crystallized into the twin doctrine of Guru-Panth and Guru-Granth. Larger and larger numbers of Sikhs came to believe that Guruship after Guru Gobind Singh was vested in the Khālsā Panth and in the Granth.

All the Sikhs at the time of Guru Gobind Singh's death were not his Khālsā, and all his Khālsā were not Singhs. The difference between the Singh and the Khālsā ended with his death and the two terms became synonymous and interchangeable. The difference between the Sikh and the Singh remained. It was yet to be seen which component would become dominant in the affairs of the Sikh Panth. It was also to be seen how the Singhs would conduct themselves in relation to the Mughal state.

Political attitude was one important element that distinguished the Singhs and the Sikhs. What is more important, the political attitude of the Singhs was not an adjunct but an essential part of their religious ideology. Bhai Gurdas had used an apt metaphor for the change introduced by Guru Hargobind in the beginning of the seventeenth century: the orchard of the Sikh faith needed the thorny hedge of armed men for its protection. The Singhs of Guru Gobind Singh were

---

[43] Bhai Gurdas, *vār* 1, *pauṛī* 87.

the orchard and the hedge rolled into one. In the entire body of the followers of the Gurus, divided into two distinct components, the Singhs represented the 'transformed' component. It was soon to become the mainstream as the result of Guru Gobind Singh's known preference.

CHAPTER 5

RISE TO POLITICAL POWER
(1708–1799)

The eighteenth century in Indian history is known for the decline of the Mughal empire and the rise of successor states and new powers like the Marathas and the British. The rise of the Singhs into power during the eighteenth century was a part of this political process. But there was nothing in the process itself to ensure their rise to power. The combination of religious piety and disciplined worldliness that was evolved by Guru Nanak and elaborated by his successors was extended to the realm of politics by Guru Gobind Singh. The political struggle of the Singhs can be appreciated not merely in terms of the growing weakness of the Mughal empire but also as an extrapolation of the pontificate of Guru Gobind Singh.

I

Only about a year after Guru Gobind Singh's death, Bahadur Shah heard of a serious uprising in the Punjab and left the Deccan for the north. This uprising was led by Banda Bahadur who had met Guru Gobind Singh at Nanded and become his follower. He was commissioned to lead the Singhs in the Punjab against their oppressors. Some of the old followers of Guru Gobind Singh accompanied him, and he was also given letters (*hukmnāmas*) addressed to the Singhs for coming to his support. Banda Bahadur and his companions moved cautiously towards Delhi, entered the *sarkār* of Hissar and started collecting men and materials for military action. By November, 1709, they had gathered enough strength to storm the town of Samana in the *sarkār* of Sarhind. The *faujdār* of Samana was overpowered, its inhabitants were killed in thousands and the town was razed to the ground. The scale as well as the suddenness of Banda's action justified the emperor's anxiety.

Before Bahadur Shah appeared on the scene in December, 1710, Banda had occupied the entire *sarkār* of Sarhind and several *parganas* of the *sarkār* of Hissar; had invaded the *sarkār* of Saharanpur in the Jamuna-Ganga Doab; and the Singhs had risen in revolt against the

Mughal authorities in the Bist Jalandhar and the upper Bari Doab. Before the fall of Sarhind in May, 1710, Banda had conquered Shahabad, Sadhaura and Banur on the east of Sarhind; after its fall he had occupied the territory on the west. In the entire area between the rivers Satlej and Jamuna, he made his own administrative arrangements, appointing his own *faujdārs*, *dīwāns* and *kārdārs*. He adopted Mukhlispur, an imperial fort now given the name of Lohgarh, as his capital and struck a new coin in the name of Guru Nanak and Guru Gobind Singh. With a similar inscription he started using a seal on his orders (*hukmnāmas*).[1] In the Jalandhar Doab, the Sikhs occupied the important town of Rahon; in the upper Bari Doab, they occupied Batala, Kalanaur and Pathankot. A long belt of territory along the Shivaliks, from the Jamuna to the Ravi, came under the influence of Banda and his supporters in less than a year. The imperial forces invaded Lohgarh towards the end of 1710. Banda escaped into the hills. While the emperor moved towards Lahore, Banda reappeared in the upper Bari Doab before the middle of 1711. At the time of Bahadur Shah's death at Lahore in February, 1712, Banda was still unsubdued.

For three years more the Mughal administrators could not crush the uprising. Due to the struggle for succession, the emperors were not in a position for one year to pay any serious attention to the affairs of the Punjab. During this short span Banda was able to recover much of the territory conquered earlier, including the fort of Lohgarh. He defeated Bayazid Khan, the *faujdār* of Jammu, and killed Shams Khan, the *faujdār* of Sultanpur in the Jalandhar Doab. Some of the hill chiefs too were obliged to pay tribute. When Farrukh Siyar ascended the throne in February, 1713, he issued a general order that the Sikhs should be exterminated. Abdus Samad Khan was appointed as the governor of Lahore and he was successful in expelling Banda Bahadur from the *sarkār* of Sarhind before the end of 1713.

A year later, however, Banda reappeared in the upper Bari Doab, and his supporters marched towards Lahore with the aspiration of occupying the provincial captial. Farrukh Siyar admonished Abdus Samad Khan for his failure to suppress the Sikhs and sent reinforcements from the imperial camp. A considerable number of Singhs withdrew their support to Banda on account of serious differences. Banda was eventually besieged by Abdus Samad Khan in the fort of

---

[1] For a facsimile of Banda Bahadur's *Hukmnāma*, Ganda Singh, *Life of Banda Singh Bahadur*, Khalsa College, Amritsar, 1935.

Gurdas Nangal near the present town of Gurdaspur. The siege lasted for eight months before Banda and his followers surrendered towards the end of 1715. Over 700 of them were taken to Delhi to be paraded in the streets before their execution in March, 1716. Banda and his close companions were executed in June near the tomb of Shaikh Qutbuddin Bhaktyār Kākī close to the Qutb Minar.

In the second decade of the eighteenth century it was still possible for the Mughal emperors to send imperial troops to support their provincial governors against rebels. Abdus Samad Khan was supported by the zamīndārs of his province too, like the Bhatti Rajputs, the Afghans of Qasur and the leaders of the Kharal and Wattu tribes. Under changed circumstances they would all become keen to carve out principalities for themselves. In any case, the circumstances of the Mughal empire were changing rather rapidly, and it is necessary to keep in view the general process of political change with all its ramifications in order to grasp the developments in the politics of the Punjab in their proper perspective.

II

Farrukh Siyar, who had ascended the throne in 1713 with the support of the Sayyids of Barah was removed and killed by those very Sayyids in 1719, and three more princes ascended the throne before the year was out. The last of them, Muhammad Shah, remained on the throne for nearly thirty years till his death in April, 1748. But he could not prevent the disintegration of his empire. The nobles at the court failed to browbeat the emperor but the emperor failed to control the nobles. Financial difficulties became more acute. While income from the crownlands (khālisa) went on decreasing with the increase in the ranks of the nobles and their jāgīrs, the provincial governors became more and more reluctant to send regular instalments of the surplus revenues to the imperial treasury. The system of revenue-farming (ijāra), which became well established in the reign of Muhammad Shah, created new vested interests for appropriating the surplus produce with serious implications for politics.

The frontiers of imperial authority began to contract rather rapidly, making room for successor states and new powers. In 1725, when Nizam ul-Mulk Asaf Jah took over the viceroyalty of the Deccan provinces, the khutba continued to be read in the name of the emperor and the coins continued to be struck in his name, but this legal fiction hardly concealed the fact that Nizam ul-Mulk was the virtual ruler of the Deccan without any binding political or administrative ties with the powers at Delhi. He had to contend rather with the Marathas whose sovereignty over the kingdom established by Shivaji had been recognized by the Mughal emperor in 1719. In 1737 they defeated Nizam ul-Mulk in a battle near Bhopal and confined him to the erstwhile territories of Golkunda, now the *nizāmat* of Hyderabad. Before Nadir Shah invaded India in 1738–1739 the Marathas had subjugated Gujarat and Malwa and extended their sway up to the river Chambal in Rajasthan.

Two years after his coronation as the Shah of Persia, Nadir Shah took over Qandahar from the Afghans in March, 1738, and occupied the Mughal province of Kabul in June. In January, 1739, he entered the province of Lahore and defeated its Mughal governor, Zakariya Khan, who was allowed to hold on to his office after paying two million rupees. Nadir Shah reached Sarhind in the first week of February to defeat the Mughal army before the end of the month. Having clearly established the superiority of the Persian bullet over the Mughal arrow, he moved to Delhi to gather its accumulated riches. When he heard of the death of his mulcting soldiers at the hands of the citizens of Delhi, he ordered a general massacre and imposed an indemnity of twenty million rupees. The Mughal emperor and his nobles made a much larger contribution in jewels, gold and silver, and precious articles. Nadir Shah celebrated the marriage of his son with a Mughal princess, put the crown back on the head of Muhammad Shah and got the *khutba* read in his name. With a long train of camels and mules loaded with spoils, he left Delhi in May after a formal treaty with the Mughal emperor by which the province of Thatta and all Mughal territories to the west of the river Indus were ceded to the Persian monarch. The four *parganas* (*chahār mahāl*) of Sialkot, Pasrur, Aurangabad and Gujrat in the province of Lahore too were ceded to Nadir Shah.

Soon after Nadir Shah's invasion, the eastern provinces of the empire were virtually lost to the Mughal emperor. Shuja ud-Daula had established his power in Bengal, Orissa and Bihar by acknowledging the authority of Muhammad Shah and by sending regular instalments of revenue or tribute to Delhi. On his death in 1740 Aliwardi Khan forcibly took over the *nizāmat* of Bengal and obtained legal recognition by paying tribute to the Mughal emperor. Gradually, however,

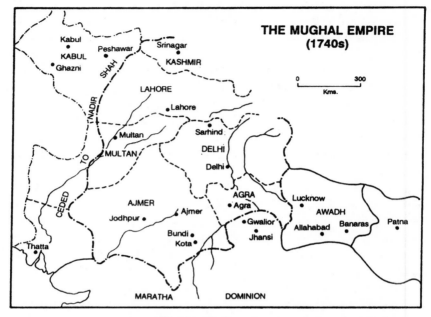

Map 3 The Mughal empire (1740s)

Aliwardi Khan started acting as an autonomous ruler, taking his own decisions without reference to Delhi and withholding payment of tribute. In the 1740s, while the Marathas were trying to increase their power and influence between the Deccan and the Gangetic provinces, Safdar Jang as the governor of Awadh strengthened his hold over the province of Allahabad as well. The Jats in the province of Agra and the Rohila Afghans in the Delhi province were trying to carve out new principalities for themselves.

Turning to the Mughal governors of the Punjab in this process of decline and disintegration, we find that Abdus Samad Khan was succeeded by his son Zakariya Khan in 1726 when the father was sent to the neighbouring province of Multan. Upon his death in 1737 Multan too was entrusted to Zakariya Khan. When Zakariya Khan died in 1745 his sons, Yahiya Khan and Shah Nawaz Khan, acted on the assumption that Lahore and Multan belonged to them almost by right. In any case, the governorship of Lahore remained in the hands of Abdus Samad Khan and his son and grandsons for nearly thirty-five years. Themselves Turanis, they were related to a powerful Turani family in Delhi. Abdus Samad Khan was married to the sister of Muhammad Amin Khan who became the *wazīr* of Muhammad Shah after the fall of the Sayyid brothers. Zakariya Khan was married to the daughter of Muhammad Amin Khan, the sister of Qamruddin Khan who also became the *wazīr* at Delhi. Qamruddin's daughter was married to Yahiya Khan. Nizam ul-Mulk Asaf Jah was a nephew of Muhammad Amin Khan. At least partly, the position of Abdus Samad Khan and Zakariya Khan was strengthened by these matrimonial ties.

Both Abdus Samad Khan and Zakariya Khan held high *mansabs* and they were regarded as competent and powerful governors. Occasionally, however, they had to face refractory vassals or *zamīndārs*. Abdus Samad Khan had to suppress the revolt of Husain Khan of Qasur. Zakariya Khan had to deal with Ranjit Dev of Jammu and the *zamīndārs* like Jang Pannah Bhatti and Jang Mir. It is not clear whether or not Zakariya Khan sent surplus revenues to the imperial treasury. It is quite clear, however, that he received no assistance from Delhi when he was faced with internal or external threat. A large measure of autonomy or initiative and nearly a total reliance on their own resources were the reverse and the obverse of the same political situation, accounting largely for their strength and weakness at the same time.

The position of the Mughal governors of Lahore weakened considerably after Zakariya Khan's death in 1745. The emperor was opposed to the idea of any of his sons becoming the governor of Lahore or Multan. Qamruddin Khan felt obliged to get these provinces for himself. Early in 1746 he was able to make Yahiya Khan his deputy at Lahore but a year later he was ousted by Shah Nawaz Khan. The emperor was not willing to recognize Shah Nawaz even as a deputy. He started negotiations with Ahmad Shah Abdali who had succeeded to the eastern dominions of Nadir Shah in 1747. To neutralize his inclination to rebel, Shah Nawaz Khan was made Qamruddin Khan's deputy at Lahore. He decided now to oppose Ahmad Shah Abdali but he was defeated in a battle near Lahore. Qamruddin himself had to march against Ahmad Shah. In a battle fought near Sarhind early in 1748 Qamruddin received a fatal wound but his son Muin ul-Mulk defeated Ahmad Shah Abdali with the support of Safdar Jang. The governorship of Lahore and Multan was now passed on to Muin ul-Mulk.

Muin ul-Mulk, called simply Mir Mannu by the Singhs, received no support from the new emperor and the new *wazirs*. In fact Safdar Jang encouraged Shah Nawaz Khan to occupy Multan. Muin ul-Mulk had to send a large force against him; Shah Nawaz was defeated and killed. When Ahmad Shah Abdali demanded the arrears of the revenue from the Four Parganas in 1750–1751, Muin ul-Mulk referred the matter to Delhi, asking for reinforcements. But he was told to pay the arrears. In 1752, Ahmad Shah Abdali defeated Muin ul-Mulk and occupied Lahore. In this situation Muin ul-Mulk had no hesitation in remaining the governor of Lahore on behalf of Ahmad Shah Abdali, though his position became even more vulnerable than before. He died in 1753 as an 'Afghan' governor. In 1757, when the province of Lahore was formally ceded to Ahmad Shah Abdali by the Mughal emperor, together with the provinces of Multan and Kashmir and the *sarkār* of Sarhind, Ahmad Shah Abdali appointed his son Timur Shah as the governor of Lahore. By this time the Singhs had occupied many pockets of territory in the eastern *doābs* of the Punjab.

III

After the death of Banda Bahadur there was no eminent leader among the Singhs. Their struggle against the Mughal government became eventually a people's war. From this viewpoint, the period from Banda Bahadur's death to Nadir Shah's invasion assumes great significance. One of the most important developments of this phase was the emergence of Ramdaspur (Amritsar) as the rallying centre of the Singhs.[2] They established their control over Amritsar against the claims of the followers of Banda in the time of Abdus Samad Khan, and appointed Bhai Mani Singh, the lifelong companion of Guru Gobind Singh and his oldest disciple, to look after the affairs of the Harmandir. Amritsar became once again the most important centre of Sikh pilgrimage. Equally important was the Singh insistence on the end of personal Guruship after Guru Gobind Singh, upholding the doctrine not only against the old dissidents but also against the new contenders like Gulab Rai, a grandson of Guru Hargobind, and the Gangu Shahi Kharak Singh, the successor of an eminent follower of

---

[2] J. S. Grewal, *The City of the Golden Temple*, Guru Nanak Dev University, Amritsar, 1985.

Guru Amar Das. A third important element in this situation was a hard core of individuals who refused to submit to the Mughals.

It was this last element which was the primary source of anxiety for the Mughal governors. Many of those who had risen against the government under the leadership of Banda returned to their old occupations. Some of them were induced to relinquish arms by concession of land revenue. Not all of them, however, gave up the stance of independence. The well-known martyr Tara Singh who humbled the *faujdār* of Patti and died fighting against the contingents sent by Zakariya Khan was only one of them. While the Sikhs in general, and even a large number of the Singhs, lived as peaceful citizens of the Mughal empire, the professed rebels, or the *tat-khālsā*, lived as outlaws in the less-accessible tracts of the province plundering or killing the government officials and their supporters.

The developments of the 1730s indicate that the number of the *tat-khālsā* was increasing and, consequently, Zakariya Khan was becoming more and more grim in his measures of suppression. Early in the decade, however, he decided to adopt conciliatory measures, to kill the Singhs with 'sugar' instead of 'poison'.[3] The emperor was persuaded to confer a robe of honour and the title of *nawāb* on their chosen leader, and a number of villages in *jāgīr* for their maintenance. The title and the robe were accepted by Kapur Singh, remembered consequently as Nawab Kapur Singh. The villages chosen for *jāgīr* were close to Amritsar. This ensured peace for a few years.

Amritsar became a converging centre for the scattered Singhs, and it became necessary for Nawab Kapur Singh to organize the increasing numbers into large units (*deras*) under different leaders from amongst the Khatrīs, Jats and the 'outcaste' Ranghretas. He entrusted the work of the common kitchen, the treasury, the stores, the arsenal and the granary for horses to experienced or competent Singhs. But he failed to contain the increasing numbers, and many of them became restive. Some of them took to plunder and adopted an attitude of confrontation with the officials.[4] Zakariya Khan resumed the *jāgīr* and adopted repressive measures with greater vigour.

The Singhs took to the roving life of outlaws in small bands. They moved with speed, and struck with effect. When Zakariya Khan failed

---

[3] Ratan Singh Bhangu, *Prachīn Panth Parkāsh*, Wazir-i-Hind Press, Amritsar, 1962 (4th edn), 210.

[4] *Ibid.*, 215–17.

to liquidate these illusive bands he turned his attention to their rallying centre. Bhai Mani Singh was given to understand that the Sikhs could visit Amritsar on the Diwālī if he would pay a stipulated amount to the government. The Singhs did come but they soon became suspicious that this was a ruse, and they dispersed. Bhai Mani Singh failed to remit the stipulated amount, and he was put to death in Lahore; his body was cut into pieces limb by limb. This did not deter the Singhs from paralyzing Zakariya Khan's administration. When they plundered the rear of Nadir Shah's army on its return from Delhi, the Shah warned the Khan against their potential threat to his rule in the Punjab.[5]

In the 1740s the rigour of repression increased, but with a diminishing effect. Zakariya Khan established a permanent post in Amritsar. Its Rajput *faujdār*, popularly referred to as Massa Ranghar, who used the precincts of the Harmandir for his amusement with dancing girls, was killed by Mehtab Singh and Sukhkha Singh. Another *faujdār* was appointed in his place. Zakariya Khan also mobilized the support of local *zamīndārs* against the Singhs, and persecuted even their sympathizers. That was why the well-known martyr Bhai Taru Singh had to suffer death. The defiant attitude of the Singhs was symbolized by a Sandhu Jat, Bota Singh, who started collecting tax from travellers on the high road to Lahore to invite martyrdom. In the time of Yahiya Khan, a band of the Singhs under the leadership of Jassa Singh Ahluwalia turned on their pursuer Jaspat Rai, the *faujdār* of Eminabad, and killed him. His brother Lakhpat Rai, the *dīwān* of Lahore, pursued the Khālsā in vengeance and killed several thousand of them in a relentless campaign.[6] By now, the Singhs were able to survive such a loss. In 1748 they felt strong enough to oust the Mughal *faujdār* from Amritsar and to build a small fortress there named Ram Rauni.

In the early 1750s the leaders of Singh bands started occupying pockets of territory in the Bari Doab in which the capital of the province was situated. Jai Singh Kanhiya, for instance, started issuing orders to local officials in 1750. A lesser-known leader named Hakumat Singh ordered the local officials not to interfere with a religious grant in the present district of Gurdaspur.[7] Jassa Singh Ahluwalia occupied

---

[5] Perhaps a post-eventum prophecy, but this is emphasized by Ahmad Shah, *Tārīkh-i-Hind*, MS, SHR 1291, Khalsa College, Amritsar, f. 315; and by Ratan Singh Bhangu, *Prachīn Panth Parkāsh*, 231–32.

[6] In Sikh tradition this event is remembered as *chhotā ghallūghārā* or the 'small carnage'.

[7] The leaders of the Khālsā bands started using their seals to issue orders after the occupation of territories. It is interesting to note in this connection that the seal of Jai Singh

Fatehabad in the present district of Amritsar in 1753, and it served as his headquarters for nearly a quarter of a century.[8] In this context the memoirs of the contemporary Tahmas Khan begin to make sense. In 1754 Khwaja Mirza Khan was appointed as the *faujdār* of Eminabad but before he could take charge he had to fight several times with the Singhs, and Qasim Beg who was appointed as the *faujdār* of Patti was not allowed by the Singhs to join his post. Towards the end of 1757, the veteran Afghan General Jahan Khan, who was appointed by Ahmad Shah Abdali to assist his son Timur Shah in the administration of the province, was nearly overpowered by the Singhs before he was saved by the timely arrival of fresh Afghan contingents. The Singhs ousted its Afghan *faujdār* Sa'adat Khan Afridi from Jalandhar early in 1758. Henceforth, in whichever direction an Afghan army was sent it came back defeated. The Singhs even attacked Lahore and plundered its suburbs.[9]

At this juncture Ahmad Shah Abdali had to contend with the Marathas who wanted to establish their own control over the Punjab on behalf of the Mughal emperor. He came to India towards the end of 1759, stayed in the neighbourhood of Delhi throughout 1760, and fought the battle of Panipat in April, 1761, to defeat the Marathas and to oblige them temporarily at least to abandon their aspiration to dominate the north. However, Ahmad Shah Abdali now found the Punjab too hot for himself. In September, 1761, the governor he had appointed to the province of Lahore was defeated by the Singhs near Gujranwala. The Singhs threw out the other appointees of Ahmad Shah Abdali like 'a fly from milk' and brought the entire land from the Satlej to the Indus under their control.[10] To strike a decisive blow, he killed more than 5,000 Singhs in a single day in a running battle in the present district of Ludhiana.[11] But only six months later he felt obliged to retire to Lahore after an indecisive engagement with the Singhs near Amritsar. After his return to Kabul his *faujdārs* were dislodged by the Singhs from the Bist Jalandhar Doab, Sarhind, Rachna and the Chaj

Kanhiya bears the date 1750 in his orders: B. N. Goswamy and J. S. Grewal, *The Mughal and the Sikh Rulers and the Vaishnavas of Pindori*, Indian Institute of Advanced Study, Simla, 1969, Documents 24, 25; for Hakumat Singh's order, Document 18.

[8] Contrary to the general impression, the founder of the Kapurthala state, Jassa Singh Ahluwalia, occupied Kapurthala towards the end of his career.

[9] Tahmas Beg Khan, *Tahmās Nāmah* (ed. Muhammad Aslam), University of the Punjab, Lahore, 1986, 106–10, 179–84.

[10] *Ibid*, 251–52.

[11] In Sikh tradition this event is remembered as *waddā ghallūghārā* or the 'great carnage'.

Doabs. When Ahmad Shah himself came to the Punjab in 1765 his authority was confined to his camp; he was on the defensive and he returned to Kabul without fighting a single battle even though the Singhs were hovering around his camp. Qazi Nur Muhammad, who had accompanied the Shah on this expedition, regretfully observed that the Singhs had divided up the country from Sarhind to the Derajat among themselves and enjoyed it 'without fear from anyone'.[12] The Singhs formally declared their sovereignty in 1765 by striking a coin at Lahore after its occupation by three of their leaders. This coin bore the inscription which Banda Bahadur had used on his seal fifty-five years earlier.[13] Sikh rule was re-established and it had come to stay.

The Singhs were not the only new rulers of the Punjab. The vassal chiefs of the hills had only to withhold tribute and contingents to become independent rulers. With the decline in Mughal authority many of them became independent of outside control. They acknowledged Ahmad Shah's suzerainty only intermitantly in self-interest. The chiefs of Jammu and Kangra in fact added to their power and prestige during the late eighteenth century. There was also a good number of new principalities under non-Sikh chiefs in the plains. Most of them were descendants of the *zamīndārs* of the Mughal times. Some of them were former *jāgīrdārs*. A few of them were heads of religious institutions enjoying revenue-free lands. They had all come into power by making use of the politico-administrative framework of the Mughal empire.[14]

By contrast, the Singhs rose from amongst the common people, setting aside the politico-administrative framework of the Mughal empire and setting themselves up against all its supporters. Their greatest assets were the arrangements they evolved on the basis of their common sense, the ties of kinship and, above all, their religious faith and doctrines which served as the motivating force and the ground for their military and political action.

The 'institutions' which enabled the Singhs to occupy territories on a large scale are known as *rākhī*, the *misl*, the *dal khālsā* and the

[12] Qazi Nur Muhammad, *Jang Nāmah*, MS, SHR 1547, Khalsa College, Amritsar, f. 177.
[13] The Persian couplet of this inscription refers to *deg*, *teg* and unlimited success which Guru Gobind Singh received from Guru Nanak and, by implication, left as a legacy for the Singhs.
[14] Not much attention has been paid to the non-Sikh chiefs of the Punjab during the late eighteenth century. For a brief discussion see Veena Sachdeva, 'The Non-Sikh Chiefs of the Punjab Plains and Maharaja Ranjit Singh', *Journal of Regional History*, Guru Nanak Dev University, Amritsar, 2 (1981), 1–11.

gurmatā.[15] They undertook to provide protection (*rākhī*) to cultivators against all outsiders, including the officials of the government, after levying only a fifth of the produce in return for that protection. The system became more and more popular as the Singhs became more and more effective, and it often served as a prelude to permanent occupation. Since all the leaders had rather limited resources it was necessary to pool them for the purposes of offence and defence. The ties of kinship among other things became the basis of small combinations which afterwards came to be known as *misls*. Territory was often occupied by the *misl* as a unit, and sometimes by a combination of two or more *misls*. A larger combination of forces became all the more necessary when the Singhs grew in power. The combination of a large number of *misls* came to be known as the *dal khālsā* which acted in concert under the command of a chosen leader for a specific purpose. Depending upon the needs of a situation the *dal khālsā* could be divided into two or more units. Invariably, before a campaign was undertaken the matter was discussed and a consensus formed by the leaders of the Singhs. Such meetings were open to every Singh and the resolution passed was called *gurmatā* or the 'resolution of the Guru'. Most of the important *gurmatās* were adopted at Amritsar where the Singhs used to meet at the time of the Baisākhī and the Diwālī. But a *gurmatā* could be adopted at any place in the presence of the Guru Granth or even on the field of battle. A *gurmatā* was morally binding on all the Singhs, even on those who were not personally present in a meeting, because of their belief in the doctrine of Guru-Panth. It is difficult to think of a better basis of cohesion than the *gurmatā* which was based on the principles of equality and freedom, which subsumed the ties of kinship and other social ties, and which imparted a large degree of flexibility to its practical application. It made the Singhs much more formidable than the other contestants for power.

The doctrine of Guru-Panth, which provided the basis for concerted action, also ensured the right of every Singh to fight, to conquer and to rule. The theoretical derivation of power from God through the grace of the Gurus, which is implied in the inscription on the coin struck at Lahore in 1765, enabled the Singhs collectively to assert their sovereignty against outsiders; it also gave equal legitimacy to every indi-

[15] For a discussion of these institutions, J. S. Grewal, 'Eighteenth Century Sikh Polity', *From Guru Nanak to Maharaja Ranjit Singh*, Guru Nanak Dev University, Amritsar, 1982 (2nd edn), 127–38; Indu Banga, *Agrarian System of the Sikhs*, Manohar Publications, Delhi, 1978, 27–38.

vidual Sikh chief. In any case, the number of identifiable Sikh principalities between the Jamuna and the Indus in the 1770s was more than three scores. The chiefs commanded varying resources in terms of territory, revenues and horsemen. A small chief could be the master of a *pargana* yielding only 50,000 rupees a year; a large chief could hold more than half a dozen *parganas* yielding nearly 10 lakhs of rupees.[16] Eminent among the Sikh chiefs in the former province of Lahore were Jassa Singh Ahluwalia, Charhat Singh Sukarchakia, Hari Singh Bhangi and his sons Jhanda Singh and Ganda Singh, Jai Singh Kanhiya, Gujjar Singh and Jassa Singh Ramgarhia. In the middle rung were the chiefs like Buddh Singh in the Jalandhar Doab, Hakikat Singh in the Bari Doab, Sahib Singh Sialkotia in the Rachna Doab and Milkha Singh Thehpuria in the Sindh Sagar Doab. There were others, followed by a score of really small chiefs. In the former Mughal province of Delhi there were about a score of Sikh chiefs, including the chiefs of Patiala, Nabha, Jind, Faridkot, Ambala, Shahabad, Thanesar, Kaithal, Jagadhari and Buriya.

In the last quarter of the eighteenth century the Sikh chief generally acted in his individual capacity in his political relations with others. The more powerful chiefs like Jassa Singh Ahluwalia, Charhat Singh Sukarchakia, Gujjar Singh, Jai Singh Kanhiya and Jassa Singh Ramgarhia asserted their suzerain claims over some of the hill principalities. Jhanda Singh and Ganda Singh Bhangi conquered Multan and held it until 1780. Some of the Sikh chiefs of the Satlej-Jamuna Divide led campaigns across the Jamuna and established *rākhī* but without any permanent gain of territory. Already in the 1770s the Sikh chiefs could range on opposite sides in alliance with non-Sikh chiefs. Even the veterans like Jassa Singh Ahluwalia, Jai Singh Kanhiya and Jassa Singh Ramgarhia could fight against one another. With a few exceptions, however, the Sikh principalities founded in the eighteenth century survived into the nineteenth to be subverted or subjugated by Ranjit Singh, the grandson of Charhat Singh Sukarchakia.

All the chiefs were completely independent of others in the government and administration of their territories. Every chief appointed his own *dīwān, thānadār* and *kārdārs* for the administration of his territory; every chief appointed his own commandant of the army.

[16] Carefully identified and studied in terms of territories and resources by Veena Sachdeva, *Polity and Economy of the Punjab During the Late Eighteenth Century*, Manohar, Delhi, 1993.

Those who served the principality at subordinate levels were generally given *jāgīrs* and not cash salaries. Arrangements for the collection of revenue from land were made with *chaudharīs* and *muqaddams*; the actual cultivators were treated rather leniently. The *qānūngos* and *paṭwārīs* continued to perform their usual functions in revenue administration. In the administration of justice many of the old courts of the *qāzī* were kept up; the individual chief gave his personal attention to matters of justice; and the *panchāyats* in villages and towns were given more importance. Non-Sikhs were associated with the administration in different capacities and at various levels. The Sikh chiefs extended their patronage to Sikhs and non-Sikhs alike, particularly for giving revenue-free land to religious personages or institutions. In spite of a total political change from the Mughal rule to the rule of the Sikh chiefs, which involved much social mobility as well, there was a great deal of continuity, including institutional continuity.[17]

IV

Towards the end of the eighteenth century, the number of Singhs was larger than ever before. However, they did not constitute the entire Sikh Panth. There were many others who had not received the baptism of the double-edged sword but who regarded themselves as Sikh. Though every Sikh was not a Singh, the Singhs were clearly the dominant component, not merely because of their large numbers or their association with government and administration, but also because of the centrality of their doctrines. They believed in the unity of Guruship from Guru Nanak to Guru Gobind Singh and in the end of personal Guruship after his death. They also subscribed to the twin doctrine of the Guru-Panth and Guru-Granth.

The Singhs constituted the bulk of the ruling class in the areas under Sikh rule. The majority of the rulers were Jat, but there were also others who had earlier belonged to the lower castes in the countryside, like *tarkhāns* and *kalāls*. At the subordinate levels in administration also there were some former barbers, water-carriers and scavengers. They enjoyed *jāgīrs* like the other members of the ruling class. In the armies too, though there was a preponderance of Jats, the others were

---

[17] Indu Banga, 'State Formation Under Sikh Rule', *Journal of Regional History*, I (1980), 15–35; Veena Sachdeva, 'Jagirdari System in the Punjab (Late 18th Century)', *ibid.*, 5 (1984), 1–13.

represented. There was a considerable number of cultivators, artisans and craftsmen, traders and shopkeepers in the Sikh Panth, including both Singhs and Sikhs. Even in the Singh component, a certain degree of social stratification was introduced by the political process, and it was being reinforced after the establishment of Sikh rule by the operation of government and administration.

The operation of the Sikh government affected the Sikh community in some other ways too. The descendants of Guru Nanak and Guru Ram Das, the Bedis and the Sodhis, came to be held in high esteem, and nearly every Sikh ruler extended patronage to them. The descendants of Guru Angad and Guru Amar Das, the Trehans and the Bhallas, also received state patronage. The improvement in their material means as much as their descent gave them a peculiar prestige in the Sikh social order. The number of *granthis*, *rāgīs* and *bhāīs* in general increased with the extension of patronage to places associated with the Sikh Gurus. Reconstruction of the Harmandir and the Akāl Takht in Amritsar was only a more pronounced example of the interest of the Sikh rulers in the sacred places of the Sikhs. Many new *gurdwāras* were built with arrangements for religious services. Revenue-free lands were granted not only to the sacred places in Amritsar but also to many others. Some of the places were maintained by Udāsī *sādhs* who traced their origin to Sri Chand, the elder son of Guru Nanak, and used Granth Sahib for their vedantic exposition of the Sikh faith. During the late eighteenth century, several of the Sikh rulers gave revenue-free lands to Udāsīs. Quite a few of their important centres were established in the late eighteenth century, including the *akhāṛa* known as Brahm Buta in the vicinity of the Harmandir. Some of the religious places were maintained by Nihangs, the remnants of the Khālsā who failed or refused to occupy any territories and who were not associated with government and administration.[18]

Largely in the hope of receiving patronage from the rulers, or the members of the ruling class, quite a few individuals started producing literature. Important among them was Sarup Das Bhalla, tenth in descent from Guru Amar Das. He compiled events (*sākhīs*) connected

---

[18] For patronage of religious persons and institutions by the Sikh rulers of the late eighteenth century, Indu Banga, *Agrarian System of the Sikhs*; Veena Sachdeva, *Polity and Economy in the Late Eighteenth-Century Punjab*; Sulakhan Singh, 'Udasi Establishments Under Sikh Rule', *Journal of Regional History*, I (1980), 70–87; and 'State Patronage to Udasis Under Maharaja Ranjit Singh', *Maharaja Ranjit Singh and His Times* (eds J. S. Grewal and Indu Banga), Guru Nanak Dev University, Amritsar, 1980, 103–16.

with the lives of the ten Gurus, adding one on Banda Bahadur, on the basis of earlier writings and oral evidence. Without much understanding of the Sikh tradition, he underlines the importance of the outward Singh form (*rehat*), extols the role of the Bhalla descendants of Guru Amar Das in Sikh history, and tries to minimize the seriousness of dissent in the past to clear the way for the acceptance of former dissidents in the contemporary Sikh social order.[19] A Sodhi descendant of Dhir Mal at Kartarpur, probably Wadbhag Singh, actually approached Jassa Singh Ahluwalia with the request to intercede with the Khālsā to rescind the old injunction regarding the excommunication of the followers of Dhir Mal. After a good deal of debate among the leaders he was allowed to join the fold.[20] The dissidents of old gradually began to receive patronage from the Singhs, or even to join their ranks.[21]

Another writer, Kesar Singh, was a descendant of Chhibber Brahmans closely associated with Guru Har Rai, Guru Har Krishan, Guru Tegh Bahadur and Guru Gobind Singh. In recognition of the services of his ancestors he expected patronage from the new rulers, but having got none he was rather resentful. He did not like the association of Hindu Khatrīs and Muslims with the government and administration of the Sikh rulers. In fact he had little appreciation for political power if it was not used to promote justice and patronage of deserving persons.[22]

Kesar Singh Chhibber's work is extremely interesting as one kind of response to the establishment of Sikh rule. Making a clear distinction between the Sikh and the Singh he shows much less appreciation for the Singhs who were associated with political power. Yet he is prepared to pronounce legitimacy on the rule of '*shūdars*'. He subscribes to the doctrine of Guru-Granth much more emphatically than to the doctrine of Guru-Panth. This enables him to become an interpreter of 'the Guru'. Indeed he is proud of his understanding of the scriptures, but he

[19] Sarup Das Bhalla's work, written around 1770, has been published now by the Punjab Languages Department as *Mahimā Parkāsh*, Patiala, 1970.
[20] Joginder Kaur (ed.), *Ram Sukh Rao's Sri Fateh Singh Partap Prabhakar (A History of the Early Nineteenth Century Punjab)*, Patiala, 1980, 204. According to Tahmas Beg Khan, Wadbhag Singh was an active leader of the Sikhs: *Tahmās Nāmah*, 182–83.
[21] The Sodhis of Kartarpur, the descendants of Prithi Chand and the descendants of Suraj Mal as well as the Udāsīs were included among the recipients of revenue-free land.
[22] Kesar Singh Chhibber's work, written around 1770, has been published by the Panjab University: *Bansāwalīnāmā Dasān Pātshāhīān Kā* (ed. Ratan Singh Jaggi, *Parakh*, Vol. 2), Chandigarh, 1972.

interprets them in his own way, presenting on the whole what may be called a Brahmanized version of Sikhism. Involuntarily a sort of alliance is implied between the new Sikh state and a Brahmanized Sikh church. Kesar Singh Chhibber upholds the distinctions of caste among the Sikhs. What was shared by all the Sikhs and Singhs, according to him, was only their religious faith; the caste *dharma* remained operative for all in matters of matrimony and commensality.

Chhibber was much more conservative than the contemporary Singhs, almost a reactionary. But he was upholding a position which differed from the contemporary social reality only to a degree, though surely a large degree. There was enough differentiation in the growing complexity of the Sikh social order to compromise the egalitarian principle of the Order of the Khālsā or even the earlier Sikh Panth.

CHAPTER 6

THE SIKH EMPIRE (1799–1849)

In 1799, a process of unification was started by Ranjit Singh virtually to establish an empire during the first quarter of the nineteenth century. He made use of an efficient army raised and trained more or less like the army of the East India Company. The use of the time-honoured suzerain-vassal polity was equally important in establishing his political control. Paying personal attention to revenue administration and trade in his large dominions he revived prosperity in the Punjab. Extending state patronage to all important sections of the population he attached them to the new empire. In the ruling class too, Hindus and Muslims came to form a substantial element.

The Sikhs formed the dominant element in the ruling class and had the largest share in *jāgīrs* assigned by Ranjit Singh and his successors. In state patronage in the form of revenue-free land, the Sikhs received a much larger share than Hindus and Muslims, but not at their cost. The state alienated more revenues now in favour of the religious grantees than in Mughal times. In fact Ranjit Singh only extended the pattern first set by Akbar and enlarged later by the early Sikh rulers. Some Sikh members of the ruling class patronized art and literature; a few took personal interest in traditional learning. The number of Sikhs was increasing during the early nineteenth century though only a small number of the new entrants were associated with government and administration or the army. In the towns and cities the increase was largely in the number of the professional and commercial middling class; in the countryside, it was largely in the number of the peasantry. Besides social differentiation, a certain degree of ideological differentiation also developed in the Sikh community.

Within ten years of Ranjit Singh's death in 1839 his empire was taken over by the British who had already established their direct or indirect political control over the rest of the subcontinent. At Lahore, a tussle for power at the top had brought in a factious nobility, and the increasing struggle for power brought in the army; the growing instability eventually brought in the British who were half inclined to annex the Punjab for reasons which had little to do with its internal affairs. After the hard-fought battles of the Satlej in 1845–1846 the army and the territory of the boy-king Dalip Singh were cut to size to make the Punjab more manageable. Lahore was garrisoned by British troops and a British adviser was given to the Lahore Darbar. The final annexation of the Punjab was only a matter of time. It came in March, 1849.

I

The occupation of Lahore by Ranjit Singh in the summer of 1799 marked a watershed in his career and in the history of Sikh rule in the Punjab. The city was unified more than three decades after its occupation and partition by Gujjar Singh, Lehna Singh and Sobha Singh in 1765. The territories of their successors, Sahib Singh, Chait Singh and Mohar Singh, were taken over by Ranjit Singh. This meant the end of two Sikh principalities. Only Sahib Singh survived as a chief with his larger territory around Gujrat. Ranjit Singh adopted Lahore as his capital. His political achievement as the ruler of Lahore has so completely overshadowed his late eighteenth-century predecessors that the year 1799 appears to many historians to mark the beginning of sovereign Sikh rule in the Punjab.

The legacy of the late eighteenth century was nevertheless relevant for Ranjit Singh's occupation of Lahore. His grandfather Charhat Singh was one of the foremost leaders of the Khālsā in their struggle for power and he had occupied large pockets of territory in three Doabs. Ranjit Singh's father, Mahan Singh, added to those territories, occupied some strategic places and asserted his suzerain rights over some of the chiefs in the hills and the plains. A large, almost contiguous, and well-administered territory from the middle of the Rachna to the middle of the Sindh Sagar Doab was the most valuable asset Ranjit Singh inherited from his father, yielding about a million rupees a year. He also came into command of 5,000 well-mounted and well-armed cavalry. This advantage was reinforced by two marriages, one in the family of Jai Singh Kanhiya in the upper Bari Doab and the other in the family of Kamar Singh Nakkai in the south of Lahore.

The invasions of Zaman Shah, the second successor of Ahmad Shah Abdali, served as a catalyst to bring out Ranjit Singh's qualities of leadership. After the first invasion Ranjit Singh recovered his own fort of Rohtas; during the second, he emerged as a leading Sikh chief; and during the third, in 1798–1799, he opposed Zaman Shah as the leader of a number of Sikh chiefs. Within six months of Zaman Shah's departure from the Punjab, Ranjit Singh occupied Lahore as much with the willing cooperation of some of its leading Hindu and Muslim residents as with the assistance of his allies, particularly his mother-in-law Sada Kaur.

With the conquest of Lahore Ranjit Singh was fairly well launched on a career of systematic aggrandisement which made him the master of an empire in less than a quarter of a century. In the first ten years of this career he subverted more than twenty principalities in the plains. Before the occupation of Amritsar in 1805, which put an end to the dominions carved out by the redoubtable Hari Singh Bhangi, Ranjit Singh annexed the territories of Jassa Singh Dulu and Dal Singh Gill in the Rachna Doab, and of Jodh Singh Bajwa in the Chaj Doab. Within the five years following, he took over Rahon and Nakodar in the Jalandhar Doab on the death of Tara Singh Dallewalia, Philaur from its Kang chief and Hariana in Hoshiarpur from the widows of Baghel Singh. In the Bari Doab he took over Pathankot from Tara Singh Sandhu, Sujanpur from Buddh Singh Bagga, Adinanagar from Gulab Singh Khaira, Chamiari from its Randhawa chief, Qasur from the Afghans, Maruf from Buddh Singh, and Hujra Shah Muqim from its Sayyid chief. In the Rachna Doab he took over Pindi Bhattian from the Bhattis and Kamalia from the Kharals. In the Sindh Sagar Doab, the territories of Nawab Khan Jodhra around Pindi Gheb and of Muhammad Khan Gheba around Fateh Jang were annexed. Thus, before Ranjit Singh signed the Treaty of Amritsar with the British in 1809, he was ruling over large areas in all the five Doabs of the Punjab.

By the Treaty of Amritsar, the British recognized Ranjit Singh as the sole sovereign ruler of the Punjab and left him free to round off his conquests in the former Mughal province of Lahore, to oust the Afghans from Multan and Kashmir and finally, to turn the tables against the successors of Ahmad Shah Abdali in the former Mughal province of Kabul.[1] The Sikh chiefs ousted now were those of Jalandhar, Hajipur and Mukerian in the Bist Jalandhar Doab; Jaimal Singh of Fatehgarh Churian, Jodh Singh Ramgarhia of

[1] In the first article of the treaty between the British and 'the Raja of Lahore' it was stipulated that 'the British Government will have no concern with the territories and subjects of the Raja to the northward of the river Sutlej'. For more than two decades then, the British did not interfere with the affairs of the chiefs on the north of the Satlej.

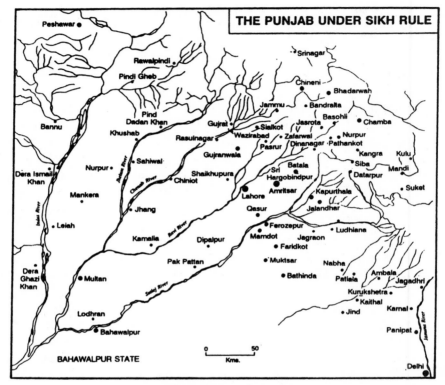

Map 4 The Punjab under Sikh rule

Sri Hargobindpur and the Nakkai chiefs in the Bari Doab; the chiefs of
Wazirabad, Hallowal and Doda in the Rachna Doab; of Daska and
Gujrat in the Chaj Doab; and Jiwan Singh of Rawalpindi in the Sindh
Sagar Doab. Batala was taken over from Sada Kaur. Fateh Singh
Ahluwalia of Kapurthala was the only Sikh chief left in the Punjab
whose territory was not taken over. The Rajput chiefs of Jammu and
Kangra, Khari Khariali, Akhnur, Bhimber, Lakhanpur, Nurpur, Guler,
Siba, Kotla, Jaswan and Datarpur also lost their territories in the hills to
Ranjit Singh. All these states were close to the plains. Attock was
wrested from the Afghans; the Awan, Gakkhar and the Tiwana chiefs
were shorn of their possessions in the Sindh Sagar Doab. The Baloch
chiefs of Khushab and Sahiwal in the Chaj Doab, and the Sial chief of
Jhang in the Rachna Doab lost their territories to Ranjit Singh before

1818. He was well poised now to oust the Afghans from the Punjab and Kashmir.[2]

In less than four years Ranjit Singh liquidated all the Afghan strongholds on the east of the river Indus. Multan fell finally in June, 1818, and all the territories of Nawab Muzaffar Khan were annexed. Kashmir was conquered a year later, in July, 1819. The chief of Mankera surrendered his capital in 1821, and all his territory in the Sindh Sagar Doab was taken over. Then for ten years Ranjit Singh did not add much to the directly administered areas. In 1831, he took over Dera Ghazi Khan from the chief of Bahawalpur to whom it had been entrusted ten years earlier. Peshawar was taken over from its Afghan governor in 1834 though he had been sending revenues and tribute since 1824. In 1836, the territories of Bannu, Kohat and Dera Ghazi Khan were taken over from the subordinate chiefs and made an integral part of the directly administered dominions of Ranjit Singh. Before his death in 1839 Ranjit Singh's authority over all the conquered and subordinated territories between the river Satlej and the mountain ranges of Ladakh, Karakoram, Hindukush and Sulaiman was recognized by the rulers of Kabul as well as by the British rulers of India.

II

Ranjit Singh's political success would have been impossible without an efficient army. Apart from his own cavalry, which went on increasing with his early conquests, he was helped by the cavalry of the chiefs who allied with him, like Sada Kaur, Fateh Singh Ahluwalia and Jodh Singh Ramgarhia, and by the contingents supplied by the chiefs whom he subordinated. There is no doubt that cavalry held great fascination for Ranjit Singh and his nobles. He raised special troops known as Orderlies and the *ghorcharha-i-khas*. As a European witness remarked, it was difficult to find a finer or a more striking body of men.[3] However, the cavalry of Ranjit Singh did not increase after 1820.

[2] For the detail of Ranjit Singh's conquests, Indu Banga, *Agrarian System of the Sikhs: Late Eighteenth and Early Nineteenth Century*, Manohar Publications, New Delhi, 1978, 22–26; Veena Sachdeva, 'The Non-Sikh Chiefs of the Punjab Plains and Maharaja Ranjit Singh', *Journal of Regional History*, Guru Nanak Dev University, Amritsar, 2 (1981), 1–11; J. S. Grewal, 'Between the Treaty of Amritsar and the Conquest of Multan', in *ibid.*, 12–20.

[3] Baron Charles Hugel, *Travels in Kashmir and the Punjab* (tr. T. B. Jervis), Light and Life Publishers, Jammu, 1972 (reprint) 330–31, 334–35. A *ghorchara* wore shirt of mail over a velvet coat; his steel helmet was inlaid with gold; his left arm was covered with a steel cuff

In fact during the second decade he had started raising cavalrymen trained on European lines. In 1820 he had three regiments of this regular cavalry consisting of about 850 horsemen. The number of such horsemen rose to 4,000 in the 1830s.

The real strength of Ranjit Singh's army lay in its infantry and artillery. Not only in the conquest of Multan and Kashmir but also in his earlier conquests, particularly after the Treaty of Amritsar, these new wings played an increasingly decisive role. Even before 1809, Ranjit Singh had raised 1,500 infantrymen and two batteries of artillery. The men who initially served in these units of the army were mostly deserters from the army of the East India Company; they were trained by Rohila Afghans in the service of Ranjit Singh. By 1820 there were thirteen infantry battalions consisting of about 10,000 trained infantrymen. At this time Ranjit Singh possessed 200 guns. Horse artillery was added in the 1820s when the most important of his European officers were also employed, Allard and Ventura in 1822 and Court and Avitabile in 1827. In 1831 there were 300 guns in the artillery and about 20,000 trained infantrymen in twenty-one battalions. Towards the end of Ranjit Singh's reign, nearly half of his army in terms of numbers consisted of men and officers trained on European lines, with a large number of Punjabis among them. In terms of its striking power, the state of Ranjit Singh was stronger than many larger states in Asia.

In the expansion of Ranjit Singh's dominions the time-honoured institution of vassalage proved to be nearly as important as the westernized wings of his army. A large majority of the chiefs whose principalities were subverted were first obliged to pay tribute in acknowledgment of his political superiority. In this respect there was no difference between a Sikh and a non-Sikh chief, or a chief of the hills and the plains. The chiefs of Khushab and Sahiwal, Jhang and Mankera, for instance, paid tribute to Ranjit Singh for several years before their territories were annexed. The chief of Multan had paid tribute regularly for nearly a decade before the annexation of Multan in 1818. The chief of Bahawalpur went on paying tribute for his territory on the west of the Satlej till 1831. In many cases, in fact, Ranjit Singh went on increasing the amount of tribute till the chief was either unable or

inlaid with gold; a damascened round shield hung over his back; he held in his right hand a long bayonet ornamented with gold; he slung a bow over his left shoulder, with a quiver on the right; he wore a pistol and a Persian dagger.

unwilling to pay, which created a situation in which annexation appeared to be called for if not justified. Before the British came in to declare that all the chiefs of the Satlej-Jamuna Divide were under their protection, Ranjit Singh had collected tribute from nearly all of them, including the chiefs of Patiala, Nabha, Jind, Faridkot, Shahabad, Thanesar, Kaithal, Malerkotla and Raikot. Nearly all the Sikh chiefs of the Punjab proper paid tribute to Ranjit Singh after his occupation of Lahore and before the annexation of their territories. Jodh Singh Ramgarhia paid tribute to Ranjit Singh for nearly a decade before his principality was subverted in 1816. The last among the Sikh chiefs to lose his sovereign status was Fateh Singh Ahluwalia. In 1825 he crossed the Satlej to seek protection with the British against Ranjit Singh's alleged or real design over his territory. Fateh Singh succeeded in retaining his territory, but when he recrossed the Satlej in 1826 he was walking into vassalage with his eyes wide open.[4]

Ranjit Singh subverted more principalities in the hills than all the Mughal rulers put together. However, Mandi, Suket, Bilaspur, Kulu and Chamba in the former Mughal province of Lahore were not annexed by Ranjit Singh, and hardly any vassal state of the province of Kashmir was taken over. Thus, a larger number of vassal chiefs went on paying tribute to Ranjit Singh. They sent contingents too whenever they were called upon to do so. Most of them were asked to provide hostages for their good conduct; succession to their position was controlled by Ranjit Singh. They could not have any political relationship with one another, or with another sovereign power. They had to allow passage to persons permitted by Ranjit Singh to pass through their territories. In the internal administration of their principalities the vassal chiefs were given more or less complete autonomy.[5]

Ironically, vassal territories did not decrease with the passage of time in Ranjit Singh's reign. This was because the Maharaja decided to create new Rajas of his own after 1820. Fateh Chand, the younger brother of Raja Sansar Chand, was made a vassal chief with the title of Raja and a small territory. A son of Raja Sansar Chand was similarly made a vassal chief all over again after the fall of the Kangra principality. Another principality to be revived in the Kangra region was that of Siba. It was

---

[4] J. S. Grewal, 'Passage to Vassalage', *From Guru Nanak to Maharaja Ranjit Singh*, Guru Nanak Dev University, Amritsar, 1982 (2nd edn), 160–68.

[5] For suzerain-vassal relations in the early nineteenth-century Punjab, Indu Banga, *Agrarian Systems of the Sikhs*, 39–62.

in the Jammu region, however, that vassalage was revived on a large scale.

Before the ouster of Raja Jit Singh of Jammu in 1815, his second cousin Kishora Singh and the latter's three sons, Gulab Singh, Dhian Singh and Suchet Singh, had joined the service of Ranjit Singh as common troopers. They rose rapidly in the estimation of the Maharaja, and in 1820 they were made *jāgīrdārs* of Jammu, Bhoti, Bandralta (Ramnagar), Chenini and Kishtwar for maintaining 400 horsemen and on the condition that they would extirpate Dido, a rebel collateral of the Jammu Rajas. Dido was killed in 1821. Kishora Singh was made the Raja of Jammu. When he died in the year following, Gulab Singh was installed in his place, while Suchet Singh was made the Raja of Ramnagar (Bandralta). Dhian Singh was given the title of Rājā-i-Rājgān and Rājā-i-Kalān Bahādur in 1827 with the territory of Bhimber. In 1837, Hira Singh, son of Raja Dhian Singh, was made the Raja of Basohli and Jasrota. More areas were added to their territories in due course so that, altogether, they came to hold much larger territories than the former chiefs of Jammu.[6]

III

The territories directly administered by Ranjit Singh were divided into a large number of primary units over which governors (*nāzims*) were appointed by the Maharaja. Each primary unit consisted of *ta'alluqas*, also called *parganas*, over which *kārdārs* were appointed for the collection of revenues and the maintenance of peace and order. The *kārdārs* were assisted by *qānūngos*, *chaudharīs*, *muqaddams* and *paṭwārīs*. Thus, there was hardly any change in the general framework of administration. The former Mughal province of Lahore remained divided into several primary units. The territories across the Indus did not form a single unit. Thus the area under a province was much less important. The size of the *pargana* or the *ta'alluqa*, however, did not always decrease, and the Sikh *kārdār* remained as important as the Mughal *'āmil*.

Administrative arrangements at the centre became more elaborate

---

[6] For the documents of *jāgīr*, *rājgī* and title, J. S. Grewal and Indu Banga, 'The Sikh Suzerain', *From Guru Nanak to Maharaja Ranjit Singh*, Guru Nanak Dev University, Amritsar, 1982 (2nd edn), 139–59. As vassals of Ranjit Singh the Jamwal brothers served the Lahore state and received large *jāgīrs* in addition to their territories.

with the expansion of territories. The entire record of income and expenditure of the state had to be maintained. *Dīwāns* and treasurers were appointed to maintain records relating to different heads of income and expenditure. The central secretariat came to be known as the Exalted Secretariat (*daftar-i-mu'allā*) to distinguish it from the provincial secretariats. Finance, however, was only one concern of Ranjit Singh. Assistance was needed for his other concerns too. Important among these was the day-to-day work of the court (*deoḍhī*). The office of the *deoḍhīdār* was therefore extremely important. It was held by Jamadar Khushal Singh till 1818 when Dhian Singh was appointed to this office. Under Raja Dhian Singh the office gradually developed into the office virtually of the Prime Minister (*wazīr*). Ranjit Singh acted as the Commander-in-Chief of the army but he appointed one of his Generals to look after the standing army (*kampū-i-mu'allā*) in accordance with his detailed instructions from day to day. For negotiations and correspondence with foreign powers Ranjit Singh generally used the services of Faqir Azizuddin. There were other courtiers who apparently held no particular office but who were consulted from time to time. The Maharaja himself was the chief source of justice, though judges (*adālatīs*) were appointed all afresh and the court of the *qāzī* and *panchāyats* were kept up in towns and villages.

Though Ranjit Singh introduced cash salaries in his battalions, regiments and batteries of artillery, *jāgīrs* remained the most important mode of payment to those who served the state. Remuneration to state functionaries was made on two accounts, for personal service and for the maintenance of troopers. Since all the functionaries of the state did not maintain troops, a large number of them received remuneration only for their personal service. Those who were paid on account of maintaining horsemen included not only the army commandants but also *nāzims* and *kārdārs*. Many a horseman too was paid in *jāgīr*. Thus, the amount of *jāgīr* given to a person could vary from a few hundred to a few lakh of rupees, or in other words from half a village to a number of *ta'alluqas*. Whereas a civilian like the Treasurer Beli Ram received about 60,000 rupees a year at one time, a General like Hari Singh Nalwa received over eight lakhs. Raja Gulab Singh at one time was getting seven lakhs of rupees as a *jāgīrdār* of the state. Altogether, nearly 40 per cent of the total revenues of the state were alienated as *jāgīrs*.

However, revenue from land was alienated not only in favour of those who served the state but also in favour of several other categories of persons. In the first place, all those chiefs, whether Sikh, Hindu or Muslim, who were displaced from power were given *jāgīrs* for subsistence. The amount of such *jāgīrs* was generally reduced with the passage of time, but a certain amount was left permanently with the descendants of the deposed chiefs. Small *jāgīrs* were given also to the descendants of persons who had served the state with zeal and distinction. Hereditary *jāgīrs* of small amounts were given by Ranjit Singh as a reward for extension of cultivation and for something out of the ordinary, like the discovery of a mine, the intelligence of a crucial significance, the defence of a fort in a desperate situation, an act of personal valour, skill or devotion or the gift of an exceptionally good horse. The total amount of revenue alienated for such purposes remained rather small.

A much larger amount of revenue was alienated in favour of persons and institutions connected with religion. Grants given by former rulers were generally continued. Additional grants were given to some old institutions, and fresh grants were given to new centres. Sikh, Hindu and Muslim institutions received state patronage. The Sodhis and the Bedis, the Harmandir and its *mutasaddīs*, *granthīs*, *ardāsias*, *rāgīs* and *rabābīs*, the Akāl Takht, Jhanda Bunga, Shahid Bunga, Ber Baba Sahib, Dera Baba Atal Sahib and Bibeksar in the precincts of the Harmandir, Gurdwara Tahli Sahib at Dera Baba Nanak, and the Gurdwaras at Keshgarh and Kiratpur, the Darbar Sahib at Tarn Taran and at Ramdas, the *udāsī akhāṛas* and Nirmala centres, the Akalis and Nihangs were prominent among the Sikh recipients of revenue-free lands. Purohits and Brahmans in general, the *purohits* of Thanesar and Hardwar, the court pandits, the Jwalamukhi Temple in Kangra, Shaiva *jogīs* and Vaishnava *bairāgīs*, particularly the Tilla of Gorakhnath in the Chaj Doab, the *jogī* centres at Kirana and Jakhbar, the *bairāgī* establishments at Pindori, Dhianpur and Dhamtal, besides a number of Shivalas and Thakurdwaras were important among the Hindu recipients. Among the Muslims there were the Gardezi Sayyids of Multan, the descendants of Shaikh Farid at Pakpattan, the descendants of Bahauddin Zakariya at Multan, the shrines of Hazratbal and Shah Hamdan in Kashmir, the shrine of Sakhi Sarwar in Dera Ghazi Khan, Shaikhs and Sayyids in Bannu and Peshawar, the *khānqah* of Pir Miththa near Wazirabad, and numerous other *khānqahs*. Altogether, more than 7 per cent of the state revenue came to be alienated in *dharmarth* by the end of Ranjit Singh's reign. The example of Ranjit Singh was often followed by the *jāgīrdārs* who gave small grants to all categories of persons and institutions from their own *jāgīrs*. Many of these continued to be enjoyed by the grantees even after the *jāgīr* was transferred to someone else.[7]

IV

The revival of cultivation and trade, which had begun in the late eighteenth century, reached a high watermark in the reign of Ranjit Singh. He was keen to extend cultivation to culturable waste land and to virgin land, and gave general instruction to this effect to *nāzims* and *kārdārs*. The *chaudharīs* and *muqaddams* who succeeded in extending cultivation in the areas under their jurisdiction were rewarded with revenue-free lands. The actual tillers of new lands were given concession for a number of years through graded rates of assessment, and also the right of occupation or even proprietary right. State loans were given for digging new wells. The Shah Nahr was re-excavated and a number of inundation canals were dug to help irrigation, particularly in the province of Multan. The state revenues from land increased considerably in the areas covered by the former Mughal provinces of Lahore and Multan. Towards the end of Ranjit Singh's reign the total income from land amounted to nearly 30 million rupees a year. If this amount was less than the figures available for the reign of Shah Jahan, it was largely because the rates of assessment in the early nineteenth century were lower than what they had been in the early seventeenth. In any case, the loss of the state was the gain of the cultivator.[8]

The state policy of ensuring larger and larger revenues through increased agricultural production was favourable to the actual cultivators of land and to those who could invest capital in wells or irrigational channels. Many large proprietors of land were reduced to the status of *ta'alluqdārs*, which meant that they lost their lands and retained only a certain share in the produce or a certain percentage in the revenue.[9] The dues of the *ta'alluqdār* varied from area to area, with a tendency towards decrease so that in certain areas they received

[7] For *jāgīrs* and grants in the early nineteenth century Punjab, Indu Banga, *Agrarian Systems of the Sikhs*, 118–67.

[8] This has been well argued by Indu Banga, *ibid.*, 113–17.

[9] The *ta'alluqdārs* of the Punjab held a widely different position from that of the *ta'alluqdārs* of Awadh.

virtually nothing. In the process many a tenant became a proprietor. The tenants gained at the cost of the peasant proprietors also in places. In any case, there was a large proportion of tenants cultivating the same lands for decades. This accounted for the preponderance of 'occupancy' tenants later under British rule in the Punjab. Towards the end of Ranjit Singh's reign, nearly 10 per cent of the land under cultivation had become *ta'alluqdārī*, which meant a certain decrease in the holdings of the large proprietors of land. The bulk of the land under cultivation was held by small proprietors who generally cultivated their own lands. The tenants were half the number of peasant proprietors and tilled only a quarter of the cultivated land. Free-peasant and free-tenant economy was helpful in agricultural production. Land in well-settled areas was certainly a commodity of some value. The trading communities in the Punjab invested some of their savings in land, particularly in the neighbourhood of cities and towns.[10] In the province of Multan many Arora families acquired proprietary rights in land by providing the means of irrigation.

Increase in agricultural production was paralleled by an increase in manufacturing and the volume of trade. Cities and towns expanded with the expansion of Ranjit Singh's dominions.[11] The capital cities of Multan, Srinagar and Peshawar regained some of their former importance, and the city of Lahore was revived on a larger scale. Towns like Wazirabad, Gujrat and Sialkot flourished more now than in the late eighteenth century. Some new towns were also founded. Amritsar became the premier city in the northwest of the Indian subcontinent. The number of important urban centres in the dominions of Ranjit Singh exceeded one hundred, and they all served as centres of trade. Many of them served as centres of manufacturing as well. The revival of Lahore, for instance, meant among other things the revival of its manufacturing of cotton, wool and silk textiles and its metal work. Multan became famous for its silks and cottons, woollen carpets, glazed pottery and enamelled silver. Amritsar was more important than Lahore and Multan, both for its manufacturing and trade. The shawl industry of Srinagar was revived, and many Kashmiri weavers

[10] A large number of Khatri proprietors of land in towns and villages are mentioned by Ganesh Das in his *Chār Bāgh-i-Panjab*: J. S. Grewal and Indu Banga (eds), *Early Nineteenth Century Panjab*, Guru Nanak Dev University, Amritsar, 1975.
[11] For trade and manufacturing in the early nineteenth century, Reeta Grewal, 'Polity, Economy and Urbanization: Early Nineteenth Century Punjab', *Journal of Regional History*, 4 (1983), 56–72.

moved into the cities and towns of the plains as well. Many towns came to be known for their specialized manufacturing, like Batala, Jalandhar, Hoshiarpur, Bajwara, Sialkot, Chandiot, Gujrat, Sahiwal and Wazirabad.

Ranjit Singh encouraged trade by ensuring safe passage for the caravans of traders and by imposing lenient duties. Banking facilities were available through the system of *hundīs*, and insurance (*bīmā*) was available at low rates. Trade and manufacturing were almost exclusively a family enterprise. There were no corporate business organizations in the dominions of the Maharaja. The state held the monopoly of salt, invested a little in trade, and maintained a good number of workshops (*kārkhānas*) for manufacturing articles needed by the army and the royal household. The items of trade in every town were rather numerous though the quantities involved were not large. Important items of trade related to agriculture, manufacturing and natural products. Wheat, sugar, rice, cotton, indigo, poppy, pepper and dried ginger were exported to Afghanistan and central Asia. Gold, silver, iron, copper, brass and zinc were among the important items of import, besides silk and wool, fresh and dry fruit, horses and some luxury goods. Internal trade was more important than external trade. Amritsar was linked by road with Lahore, and through Lahore with Multan, Srinagar and Peshawar. All these cities were linked with a number of towns which in turn were linked with smaller towns and villages.

The socio-political situation created by the establishment of a large state by Ranjit Singh was conducive to new developments of great cultural significance. A new style of architecture is visible in the religious and secular buildings of the period. A new style of painting also emerged in the Punjab during the early nineteenth century as a result of the patronage given to artists by the rulers and the nobles.[12] Historical literature in Persian was encouraged by Maharaja Ranjit Singh. Sohan Lal Suri's monumental *Umdat ut-Tawārīkh* is only one example of the historical works on the Punjab produced in Persian during the first half of the nineteenth century.[13] Ram Sukh Rao, a chronicler patronized by Fateh Singh Ahluwalia, wrote a volume each on Jassa Singh Ahluwalia, his successor Bhag Singh and Fateh Singh

[12] W. G. Archer, *Paintings of the Sikhs*, London 1966; B. N. Goswamy, 'The Context of Painting in the Sikh Punjab', *Journal of Regional History*, 2 (1981), 85–105.

[13] It is not generally known that under Colonel Mihan Singh as the governor of Kashmir a detailed work on its fiscal resources was prepared under the title *Tarīkh-i-Kalān*.

Ahluwalia himself, not in Persian but in Gurmukhi script in a language easily understandable to the people of the Punjab.[14] Some of the poets also wrote in Punjabi in the hope of patronage from the members of the ruling class if not from the rulers themselves. Only in this context can we appreciate Sawan Yar's *Sīharfī Sarkār Kī* praising the rule of Ranjit Singh, Jafar Beg's *Sīharfī* lamenting his death, and Hakam Singh's *Sīharfī* celebrating the exploits of Hari Singh Nalwa. Qadir Yar identified himself with the Punjabi ruling class against their Afghan opponents.

Not all the Punjabi works were written for the rulers or the members of the ruling class. Many of them were clearly meant for the common Punjabis, like Qadir Yar's *Qissa Sohni Mahīwāl* or his *Pūran Bhagat*. His *Raja Rāsālū* was actually meant to be sung by popular minstrels (*dhāḍis*). Ahmad Yar, who wrote the *Shāhnāma* of Ranjit Singh in Persian was nonetheless a poet of the people. All his life he had written in Punjabi and quite deliberately too. He cannot help mentioning this in the *Shāhnāma*. Having been born in the Punjab, lived in the Punjab, breathed its air and tasted its water, he was naturally inclined, he says, to write on all old or new themes in Punjabi, a language that was much easier for the people to understand than any other language. Obviously, Ahmad Yar was writing for the common people of the Punjab. The themes of his works indicate that he was writing for members of all the three communities.[15] This articulation of regional identity may be regarded as the cultural counterpart of the secularization of polity by Ranjit Singh which ensured participation of all important sections of society on a significant scale.

However, the new interests of the early nineteenth century did not eliminate the works produced for the consumption of a particular community. Nor did they undermine the traditional branches of learning or knowledge. This was partly because of the continuance of Persian as the language of administration. There were scholars in cities and towns who went on studying books written in Persian or Sanskrit. These books related to several areas of interest, like jurisprudence, politics, poetry, composition, calligraphy, mathematics, medicine, astronomy and astrology. Jurisprudence was exclusively the domain of

---

[14] One of these works has been edited and published by Dr Joginder Kaur as *Ram Sukh Rao's Sri Fateh Singh Partap Prabhakar*, Patiala, 1980.

[15] Daljinder Singh Johal, 'Heroic Literature in Punjabi (1800–1850)', *Journal of Regional History*, 2 (1981), 57–84; 'Punjabi Literature: Late Eighteenth-Early Nineteenth Century', *ibid.*, 20–42.

Hindu scholars, particularly Brahmans. All other interests were cultivated by Muslims, Hindus and Sikhs alike.[16]

V

The Austrian traveller Baron Charles Hugel remarked that the state established by Ranjit Singh was 'the most wonderful object in the whole world'. Like a skilful architect the Maharaja raised a 'majestic fabric' with the help of rather insignificant or unpromising fragments.[17] In retrospect it is possible to see that Ranjit Singh did evolve a structure of power by which he could reconcile all important sections of his subjects to his rule, and he could induce many of them to be enthusiastic in his support. He revived prosperity and minimized oppression. He created opportunities for members of several sections of the society to improve their social position. It is in this context that we can appreciate the position of the Sikh community during the early nineteenth century.

We can form a general idea of the number of Sikhs and their distribution in the dominions of Ranjit Singh. In the areas covered by the former Mughal provinces of Lahore, Multan and Kabul there were about 12 million persons. In this population there were about a million and a half Sikhs who accounted for about 12 per cent of the total population. Furthermore, the Sikh population in the dominions of Ranjit Singh was concentrated in the upper Bari, Jalandhar and the upper Rachna Doabs. In fact, though this region was much smaller in area than the rest of the dominions of Ranjit Singh in the plains, it contained more than 50 per cent of the total population, and nearly 90 per cent of the total Sikh population. Nearly half of the Sikh population of this core region was concentrated in the area covered by the later districts of Lahore and Amritsar. The impression formed by Alexander Burnes in the 1830s was not off the mark when he observed that the Sikhs formed about one-third of the total population in the area of their greatest concentration. Burnes carried the impression that the number of Sikhs had been increasing year by year.[18]

However, the importance of the Sikhs in the early nineteenth

---

[16] J. S. Grewal, *The Reign of Maharaja Ranjit Singh: Structure of Power, Economy and Society*, Punjabi University, Patiala, 1981, 34.

[17] Baron Charles Hugel, *Travels in Kashmir and the Punjab*, 293–94.

[18] Alexander Burnes, *Travels into Bokhara*, Oxford University Press, 1973, Vol. 1, 11–13, 44–45, 80; Vol. 3, 102, 119 and 146.

century was not due to their number. Rather, their number was increasing partly due to their importance. Over 50 per cent of the ruling class was formed by the Sikhs. It is true that Ranjit Singh inducted a considerable number of persons on merit, irrespective of their creed or country. Apart from the well-known European officers in the army, there were several important civil functionaries like Diwan Bhawani Das, Diwan Ganga Ram, Diwan Ajudhya Prashad and Diwan Dina Nath, who did not belong to the Punjab. Among them were also persons like Jamadar Khushal Singh and his nephew Tej Singh who accepted the baptism of the double-edged sword to join the Sikh fold. However, the number of Punjabis among the members of the ruling class remained much larger. There were men like Diwan Muhkam Chand, Misr Diwan Chand, Diwan Moti Ram, Diwan Kirpa Ram, Diwan Sawan Mal, Faqir Azizuddin, Faqir Nuruddin, Faqir Imamuddin, Diwan Sukh Dayal and Sarab Dayal who belonged to the Punjab. The Dogra brothers, Gulab Singh, Dhian Singh and Suchet Singh, and Dhian Singh's son Hira Singh, who all served the Maharaja as *jāgīrdārs* and vassal chiefs, were matched in importance by the Sikh vassal chief Fateh Singh Ahluwalia who served the Maharaja with great distinction.

Furthermore, since Ranjit Singh gave service *jāgīrs* to many dispossessed chiefs, and the number of Sikh chiefs among them was the largest, they became a part of the ruling class. This was equally true of the *jāgīrdārs* of the former chiefs. In fact men like Hukma Singh Chimni, and the Majithia and Atariwala Sardars, who were among the most important members of the ruling class, belonged to this category. Even the new men, like Hari Singh Nalwa and the Sandhanwalia Sardars, rose to eminent positions. A commoner like Colonel Mihan Singh, or Dhanna Singh Malwai, could rise to nearly the highest rung. There is hardly any doubt that the Hindus, Muslims and the Sikhs of the core region constituted the large majority of the ruling class, and within this majority the Sikhs formed the largest component. There were some *khatrīs*, *kalāls*, *nāīs* and *jhīwars* among the Sikh nobles. By far the largest bulk, however, consisted of Jats who constituted also the dominant agricultural caste in the core region. Among the hereditary *jāgīrdārs* also the Jat Sikhs formed the largest bulk.[19]

---

[19] Indu Banga, 'The Ruling Class in the Kingdom of Lahore', *Journal of Regional History*, 3 (1982), 15–24; J. S. Grewal, *The Reign of Maharaja Ranjit Singh: Structure of Power, Economy and Society*, 32–33.

In the army of Ranjit Singh the Sikhs were represented in large numbers. The Khālsā horsemen had initially established Sikh rule in much of the Punjab. The new rulers depended almost exclusively on cavalry, and their forces consisted very largely of Sikh horsemen. Many of these forces were taken over by Ranjit Singh when he subverted the Sikh principalities. The regular cavalry too was raised mostly by recruiting Sikhs as horsemen. Ranjit Singh encouraged the Punjabis in general and the Singhs in particular to join the infantry and the artillery raised on European lines. In the 1830s, several commanders of the infantry and artillery units were Sikh; the number of Sikhs increased as the ranks became lower till the foot soldier or the gunner was reached. We have no exact figures, but it may be safe to suggest that more than half of the men in the army of Ranjit Singh were Sikh, which would mean about 50,000. Among these too the representation of the Jats of the core region was the largest.[20]

The share of the Sikhs in revenue-free grants given by Ranjit Singh was the largest. The Sodhis and Bedis, who did not belong strictly to religious classes and who in fact maintained a considerable number of horsemen, got a very large share. Towards the end of Ranjit Singh's reign the Sodhis were enjoying *jāgīrs* worth 500,000 rupees a year, and the Bedis were receiving 400,000 rupees. A descendant of Dhir Mal at Kartarpur, Sodhi Sadhu Singh, was lavishly patronized by Ranjit Singh; several villages were given for the Granth Sahib compiled by Guru Arjan which was in his possession. Eminent among the Bedis was Baba Bikram Singh of Una, son of Baba Sahib Singh. Their importance in the early nineteenth century was no less than that of any courtier of the Maharaja. Bhai Ram Singh and Bhai Gobind Ram, sons of Bhai Wasti Ram, figured prominently at the court of Ranjit Singh and his successors. They were more important than the court *granthī*, Bhai Gurmukh Singh. The revenue-free grants received by Sikh individuals and institutions, apart from the Sodhis and the Bedis, amounted to hundreds of thousands of rupees. Nearly 60 per cent of the total revenue alienated by the state in favour of religious personages and institutions was enjoyed by the Sikh grantees. The Nirmalas, the Nihangs and the Akalis were among them, and they all represented the Singh component of the Sikh community.

[20] A set of over 450 orders of Ranjit Singh to Tej Singh as the officer in charge of the *kampū-i-muʿallā* provides valuable insights into the working of the military system of Ranjit Singh: *The Civil and Military Affairs of Maharaja Ranjit Singh* (eds J. S. Grewal and Indu Banga), Guru Nanak Dev University, Amritsar, 1987.

The Singh component of the community spread into the countryside more in the early nineteenth century than ever before. During the grim struggle between the Khālsā and the Mughal administrators it was difficult to find a village entirely of the Singhs. The number of such villages in the early nineteenth century ran into hundreds. The largest addition to the number of Singhs from the countryside came from amongst the Jats of the core region. The bulk of the Sikh peasantry belonged to the areas which had produced the largest number of Sikh rulers and Sikh *jāgīrdārs*. Agricultural clans other than those of the Jats were represented in the Sikh peasantry by Mahtons, Kambos and Sainis. The gulf between the economic means of the Sikh peasant and the Sikh noble was conspicuously wide, giving support to the observation of a contemporary that the difference between the rich and the poor classes in the Punjab was greater than elsewhere in India.[21] Service in the army of the state mitigated the poverty of a large number of the Sikh peasant families. There was a considerable number of Sikh artisans and service-performing individuals in the villages. The Mazhabi Sikhs were represented in the army.[22]

The number of the non-Singh or Sehajdhārī Sikhs in the dominions of Ranjit Singh appears to have been pretty large. All the Sikhs had not become Khālsā during the eighteenth century. Those who did not take up arms against the Mughal authorities, or did not openly support the Khālsā, had not been persecuted. They went on living in villages and towns following their ordinary pursuits. In the late eighteenth century the Udāsī protagonists of the teachings of Sikhism had been patronized by the Sikh rulers, and their centres began to proliferate more in the early nineteenth century. Before the advent of Sikh rule their centres numbered about a dozen; in the late eighteenth century, this number reached about fifty; and by the end of Ranjit Singh's reign there were nearly 250 Udāsī centres in his dominions. Most of them were patronized by the state, and the majority of the patronized centres were in the core region. Though dispersed over the country-side in large numbers, the Udāsī centres in cities and towns were much larger in size. Presumably, they catered more for the town-dwellers than for the people living in the countryside. They were

---

[21] H. L. O. Garrett (trans.), *The Punjab a Hundred Years Ago*, Patiala, 1971 (reprint), 66–67.
[22] The outcaste *chūhra* Sikhs were generally known as Mazhabi.

useful allies of the state which needed a broad base for the willing acceptance of its authority. Not for nothing did they receive revenues worth 200,000 rupees a year which was nearly 10 per cent of the state revenues alienated by way of *dharmarth*.[23]

The Udāsī version of Sikhism was in some essential ways different from what the Singhs believed in. The Udāsīs traced their origin to Guru Nanak but gave more prominence to Sri Chand as the real founder of the path of renunciation (*udās*). They did not reject the line of succession from Guru Nanak to Guru Gobind Singh, but they attached greater importance to the chain of succession from Guru Nanak, through Sri Chand and the Ādi Udāsīs, to the reigning Mahant of an Udāsī establishment.[24] They showed no great respect for the Granth Sahib, and interpreted its essential message in Vedantic terms, shifting the emphasis from a personal God to an impersonal reality. They did not subscribe to the twin doctrine of Guru-Panth and Guru-Granth. The mark of their ideas is left on the literature they produced in the early nineteenth century. They wrote expositions of several important compositions in the Granth Sahib; they wrote original *mātras* of their own; they produced new versions of *janamsākhīs* and *gurbilāses*; and they wrote about their own past.[25] In the process they produced an interpretation of Sikhism that made them rather 'unorthodox' from the viewpoint of the Singhs.

New representatives of Sehajdhārī Sikhism were arising towards the close of Sikh rule in the Punjab. They were working outside the core region, addressing themselves to the small number of Hindu traders and shopkeepers in the towns of the Sindh Sagar Doab. They regarded Guru Nanak as the founder of a new faith and paid equal reverence to his nominated successors. They regarded Granth Sahib as the Guru but not as the exclusive Guru, because the founders of the movements were also regarded as *gurūs*. They advocated adoption of specifically Sikh ceremonies for birth, marriage and death. However, they did not insist on the baptism of the double-edged

---

[23] Sulakhan Singh, 'Udasi Establishments Under Sikh Rule', *Journal of Regional History*, 1 (1980), 70–87; 'State Patronage to Udasis under Maharaja Ranjit Singh', *Maharaja Ranjit Singh and His Times* (eds J. S. Grewal and Indu Banga), Guru Nanak Dev University, Amritsar, 1980, 103–16.

[24] Founder of four branches of Udāsīs, the Ādi Udāsīs were Almast, Balu, Hasna and Goinda who are believed to have lived and worked in the seventeenth century.

[25] Sulakhan Singh, 'The Udasis in the Early Nineteenth Century', *Journal of Regional History*, 2 (1981), 35–42.

sword. Both the Singhs and the Sikhs with shorn hair could become their followers.[26]

The Sikh Panth in the early nineteenth century was thus marked by ideological differences. Not exactly a vertical division, the first line of difference was between the Singhs and the Sehajdhārīs. The Singhs believed in the indistinguishability and the unity of Guruship from Guru Nanak to Guru Gobind Singh, and in the end of personal Guruship after Guru Gobind Singh. The doctrine of Guru-Granth was coming to the fore in place of the doctrine of Guru-Panth. This is understandable because the doctrine of Guru-Granth was better suited to the situation of the early nineteenth century when social inequalities had to be reconciled to the ideal norm of equality. Every Sikh was equal in the presence of the Granth Sahib, in the *sangat* and the *langar*, but in the life outside social differences were legitimized.

The Sikh community in the early nineteenth century was not a caste-ridden society, but there was enough social differentiation in the community to infringe the idea of equality on which the Sikh Panth was based in theory and which was still espoused by a handful of the Khālsā, like the Akalis and the Nihangs. Between the ruling class and the ordinary peasant there was a wide social gulf. Among the peasants, artisans and the service-performing groups in the Sikh community, there were subsistence *jāgīrdārs*, petty functionaries, *chaudharīs* and *muqaddams*, and the well-paid soldiers of the state. In addition to these, there were Sikh traders and shopkeepers in cities and towns, some of whom were Sehajdhārīs but a considerable number of them were Singhs. However, all ideological differences and social stratification in the Sikh community appear to have been overshadowed by an awareness of political power. The Sikhs had a vague feeling that the rulers of the land were their own people.

Identification with the sovereign Sikh rule found clear expression in Ratan Singh Bhangu's *Gurū-Panth Prakāsh* completed at Amritsar in 1841.[27] He refers to the expulsion of the Marathas from Delhi and from the *sarkār* of Hissar in the early years of the nineteenth century, the declaration of British 'protection' over the chiefs of the Satlej-Jamuna Divide, and the establishment of a British Agency at Ludhiana. A recurrent question which, according to Bhangu, the British were

---

[26] They came to be known as *nirankārīs* and *nāmdhārīs* in the late nineteenth century.
[27] Ratan Singh Bhangu's work has been published as *Prāchīn Panth Parkāsh*, Wazir-i-Hind Press, Amritsar, 1962 (4th edn).

asking was about the 'right' of the Singhs to rule. Men like Ochter-
loney and Murray were given to understand that the Singhs were the
subject people of the Mughals and, during the invasions of Ahmad
Shah Abdali, they had illegitimately occupied Mughal territories. The
implication of this view was that these territories could be taken back
by the Mughal emperor, or by someone else on his behalf.

In presenting his own view on this issue, Ratan Singh Bhangu
presents in fact the Singh view of Sikh history. He looks upon Guru
Nanak's mission as transcending all previous dispensations; he sees no
difference between the first Guru and his successors; the personal
Guruship ends for him with Guru Gobind Singh; Guruship henceforth is vested in the Khālsā and the Granth; but Ratan Singh Bhangu
attaches greater importance to the doctrine of Guru-Panth. In his
presentation Mughal oppression is the cause of conflict between the
emperors and the Gurus who had no temporal ambition, being the
'true emperors' of the spiritual realm. Guru Gobind Singh instituted
the Khālsā to put an end to Mughal oppression. From the very
beginning the Khālsā was sovereign. Men from all the four *varṇas* were
merged into one *varṇa*, that of the Khālsā. That was why '*khatrīs,
tarkhāns, kalāls, nāis* and *jhīwars*' laid down their lives for the
establishment of the sovereign rule of the Khālsā.

Far from taking undue advantage of the anarchy caused by Ahmad
Shah Abdali, the Khālsā in reality wrested from Ahmad Shah Abdali
those provinces which the Mughals had lost to him. Obviously, the
Khālsā ruled over the Punjab in their own right, justified by the
sacrifices they had made and upheld by the sword they had come to
wield against oppression. This was how the sovereignty of the Khālsā
Panth was made manifest to the world. Ratan Singh Bhangu's assertion
of Sikh sovereignty sprang partly from his apprehensions about its
continuance.

VI

Maharaja Ranjit Singh died at Lahore on June 27, 1839, after nominat-
ing his eldest son Kharak Singh as his successor, with Raja Dhian Singh
as the *wazīr*, a position he had held under the Maharaja. The formal
investiture of Kharak Singh as Maharaja was arranged in the capital on
the first of September, deliberately before the arrival of his son, Prince
Nau Nihal Singh, who was in the Peshawar region at the time of Ranjit

Singh's death. The increasing influence of a close relative, Chet Singh Bajwa, on the new Maharaja, and Chet Singh's aspiration to oust Dhian Singh, induced the latter to conspire with Prince Nau Nihal Singh. Chet Singh was murdered in early October.[28]

Prince Nau Nihal Singh became *de facto* ruler, and ruled generally in consultation with Raja Dhian Singh. For a little over a year, their administration was successful. Unrest in the Hazara region was put down by Sardar Chattar Singh Atariwala; the governors of Kashmir and Multan, Colonel Mihan Singh and Diwan Sawan Mal, were called to Lahore to pay up the arrears; expeditions sent to Iskardu, Mandi and Kulu were successful; and the attempts of the British officers like MacNaughten to favour the fugitive Shah Shuja at the cost of Maharaja Kharak Singh in the Peshawar region were foiled. Maharaja Kharak Singh died of ill health on 5 November 1840. Returning from his funeral Nau Nihal Singh, accompanied by Raja Gulab Singh's son Mian Udham Singh, died due to the accidental fall of a gate. With him died the great expectations associated with that 'Alexander-like Prince'.[29]

There were six princes left after the death of Maharaja Kharak Singh and his son. Sher Singh and his twin brother Tara Singh were in their mid-thirties; Pashaura Singh, Kashmira Singh and Multana Singh were in their early twenties; and Dalip Singh was less than three years old. The accession of Sher Singh as the new Maharaja was proclaimed on November 9. But the mother of Nau Nihal Singh, Maharani Chand Kaur, asserted her claim to be the Regent till the birth of the child by his widow. Raja Dhian Singh became her adviser but only in addition to Sardar Attar Singh Sandhanwalia, Jamadar Khushal Singh and Sardar Lehna Singh Majithia. Dhian Singh discovered very soon that he could not have his way. His opponents were supported by the Maharani who listened to the Sandhanwalia Sardars more than to him. To obviate his eclipse at the court, Dhian Singh incited the already eager Sher Singh to make a fresh bid for power, telling some of the army commanders to support him.

Prince Sher Singh occupied the fort of Lahore on 20 January 1841, but only after meeting resistance from the troops of Raja Gulab Singh

---

[28] The contemporary poet Shah Muhammad in his *Vār* looks upon this incident as the beginning of the violence: *Vār Shah Muhammad* (eds Sita Ram Kohli and Sewa Singh Giani), Punjabi Sahit Academy, Ludhiana, 1972, 136.

[29] In one of his orders to Tej Singh, the Maharaja refers to the prince as *sikandar-misāl*: *The Civil and Military Affairs of Maharaja Ranjit Singh*, Document 454.

who was in the fort in support of Maharani Chand Kaur. The use of the army to decide the issue of succession, with Raja Dhian Singh and Raja Gulab Singh ranged on opposite sides, had a disastrous effect on discipline in the army. Commanders were humiliated and coerced at many places in the empire, some of them were in fact murdered, like Mihan Singh in Kashmir, Foulkes in Mandi, Ford in Hazara and Sobha Singh in Amritsar. The civilians of Lahore were molested by the soldiers of the *kampū-i-muʻallā*. Maharaja Sher Singh and Raja Dhian Singh felt obliged to give a raise in pay, in addition to gratuity and promotions, after parleying with the representatives of the soldiers. This was the beginning of the army *panchāyats* which became a crucial factor in the deteriorating situation.[30]

During the reign of Maharaja Sher Singh, the British diplomats and even the Governor-General developed an increasing interest in the affairs of the Punjab. Maharani Chand Kaur and Maharaja Sher Singh had both approached the British with the offer of a large slice of the empire as the price of their support against each other. The discomfiture of the Maharani was at the same time a defeat of the Sandhanwalias in their drive against Dhian Singh. Sardar Attar Singh Sandhanwalia and his nephew Ajit Singh sought protection with the British. Sardar Lehna Singh Sandhanwalia and his nephew Kehar Singh were placed under detention. All their *jāgīrs* were resumed. Out of a feeling of insecurity, Maharaja Sher Singh used Dhian Singh's manipulative skills to ensure first the abortion of Nau Nihal Singh's child and then the death of Maharani Chand Kaur who had not stopped her intrigue with either the nobles or the soldiers or the British. The Maharani and the Sandhanwalia Sardars were not alone in cultivating the British in self-interest. The European Generals Avitabile and Ventura, who were keen to take back their earnings to Europe, and Gulab Singh who was eager to retain his territories, entered into small conspiracies with the British officers and diplomats. Their inclinations were conveyed to higher authorities. It was on the suggestion of a British political Agent that Maharaja Sher Singh pardoned Sardar Attar Singh and Ajit Singh Sandhanwalia and allowed them to return to Lahore. Lehna Singh and Kehar Singh were released. They were all reinstated in their *jāgīrs*. Regaining the Maharaja's confidence and trust, Lehna Singh and Ajit

---

[30] An interesting dimension of this situation was the assumption of the Sikh soldiery and the junior officers that they were the truer representatives of the Panth than the courtiers and nobles. In Shah Muhammad's *Vār*, they refer to themselves as the 'Khalsa Panth': *Vār Shah Muhammad*, 167.

Singh murdered him and his son, Prince Pratap Singh, on 15 September 1843. They also murdered Raja Dhian Singh who had served himself well but who had also served the state faithfully for nearly a quarter of a century.

The intention of the Sandhanwalia Sardars was to install the boy-prince Dalip Singh, with his mother Maharani Jindan as the Regent to perpetuate their indirect control over the affairs of the state. But Dhian Singh's son Raja Hira Singh was able to win the support of the army against them. About a thousand men, including Lehna Singh and Ajit Singh, were killed in action when Hira Singh occupied the fort. The palace revolution of 1843 was thus bloodier than that of 1841. To have Dalip Singh on the throne, with himself as the *wazīr*, was in Hira Singh's interest too. In fact he tried to eliminate Prince Pashaura Singh and Prince Kashmira Singh with the help of Raja Gulab Singh. The grimness of the whole situation comes out clearly from the fact that when Raja Suchet Singh made a bid for the office of the *wazīr* against his nephew Hira Singh, the nephew had no hesitation in eliminating the uncle. Raja Suchet Singh died fighting against overwhelming numbers on 27 March 1844. Hira Singh made a move against Gulab Singh too, who was eventually obliged to send his son Sohan Singh to Lahore virtually as a hostage.

Sardar Attar Singh Sandhanwalia who had escaped into the British territories returned to the religious centre of the much-venerated Bhai Bir Singh at Naurangabad near Tarn Taran. Hira Singh struck at the centre, treating it as a source of disaffection. Both Bhai Bir Singh and Attar Singh were killed. This action made Hira Singh a little unpopular. A greater cause of his unpopularity with the army was the attitude of Misr Jalla, his factotum at the court who gave offence to all and sundry. The army *panches* demanded his surrender. But Hira Singh tried to escape with him to the hills. They were pursued and killed on 21 December 1844. With them died Sohan Singh, the second son of Raja Gulab Singh, and Mian Labh Singh, a distant cousin of the Raja. Of the Jammu Rajas thus only Gulab Singh survived, with only one son left to succeed him.

In military matters the army *panches* were now supreme. For civil affairs, Maharani Jindan acted as the President of a Council consisting of her brother Jawahar Singh, Bhai Ram Singh, Bakshi Bhagat Ram, Diwan Dina Nath and Faqir Nuruddin. With the *nāzims* and *kārdārs* reluctant to submit revenues, and the increasing expenditure on a larger army, it became difficult to run the administration. The total strength of the army in 1844 was about 120,000 whereas at the end of Ranjit Singh's reign it had been about 85,000. The total expenditure on the army in 1844 amounted to about six million rupees whereas in 1839 it had been about four million.[31] The revenue alienated in favour of *jāgīrdārs* was in addition to this amount. Among those who had not paid large arrears to the Treasury were the governors of Multan and Kashmir, and Raja Gulab Singh.

Troops were sent to Jammu to collect arrears from the Raja. He accompanied them to Lahore, paid 2,700,000 rupees, but got his contracts (*ijāra*) renewed for two years. Asked to become the *wazīr*, he declined the offer politely and hurriedly marched back to Jammu. Prince Pashaura Singh rose in revolt; he was killed on 31 August 1845, on Jawahar Singh's instructions. The army demanded Jawahar Singh's head. He was killed on September 21.

Maharani Jindan and the Sardars who supported her decided to approach the British with the suggestion that they may destroy the army and take the Maharaja under their 'protective wings'. Gulab Singh had already offered cooperation on the understanding that Jammu and some other territories should be left with him. The British had been collecting men and war materials on the Punjab frontiers. The stage was set for a war. Lal Singh was appointed as the *wazīr* and Tej Singh as the commander of the army.[32] Reports of British preparations were assiduously spread among the soldiery and solemnly confirmed by Diwan Dina Nath. After a pledge on the *samādh* of Ranjit Singh to save his state, the authority of the *panches* was suspended. The stage was set for a defeat.

One important element in the understanding between the British agents and the junta at Lahore was that the army of Lahore should cross the river Satlej to make it appear that the state of Lahore was the aggressor. The army of Lahore crossed the river on 11 December 1845. Lord Hardinge declared war on the state of Lahore on December 13. The first battle was fought near Mudki on December 18. The British forces suffered heavy losses.[33] But in the second battle fought near

---

[31] Sita Ram Kohli, *Sunset of the Sikh Empire*, Orient Longmans, Bombay, 1967, 85–97.

[32] This position was different from the position of Tej Singh under Maharaja Ranjit Singh when he was looking after the *kampū-i-mu'allā* on behalf of the Maharaja as discussed in *The Civil and Military Affairs of Maharaja Ranjit Singh*.

[33] 'British losses in men and officers, considering the brevity of the action, were heavy; 215 killed, including Sir Robert Sale, Sir Joseph McGaskill and two aides of the Governor-General; and 657 wounded': Sita Ram Kohli, *Sunset of the Sikh Empire*, 107.

Pherushahr on December 21 they could claim a victory. Both Lal Singh and Tej Singh played their premeditated treacherous roles, informing the British officers of the disposition of their armies, not attacking the British critical situations and leaving the field of battle after the commencement of action. The replacement of Lal Singh by Gulab Singh before the battle of Sabraon, fought on 10 February 1846, was a change for the worse. Tej Singh not only left the field of battle but also destroyed the bridge of boats which could be used for retreat. Thousands lost their lives in this battle, including the grey-beard Sardar Sham Singh Atariwala. Ranjodh Singh Majithia had been defeated in the battle of Aliwal near Ludhiana after his initial success in the battle of Baddowal in January, 1845. Gulab Singh was eager to negotiate the terms of peace.

According to a treaty signed on March 9, the Jalandhar Doab was taken over by the British, Jammu and Kashmir were given to Gulab Singh under a separate treaty, and the strength of the Lahore army was reduced. By a supplement added on March 11, a British force was kept in Lahore at the expense of the state; a British political officer was stationed there for 'advice and guidance'. Dalip Singh remained on the throne, with Lal Singh as the *wazir* and Tej Singh as the commander of the army, while Maharani Jindan became the Regent. This was the reward for their helpful role in the late war. Henry Lawrence was sent to Lahore with a British force which was to remain there only until the end of 1846. The state of Lahore was not merely smaller and weaker now, it was also a 'protected' state for all practical purposes. In a letter to Henry Lawrence it was made clear by Hardinge that 'the native prince is in fetters and under our protection, and must do our bidding'.[34]

VII

If there was any doubt about the status of Maharaja Dalip Singh, it was formally clarified by the Treaty of Bhyrowal signed on 22 December 1846, before the expiry of the time for the British force to leave Lahore. Lal Singh had already been pensioned off to Dehra Dun because of his complicity in the refusal of the Governor of Kashmir to hand over the province to Raja Gulab Singh. No one was appointed as *wazir* in his place. Instead, a Regency Council had been formed, consisting of Tej

[34] *Ibid.*, 119.

Singh, Diwan Dina Nath, Faqir Nuruddin and Sher Singh Atariwala, whose sister had been betrothed to Prince Dalip Singh in the reign of Maharaja Sher Singh, and who was now given the title of Raja. By the new Treaty, four other members were added to the council: Attar Singh Kalianwala, Shamsher Singh Sandhanwalia, Ranjodh Singh Majithia and Bhai Nidhan Singh. More important than the enlargement of the Council was the removal of Maharani Jindan from her position as the Regent; she was given 150,000 rupees a year as pension. The most important clause of the treaty, however, was the one that empowered the Resident at Lahore 'to direct and control the duties of every department'. These arrangements were to continue till Maharaja Dalip Singh reached the age of 16 on 4 September 1854.

In the first week of October, 1848, Governor General Dalhousie's secretary wrote to Frederic Currie, the Resident at Lahore, that he should consider 'the State of Lahore to be, for all intents and purposes, at war with the British Government'.[35] Dalhousie's own letter reveals his satisfaction with the crisis developing in the Punjab: 'I have for months been looking for, and we are now not on the eve of but in the midst of war with the Sikh nation and the kingdom of the Punjab.'[36] Ironically, the 'Sikh nation' and the 'kingdom of the Punjab' were represented by two rebel governors and not by the Maharaja or the Regency Council.

Initially, in fact, there was only one rebel, Diwan Mul Raj, the governor of Multan. The actions of the representatives of the British Government in the Punjab were partly the cause of his revolt. In 1846, Mul Raj had accepted all the conditions imposed on him as the governor of Multan, knowing that Lal Singh was keen to dislodge him. Subsequently, certain duties were abolished in the province without reducing the amount of ijāra to be paid by the governor. A simultaneous reduction in his judicial powers undermined his authority to make even the usual collection.[37] He offered to resign in December, 1847. John Lawrence, as the officiating Resident, agreed to accept his resignation but with effect from March, 1848. By then, Frederic

---

[35] S. S. Bal, *British Policy Towards the Punjab 1844–49*, New Age Publishers, Calcutta, 1971, 204.

[36] N. M. Khilnani, *British Power in the Punjab 1839–1858*, Asia Publishing House, New Delhi, 1972, 154.

[37] For changes made in the judicial, civil and revenue matters by the Resident at Lahore before the second Anglo-Sikh War which created resentment among various sections of the Punjabis, *ibid.*, 96–125; S. S. Bal, *British Policy Towards the Punjab*, 148–85.

Currie had become the Resident and he sent Kahn Singh Man to the governorship of Multan, appointing Vans Agnew as his political adviser with Lt Anderson to assist him. Mul Raj handed over the keys of the fort of Multan to Kahn Singh Man. Soon afterwards, however, Agnew was attacked by some men without incitement from Mul Raj. His troops, the largest losers due to the impending change, now forced him to lead their revolt. A rebel commandant, Godar Singh Mazhabi, on his own attacked both Agnew and Anderson, and killed them. Currie did not order the British force at Lahore to march against Mul Raj. In fact he told Herbert Edwardes, posted in Bannu to 'advise' its governor, only to contain Mul Raj and not dislodge him from Multan.

James Abbott, posted at Haripur in Hazara to 'advise' its governor, Sardar Chattar Singh Atariwala, suspecting him of sympathies with the rebels, moved away from Haripur and recruited unauthorized levies. When Colonel Canora refused to obey Sardar Chattar Singh's orders, he was killed and Abbott presented the incident as the cold-blooded murder of a loyal officer. Currie knew that Chattar Singh was not at fault, but Dalhousie wanted the Sardar 'smitten'. He was dismissed from governorship and his *jāgīrs* were resumed. Chattar Singh decided to defy the Resident's orders. He tried to enlist the support of army units posted in the Sindh Sagar Doab and the Peshawar region, approaching Dost Muhammad Khan of Kabul and Raja Gulab Singh for help in the cause of the Punjabis to overthrow the British usurpers. He wrote to his son, Raja Sher Singh, to join him.

Raja Sher Singh had joined Edwardes in his campaign against Mul Raj. When General Whish appeared on the scene, he issued a proclamation demanding unconditional surrender from the rebels of Multan on hearing the salute to be fired on the morning of September 5 'in honour of her Most Gracious Majesty, the Queen of Great Britain, and her ally, the Maharaja Dalip Singh'. The British intention of annexation had been noised abroad; this proclamation came as a confirmation. General Whish suspected the loyalty of the Sikh units and ordered them to leave on September 11. They decided to join Mul Raj. Raja Sher Singh went over to the rebels on September 14. In joint proclamations with Mul Raj, he exhorted the Hindus and Muslims of the Punjab to join them against the English, and asked the chiefs of the Satlej-Jamuna Divide for support. No chief joined the rebels. A forged letter arranged by Edwardes to fall into the hands of Mul Raj made him suspicious of Raja Sher Singh who felt obliged to leave Multan on

October 9, eventually to join his father in Hazara. Mul Raj was left alone to defend himself against the British forces. He was compelled to lay down arms on 22 January 1849.

The Commander-in-Chief Lord Gough had crossed the Satlej in November, 1848, at the head of a large army to suppress the revolt of the Atariwala Sardars. In a battle fought on November 22 near Ramnagar, close to the river Chenab, Brigadier General Campbell's force was routed. A Lt Colonel and a Brigadier General of the British army were killed in this action. In the battle of Chillianwala, fought on 13 January 1849, three British regiments lost their colours, and Brigadier Pennyuick was killed in action along with 3,000 British officers and men. This was the worst defeat suffered by the British in the Indian subcontinent. In the battle of Gujrat, however, Raja Sher Singh suffered defeat on February 21, and his retreat towards Kabul was barred by Abbott with the help of Raja Gulab Singh who by now was bound by a treaty to help the British. On March 14, Sardar Chattar Singh and Raja Sher Singh surrendered to General Gilbert near Rawalpindi. Laying down his sword a few days later a greybeard veteran could not help feeling, 'today Ranjit Singh is dead'.[38]

Lord Dalhousie kept up the charade till the end. He sent H. M. Elliot to Lahore with the document of annexation. Elliot coerced Raja Tej Singh and Diwan Dina Nath first to sign this document, and then approached Bhai Nidhan Singh and Faqir Nuruddin. The representatives (*vakīls*) of Shamsher Singh Sandhanwalia and Attar Singh Kalianwala, both of whom had stuck to Edwardes when Raja Sher Singh had gone over to the rebels, signed in the absence of the Sardars. On 29 March 1849, Maharaja Dalip Singh held his court for the last time in his life to sign the document of annexation in Roman letters and to become a pensioner of the British. The 'majestic fabric' raised by Maharaja Ranjit Singh was a thing of the past.

[38] Khushwant Singh, *A History of the Sikhs*, Oxford University Press, Delhi, 1986, Vol. 2, 82.

CHAPTER 7

RECESSION AND RESURGENCE
(1849–1919)

I

The Punjab as a province of the British empire was larger than the kingdom of Ranjit Singh and it was also placed in a context almost of global economy and polity. The colonial rulers introduced a large measure of bureaucracy and the rule of law, which established a new kind of relationship between the individual and the state. The 'paternal' rule of the early decades was eventually replaced by the 'machine rule' of laws, codes and procedures. The executive, financial and judicial functions were separated. An elaborate administration was geared to the purposes of peace and prosperity. For political and economic purposes as well as for administration, new forms of communication and transportation were developed, symbolized by the post office, the telegraph office, the metalled road, the railway and the press.

To increase agricultural production and revenue from land the British administrators of the Punjab introduced reform in the agrarian system with periodic settlements and records of rights as its major planks. Land revenue began to increase steadily. New sources of revenue were tapped. Irrigation projects completed between 1860 and 1920 brought nearly 10,000,000 acres of land under cultivation, creating a 'prosperous, progressive and modern' region in the province and changing not only its agrarian economy but also its demographic distribution and even its physical appearance. The increase in production was reflected in the increasing volume and value of trade.

Colonial rule in the Punjab as elsewhere in the subcontinent was marked by economic exploitation. Geared largely to export needs, the bulk of external trade was controlled by British exchange banks, export–import firms and shipping concerns. Payment of home charges out of Indian revenues drained wealth and converted rupees into sterling at the officially determined rate to the advantage of the British. The imperial government exercised control over the finances of the Punjab and shared income and expenditure in a manner that tilted the

Map 5 British India (twentieth century)

financial balance in its favour, making it a major co-sharer in the increasing wealth of the Punjab.

From the very beginning, the British administrators of the Punjab gave importance to education in English literature, western sciences and social studies. For about two decades Dr G. W. Leitner tried to revive the learning of Arabic, Persian and Sanskrit, to introduce western sciences in vernacular languages and to raise the standard of contemporary Indian literatures. Even his conception of a university was different from what had been established at Bombay, Calcutta and Madras. Nevertheless, when the Punjab University was established at Lahore in 1882 its character was no different from that of the other universities. The cause of indigenous education in the Punjab was finally lost. Urdu was introduced as the medium of education in government schools up to the matriculation level, though Punjabi was the dominant language of the province.

Christian missionaries proved to be the greatest allies of the government in spreading English education. The system of grant-in-aid at the time of its introduction was meant primarily for their schools. They made the press an effective medium of communication in Punjabi, Urdu and Hindi for evangelization. In the process they denounced indigenous religious beliefs and practices, social evils and morals of the Punjabis rather openly and aggressively, partly because of their own theological assumptions and partly because they regarded the colonial rule as providential.[1] In the popular mind they were closely allied with the rulers, and their socio-cultural programme carried a sharper edge because of this real or supposed alliance. The Punjabis reacted to the presence of the Christian missionaries also because of their spectacular success. Starting from about 4,000 in 1881, the number of Indian Christians in the Punjab rose to over 300,000 in 1921.

The colonial regime produced a certain degree of social transformation in the Punjab. The collapse of peasant prosperity by the 1880s was attributed by one contemporary administrator 'particularly to the innovations of fixed assessments, freedom of contract, individual property in land, and the series of technical laws which benefited the rich and astute at the expense of the poor and the ignorant'.[2] The impoverishment of the small landholder was reflected in the increasing number of the tenants-at-will. An unprecedented degree of commercialization of agriculture facilitated the emergence of petty commodity producers in the central districts of the province first and then in the canal colonies. Socio-economic differentiation among landholders was accentuated by the Punjab Land Alienation Act of 1900 which brought the agricultural moneylender into greater prominence during the early decades of the twentieth century.

Traders and moneylenders, the unconscious accomplices in the commercialization of agriculture, were the subordinate beneficiaries of colonial exploitation. The traditional business communities like the Khatrīs, Aroras and Banias among the Hindus and the Shaikhs, Khojas

---

[1] For the missionary work of the Presbyterians in the Punjab and their attitudes and assumptions, John C. B. Webster, *The Christian Community and Change in Nineteenth Century North India*, Macmillan, Delhi, 1976.

[2] S. S. Thorburn, *The Punjab in Peace and War*, Punjab Languages Department, Patiala, 1970 (reprint), 252.

and Pathans among the Muslims provided commercial leadership. Looking for new opportunities they invested capital in small-scale industries. The Punjab National Bank, a purely Indian concern, was founded in 1895, followed by a number of other enterprises like the Bharat Insurance Company and the People's Banking and Commercial Association. The old moneylender blossomed into usurer through high interest charges and forced sale of land at below market price, virtually in collusion with *munsifs* and lawyers thrown up by the new regime.

Indeed, to the agrarian and commercial middle classes was added a professional middle class, through English education, which opened the door to employment on the middle of bureaucratic rungs and in professions like law, teaching and medicine. At the end of the nineteenth century, the Punjabi Hindus outnumbered the Punjabi Muslims on the middle and upper rungs of administration open to Indians. The Khatrīs among the Hindus occupied the largest proportion of gazetted positions, followed by Brahmans, Aroras, Banias and Rajputs. Among the Muslims, foremost in employment were Shaikhs, followed by Pathans and Sayyids. The new professions too were generally dominated by Hindus, particularly by the Khatrīs. All educated Punjabis were trying to climb up, and those who were lagging behind wished to catch up with the others.

Numbers began to count, in argumentation as well as in census reports, strengthening democratic assumptions without even the semblance of a democratic system. Numerically both Hindus and Muslims lost to Christians and Sikhs, the Hindus much more than the Muslims. Since numbers were generally equated with strength, particularly for employment under the government, change in numbers was viewed with concern. As yet, however, there was little representation on legislative or executive bodies on the basis of people's will. The Indian Councils Act of 1861 was made operative in the Punjab only in the last decade of the century, and all the nine members of the provincial council were nominated by the Lieutenant Governor. The Act of 1909 raised the number of the legislative council to 30, but only a fifth of them were to the elected members.

The political and socio-cultural concerns of the Punjabis were reflected in their journalistic activity.[3] More than half of the publi-

---

[3] This is well brought out in Emmett David, *Press and Politics in British Western Punjab (1836–1947)*, Academic Publications, Delhi, 1983.

cations were brought out in Lahore. Next in importance was Amritsar but with a wide margin; it brought out only a fourth of the number published in Lahore. Books too began to be published in increasing numbers. In 1911, nearly 600 books were published in Urdu, over 450 in Punjabi, and about eighty each in English and Hindi, not only in the traditional forms of prose and poetry but also in the new forms of drama and fiction. This literature and journalism reflected the communal concerns of the Punjabis as well as their interest in religious and social reform, history and biography, sciences and arts.

The first to own a press for the propagation of their ideas in the Punjab, besides the Christian missionaries and the government, were the leaders of the Brahmo Samaj who started bringing out their monthly *Hari Hakikat* in 1877. The Brahmo Samaj in the Punjab was an offshoot of the movement started initially by Raja Ram Mohan Roy in Bengal. Based on Upanishadic thought and appreciative of western science and the Christian ethic, this rational yet theistic, tolerant yet socially radical movement stood for the freedom of the press and English education and espoused the cause of the low castes and the Hindu woman. Though willing to make use of Urdu and Punjabi for the propagation of their own ideas, the leaders of the Brahmo Samaj had a decided preference for Hindi in Devanagri script. As Lajpat Rai put it rather negatively, the 'atmosphere' of Brahmo literature was not free from 'Hindu nationalism'.[4]

Swami Dayanand Sarswati, the founder of the Arya Samaj, had published his *Satyarth Prakash* in Hindi before he came to the Punjab in 1877. He had discarded the Vedantic monism of the Upanishads in favour of a faith in an eternal, omniscient, all-pervading, just and merciful God who revealed all true knowledge in the Vedas, the source of all true virtue. The post-Aryan history of India was a long tale of degeneration, particularly after its invasion by foreign peoples and their alien faiths. The time had now come to regenerate Aryavarta with true knowledge and virtue and to turn the tide against the invaders of its culture. In the *Satyarth Prakash* there is a stronger argument against Christianity and Islam than against Puranic Hinduism or Sikhism. Swami Dayanand discarded idol-worship, traditional rites and rituals, and pilgrimage to sacred places. He was opposed to child marriage, discrimination against widows, distinctions of caste and restriction on

---

[4] Quoted, Kenneth W. Jones, *Arya Dharm*, University of California Press, Berkeley, 1976, 65.

travel to foreign countries. He retained only the ritual of *havan* and the ideal of cow protection.

After Dayanand's death in 1883 the Lahore Arya Samaj decided to establish a college *in memorium*. In the last decade of the nineteenth century a system of Arya education was set up from primary to college level, geared largely to the needs of the westernized Hindu middle class. English literature, western science and social studies were combined with Sanskrit and Hindi to evolve what was generally known as the Anglo-Vedic system of education. Social reform went ahead with simpler ceremonies for marriage, birth and death, remarriage of 'virgin widows', founding of orphanages, education of girls, Ved *parchār* for the propagation of new ideas and *shuddhī* for reconversion to Arya *dharma*. After a split in 1893–1894, the 'militant' Aryas in particular waged a war in print against Christians, Muslims, Sikhs and the traditionist Hindus. The Arya leaders hobnobbed with the Indian National Congress to promote the interests of Punjabi Hindus. When the government became hostile to the urban leaders in general and the Arya Samaj leaders in particular after the agitation of 1907, the Aryas declared the Samaj to be a non-political body and tried to remove the impression that they were 'seditious'. Hindu Sabhas sprang up in the province and the Punjab Hindu Conference was held successively for six years from 1909 to 1914. The 'Arya' consciousness was being transformed into 'Hindu' consciousness.

The British policy of impartiality towards all religious communities encouraged corporate action within each, and leaders talked as if they represented their entire community. The British policy of maintaining 'balance' between the various communities encouraged competition between them. Communal consciousness, therefore, was not confined to the Aryas or the Hindus. Muslim associations known as Anjuman-i-Islamia and Anjuman-i-Himayat-i-Islam were founded over the entire province and formed a network to embrace education, social reform, religion and politics during the last two decades of the nineteenth century. Schools were established with western education as an essential element in their programme, orphanages for boys and girls were founded, preachers were sponsored, pamphlets and tracts were printed and distributed, memorials and petitions were presented to safeguard and promote Muslim interests.[5] The influence of Sir Syed

[5] Edward D. Churchill Jr., 'Muslim Societies of the Punjab, 1860–1890', *The Punjab Past and Present*, Vol. 8, Part 1 (April 1974), 69–91.

Ahmed Khan was palpable in the Punjab in the field of education as well as politics. In 1887–1888 he advised the Muslims to remain aloof from the Indian National Congress and his call proved to be effective in the Punjab. There was a general fear among the Muslims that representation based on elections and employment based on open competition were not in their interest.

The 'Anglo-Muslim' programme of education and politics did not exhaust the concerns of the Punjabi Muslims. In the 1870s there were still a few hundred Wahhabis in the province, drawn generally from the pre-industrial lower middle class, but their idea of *jihād* to get rid of non-Muslim domination by armed force had lost its appeal.[6] There were a few hundred Ahl-i-Hadīs too, who dwelt on the past alone for reform, which had no appeal for the westernized middle-class Muslims. Mirza Ghulam Ahmad of Qadian, the founder of the Admadiya movement, made a contribution to religious controversy out of all proportion to the number of his followers. In his *Burāhīn-i-Ahmadiya* (1880–1884), which was meant to rejuvenate Islam on the basis of the Quran, he tried to refute the Christian missionaries, the Ayra Samajists and the Brahmos. In another work he argued that Guru Nanak was in fact a Muslim. Interpreting *jihād* as a peaceful propagation of Islam (*tablīgh*), he put all his energies into *tablīgh*, assuming for himself the position of the promised Messiah (*masīh-i-maw'ūd*), which made him rather heterodox. Muslims as well as Hindus, Sikhs and Christians reacted to Ghulam Ahmad's publications to make the last decade of the nineteenth century the highest watermark of religious controversy in the Punjab.[7]

In the first and second decades of the twentieth century the idea of Hindu Muslim separation was given constitutional and political recognition in the Punjab as in the rest of the country. Two years after the founding of the All India Muslim League the demand for separate electorates for Muslims was made at Amritsar in 1908. The principle was conceded and embodied in the Councils Act of 1909. To hasten political and constitutional change, the Muslim League and the Congress entered into a pact at Lucknow in 1916, ensuring separate electorates for Muslims in every province and weightage in those in

[6] Peter Hardy, 'Wahhabis in the Punjab, 1876', *The Punjab Past and Present*, Vol. 15, Part 2 (October 1981), 428–32.
[7] Spencer Lavan, 'Communalism in the Punjab: The Ahmadiyah Versus the Arya Samaj During the Lifetime of Mirza Ghulam Ahmad', *The Punjab Past and Present*, Vol. 5, Part 2 (October 1971), 320–42.

which they formed a minority. There was only a small and a logical step from the Lucknow Pact to the Reform Act of 1919 in which both weightage and separate electorates for the Muslims were enshrined. In the Punjab they got only separate electorates; weightage was to go to the minorities.

II

To the British administrators of the Punjab in the early 1850s, the decline of the former ruling class, the 'pillars' of the Sikh empire, appeared to be inevitable. The gaudy retinues of the former *jāgīrdārs* had disappeared, their country seats stood rather neglected and their city residences were not thronged by visitors. The British administrators hoped to 'render their decadence gradual' by allowing them pensions, or a part of their *jāgīrs*.

However, all of them were not treated alike. Jawahar Singh, the son of Sardar Hari Singh Nalwa, who had fought against the British with conspicuous gallantry at Chillianwala and Gujrat, lost all his *jāgīrs* and got no pension. Sardar Chattar Singh Atariwala and his son Raja Sher Singh, the arch rebels, were banished from the Punjab but with pensions. The 'rebels' generally lost *jāgīrs* and got merely pensions for life. The loyal members of the nobility retained a part of their *jāgīrs* in perpetuity. Raja Tej Singh, for instance, got a *jāgīr* worth about 20,000 rupees a year in perpetuity out of a *jāgīr* of over 90,000 rupees for life. Sardar Shamsher Singh Sandhanwalia, a former member of the Regency Council, retained a fourth of his *jāgīr* in perpetuity out of 40,000 rupees a year for life. The hope of reward induced a large number of *jāgīrdārs* of the Punjab to demonstrate their loyalty to the British rulers during the uprising of 1857–58, and the reward came in terms of increase in pensions and *jāgīrs*, grant of land in proprietorship and employment in service, proving to be a turning point in their fortunes. They began to be looked upon as the 'natural leaders' of the society. Nearly half of the Sikh aristocratic families survived into the twentieth century, readjusting themselves to the new situation. Many of them played a leading role in socio-religious reform and constitutional politics.[8]

[8] The changing fortunes of the former *jāgīrdārs* of the Punjab come out clearly from an analysis of Lepel Griffin's *The Panjab Chiefs*, published in 1865, and its subsequent editions published in 1890, 1909, 1940.

The *dharmarth* grantees of the days of Ranjit Singh and his successors were allowed to retain a part of their grants, and the Sikhs remained the major recipients of revenue-free grants now as before. Many Udāsī *mahants* got proprietary rights over lands granted earlier for their establishments or for the *gurdwāras* they maintained on behalf of the Sikhs. The number of important *gurdwāras* enjoying grants was not less than three scores, including a score of those associated with Guru Nanak and his successors. The descendants of Bhai Ram Singh, Gobind Ram and Bhai Gurmukh Singh, who had been patronized by the former rulers, were treated with special consideration by the British administrators.

The influence of Bhāīs and Sardars was utilized by the new rulers to maintain effective control over the Golden Temple and the institutions in its precincts. A committee headed by Raja Tej Singh was formed to advise Sardar Jodh Singh who was appointed as an Extra Assistant Commissioner at Amritsar to manage the affairs of the Golden Temple complex. Through an administrative manual (*dastūr al-'aml*), signed by a large number of Sardars and the functionaries of the Golden Temple in the presence of the Deputy Commissioner of Amritsar in 1859, its management was transformed into 'simple magisterial and political control' to maintain influence over the 'high spirited and excitable Khālsā'. It was conceded, however, that Guru Ram Das was the sole proprietor of the institution and the entire body of the Khālsā constituted the 'noviciate'.[9] With the passage of time the Singhs would claim not only the Golden Temple but all the historic *gurdwāras* as an inheritance of the Sikh Panth.

Retrenched after 1845–46 and virtually disbanded after 1848–49, the Khālsā came to form nearly a third of the 60,000 men raised from the Punjab during 1857–58. Raised at a most critical time when other recruiting grounds were in the hands of the rebels, the Khālsā were called out to 'save the Empire' and they 'fulfilled their mission'.[10] Henceforth they were to hold an honoured position in the Indian army and to fight in nearly all major wars fought by the British in all the three continents of the world. The proportion of the Sikhs in the Indian army remained much larger than their proportion in the

[9] Ian J. Kerr 'The British and the Administration of the Golden Temple in 1859', *The Punjab Past and Present*, Vol. 10, Part 2, (October 1976), 306–21.
[10] A report of 1858, quoted, Khushwant Singh, *A History of the Sikhs*, Oxford University Press, 1978, Vol. 2, 114, n 47.

population. Their 'gallant and faithful service in all climes' made them the 'pride of the Punjab'.[11]

The Sikh peasantry suffered economically in the late nineteenth century with the rising tide of indebtedness but much less than others. 'Their love of gain and inherited shrewdness', observed a contemporary British administrator, 'have, since the establishment of our reign of law, enabled them to avoid the pitfalls of the system of administration which has demoralised so many of the less efficient agricultural communities of the province.'[12] Many Sikh landholders prospered as commodity producers in the central Punjab and in the canal colonies. However, prosperity and debt travelled together for the Sikhs as for others. If some of the Sikh proprietors became richer, others became poorer. Differentiation among the Sikh landholders was in evidence everywhere but more so in the central districts of the Punjab. Apart from service in the army, which played a sustaining role in rural economy, emigration promised better opportunities of employment. In the first decade of the twentieth century, the percentage of net outmigration from the central Punjab rose from about 1.5 to nearly 4.75, and Sikh agriculturists represented a substantial portion of the emigrants to other parts of the country and to other countries and continents.

Much more striking than the increasing richness and poverty of the Sikh peasantry, the employment of the Sikhs in the Indian army, the conciliation of the Sikh priestly class or the partial rehabilitation of the Sikh aristocracy from the viewpoint of Sikh resurgence was the sheer increase in the number of Sikhs, from less than 2 millions in 1881 to over 4 millions in 1931, raising the percentage in the total population of the province from about 8 to over 13. In 1891 the number of Sikhs had increased by more than 8 per cent but the percentage of increase in the population of the Punjab was more than 10. In 1901, the corresponding percentages were about 13.5. In 1911, when the total population of the province was actually 2 per cent less than in 1901, the Sikh population increased by more than 37 per cent.

Equally remarkable was the increase in the proportion of Keshdhārī Sikhs in the Sikh population. When the British administrators talked of the declining number of the Sikhs in the early decades of British rule in

---

[11] Major G. F. Macmunn, 'The Martial Races of India', *The Punjab Past and Present*, Vol. 3, Part 1 (April 1970), 75–77; Regionald Hodder, 'The Sikhs and the Sikh Wars', *ibid.*, 86–105.

[12] S. S. Thorburn, *The Punjab in Peace and War*, 265.

the Punjab they had actually the Keshdhārī Singhs in mind.[13] The early census operators were instructed to return only those Sikhs as 'Sikh' who wore *kesh* and refrained from smoking. In 1911 for the first time all those persons were returned as Sikhs who thought of themselves as 'Sikh', whether Keshdhārīs or Sehajdhārīs. By now the number and proportion of Keshdhārī Sikhs was increasing, rising from about 840,000 in 1891 to nearly 3,600,000 in 1931. The number of Sehajdhārīs fell from nearly 580,000 in 1891 to less than 300,000 in 1931. Thus, the percentage of Keshdhārī Sikhs rose from less than seventy to more than ninety in less than half a century.

Increase in the number of Sikhs was generally attributed to the policy of the British to give preference to Sikhs in many branches of government service as well as in the army. However, only in 1911 were the Sikhs able to catch up with the Hindus in literacy, with 10.6 per cent of literates among them. In 1921 they formed nearly 16 per cent of the literates in the province, but literacy among them was still not higher than among the Hindus. If the number of literates in the army was not to be counted, the percentage of literacy among the Sikhs was in fact much lower. Literacy in English was even lower than the literacy in general. This position was reflected in the number of Sikhs in the government services. In 1911, nearly 15 per cent of the Sikhs were in the employment of the government but their percentage in the civil service was less than eight. Even in the police force in which they were believed to be well represented their percentage was less than nine. If 'preference' for the Sikhs in many branches of government service was the cause of increase in the number of Sikhs it was not because of the partiality of the British but the smaller representation of the Sikhs in the services other than the army.

Another cause of increase in the number of Sikhs was thought to be 'conversions' due to concern for religious reform among the educated Sikhs. There is no doubt that many persons were influenced directly by *parchār* or the propagation of reform. Many more, however, were affected by the growing consciousness of a distinct identity. 'A change of sentiment on the part of the Sikh community has led many persons recording themselves as Sikhs who were formerly content to be

---

[13] This is evident from the statement of Lord Dalhousie quoted by Khushwant Singh in his *History of the Sikhs* (Vol. 2, 96 n 20) and the statement of Richard Temple quoted by Rajiv A. Kapur in his *Sikh Separatism*, Vikas Publishing House, New Delhi, 1987, 8.

regarded as Hindus.'[14] This phenomenon was best exemplified among the Jats of the central districts of the Punjab: The percentage of Sikhs among the Jats rose from less than fifty four in 1881 to nearly eighty in 1921, while the percentage of Hindus among the Jats decreased from about forty in 1881 to less than ten in 1921. This was not a peculiarity of the Jats. Their proportion among the Sikhs did not appreciably change during all these decades. In fact the percentage of many other caste groups among the Sikhs actually increased by 1921 when the percentage of the Jats was slightly less than what it had been in 1881.

In terms of traditional professions, the number of agriculturists and their percentage in the Sikh population increased only slightly during these four decades, rising from about 1,190,000 persons in 1881 to over 2,000,000 in 1921, from 72.76 per cent to 73.53 per cent. Besides the Jats they were represented by Kambos, Sainis, Rajputs and Mahtons. The trading communities were represented by Khatris and Aroras. Their number rose from about 73,000 to over 177,000, improving their percentage from 4.46 to 6.41 during these decades. The number of Sikh artisans and craftsmen rose from about 122,000 to nearly 324,000 but their percentage fell from 13.58 to 11.71 during this period. They were represented by Tarkhāns, Lohārs, Jhīwars, Nāīs, Kumhārs, Sunārs, Julāhās, Darzīs and Chhīmbas. The number of traditional outcastes, represented by Chuhrās and Chamārs among the Sikhs, rose from over 140,000 in 1881 to over 200,000 in 1921, but their percentage fell from 8.59 to 7.31 during these decades. But this could be partly due to the fact that some of them did not return themselves as Chuhrās or Chamārs. By 1921, the Sikhs coming from the traditional occupations of agriculture, commerce, artisanry and scavenging constituted nearly 99 per cent of the Sikh population in the Punjab.

However, all the Sikhs were not pursuing their traditional occupations. The Khatrīs, Aroras and Brahmans among the Sikhs led in literacy, followed at a considerable distance by Jats and other agriculturist groups, followed in turn by Tarkhāns and by Jhīwars, Chamārs and Chuhrās. In the early twentieth century they were all represented in the new professions and occupations, though not in proportion to their numbers. The agriculturists were represented adequately in the army and the police; the trading groups were represented more than

---

[14] James Douie, *The Panjab, North-West Frontier Province and Kashmir*, Seema Publications, Delhi, 1974 (reprint), 117. Douie also observed that the future of Sikhism was with the Keshdhārīs: *ibid.*, 118.

adequately in civil services and in the new professions of teaching, medicine and law. However, there were also Khatrīs, Kalāls, Tarkhāns and Chuhrās in the army; and there were Labānas, Nāis, Jhīwars and Chhīmbas too in the police. They were all represented in the professions of law, medicine and teaching. In 1921, there were nearly seventy factories owned or managed by Sikh Jats and thirty by Sikh Tarkhāns. Several of the non-agriculturist groups owned or cultivated land. However, the largest bulk of land was still held by the traditional land-owning groups, just as the bulk of the trade and shopkeeping was still handled by the traditional business communities. In the professions of law, medicine and teaching, the Khatrī, Arora and Brahman Sikhs found the largest representation, followed by the Jats. These were the groups which had played a conspicuous part in the politico-administrative and the socio-economic life of the Punjab during the early nineteenth century. In the early decades of the twentieth century they were back on the stage to participate in the growing resurgence in the Sikh community and to feel their way towards wealth and power.

III

Religious ferment among the Sikhs was in evidence already at the time of the annexation of the Punjab to the British empire. Baba Dayal, a Malhotra Khatrī of Rawalpindi, was asking his fellow Sikhs to believe in only the Formless One (nirankār), to reject all gods and goddesses, to discard all Brahmanical rites and ceremonies and to conform their lives to the teachings of the Granth Sahib. He came to have hundreds of followers before he died in 1853. His eldest son, Baba Darbara Singh, established many centres in towns and villages outside Rawalpindi, appointing his representative (birādār) for every local congregation (sangat). For their guidance he prepared a hukmnāma containing the essential teachings of Baba Dayal. Though divine sanction is invoked for the mission of Baba Dayal in this hukmnāma and he is referred to as 'the true guru,' the doctrine of Guru-Granth is clearly enunciated.[15]

On his death in 1870, Baba Darbara Singh was succeeded by his younger brother, Sahib Rattaji. He consolidated the work of his predecessors by an uncompromising insistence on the Nirankārī code (rehat). He transformed the mission at Rawalpindi into an impersonal

---

[15] An English version of this hukmnāma is given by John C. B. Webster in The Nirankari Sikhs, Macmillan, Delhi, 1979, 83–99.

institution in 1903, through a formal will which also reflects its prosperity. The Nirankārīs were now counted in thousands, consisting of the Khatrī, Arora and Bhatia traders, bankers and shopkeepers of the towns and villages of the upper Sindh Sagar Doab. Even there, however, some of them were turning to a new movement called the Singh Sabha.[16] True to their advocacy of a peculiarly Sikh ceremony of marriage, the Nirankārīs supported the Anand Marriage Bill in 1908–1909 but the initiative for the bill had come from the Singh Sabha reformers. Indeed, during the early twentieth century, under the guidance of Baba Gurdit Singh who succeeded his father Sahib Rattaji in 1909, the Nirankārī participation in Sikh resurgence remained rather marginal. Geographically on the fringe, the Nirankārīs could never hold the central position even doctrinally. They remained as much true to the mission of Baba Dayal as Baba Dayal was true to the mission of Guru Nanak. But that was not the whole of the Sikh tradition. They did not take Guru Gobind Singh fully into account, and they were bound to lag behind when the Singh identity was coming to the fore.

The first reformer to emphasize the importance of Singh identity under colonial rule was Baba Ram Singh. He was a disciple of Baba Balak Singh, a Batra Arora, who too had invoked the authority of Sikh scriptures, emphasized the importance of the Name (*nām*) for salvation and addressed himself to both Sehajdhārī and Keshdhārī householders, from his centre at Hazro near Attock. A new direction was given to his *nāmdhārī* movement by Baba Ram Singh who worked in the central districts of the Punjab, instituting the Sant Khālsā in 1862, the year of Baba Balak Singh's death.[17]

By the middle of 1863, Baba Ram Singh was ordered by the British administrators not to move out of his native village Bhaini in Ludhiana district and not to hold a religious assembly (*dīwān*). Baba Ram Singh subscribed to the doctrine of Guru-Granth but the mission of Guru Gobind Singh was more important in his eyes. His followers were administered the baptism of the double-edged sword (*khande kī pauhl*)

---

[16] Bhai Manna Singh, 'a saintly Sikh and the most illustrious member of the Nirankari community, next to the Guru of this sect', performed *kīrtan* and *kathā* for the founding of Singh Sabha at Gujar Khan. Bhagat Lakshman Singh, *Autobiography* (ed. Ganda Singh), Calcutta, 1965, 107–09.

[17] There are references to the Sant Khālsā in the official records of the 1860s and Baba Ram Singh refers to its institution in 1862 in one of his letters. According to Bhagat Lakshman Singh, Baba Ram Singh was a disciple of Baba Balak Singh who was a disciple of Bhagat Jawahar Mal, a Kohli Khatri of Rawalpindi, and Baba Ram Singh was known to Jawahar Mal as well: *Autobiography*, 3–6.

and, since there was a legal ban on carrying a sword, they were asked to carry some other simple weapon or merely a staff. Like many of his contemporary Sikhs, Baba Ram Singh believed that Guru Gobind Singh had invoked the goddess Chaṇḍī when he instituted the Khālsā. Many of his followers believed in the veracity of the *Sau Sākhī* attributed to Guru Gobind Singh in which the end of British rule in the Punjab was foretold as a prelude to the establishment of Sikh rule under a carpenter named Ram Singh.[18] With the background of the uprising of 1857–1858, the activity of his followers appeared to be potentially dangerous. A circular letter of Baba Ram Singh, asking his followers to come to Amritsar at the time of the Diwālī, convinced the British administrators that his internment at Bhaini could contain his increasing popularity.

Within a few years of Baba Ram Singh's internment, however, the number of his followers was estimated to have shot up to over 100,000. Organizational improvement was reflected in the 'postal arrangements' he evolved and the appointment of 'provincial governors' (*sūbas*) he made to look after the Nāmdhārīs, now popularly known as Kūkās.[19] The millenarian hopes of his followers increased with the popularity of his ideology among the peasantry in the central districts of the Punjab. Invocation of the goddess Chaṇḍī, through *chaṇḍī-pāṭhs*, became an important ritual, giving a long leverage to the 'frenzied' (*mastāna*) among his followers. They expressed their icono-clastic zeal in the destruction of idols, tombs, *maṛhīs* and *samādhs*. In 1866–1867, a number of them were sentenced to an imprisonment of three months to two years in the districts of Ludhiana, Ferozepur, Hoshiarpur, Amritsar, Gurdaspur, Gujranwala and Sialkot.

One great resentment which Baba Ram Singh developed against the British was over the killing of kine for beef. The more irate among the Kūkās struck at the butchers in Amritsar first and then in Raikot in Ludhiana district, killing seven persons and wounding twelve. Eventu-ally, eight Kūkās were sentenced to death. The Commissioner of Ambala Division now marshalled every known fact and plausible

---

[18] This prophecy, included in the *Sau Sākhī*, was known to the British administrators in 1863: Nahar Singh (ed.), *Gooroo Ram Singh and the Kuka Sikhs*, Amrit Books, New Delhi, 1965. This volume contains official documents from 1863 to 1871.

[19] In the reports of 1863, the followers of Baba Ram Singh are referred to as Kūkās by some of the administrators. They had acquired this name because of their ecstatic cries (*kūks*) during the singing of hymns. Baba Ram Singh, who preferred to call them Nāmdhārīs or Sant Khālsā, was also aware that others referred to his followers as Kūkās.

argument to convince the higher authorities that murders could not have taken place without Baba Ram Singh's approval. In any case, Baba Ram Singh, according to the Commissioner, was oppposed to British rule in the Punjab and he was hoping if not actually working for the return of Sikh rule. While the suggestion of his removal from the Punjab was under consideration, a band of the Kūkās struck at Malaud and Malerkotla in January, 1872, in search of arms to overawe the kine-killers all over the Punjab. They killed ten and wounded seventeen persons in the process of getting one double-barrelled gun, five horses and some swords. The Deputy Commissioner of Ludhiana, L. Cowan, acted with undue promptness to save the empire from what he felt was the beginning of a holocaust like the one of 1857–1858. He blew forty-nine Kūkās from guns at the spot. The Commissioner of Ambala, T. W. Forsyth, put his stamp of approval on what his subordinate had done illegally: Forsyth ordered sixteen more Kūkās to be blown from guns. Cowan was removed from service and Forsyth was removed from the Punjab. Baba Ram Singh and eleven of his *sūbas* were sent to distant jails in or outside the subcontinent.

The devotees of Baba Ram Singh established contact with him at Rangoon and letters began to exchange between Burma and the Punjab with increasing frequency till 1880 when he was removed to Mergui where he died five years later.[20] His letters refer to the practice of Anand marriage among his followers. Subscribing emphatically to the doctrine of Guru-Granth, he refers to himself as the Guru's drummer, his *reporteur*, a dog sitting at his door. But he was aware of the prophecies which implied that he was the twelfth Guru. He came to pay more and more attention to prophetic literature attributed to Guru Gobind Singh: the *Sau Sākhī*, the *Prem Sumārg* and a *Pothī* discovered at Prahladpur in the Hissar district. He was convinced of the impending fall of British rule through a political upheaval between 1877 and 1883. In this context he emphasized the importance of *chanḍī-pāṭh* and the *bhogs* of Guru Granth Sahib and asked his followers not to join the service of the British.

In the context of the prophecies of political turmoil, there was a certain degree of excitement among the Kūkās in the Punjab due to the worsening relations of the British with Afghanistan and Russia. The Police Superintendent of Ludhiana observed in 1878 that in the case of

[20] About sixty letters of Baba Ram Singh are published by Ganda Singh in his *Kūkiān dī Vithya* (Pbi), Amritsar, 1944.

a reverse to British arms the Kūkās were sure 'to show their teeth' and to get support from a large portion of 'ignorant agriculturists'. However, the expected turmoil did not take place and the Kūkā unrest gradually merged into the issue raised by the expected return of Maharaja Dalip Singh to India. In 1885 they were eagerly looking forward to Dalip Singhs's visit to the Punjab, hoping that 'this would be followed by the release and the return of their exiled Guru Ram Singh'.[21] In the late 1880s the Kūkās were potentially his most important supporters. Uneasy excitement among them began to subside, however, when the Maharaja returned to his loyalty to the Queen Empress in 1890. In the census of 1891 only about 10,500 persons returned themselves as Nāmdhārīs. They were now guided by Baba Ram Singh's younger brother, Baba Hari Singh, who had taken his place at Bhaini after his deportation in 1872. On Baba Hari Singh's death in 1906, the leadership of the Nāmdhārīs devolved upon his son, Mahraj Pratap Singh, who led them into free India as a sect within Sikhism.

Before the end of the nineteenth century the Nāmdhārīs had discarded militancy and stuck to the ideals of personal piety and earnest living. They retained the idea and practice of 'intoxication'. They developed the idea of a living *guru*. They could not be the precursors of the movement known as the Singh Sabha which was characterized by serious interest in modern education, including science and English literature, and in the politics of numbers, municipalities, councils and legislatures. The Nāmdhārī idea of a living personal *guru* could not be reconciled to the doctrines of Guru-Granth and Guru-Panth which were reinforced by the Singh Sabha reformers with an uncompromising zeal.

IV

The Sri Guru Singh Sabha of Amritsar was founded in 1873 and followed by the Lahore Singh Sabha in 1879. Then for twenty years, six Singh Sabhas on the average were added every year. At the end of the First World War there were Singh Sabhas in nearly all the cities of the Punjab, in most of its towns and some of its villages. Nearly all these associations had formal constitutions. Each Singh Sabha catered to a

---

[21] Ganda Singh (ed.), *Maharaja Duleep Singh Correspondence*, Punjabi University, Patiala, 1977, 387–88.

small area in practice but in theory regarded itself as the representative of the whole community. A new consciousness of common identity was imparted by common concerns and a kindred outlook on the world around in spite of rivalries due to differences in the social background of the leaders, their image of the past or their vision of the future.

The need for coordination brought into existence the Khalsa Diwan at Amritsar in 1893 and the Khalsa Diwan at Lahore in 1896. Khalsa Diwans were founded in a few other cities and towns as well. The Chief Khalsa Diwan, founded at Amritsar in 1902, had about thirty Sabhas and Diwans affiliated to it. By 1920, the number of associations affiliated to the Chief Khalsa Diwan was more than a hundred. Between 1890 and 1910, about a dozen allied or ancillary associations were founded, like the Gurmat Granth Pracharak Sabha of Amritsar, Gurmat Granth Sudharak Sabha of Amritsar, Gurmat Granth Sudharak Sabha of Lahore, Khalsa Dharam Pracharak Sabha of Rawalpindi, the Khalsa Tract Society, the Central Khalsa Orphanage, the Sikh Education Conference, and the Punjab and Sind Bank. The leaders of the Sikh associations came from all sections of the Sikh community in varying proportions from place to place. The ruling families were represented by the Princes of Nabha, Faridkot and Kapurthala. The aristocracy was represented by men like Sunder Singh Majithia and Harbans Singh Atariwala. The new middle class was represented by teachers like Gurmukh Singh and Bhai Jodh Singh, petty bureaucrats like Bhai Jawahar Singh and Babu Teja Singh, businessmen like Trilochan Singh, scholars like Giani Gian Singh and Bhai Kahn Singh, writers like Bhai Vir Singh and Bhai Mohan Singh Vaid and publicists like Bhai Dit Singh Giani.

Whatever the differences between one Sabha or Diwan and another, they were all concerned with religious reform. They felt a threat from Christian missionaries who continued to gain converts from amongst the Sikhs, besides the conspicuous conversion of Maharaja Dalip Singh and Kanwar Harnam Singh Ahluwalia in the early decades of British rule. Fear of conversion to Christianity was articulated in Sikh publications even in the early twentieth century. There were stray conversions to Islam as well. But more than the threat of Islam and Christianity, the Singh reformers felt a threat from the Arya Samaj. Despite Swami Dayanand's dim view of Sikhism in the *Satyarth Prakash*, several eminent Sikhs had joined the Arya Samaj, but a decisive break came in 1888 when the Arya 'fire-brands' mounted a 'thoughtless attack' on the Sikh Gurus.[22] Bhai Jawahar Singh and Bhai Dit Singh Giani felt obliged to leave the Arya Samaj leaders of Lahore and to join the Singh Sabha reformers.

The Sikh–Arya confrontation sharpened the issue of Sikh identity. The Sikh leaders in their farewell address to the Governor General in 1888 at Lahore expressed the view that the Sikhs should not be 'confounded with Hindus but treated in all respects as a separate community'.[23] The death of Dyal Singh Majithia in 1898 made the question of Sikh identity a legal issue because his widow went to the court to contest his will on the plea that he was not a Hindu. But the court ruled that he was. This gave new impetus to the Sikh–Arya debate. In this context Bhai Kahn Singh published his well-known work *Ham Hindu Nahīn* which is regarded now as a classic exposition of a distinct Sikh identity. Bhagat Lakshman Singh refuted Bawa Chajju Singh's contention that the Sikh Gurus were 'only Hindu reformers', or that the Sikh scriptures were 'only mutilated copies' of Hindu works. For Lakshman Singh, 'the Sikh dispensation was an independent entity and not a subsidiary system, based on Hindu philosophy'.[24] In 1900, the Arya Samaj leaders reconverted some Rehatia Sikhs through a ceremony involving the shaving of their heads in public. The Singh reformers evolved their own programme of purification (*shuddhī*) and their confrontation with the Aryas continued into the twentieth century.

On several vital issues the Singh reformers had to contend not only with outsiders but also with their fellow Sikhs. If some Sehajdhārīs insisted that they were Sikh and not Hindu, some Keshdhārīs insisted that they were Hindu. Baba Gurbakhsh Singh Bedi, son of Baba Sir Khem Singh Bedi, made a public statement in 1910 that the Sikhs were Hindus. Bhai Avtar Singh, a protégé of Baba Sir Khem Singh Bedi, maintained in a couple of tracts published a year later, that the Sikh Gurus had worshipped gods and goddesses, accepted no Muslims as their followers and maintained the distinctions of caste. A conservative interpretation of Sikhism was built into the commentary of Sant Badan Singh on the Ādi Granth, sponsored by the ruling chief of Faridkot and published in 1905. The Singh reformers did not appreciate this

[22] Bhagat Lakshman Singh, *Autobiography*, 58.
[23] 'Bhai Jawahar Singh – Arya Samaj –Singh Sabha', *The Punjab Past and Present*, Vol. 7, Part 1 (April 1973), 92.
[24] Bhagat Lakshman Singh, *Autobiography*, 132–33.

'Hinduized' commentary and supported the religious views expressed by Bhai Kahn Singh in his *Gurmat Prabhākar* and *Gurmat Sudhākar*, both of which were published around 1900. A similar preference was shown by the Singh reformers for M. A. Macauliffe's *Sikh Religion*, published in 1909, over Ernest Trumpp's *Adi Granth* published three decades earlier.

The volume of tracts and pamphlets expressing the social and religious concerns of the Singh reformers increased sharply in the early decades of the twentieth century. Apart from the general appeals for return to the teachings of the Gurus, there were arguments against idol worship, observance of fasts, notion of auspicious and inauspicious days, the practice of *shrādhs*, the celebration of Holi and other 'Hindu' elements of belief and ritual. For 'Sikh' ceremonies and rites, a comprehensive code was published by the Chief Khalsa Diwan in 1915 as the *Gurmat Parkāsh Bhāg Sanskār*. The authenticity of the Dasam Granth was questioned because its contents appeared to compromise the ideal of monotheism. The idea of Guru-Panth became stronger with the increasing importance of Singh identity. In a tract published in 1919, it was argued that no human being could be the Guru of the Sikhs after Guru Gobind Singh decided to vest Guruship in the Ādi Granth. The Sikhs were 'to view themselves as the Panth and not to recognize any single person as their sole leader'. The idea of Guru-Panth was emerging as clearly as the equation of the Guru with the Ādi Granth.[25]

Interest in the past was a reflection of the concern for the present. Giani Gian Singh led the way by publishing his *Panth Parkāsh* in 1880, followed by his *Tawārīkh-i-Gurū Khālsa* in 1892. A number of books in Punjabi were published on the lives of the Sikh Gurus, the institution of the Khālsā, and the political struggle of the Sikhs against the Mughals and the Afghans. Bhai Vir Singh, by far the most important literary figure among the Singh reformers, recreated the heroic age of the Khālsā in his *Sundarī, Bijai Singh, Satwant Kaur* and *Bābā Naudh Singh*, producing historical fiction far more attractive than history. The creative literature produced by the Sikh writers of the early twentieth century also reflected concern for reform.[26]

[25] The entries in N. Gerald Barrier's *The Sikhs and Their Literature*, Manohar Book Service, Delhi, 1970, contain ample evidence of the concerns, ideas and attitudes of the Sikhs in the early decades of the twentieth century.

[26] J. S. Grewal, 'The Emergence of Punjabi Drama: A Cultural Response to Colonial Rule', *Journal of Regional History*, Guru Nanak Dev University, Amritsar, Vol. 5 (1984), 115–55.

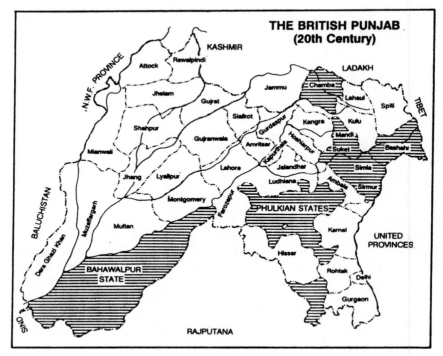

Map 6 The British Punjab

The Singh reformers welcomed English education and appreciated western science and technology but they did not like the idea of Christian instruction in missionary schools and no religious instruction in government institutions. They were keen to teach Sikh tenets and Sikh history to their boys and girls as well as western science and literature. This Anglo–Sikh system of education was an important plank of reform. The proposal for a Khalsa College at Lahore was made as early as 1885. In 1890, there was a hot debate about its location.[27] The foundation stone of Khalsa College was eventually laid at Amritsar in March, 1892, and the College soon became the premier educational institution of the Sikhs. Equally symbolic of the Singh reform was the Kanya Maha Vidyalaya founded at Ferozpore by Bhai Takht Singh in 1892, and run without any grant from the government and without any tuition fees from the girls. It was followed by girls'

[27] Some of the Arya Samaj leaders were not happy about the establishment of a Khalsa College at Lahore: Bhagat Lakshman Singh, *Autobiography*, 90–93.

schools at Lahore, Amritsar, Rawalpindi and Ropar. High Schools were established not only in cities but also in small towns like Damdama Sahib and new towns like Lyallpur. A college was established at Gujranwala before 1920 when the number of Sikh educational institutions was more than three scores.

Like the Brahmos and the Arya Samajists, the Singh reformers were opposed to Urdu as the medium of education and administration. Unlike them, however, they supported Punjabi in Gurmukhi script rather than Hindi in Devanagri script. They argued strongly that school education should be based on 'the language of the people'.[28] The traditional Punjabi literature was still dear to Muslim and Hindu writers but the number of Hindu and Muslim writers taking to the new literary genres in Punjabi was rather small. The Singh reformers espoused the cause of new Punjabi literature. In their minds, Punjabi language and literature were inseparable from the Gurmukhi script in which were written their sacred scriptures.[29] In the opening decade of the twentieth century, the Singh reformers and the Arya Samajists were fighting over the linguistic issue as well as the issue of religious identity. Differences in language and script came to be progressively associated with differences in religion, deepening communal consciousness and its appeal.

Like most of the educated Punjabis, the Singh reformers tried to promote their interests through journalism. The average number of tracts by the Sikhs and on the Sikhs increased from about sixty a year in the 1870s to about 160 a year in the late 1890s. Compared with the 'Hindu' press, however, the 'Sikh' press was rather weak. The most important Sikh publications were the *Gurmukhi Akhbār* and the *Khālsā Akhbār* in Punjabi and *The Khālsā* in English, which were brought out from Lahore. *The Nirguniārā* and the *Khālsā Samāchār* in Punjabi and the *Khalsa Advocate* in English were brought out from Amritsar.

In the early twentieth century, the viewpoint of the Singh reformers was consistently represented by the *Khālsā Samāchār*. Apart from an attempt in its numbers to counter the propaganda of Christian missionaries, the Arya Samajists and the Ahmadiyas, there is an insistence on the separate socio-religious identity of the Sikhs, an

---

[28] Note 23, above.
[29] As an example of contemporary attitudes towards languages and scripts, Bhagat Lakshman Singh, *Autobiography*, 110–13.

emphasis on the study of Sikh religious literature and Sikh history, an increasing criticism of Udāsīs, *pujārīs* and *mahants*, argument for the good treatment of the Ramdāsia and the Rehatia Sikhs, and an advocacy of the education of women. There are pleas for the use of Punjabi in Gurmukhi script at least up to primary level in education, in courts, in post offices and in railway carriages. There is advocacy of the Anand marriage. There is criticism of the management of *gurdwāras* and there is the argument that they should be handed over to committees of Singhs because they belong to the Panth. There is a general expression of loyalty to the British Government with pleas for separate representation for the Sikhs in municipalities, local boards, the provincial council and the imperial legislature. The dominantly religious concerns of the late nineteenth century were thus spilling over into the political concerns of the early twentieth century.[30]

V

The British intelligence officer David Petrie thought of the neo-Sikhs in 1911 as the source of disaffection among the Sikhs. These neo-Sikhs were equated by him with the *tat-khālsā* or the Singh reformers. The activities even of the Chief Khalsa Diwan and its leading light, Sunder Singh Majithia, appeared to him to be potentially subversive. In any case, he saw a political dimension in the programme of *shuddhī* because representation, and consequently power, was expected to flow from numerical strength. Furthermore, he disliked loose talk among the Singh reformers about the fallen estate of the Sikhs because it carried the implication that it was due to their loss of power. Their wretched condition under the Mughals was obliquely suggestive of their miserable plight under the British. Finally the past was invoked to carry implications for the present; what the sword of Guru Gobind Singh did to the empire of Aurangzeb, the might of the Khālsā could do now to the British empire. Seditious ideas were expressed through quotations from the Sikh scriptures: 'the brave is he who fights in the cause of religion; the rulers are lions and *muqaddams* are dogs; the times are a dagger and

---

[30] Joginder Singh, 'Resurgence in Sikh Journalism', *Journal of Regional History*, Vol. 3 (1982), 99–116; Satpal Kaur, 'Journalism in the Punjab and the Khālsā Samachār (1899–1919)', M. Phil. Dissertation, Guru Nanak Dev University, Amritsar, 1985.

the rulers are butchers'. Petrie was inclined to attribute this new mood to the increasing number and influence of the Singh reformers.[31]

There is no doubt that one of the professed objectives of the Chief Khalsa Diwan was to safeguard 'the political rights' of the Sikhs. However, their idea was to make representations to gain constitutional positions or advantages from the British. In the late nineteenth century, some of the Sikh leaders had worked with the Lahore Indian Association and the Indian National Congress. The most eminent among them was Dyal Singh Majithia who was closely associated with the activities of the Brahmo Samajists and left behind the legacy of a college, a library and *The Tribune*. Before the end of the nineteenth century, however, he had come to be looked upon as an apostate by a large number of Sikhs who did not like even to cast their eyes on him.[32] Those of the Singh reformers who wanted to retain their image of loyalty to the British did not appreciate Dyal Singh's politics either. In any case, Bhai Jawahar Singh was telling the Sikhs not to associate themselves with the Congress which was looked upon by the British administrators with suspicion if not hostility.

Only some members of the ruling and aristocratic families were representing the Sikhs on councils and legislatures, like the Maharaja of Patiala, the Yuvraj of Nabha, Kanwar Harnam Singh Ahluwalia, Sir Ranbir Singh, Baba Sir Khem Singh Bedi and Sunder Singh Majithia. However they did not remain unaffected by the concerns of the Singh reformers. The Anand Marriage Bill was proposed by Yuvraj Ripudaman Singh and introduced in the Imperial Council in October 1908. It was meant to give legal recognition to the Sikh ceremony of marriage. Not only the Arya Samajists but also many Sikhs were opposed to the Bill, including the *granthīs* of the Golden Temple. The Anand marriage was regarded as an innovation of the Singh reformers by the opponents of the Bill. Hundreds of communications were sent for and against the Bill. The Nirankārīs and the Nāmdhārīs wrote to the government in its support. The support of the Nirankārīs, who were basically Sehajdhārīs, proved to be rather crucial in a tussle between the conservative Sikhs and the Singh reformers. The Bill was eventually passed in October 1909, when Sunder Singh Majithia was a member of the Council.

[31] D. Petrie, 'Recent Developments in Sikh Politics', *The Punjab Past and Present*, Vol. 4, Part 2 (October 1970), 302–79. This comprehensive report was compiled in August, 1911.
[32] Bhagat Lakshman Singh, *Autobiography*, 128–29.

If the Anand Marriage Act was a triumph for the Singh reformers, the Act of 1909 proved to be a disappointment. The Provincial Council was enlarged with the provision for eight of its members to be elected. For nearly a decade, only one Sikh was elected. The Sikhs could find representation only through nominated members like Partap Singh Ahluwalia, Daljit Singh of Kapurthala, Baba Gurbakhsh Singh Bedi, Sunder Singh Majithia and Gajjan Singh Grewal. The Singh reformers felt more and more convinced that the Sikhs needed separate electorates like the Muslims. Soon after the Lucknow Pact, Sunder Singh Majithia wrote to the Lieutenant Governor that the Sikhs should be given a share in the councils and administration with due regard to their importance, their status before the annexation of the Punjab, their present stake in the country and their services to the British empire. Asking for a share in excess of the proportion of the Sikh population in the province, Sunder Singh Majithia had in mind the Lucknow Pact which gave such weightage to Muslims in the provinces where they were in the minority.

A Sikh deputation met Chelmsford, the Governor General, in November, 1917, to plead for separate electorates and weightage for the Sikhs on the basis of their 'unique position'.[33] In the Montford Report it was noted that the Sikhs had remained unrepresented in spite of their services to the empire. 'To the Sikhs, therefore, and to them alone, we propose to extend the system already adopted in the case of Muhammadans.'[34] In September 1918, representatives of the entire Sikh community prepared a memorandum on the initiative of the Chief Khalsa Diwan to impress upon the government that the principle conceded in the Montford Report should be 'carried out and fulfilled in the fullest measure and in all its consequences'. However, the proposal of 30 per cent share for the Sikhs in the provincial council was not acceptable to its Hindu and Muslim members. On a strong recommendation from the Punjab government, nonetheless, the Franchise Committee conceded 'a separate electoral role and separate constituencies for the Sikhs'. In terms of weightage, however, the Sikhs got merely half of what they had demanded, ten out of fifty eight seats and not 30 per cent.

Sikh politics was not confined to constitutional politics. During

[33] Ruchi Ram Sahni, *Struggle for Reform in Sikh Shrines* (ed. Ganda Singh), SGPC, Amrtsar, nd, 45–46.
[34] *Ibid.*, 46–47.

the unrest of 1907, Denzil Ibbetson had observed with some
concern that 'if the loyalty of the Jat Sikhs of the Punjab is ever
materially shaken, the danger will be greater than any which could
possibly arise in Bengal'.[35] The leader of the agitation, Ajit Singh,
was paying special attention to the Sikhs, including soldiers and
pensioners. The Sikh peasants did participate in the agitation more
than the Muslim or Hindu peasants in proportion to their
numbers.

David Petrie had looked upon Sikh participation in the agitation of
1907 as an example of their disaffection. But the Singh reformers had
little to do with that agitation. As if to bear him out, they felt much
exercised when in 1913 the outer wall of the Rakabganj Gurdwara in
Delhi was dismantled to construct a road through its estate to the
Viceregal Lodge. When the Sikhs came to know of the demolition of
the wall, they sent telegrams, petitions and memoranda to the
Viceroy, the Lieutenant Governor of the Punjab, the Commander-in-
Chief and the Commissioner of Delhi. *The Sikh Review* was
launched in Delhi, with Sardul Singh Caveeshar as its editor, to
inform Sikh opinion on Sikh interests. However, Sunder Singh Majithia and the Chief Khalsa Diwan tried to support and to accommodate the government. In the Sikh Education Conference held at
Jalandhar in April 1914, a Sikh leader from Lyallpur was not allowed
to raise the Rakabganj issue. In a meeting held at Amritsar, Sunder
Singh Majithia and his associates tried to support the official
viewpoint. Protest meetings were held in several places as much
against the Chief Khalsa Diwan as against the government. The
Rakabganj agitation was beginning to gain momentum when the war
broke out in September. The agitation was shelved but only to be
taken up after the war.[36] In 1912 David Petrie had 'sufficient evidence
available to prove that a spirit of anti-British disaffection is com-
monly prevalent among the Sikhs in Canada'. Indeed the executive
committee of the Sikh Temple at Vancouver had resolved in October,
1909, that none of its members should wear 'any kind of medal,
buttons, uniforms or insignia which may signify that the position of
the party wearing the article is nothing but of a slave to the British

[35] 'Sir Denzil Ibbetson's Report on Political Situation in Punjab (1907)', K. K. Khullar,
Shaheed Bhagat Singh, Hem Publishers, New Delhi, 1981, 98–110. This report was written
on 30 April 1907.
[36] Harjot Singh, 'From Gurdwara Rakabganj to the Viceregal Palace – A Study of
Religious Protest', *The Punjab Past and Present*, Vol. 14, Part 1 (April 1980), 182–98.

supremacy'.[37] The resentment which thousands of Indians felt against the blind racial prejudice of their white neighbours was transferred to the colonial rulers of India. In a meeting of the United India League and the Khalsa Diwan Society held in February, 1913, it was decided to send a delegation to the Colonial Secretary and the Governor General of India to present the case of Indian emigrants against the legal disabilities and statutory discrimination they were suffering at the hands of the states and the federal government in Canada. This delegation was well received by the press in the Punjab, but the Lieutenant Governor merely warned its members against inflammatory speeches; Lord Hardinge expressed his inability to help them, and the Colonial Secretary in London refused to meet them.

Before the delegation returned to Canada, a new organization called the Hindi Association of the Pacific Coast, had been founded. It was given the popular name of Ghadar Party by Har Dayal in the very first issue of its weekly, the *Ghadar*. The Urdu and Gurmukhi editions of the *Ghadar* began to circulate among the Indian settlers in three continents. This propaganda had gone on for about six months when in May 1914 the Japanese steamer *Komagata Maru* reached Vancouver with 376 emigrants. Their entry into Canada became a legal issue in which the validity of the new laws was upheld and their efficacy was reflected in the return of the *Komagata Maru* in July with the bulk of its passengers. The steamer was on the high seas when the war broke out. None of its passengers was allowed to disembark before it reached Calcutta. There, at Budge Budge, the passengers refused to be sent straight to the Punjab and eighteen of them were killed when the troops opened fire. The first batch of the Ghadarites had already left America. The *Komagata Maru* affair appeared to merge into the revolutionary programme of the Ghadar Party.

Batches of Ghadarites started coming to India from Canada, the United States, Hong Kong and Shanghai, including their president Sohan Singh Bhakna. The Indian government was much better informed about their intentions and movements than they ever imagined. Even their entry through the southern ports did not save them all from the British dragnet. Of over 3,000 returning emigrants who were handled by the police at Calcutta and Ludhiana, nearly 190 were interned and more than 700 were restricted to their villages.

[37] Harish K. Puri, *Ghadar Movement: Ideology, Organisation and Strategy*, Guru Nanak Dev University, Amritsar, 1983, 46.

Those of the revolutionaries who escaped the police started telling the people openly to rise against the British. They addressed the Sikh gatherings at Amritsar, Tarn Taran, Muktsar and Nankana Sahib, with mixed response from their audiences. If Randhir Singh Grewal, who had earlier participated in the Rakabganj Gurdwara agitation joined the Ghadarites, Gajjan Singh Grewal condemned their seditious ideas and passed their propaganda material on to the police. The leaders of the Chief Khalsa Diwan looked upon them as dupes, and regarded their activity as discreditable. The Zaildārs and Lambardārs in the villages were ready to inform the police against the revolutionaries. Their activities during 1914 were confined to a few robberies, an attack on a railway station and an unsuccessful attempt at looting a treasury. Disillusioned with the people, the revolutionaries turned to the army units in the beginning of 1915.

Rash Bihari Bose and a few other revolutionary leaders, the only category of political activists who had any sympathy for the Ghadarite cause, arrived at this juncture. The revolutionaries were able to contact a number of regiments, particularly the 23rd Cavalry at Lahore, the 28th Punjabis at Ferozepur, the 28th Pioneers and the 12th Cavalry at Meerut. They were optimistic about their response. February 21 was fixed as the date of general rising, advanced to February 19 in view of suspected leakage. This date too was known to the authorities. The disaffected regiments were disarmed; suspects were court martialled and executed. The attempt of the revolutionaries to capture arms from the arsenals at Lahore and Ferozepur and the police station at Sarhali in Amritsar district proved abortive. The revolutionaries blamed the informers and the loyalist supporters of the administration for this fiasco and killed a few of them. By about the middle of 1915 the hope of a popular rising was over. All that was now left of the *ghadar* was a series of conspiracy trials in which forty-two of the accused were sentenced to death, 114 were transported for life and ninety-three were given long or short terms of imprisonment. A few of them left a legend behind, like the young Kartar Singh Sarabha who had gone about seducing the soldiers with astounding audacity and faced the trial with cool courage, ready to lay down his life in 'the struggle for India's freedom'.[38]

Like the Punjabi labourers repatriated in 1914 and 1915, the Ghada-

---

[38] *Ibid.*, 161; 'Sarabha, Kartar Singh', *Dictionary of National Biography* (ed. S. P. Sen), Institute of Historical Studies, Calcutta, 1974.

rites who returned to the Punjab to fight for the freedom of the country belonged overwhelmingly to the central Punjab, and they were overwhelmingly Sikh. Some of their leaders recalled later that they had been inspired by the novels of Bhai Vir Singh and the *Panth Prakāsh* of Giani Gian Singh to live or die heroically. The non-Sikh revolutionary leaders made an important contribution in terms of the goal and the direction. In the process, the rank and file of the Ghadarites as well as their Sikh leaders acquired a genuinely 'national' outlook. Their source of inspiration, however, remained almost exclusively Sikh. Appeal to their religious sentiment was made in many an article or a poem in the *Ghadar*, though for a secular end. It was implied that love, whether of God or the country, demanded sacrifice. To fight against tyranny of this kind was presented as the duty of a true Sikh. To take up the sword as a last resort was an injunction of Guru Gobind Singh. The memory of Sikh heroes and martyrs was evoked. The Sikh heritage of struggle was presented in terms of a struggle for liberation, substituting the Khālsā Panth by the country. Not indifference to faith but secular interpretation of the heritage came to divide them from the Singh reformers of the Punjab.

CHAPTER 8

IN THE STRUGGLE FOR FREEDOM
(1920–1947)

The phase of about three decades from the end of the First World War to the Act of Independence in 1947 was marked by intense political activity appearing first in the form of the Act of 1935 and then in the form of independence and partition. However, the struggle for freedom was not always constitutional; it was also agitational, and even militant. The Sikhs participated in the struggle for freedom in all its forms.

I

In a general meeting of the Sikh leaders at Lahore in March, 1919, a new political party known as the Central Sikh League was announced, and it was formally inaugurated at Amritsar in the last week of December. The immediate and long-term objectives of the new party were put forth in the first issue of its organ, the *Akālī*: to rebuild the demolished wall of the Rakabganj Gurdwara, to bring the Khalsa College at Amritsar under the control of the representatives of the Sikh community, to liberate *gurdwāras* from the control of the *mahants*, and to inspire the Sikhs to participate in the struggle for the country's freedom.[1]

The Rakabganj issue was taken up by the Central Sikh League when a few of the prominent individuals who had participated in the agitation of 1914 approached Sardul Singh Caveeshar at Lahore to revive the agitation. Caveeshar issued an appeal in the *Akālī* of September 2, 1920: 'Wanted 100 martyrs to save *gurdwāras*'. Within a fortnight, he received 700 offers. The method and the mood had changed. Before the band of martyrs (*shahīdī jathā*) led by Sardul Singh reached Delhi to construct the demolished wall, the government had reconstructed the wall at its own expense and handed over the Gurdwara to the Khalsa Diwan of Delhi.

[1] Harjot Singh, 'From Gurdwara Rakabganj to the Viceregal Palace – A Study of Religious Protest', *The Punjab Past and Present*, Vol. 14, Part 1 (April 1980), 182–98. The *Akālī* was the new name given in May 1920, to the *Khālsā Akhbār*, a weekly published by Harchand Singh of Lyallpur.

The control of the Khalsa College at Amritsar was restored to the representatives of the Sikhs in November, 1920. The Central Sikh League in its second annual session at Lahore on 20 October 1920, had resolved to support the non-cooperation movement. The teachers and students of the Khalsa College demanded that the College should refuse grant-in-aid from the government. The management of the College since 1908 had been entrusted to the Deputy Commissioner of Amritsar ostensibly on financial but intrinsically on political grounds. When the College Council passed a resolution on October 31 against receiving any grant from the government, no basis was left for government control over the management of the College. Sunder Singh Majithia became President of the Managing Committee in place of the Deputy Commissioner of Amritsar.[2]

This development was overshadowed by what was happening at the Golden Temple. The Central Sikh League had demanded that 'this foremost seat of Sikh faith should be placed in the hands of a representative body of the Sikhs, constituted on an elective basis and responsible for its action to the Panth at large'.[3] In the month of October, the Golden Temple and the Akāl Takht were taken over by the Singh reformers and placed under the management of a committee. The government appointed another committee consisting of thirty-six members, mostly from the Sikh aristocracy. The leaders of the Central Sikh League called a general meeting of the Sikhs in November. It was attended by more than 10,000 Sikhs who elected 175 members to form a managing committee for all Sikh gurdwāras. The comprehensive scope of its authority was implied in the name chosen for this committee: Shiromani Gurdwara Prabandhak Committee. It became responsible for launching a movement for liberating all gurdwāras from their custodians on behalf of the Sikh Panth. In this self-assigned task the Shiromani Committee was assisted by the Shiromani Akali Dal, formed at Amritsar in December, 1920, to coordinate the local bands of volunteers known as Akālī Jathās. Thus, within one year of the inauguration of the Central Sikh League, its concerns resulted in the formation of two organizations which were to play a vital role in the history of the Sikhs after 1920.

---

[2] Kashmir Singh, 'Managing Committee of Khalsa College Amritsar: Its Relations with British Government', *Proceedings Punjab History Conference*, Punjabi University, Patiala, 1983, 221–24.
[3] Quoted, Mohinder Singh, *The Akali Movement*, Macmillan, Delhi, 1978, 21.

II

With the direct and indirect support of the Central Sikh League and the Indian National Congress, the Shiromani Gurdwara Prabandhak Committee and the Shiromani Akali Dal started what a contemporary called 'the third Sikh war', a non-violent struggle against the government for the control of *gurdwāras*. On 25 January 1921, a band of about forty Akalis took over the Darbar Sahib at Tarn Taran from its *mahants* but not before two Akalis were killed and several of them were wounded by the henchmen employed by the *mahants*. In fact, a local *jathā* had been beaten up only a fortnight earlier. The *mahants* were ejected now and a managing committee was appointed by the Shiromani Gurdwara Prabandhak Committee.

The British administrators did not like the *gurdwāras* to pass under the control of managing committees appointed by the Shiromani Gurdwara Prabandhak Committee on behalf of the Sikh Panth. Their earlier posture that the control of a *gurdwāra* could be contested in a court of law was of little use to the *mahants* against the direct action launched by the Akalis. When the *mahant* of Nankana Sahib, Narain Das, approached the administrators for advice and support against the Akali threat of direct action, he was encouraged to make his own arrangements to meet the threat. Consequently when over a hundred Sikhs entered the Gurdwara at Nankana Sahib on 20 February 1921, without any intention yet of taking it over, they were attacked by the hired assassins of Mahant Narain Das. Most of them were killed or wounded, and burnt at the spot. The Akalis reached Nankana Sahib in thousands. The authorities arrested Mahant Narain Das and over a score of his hired assassins. On 3 March 1921, the Gurdwara was handed over to a committee, with Harbans Singh Atariwala as its President.[4]

In May, 1921, the Shiromani Gurdwara Prabandhak Committee passed a resolution in support of non-cooperation. It was clear that the Singh reformers had thrown in their lot with Mahatma Gandhi. The British administrators felt obliged to revise their policy of acquiescing in the increasing control of the Shiromani Gurdwara Prabandhak Committee over the *gurdwāras*. In October, 1921, the executive of the Shiromani Gurdwara Prabandhak Committee asked its secretary,

---

[4] Nankana Sahib was visited in the first week of March by Mahatma Gandhi, Maulana Shaukat Ali, Dr Saifuddin Kitchlew and Lajpat Rai, among others.

Sunder Singh Ramgarhia, who was also the officially appointed manager of the Golden Temple, to hand over the bunch of its fifty-three keys to Baba Kharak Singh, the President of the Shiromani Gurdwara Prabandhak Committee. Sunder Singh Ramgarhia sought the advice of the Deputy Commissioner who deputed his subordinate Lala Amar Nath to collect the keys from Sunder Singh Ramgarhia. The Shiromani Gurdwara Prabandhak Committee decided to hold protest meetings against this interference. The Akali protesters were arrested and awarded punishments. However, the number of protest meetings, arrests and punishments went on increasing till 17 January 1922, when all the Akali workers and leaders were released unconditionally and the keys of the Golden Temple were handed over to Baba Kharak Singh. The 'first decisive battle for India's freedom won' was the telegraphic message sent by Mahatma Gandhi to Baba Kharak Singh.[5]

The keys were delivered to the Shiromani Committee as a politic measure in view of the large proportion of the Sikhs in the army, a large number of disbanded Sikh soldiers, an unprecedented Hindu–Muslim solidarity on the Khilafat issue and the threat of an intensive civil disobedience at the beginning of 1922.[6] After the middle of the year, however, the situation appeared to have changed and the British administrators were inclined to humble the Akalis who, for their part, were feeling that Swaraj was the only remedy of all their troubles.[7]

The Mahant of the Gurdwara Guru Ka Bagh, near Ajnala in the Amritsar district, who had submitted to the Shiromani Committee nearly a year earlier was encouraged by the administrators to treat the Akalis as trespassers. The Akalis accepted the challenge and launched a *morchā* which became the most famous in the Akali struggle for the control of *gurdwāras*. On 9 August 1922, five Akalis who had chopped wood from the land adjoining the Gurdwara for the community kitchen (*langar*) were arrested and put on trial for theft. By August 25, the number of Akalis arrested rose to over 200. Pickets were placed on the road to Guru Ka Bagh and the gathering at the Bagh was declared to be an unlawful assembly. Akali volunteers continued to reach Amritsar

[5] Ganda Singh (ed.), *Some Confidential Papers of the Akali Movement*, SGPC, Amritsar, 1965, 11.

[6] John Maynard, 'The Sikh Problem in the Punjab, 1920–23', *The Punjab Past and Present*, Vol. 11, Part 1 (April 1977), 129–41. This article was originally published in the *Contemporary Review* in September, 1923.

[7] Sardul Singh Caveeshar, 'The Akali Movement', *The Punjab Past and Present*, Vol. 7, Part 1 (April 1973), 136.

and bands of fifty to 100 and even 200 Akalis continued to march from the Akāl Takht to the Guru Ka Bagh to suffer blows in passive resistance. By October 19, the number of Akalis arrested was more than 2,450. On October 25, a *jathā* consisting entirely of army pensioners reached Guru Ka Bagh under the leadership of a retired Subedar Major. This development was deemed to have dangerous implications. The Mahant was persuaded to sell the entire establishment to Sir Ganga Ram who, in turn, handed it over to the Akalis on 17 November 1922. In March, 1923, more than 5,000 Akali volunteers were released from jails in appreciation of the role of the Akalis in a situation of Hindu–Muslim riot in Amritsar. C. F. Andrews, who had visited the Guru Ka Bagh in September 1922 to be shocked by the brutality and inhumanity of the British administrators and their henchmen, admired the Akalis for their patient suffering without any sign of fear. In his eyes the Guru Ka Bagh *morchā* was a 'new lesson in moral warfare'.[8]

The last battle of 'the third Sikh war' was fought outside British territory in a neighbouring princely state. Maharaja Ripudaman Singh of Nabha was forced to abdicate in favour of his minor son on 9 July 1923. Because of his sympathy for the Singh reformers, the Shiromani Gurdwara Prabandhak Committee decided on August 4 to take up his cause. Meetings were held in protest. In a meeting held at Jaito in the Nabha state on August 25, the action of the government was condemned. The organizers of the meeting were arrested. New leaders started an *akhand-pāth*. It was disrupted. The Shiromani Gurdwara Prabandhak Committee condemned the official action and resolved to restore the Sikh right to free worship.

It was decided to send *jathās* from the Akāl Takht to Jaito for completing an *akhand-pāth* as a matter of right. On 12 October 1923, the Shiromani Akali Dal as well as the Shiromani Gurdwara Praban-dhak Committee were declared to be unlawful associations. All the sixty members of the *morchā* committee were arrested and charged with treason against the King–Emperor. New members replaced the old ones and *jathās* continued to reach Jaito. On 21 February 1924, a special *jathā* of 500 Akalis was sent to mark the third anniversary of the Nankana Sahib massacre. Its departure from the Golden Temple was witnessed by 30,000 people. The British administrators in Nabha decided to stop the *jathā* by firing at the Akalis. Three hundred

[8] Ruchi Ram Sahni, *Struggle for Freedom in Sikh Shrines*, SGPC, Amritsar nd, 176–83.

volunteers were injured, of whom a hundred eventually died. Nevertheless, *jathās* continued to march to Jaito till 101 *akhand-pāṭhs* were completed on 6 August 1925, and the right to free worship was firmly established.

Jawahar Lal Nehru who had marvelled at the courage and sacrifice of the Akalis during the Guru Ka Bagh *morchā*, was looking for an opportunity to show his deep admiration for them by some form of service. He visited Jaito during the *morchā* to be arrested, and rejoiced at being tried for a cause which the Sikhs had made their own. Indeed, the leaders of the Indian National Congress supported the Akalis in the Jaito *morchā* as they had supported them during the *morchā* at Guru Ka Bagh. However, after the release of Mahatma Gandhi on 5 February 1924, the Congress support became less enthusiastic. Mahatma Gandhi wanted the political issue of abdication to be completely separated from the religious issue. The Punjab Governor, Malcolm Hailey, was as much keen to separate the religious from the political issue as to split the Akali leadership, to divide their resources by opening new fronts and to alienate Hindus and Muslims from their cause by attributing political designs to them.[9]

Malcolm Hailey was nonetheless prepared to go a long way in conceding the demand with which the Akali movement had started. On 7 May 1925, a Bill was introduced in the Legislative Council and adopted on July 7. It received the assent of the Governor General in Council on July 28 and came into force on 1 November 1925. This Act recognized the Shiromani Gurdwara Prabandhak Committee as the legal authority to manage and control Sikh *gurdwāras*. With this constitutional recognition added to its links with the Sikh masses and control over a large number of important *gurdwāras*, the Shiromani Gurdwara Prabandhak Committee, popularly referred to as the SGPC, was well poised to overshadow the Chief Khalsa Diwan and to become the foremost Sikh institution of the twentieth century.[10]

During the five years of the Akali movement 400 persons suffered death, 2,000 were wounded and 30,000 men and women were jailed. The pensions and *jāgīrs* of many were withdrawn, fines were imposed and property was confiscated in the case of many others; many lost their jobs; soldiers were court-martialled for wearing *kirpān* or a black

---

[9] Mohinder Singh, *The Akali Movement*, Macmillan, Delhi, 1978, 62–86, 126–36.

[10] Gobinder Singh, *Religion and Politics in the Punjab*, Deep and Deep Publications, New Delhi, 1986.

turban; printers, publishers and editors suffered for their sympathy with the movement. As a contemporary put it, the British authorities soon came to believe that the Gurdwara Reform Movement was a subversive movement which aimed at overthrowing the British Raj and which therefore, it was necessary to suppress.[11] For Sardul Singh Caveeshar, freedom of religion and the freedom of the country went together. He regarded the Akali movement as 'only an offshoot of the national movement. The national spirit impregnated the Sikh hearts through and through; they desired to assume responsibility as much for the control and management of the temples as for the administration of the country.'[12]

In 1920 almost two-thirds of the Akalis were Jats, and 15 per cent of the protesters belonged to the low castes. This was broadly in proportion to their numbers in the Sikh population. The urban Singhs, who were mainly Khatrīs and Aroras, constituted nearly 19 per cent of the protesters, representing a much larger proportion than their number in the Sikh population. The number of recently returned immigrants was considerable among the Akali protesters and so was the role of former soldiers in the movement. The general impression carried by the contemporaries that the Akali movement found support from nearly all sections of the Sikh community was not wrong. According to Sardul Singh Caveeshar the Akali movement was 'preeminently the movement of the masses, of the humble folk recruited from among peasants, artisans and the labourers. Doctors, pleaders, editors, merchants and the professors were all in the movement but their number was very small.'[13]

III

All the Akalis did not appreciate passive resistance or non-violence as the political weapon to fight against the colonial rulers. A few of the Akali leaders and some old Ghadarites reacted sharply to the cold-blooded murder of a large number of Singh reformers at Nankana Sahib in February, 1921. A month later, when the Sikh Education Conference

[11] Bhagat Lakshman Singh, *Autobiobraphy* (ed. Ganda Singh), the Sikh Cultural Centre, Calcutta, 1965, 256.

[12] Sardul Singh Caveeshar, 'The Akali Movement', *The Punjab Past and Present*, Vol. 7, Part 1 (April 1973), 135.

[13] Sardul Singh Caveeshar, 140; Teja Singh, 'The Singh Sabha Movement', *The Punjab Past and Present*, Vol. 7, Part 1 (April 1973), 42.

met at Hoshiarpur, a few militant leaders found the opportunity to conspire revenge upon the persons who were deemed to be essentially responsible for the massacre at Nankana Sahib. Before the end of May, 1921, an unsuccessful attempt was made on the life of G. M. Bowring, the Superintendent of Police, and Sunder Singh Majithia. A few of the conspirators were arrested and the others absconded, including Master Mota Singh and Kishan Singh popularly known as Gargajj.

During the year following some of the militant leaders were arrested but the others were able to enlist more supporters to their programme. In August, 1922, an organization known as the Babbar Akali Jatha was formed with the twin objective of vindicating the Sikh faith and gaining political independence. The Babbar Akalis addressed themselves to demobilized soldiers as well as to the Singh reformers. They invited Hindus and Muslims too, for eliminating the British officials and their Indian and Punjabi supporters. They brought out fifteen issues of the *Babbar Akālī Doāba* from August 1922 to May 1923, from a press that moved from place to place to propagate their ideas in the districts of Jalandhar and Hoshiarpur. In 1923, they also undertook a campaign of political murders. Consequently, in August, 1923, the Babbar Akali Jatha was declared to be an unlawful association. In less than a year then, almost all the important Babbar Akalis were either eliminated or arrested. They were tried in courts and in the verdict given in February, 1925, it was imputed that their aim was to gain independence in India and Sikh rule in the Punjab. Six Babbars were hanged a year later, in February, 1926. Several organizations, including the Central Sikh League, issued appeals for raising a fund for the families of the Babbars who were hanged. Many a poet glorified their martyrdom.

Bhagat Singh, a nephew of Ajit Singh, founded the Naujawan Bharat Sabha which organized public meetings in Lahore from March, 1926 to April, 1927. It remained dormant for about a year till it was revived in April, 1928. The declared aim of the Sabha was to organize labourers and peasants for establishing an independent Republic in India with all its inhabitants forming a united Indian Nation. Bhagat Singh and his comrades subscribed to the idea that 'a single deed makes more propaganda in a few days than a thousand pamphlets'. Nevertheless, in the sessions of the Naujawan Bharat Sabha in 1929, the ideas expressed were not only anti-British and revolutionary but also socialistic. One session was presided over by Sohan Singh Josh who is well known as both an Akali and a Communist leader; the other session held at

Amritsar in August was attended by Jawaharlal Nehru. There was rather a close link between the Indian National Congress and the Naujawan Bharat Sabha. In 1928, the Sabha supported the Congress in its protest demonstration against the Simon Commission. Lord Irwin observed that the activities of the Sabha and the Congress in the Punjab had been 'identical'.

At about his time, however, Bhagat Singh was activating the Hindustan Socialist Republican Association with the help of Sukhdev and Bhagwati Charan. The objective of the Association was not merely the freedom of India from foreign rule but also the restructuring of society on socialist principles. However, their approach was militant. In fact, they came to regard the civil disobedience movement as a failure. They favoured violence in the cause of justice. In their 'philosophy of the bomb', it was legitimate to make 'loud noise to make the deaf hear'. The two best-known incidents in which the leaders of the Association took an active part exemplified their basic attitude: the murder of J. P. Saunders, who was thought to be responsible for Lajpat Rai's death, on 17 December 1928 and the throwing of a bomb in the Legislative Assembly in Delhi on 8 April 1929. Such activities continued for some time more under the leadership of Yash Pal but militant nationalism lost its appeal soon after the execution of Bhagat Singh, Sukhdev and Rajguru on 23 March 1932.[14]

Of all the militant revolutionaries, Bhagat Singh, towards the end of his life, had probably the best grasp of the rationale and the implications of socialist revolution. In one of his articles published in September 1931 he states that before the end of 1926 he was convinced of the baselessness of 'the theory of existence of an almighty supreme being who created, guided and controlled the universe'. Such a theory, in his view, was refuted by the existence of human misery. Furthermore, it went against the progressive assumption that it was necessary for man to establish his domination over nature. Thus, there was a close connection between Bhagat Singh's atheistic position and his ideology of social progress. To fight against the alien rulers was a laudable objective but not a 'revolutionary idea'. Revolution for Bhagat Singh meant a 'systematic reconstruction' of society after a 'complete destruction' of the existing order. Such a revolutionary social reconstruction could not be based on a teleological or meta-

[14] Kamlesh Mohan, *Militant Nationalism in the Punjab, 1919–1935*, Manohar, New Delhi, 1985, 146–95.

physical interpretation of the universe; it needed a rational and causal world-view.[15]

The influence of the Russian Revolution was more clearly visible in the Kirti Kisan Party which drew its support from the former Ghadarites as well as from some Akalis and Babbars. The Ghadar Party in California had sent Santokh Singh and Rattan Singh as its representatives to the fourth Congress of the Communist International in November, 1922. They left Moscow for India in 1923 but Santokh Singh, who was a founder member of the Ghadar Party, was confined to his village for two years by the police authorities of the Punjab. Towards the end of 1925 he moved to Amritsar and started the *Kirti* with the help of two other Ghadarites, Bhag Singh Canadian and Karam Singh Cheema. Like the *Ghadar* and the *Babbar Akāli Doāba*, the *Kirti* made use of verses from the Sikh scriptures. It showed great concern for liberating the working class from the bourgeois ideology. In April, 1928, in a meeting called by Sohan Singh Josh and Bhag Singh Canadian and held at the Jallianwala Bagh in Amritsar, it was resolved to establish a party to organize workers and peasants. The name chosen for it was appropriately the Kirti Kisan Party. Nearly all the leaders of the party were Sikhs, with a rural or revolutionary background. Unlike the Naujawan Bharat Sabha, the Kirti Kisan Party was opposed to the Indian National Congress. The Kirtis supported the idea of expropriating large landholders though they did not subscribe to cooperative farming. They advocated an increase in wages and a reduction in revenues and water rates. In September 1934, the Kirti Kisan Party was one of several organizations which were declared illegal and dissolved.

IV

Notwithstanding the preoccupation of the majority of the politically articulate Sikhs with agitational and militant politics, the working of the Act of 1919 and the formulation of the Act of 1935 remained central to the politics of the Punjab. Sikh representation in the Imperial Council and Legislature was rather marginal. The Sikhs had only one out of the four seats meant for the Punjab in the Council of States. In the Legislative Assembly they had only two seats out of the eleven for the Punjab. The twelfth seat for the Punjab was meant for landholders,

---

[15] Bhagat Singh, *Why I Am An Atheist*, Shahid Bhagat Singh Research Committee, Delhi, 1979.

including the Sikhs. In all, thirteen Sikhs were represented on both these bodies between 1919 and 1947.[16]

Sikh participation in the Legislative Council of the Punjab was only a little more satisfactory. The Sikhs had thirteen seats out of a total of seventy-one. One of these thirteen seats was meant for the urban contituency and another for the constituency of landholders. Elections to the Council were held in 1920, 1923, 1926 and 1930. During all these years, forty-six persons represented the Sikhs in the Legislative Council, which indicates that the membership of the Council changed rather frequently. Only a few candidates were elected twice or thrice. Though most of the candidates fought elections in their individual capacity, parties began gradually to be formed.[17]

Between 1920 and 1937, the Punjab Legislative Council was dominated by the Unionist Party. Formed initially by Fazl-i-Husain as the Rural Party from amongst the Muslim, Hindu and Sikh members elected to the Council in 1920, it came to be known as the Unionist Party by the time of the second elections and dominated the constitutional politics of the Punjab for nearly a quarter of a century till its defeat in the elections of 1946. Two other political parties contested the elections in 1923, namely the Swarajists and the Hindu Nationalist Party. Two of the Sikh members elected to the Council were sponsored by the Shiromani Gurdwara Prabandhak Committee. The Congress contested elections only in 1926 and won a few seats. In 1930, the elections were boycotted not only by the Congress but also by the Central Sikh League and the Akalis. The field, thus, was left wide open for the Unionists. The Sikh legislators who collaborated with them were either independents or leaders of the Chief Khalsa Diwan. The ministers were appointed by the Governor without reference to any political party. The Sikh legislators who became ministers were Sunder Singh Majithia and, in his absence, Joginder Singh. Sikh representation in the Government as well as the Council remained rather unsatisfactory from the viewpoint of the new Sikh leaders.[18]

The Unionist Party professed to be representative of the rural classes, irrespective of religious differences, and to safeguard the interests of all landholders. In actual operation, however, its Muslim

---

[16] The federal provisions of the Act of 1935 were never implemented. Therefore the Act of 1919 remained operative till the formation of the interim government in 1946.

[17] Kripal C. Yadav, *Elections in Panjab, 1920–1947*, Manohar, Delhi, 1987.

[18] The Sikh minister did not represent the Sikh legislators; they, in turn, did not necessarily represent the Singh reformers.

leaders gave preference to Muslim interests and the interests of the richer landholders. The Reform Enquiry Committee observed in 1924 that the Ministry of Education, which was headed by Fazl-i-Husain himself, had subordinated the interests of its departments to 'the support of the communal interests of the Mohammadans'.[19] Separate electorates were extended by the Unionists to municipal bodies, and reservation was introduced in educational institutions. In 1932, they improved the proportion of Muslims in services from the older ratio of 40, 40 and 20 for Muslims, Hindus and Sikhs respectively to 50, 30 and 20.

The working of the 'transferred' departments under the Unionists largely determined the attitude of the Sikhs towards constitutional reform. The Central Sikh League asked for abandoning communal representation or weightage for the Sikhs. The Akalis as well as the Central Sikh League decided to boycott the Simon Commission and to hold protest demonstrations jointly with the Congress. The Chief Khalsa Diwan submitted a memorandum to the commission asking for reservations and constitutional safeguards for the Sikhs. The moderate Sikh leaders formed the Central Sikh Association to represent the Sikh case before the Commission; they asked for 30 per cent representation each for the Sikhs and the Hindus. The Unionists, who appeared to represent the majority view, asked for the maintenance of communal electorates and for greater autonomy and power for the province.

The Akali and the Central Sikh League leaders attended the All Parties Conference at Delhi in February, 1928 and Mangal Singh Gill became a member of the Moti Lal Nehru Committee to frame a constitution for India as an alternative to the proceedings of the Simon Commission. The report prepared by the committee recommended separate electorates for Muslims in provinces other than the Punjab and Bengal. When the report was taken up in the All Parties meeting at Lucknow in August, the Sikh delegates raised the issue regarding their position in the Punjab. Some of them demanded that if separate electorates or weightage was to be maintained for minorities in other provinces then a similar provision should be made for the Sikhs. Most of the Sikh leaders dreaded the prospect of universal suffrage without reservation of seats for the Sikhs as a minority.

The Central Sikh League decided to reject the Nehru Report and to

---

[19] Quoted, K. L. Tuteja, *Sikh Politics (1920–40)*, Vishal Publications, Kuruskshetra, 1984, 136.

boycott the Congress session scheduled to be held at Lahore. Mahatma Gandhi, Moti Lal Nehru and M. A. Ansari met Master Tara Singh and Baba Kharak Singh to inform them that the Congress Working Committee had replaced the goal of Dominion Status by 'complete independence', an objective on which Baba Kharak Singh had been insisting. The Sikh leaders were persuaded to participate in the Congress session at Lahore towards the end of 1929. In this session the resolution for 'complete independence' was passed. Furthermore, the Congress gave explicit assurance to the minorities that no constitution would be acceptable to the Congress if it did not give 'full satisfaction' to the Sikhs and the Muslims as minorities. Baba Kharak Singh, Master Tara Singh and other Sikh leaders felt satisfied with this declaration of Congress intentions. Sikh participation in the celebration of Independence Day on 26 January 1930 was marked by enthusiasm. When Mahatma Gandhi launched Civil Disobedience in March, 1930, Baba Kharak Singh refused to join unless the Sikh colour was included in the national flag, but the Shiromani Akali Dal and the Central Sikh League decided to join the Civil Disobedience. The Shiromani Gurdwara Prabandhak Committee joined the movement after the firing incident at the Sisganj Gurdwara in Delhi.

The report of the Simon Commission appeared in June, 1930, retaining communal electorates and reservations. It was rejected by the Sikh leaders. In response to a call from the Congress they decided to boycott the elections in August. They also decided to boycott the First Round Table Conference. Ujjal Singh and Sampuran Singh, who were invited to the Conference, did not represent the Akalis or the Central Sikh League. In March, 1931, when the Gandhi-Irwin Pact was signed, the Central Sikh League decided to participate in the Second Round Table Conference. Master Tara Singh presented a memorandum to Mahatma Gandhi which contained a proposal to alter the boundaries of the Punjab to give larger representation to Hindus and Sikhs in addition to reservation of seats for the Sikhs on the basis of joint electorates.

In August, Ramsay MacDonald announced his award, popularly known as the Communal Award, which retained separate electorates and reinforced reservations. What was galling for the Sikh leaders was the proposed distribution of seats in the Punjab Legislative Council: eighty-eight for Muslims, forty-four for Hindus and thirty-three for Sikhs. The only party that found the award satisfactory was the

Unionist party. The Sikh leaders were strongly opposed to the award but the Congress remained neutral. This award was to become the basis of the Act in 1935 with greater autonomy to the provinces.[20]

The Sikh leaders tried unsuccessfully to ensure that the 'communal award' did not become the basis of formal legislation. As a significant result of their activity of these few years the Shiromani Akali Dal emerged as an important political party of the Sikhs. In a general meeting of the Sikhs held in September, 1932, it was decided to form the Khalsa Darbar to present a united front against the 'communal award'. However, in its second meeting held in the year following, Baba Kharak Singh and his supporters dissociated themselves from the Darbar and tried to raise parallel organizations, while the Central Sikh League was merged with the Khalsa Darbar. A further split in the Darbar on the eve of the elections of 1937 divided its leaders into two camps: the Shiromani Akali Dal and the Congressite Sikhs. The Central Sikh League became extinct in the process.

V

In the election to the Punjab Legislative Assembly in 1937 about a dozen political parties took part. The most successful were the Unionists who won ninety-five out of the total 175 seats. In forming the government, they were joined by the legislators elected on the ticket of the Khalsa National Party which represented the leaders of the Chief Khalsa Diwan and the Hindu Election Board which represented the non-Congress Hindu leaders. In the opposition eighteen legislators belonged to the Indian National Congress and ten to the Shiromani Akali Dal. One or two seats each were won by the Muslim League, the Congress Nationalists, the Socialists, the Majlis-i-Ahrar and the Itihad-i-Millat, and there were nineteen independent legislators. Prominent among the Khalsa Nationals were Sunder Singh Majithia, Ujjal Singh, Joginder Singh and Dasaundha Singh. Among the Akalis, there were Baldev Singh, Giani Kartar Singh, Partap Singh Kairon, Sampuran Singh and Kapur Singh. Under Sikandar Hayat and Khizr Hayat Khan as the Unionist Premiers, Sunder Singh Majithia was succeeded on his death in 1941 as a minister by Dasaundha Singh who

---

[20] By the Act of 1935 the provincial governments were made 'completely autonomous and they and the central government acted in mutually excluded spheres of administration': V. P. Menon, *The Transfer of Power in India*, Orient Longman, New Delhi, 1979 (reprint), 52.

was replaced by Baldev Singh in June, 1942. There remained only one Sikh minister at a time now as before, though the number of ministers in the province increased from three in the 1920s to six in the 1940s.[21]

After the formation of the ministry in 1937 the first important political development was Sikandar Hayat Khan's agreement with Jinnah at Lucknow in October, 1937. It made all Muslim legislators of the Punjab Unionists within the province but Muslim Leaguers outside the province. In reaction, Gokul Chand Narang left the Unionists. Sunder Singh Majithia did not leave the Unionists but only because of Sikandar's reassurance that there would be no change in the policies of the Unionist Party. There was no need. As Khizr Hayat Khan was to point out later, the policies of the Unionist Party had enabled 'the backward' Muslim community of the Punjab to compare 'favourably with any in India or even elsewhere' and the Muslims were surely the 'predominant community' of the province.[22] The Sikandar-Jinnah agreement brought the Akalis and the Congress leaders formally closer to one another. In November, 1938, when the All-India Akali Conference was held at Rawalpindi, the Akali and Congress flags were hoisted together, and the Akali leaders appreciated the Congress as the only representative political party in the country, a true trustee of national honour and self respect.

Much more important than the Sikandar-Jinnah agreement was the outbreak of war in September, 1939. The Unionists offered unconditional support. The Chief Khalsa Diwan was equally prompt, though it wished the government in turn to safeguard Sikh rights and privileges, culture and religious liberty. The Shiromani Akali Dal wanted the government to declare its war aims, following thus the Congress lead on this issue. Unlike the Congress, however, the Akali Dal did not relish the prospect of being isolated in the Punjab on the issue of war effort. Master Tara Singh tried to persuade the Congress through Mahatma Gandhi that the Sikhs might participate in the war effort, but only to receive a categorical and rather strong disapproval from the Mahatma. Before the end of 1940 Master Tara Singh felt obliged to resign from the Congress Working Committee.[23]

[21] This fact was pointed out as a grievance by Sikh leaders in the 1940s.
[22] Khizr Hayat Khan Tiwana, 'The 1937 Elections and the Sikandar-Jinnah Pact' (ed. Craig Baxter), *The Punjab Past and Present*, Vol. 10, Part 2 (October 1976), 356–85.
[23] K. L. Tuteja, *Sikh Politics (1920–40)*, 193–95; Jaswant Singh (ed.), *Master Tara Singh*, Pbi, Amritsar, 1972, 168–70. Combining the evidence cited in these works it becomes clear how thin was the line between 'communalism' and 'nationalism' in the minds of the leaders.

By this time, the Akali leaders were not feeling happy with the Congress because of its indifference to the resolution of the Muslim League, passed at Lahore in March, 1940, which appeared to demand separate states in the Muslim majority areas in the north-west and the north-east of the subcontinent. Sikandar Hayat Khan clarified his position in a forceful speech in the Assembly, making an appeal to the Punjabi sentiment of its members.[24] Nevertheless, the resolution of the Muslim League, popularly referred to as the 'Pakistan Resolution', was denounced at the All-India Akali Conference. Dr V. S. Bhatti of Ludhiana published a pamphlet demanding 'Khalistan' as a buffer state between India and 'Pakistan'. That the idea of Khalistan was meant merely to oppose the idea of Pakistan is evident from the frequent use of the phrase 'if Pakistan is to be conceded'. On 1 December 1940, a general conference of the Sikhs was convened at Lahore to pass a resolution against the formation of Pakistan. Throughout 1940, however, the Congress did not formally react to the 'Pakistan Resolution', treating the idea as fantastic.

By the beginning of 1941, the Shiromani Akali Dal was finally committed to support the war effort. The Khalsa Defence League was formed in January, 1941, under the leadership of the Maharaja of Patiala with the sympathy and support of Master Tara Singh and Giani Kartar Singh among others. Confrontation with the government in the early 1920s had resulted in the decrease of Sikh soldiers in the Indian army. The Akalis were afraid of further loss on this account. The government was equally keen to enlist their entire support during the war. Sikandar was encouraged to forge a link with the Akali leaders. In March, 1942, Baldev Singh formed a new party in the Assembly under the label of United Punjab Sikh Party, consisting initially of a few Akali and independent legislators. Three months later he joined the ministry on the basis of an agreement with Sikandar Hayat Khan. The British administrators looked upon the pact with great satisfaction. Like the leaders of the left parties, only a handful of Akalis took part in the Quit India Movement in August, 1942. For the time being, the Second World War became for them all 'the war for freedom' (jang-i-āzādī).

---

[24] V. P. Menon, *The Transfer of Power in India*, 443–58. Sikandar was applauded when he referred to 'our province, our motherland' as 'the sword arm' of India and asked the Punjabis to stand united to tell the meddling busybodies from outside, 'hands off the Punjab'.

Neither the Sikandar-Baldev Singh pact nor the Quit India Resolution of the Congress was so important to the Sikhs as the spectre of partition which appeared on the horizon of Indian politics in 1942. The mission of Stafford Cripps appeared to concede Pakistan in principle. The experience of 'Muslim' domination in the province in the form of the Unionist politics which concealed Muslim partialities under a Punjabi front obliged the Akalis to dread the prospect of its perpetuation. Therefore, the Sikhs in general and the Akalis in particular denounced the principle of partition even more than the fact of the constitutional domination by a single community in the province. Master Tara Singh and Giani Kartar Singh declared that Pakistan could be formed only over 'their dead bodies'.

The idea put forth by Master Tara Singh in his memorandum to Mahatma Gandhi in 1931 became much more relevant now. Master Tara Singh wrote to Stafford Cripps that, since the Sikhs could not dominate in any large area because of their more or less thin distribution over the province, it was unthinkable to demand domination. However, a province could certainly be carved out 'in which the Sikhs are dominated by no single community'.[25] This was the basis of the Azad Punjab Scheme which the Akalis tried to clarify and popularize for about two years as an alternative to the Cripps Proposals.

The use of the word *āzād* gave the wrong impression that the proposed Punjab was meant to be an independent state. The Sikhs and Hindus of the western districts, particularly in the Rawalpindi Division, were opposed to it because of their implied exclusion. The Akali leaders tried to clarify their position and to justify their demand to all fair-minded Punjabis. Master Tara Singh declared in December, 1942, that the Punjab he visualized would consist of 40 per cent Muslims, 40 per cent Hindus and 20 per cent Sikhs. Again, in March, 1943, he asserted that by creating Azad Punjab, the Sikhs and Hindus will get rid of the spectre of Pakistan. By the middle of 1943, Master Tara Singh felt obliged to refer to his memorandum of 1931 to make it clear that the Sikhs were not in a majority anywhere to ask for a Sikh state. He insisted that they wished to remain in India and should not be forced to get out. In this context Sadhu Singh Hamdard published a booklet in

[25] Quoted, Kirpal Singh, *The Partition of the Punjab*, Punjabi University, Patiala, 1972, 10.

1943 giving the background, the objectives and the boundaries of the Azad Punjab.[26]

In 1944 C. Rajagopalachari came out with his famous formula involving the principle not only of the partition of the country but also of the possible partition of Bengal and the Punjab. Apparently, he had the blessings of Mahatma Gandhi and his proposal in the popular mind came to be associated with the Congress. The Sikhs reacted sharply to the formula. In August, 1944, an All Parties Sikh Conference under the presidentship of Baldev Singh came to the conclusion that, since it set aside the Lahore resolution of 1929, it was a breach of faith by the Congress. Therefore, in a general meeting of the Sikhs on August 20–21 at Amritsar it was resolved that no settlement would be acceptable to the Sikhs if it was not based on their prior consent. In October, 1944, the Akali leaders thought of a Sikh state as an alternative to Pakistan but their main grievance was that the Congress had not kept its promise of 1929. Mahatma Gandhi reassured Durlabh Singh that the Lahore resolution of the Congress was still valid. By this time Gandhi-Jinnah talks had broken down and Jinnah had rejected Rajagopalachari's formula as the basis of any understanding with the Congress. In their memorandum to the Sapru Committee, the Sikhs reiterated that if Pakistan was to be conceded the Sikhs would insist on the creation of a state with a substantial Sikh population and provision for transfer of population and property. But even after the Simla conference in 1945 the Sikh leaders were hoping that the demand for Pakistan would not be conceded.

VI

The Akalis fought the elections of 1946 independently of the Congress but in support of the unity and integrity of the country. They could come to an understanding with the Congress only in four constituencies which were believed to be the stronghold of the Communists whom the Congress leaders had not forgiven after what was regarded as their betrayal at the time of the Quit India Movement, and whom the Akalis denounced as atheists. Ironically, the election manifesto of the Communists underlined the justification for a Sikh state as much as for

[26] Published anonymously in the middle of 1943, the *Āzād Punjab* was brought out for the second time under the author's name before the year ended. It contains a map showing the area of the proposed Āzād Punjab from the Jamuna to the Chenab.

Pakistan.[27] They believed that in espousing the principle of self-determination for cultural minorities they were only being consistent. They failed to win even a single seat. The largest number of seats were won by the Muslim League, seventy-four out of 175; the Congress came out second with fifty-one seats, including ten Sikh seats; the Akalis won the remaining twenty-three of the Sikh seats, the Unionists won only twenty-one seats, with only twelve Muslim legislators. The Muslim League and the Akalis had fought elections on the issue of Pakistan, ranged on opposite sides. The cleavage was clearly reflected in the election results. The Akalis emerged as the sole representatives of the Sikhs on the issue of Pakistan and partition.

The single largest party in the legislature, the Muslim League failed to form a ministry primarily because no other political party in the Punjab was willing to form a coalition with its leaders. Jawaharlal Nehru was inclined to support the League in principle because of its mass base, but Maulana Abul Kalam Azad as the Congress President had already decided in favour of a coalition with the Unionists and the Akalis, and he had the support of Mahatma Gandhi. Khizr Hayat Khan Tiwana formed the coalition ministry in March, 1946. This 'makeshift coalition' merely glossed over a position in which practically all Muslims were on one side and nearly all non-Muslims on the other. Punjabis ceased to be Punjabis and became Muslims, Hindus and Sikhs. Until the ministry resigned in March, 1947, the Punjab Governor thought he was 'the only member of the Government who could meet members of the opposition naturally and without constraint'.[28] The major concern of the ministry was to maintain law and order in face of the mounting communal tension.

The results of the elections convinced the Sikhs that the possibility of Pakistan had turned into a probability. In any case, when the mission of the British Cabinet ministers arrived in New Delhi, the most outstanding issue of the moment was a united India versus Pakistan. The case of the Sikh community was presented to the Cabinet Mission first by Master Tara Singh, Giani Kartar Singh and Harnam Singh together as the Sikh leaders and then by Baldev Singh alone as the Sikh minister. They were asked specially to express their views on whether they favoured a united India or its division, and in the case of its

---

[27] Dr G. Adhikari, the author of the *Sikh Homeland Through Hindu-Muslim-Sikh Unity*, Bombay, 1944, wrote the election manifesto of the Communist Party.

[28] Larry Collins and Dominique Lapierre (eds), *Mountbatten and the Partition of India*, Vikas Publishing House, New Delhi, 1982, 133.

division whether they would join India or Pakistan, or would they like to have a state of their own. They were all opposed to the creation of Pakistan. But if Pakistan was to be created they opted for a Sikh state. Master Tara Singh wanted the right for a separate independent Sikh state to federate with Hindustan or Pakistan. However, the Sikh state or Khalistan of the Sikh leaders was still synonymous with an area in which no single community was in absolute majority.[29]

The proposals of the Cabinet Mission, embodied in their statement of 16 May 1946, gave a serious jolt to the Sikhs. Whereas the Congress leaders could see in this statement the possibility of a virtual federation in a united India and the Muslim League a virtual Pakistan, the Sikhs could see nothing but their perpetual subjection to a Muslim majority in the Punjab. Master Tara Singh wrote to Pethic-Lawrence on May 25 that a wave of dejection, resentment and indignation had run through the Sikh community because the Cabinet Mission Proposals would place the Sikhs permanently at the mercy of the Muslim majority. In an all-parties conference of the Sikhs at Amritsar on 10 June 1946, the Cabinet Mission Proposals were rejected.[30]

Before the Cabinet Mission left India on June 29, the Akali leaders rejected the interim proposals as well. An organization called the Panthic Pratinidhi Board was formed as a representative body of nearly all Sikh organizations. Its formation symbolized the will of the Sikh community to fight against the dreaded domination of Pakistan. It resolved to accept no constitution that did not meet their just demands. Within a fortnight of this resolution the Panthic Board was faced with the concrete issue whether or not Baldev Singh should join the interim government. The Board decided against his joining the government.

By early September, however, the Sikh leaders accepted both the long-term and the interim proposals. On June 25, the Congress Working Committee had noted among other things the unfairness of the Cabinet Mission Proposals to some of the minorities, especially the Sikhs; the Congress rejected the idea of joining the interim government but decided to join the Constituent Assembly. At Wardha on August 8, however, the Congress Working Committee turned in favour of Jawaharlal Nehru forming the interim government. Baldev Singh asked Attlee to intervene for undoing the wrong done to the Sikhs. Attlee

[29] V. P. Menon, *The Transfer of Power in India*, 242–43. Even when the Sikh leaders talked of a 'Sikh State', or 'Khalistan', or 'Sikhistan', they did not think of a territory in which the Sikhs would form a majority.

[30] *Ibid.*, 272.

referred the matter to the Congress President through the Viceroy, advising Baldev Singh at the same time that the Sikhs should join the Constituent Assembly. The Congress Working Committee passed a resolution assuring the Sikhs of all possible support in removing their legitimate grievances and in securing adequate safeguards for the protection of their just interests in the Punjab. In response, the Panthic Pratinidhi Board decided to accept the statement of 16 May 1946, and to send their representatives to the Constituent Assembly. Baldev Singh joined the interim government as Defence Minister on 2 September 1946.

VII

Early in August, 1946, the Punjab Governor had noticed that the League resolution of direct action passed in July was bringing the Sikhs closer to the Congress. After Baldev Singh joined the interim government, Swaran Singh became the leader of the Akali legislators and signed a pact with Bhim Sen Sachar to ensure unity of action among the Congress and Akali members of the Assembly. The opponents of Sachar in the Punjab Congress raised objection to the Akali-Congress pact but the Congress President, Acharya Kriplani, ruled that Sachar was within his rights to enter such an understanding with the Akalis in the Legislative Assembly.

This renewed understanding enabled the Akalis to convince the leaders of the Congress that the best way to safeguard the interests of the minorities in the Punjab was to divide the province into two units. The Sikh leaders were against the idea of compulsory grouping of provinces. On 5 January 1947, in a meeting of the All India Congress Committee, Jawaharlal Nehru moved the resolution that the Congress could not be a party to compulsion. 'In the event of any attempt at such compulsion, a province or part of a province has the right to take such action as may be deemed necessary in order to give effect to the wishes of the people concerned.'[31] A few days later Mangal Singh Gill made the statement that partition of the Punjab into two parts was the 'only solution which would help the Sikhs'. When Wavell pressed upon Nehru the necessity of getting the Muslim League into the Constituent Assembly, Nehru argued that 'it was only logical that large minorities inside a province, such as the Hindus in Bengal and the Hindus and

[31] *Ibid.*, 332.

Sikhs in the Punjab, could also not be compelled into an unacceptable constitution'.[32]

To the attraction of the idea of partition was added an element of necessity by the mounting violence in the Punjab. Balked in their aspiration to form a ministry the leaders of the Muslim League had concentrated their energies upon bringing down the ministry of Khizr Hayat, resorting to direct action against what they regarded as the suppression of civil liberties. In January, 1947, Khizr Hayat Khan banned the National Guards, and the Muslim League started a civil disobedience movement. With the pace of this movement rose the pitch of communal tension. The Hindu and Sikh legislators of the Punjab wanted Khizr Hayat Khan to suppress the agitation; the agitators wanted him to join the League or resign. On March 2, he decided suddenly to resign. On March 3 the leaders of the Congress and the Sikhs made violent speeches to leave no scope for the League to form a coalition. Riots broke out in Lahore on the day following, and spread later to Amritsar, Multan, Rawalpindi, Jalandhar and Sialkot. With reference to these events the Congress Working Committee, in its meeting on March 5, resolved that 'in order to avoid compulsion of any section, the province should be divided into two parts so that the predominantly Muslim portion might be separated from the predominantly non-Muslim portion'.[33] This resolution had 'a tremendous reassuring effect' on the Hindus and Sikhs of the Punjab.

Ten days after his arrival in India in March, 1947, Mountbatten noted that all parties in the Punjab were seriously preparing for civil war, and of these 'by far the most business-like and serious are the Sikhs'.[34] He was inclined to think that the partition of the province was really inevitable. On the Governor's suggestion he decided to meet the Sikh leaders. He met Master Tara Singh, Giani Kartar Singh and Baldev Singh on April 18. They were emphatic that the Sikhs would fight to the last man if put under Muslim domination. They invoked property and religious or historical associations as the criteria of partition and talked of 'Sikhistan' with the option to join either Hindustan or Pakistan to extort the largest possible concessions in terms of territory. Mountbatten, however, was not yet inclined to give them any areas

[32] *Ibid.*, 339.
[33] *Ibid.*, 346–47. This resolution was approved by the Congress on 8 April 1947: Kirpal Singh, *The Partition of the Punjab*, 28.
[34] Larry Collins and Dominique Lapierre (eds), *Mountbatten and the Partition of India*, 118.

where Muslim population was predominant.[35] By April 30, the Punjab Governor reported to Mountbatten that the Sikhs were deeply, almost finally, committed to partition. Nehru had declared in a public speech already on April 20 that the Muslim League could have Pakistan on the condition that 'they do not take away other parts of India which do not wish to join Pakistan'.[36] Rajendra Prasad as the President of the Constitutent Assembly told its members a week later that they might have to draw up a constitution based on the division of provinces. At the beginning of May a resolution was passed by the non-Muslim legislators of the Punjab that a just and equitable division of the province was the only solution of the political problem of the Punjab.

In the month of May, events took a dramatic turn. The idea of Dominion Status was brought back into focus. Mountbatten was able to present a new plan on June 2 in a conference with Nehru, Patel, Kriplani, Jinnah, Liaqat Ali Khan, Abdur Rab Nishtar and Baldev Singh. Partition of the country and partition of the Punjab and Bengal was built into the new proposal. Therefore, the question now before the Congress and the Akalis was to get as much territory as they possibly could from the British province of the Punjab for the East Punjab of the Indian Union. As it could be easily anticipated by now, all the non-Muslim legislators of the Punjab opted for the Indian Union, making the option of the Muslim members for Pakistan totally irrelevant according to the terms of the new plan. The question of territory, however, was not so simple. The Muslim majority districts covered even the Bari Doab with the only exception the district of Amritsar. But the Akalis were staking their claims to nearly the whole of the Rachna Doab on the basis of religious and historical associations as well as property. For the labour leaders in Great Britain and for Mountbatten, however, population was virtually the only criterion of division. Not much discretion was left for the Boundary Commission after the notional division of the Punjab had been declared on the basis of population. Nevertheless, the award of Cyril Radcliffe brought the larger part of the district of Gurdaspur and a small area of the district of Lahore to the East Punjab.

The Bill for the Independence of India, introduced in the House of Commons on July 4, was passed on July 15. The House of Lords

[35] Larry Collins and Dominique Lapierre (eds), *Mountbatten and the Partition of India*, 91.
[36] V. P. Menon, *The Transfer of Power in India*, 354.

passed it on the day following, and it received the royal assent on July 18. On 15 August 1947, India became a free subcontinent, with India and Pakistan as its two sovereign states, and with the larger proportion of the Sikhs in India. The 'East Punjab' became in a sense a gift of the Akalis to the Indian Union.

CHAPTER 9

TOWARDS THE 'PUNJABI PROVINCE' (1947–1966)

I

To the task of framing a constitution for free India was added the problem of resettlement and rehabilitation almost immediately upon Independence. The integration of princely states with the Indian Union too was urgent. Equally important were a long-term territorial reorganization and economic growth. The politics of the Sikhs in the early decades of Independence were linked up with these major issues.[1]

The political decision to partition the subcontinent into two sovereign states resulted eventually in the largest transfer of population known to history. Nearly a million persons perished, and over 13 million crossed the borders. Over 4 million refugees from West Pakistan crossed into the Punjab and a larger number of Muslims from the Indian side went to Pakistan. In 1951, when the total population of the Indian Punjab was over 12½ millions, there were nearly 2½ million refugees, forming a fifth of its population.

Resettlement of refugees became the most urgent task of the new governments. The Indian Government retained the responsibility of rehabilitating urban refugees, delegating the responsibility of rehabilitating rural refugees in the Punjab to the Punjab Government. The non-Muslim landowners, who had left 5,700,000 acres of land in the West Punjab, had to be settled on 4,500,000 acres left by Muslim landowners in the East Punjab. The government evolved a scheme of graded cuts by which the refugees lost land in increasing proportion to the size of their holdings, putting a virtual end to large landholdings. Several legislative measures from 1951 to 1957, including the abolition of the Land Alienation Act of 1900, ensured that the occupancy tenants did not lose, and the 'superior owners' did not retain, their rights. Land tenures were made more secure; *jāgīrs* were made liable to resumption. Combined with the consolidation of landholdings, these measures proved to be effective in increasing agricultural production.

---

[1] For a brief outline of the developments in the first decade, S. S. Bal, *British Administration in the Punjab and its Aftermath*, Guru Nanak Dev University, Amritsar, 1986, 19–30.

Equally important was the attention given to schemes of irrigation. The Punjab Government built a new dam at Harike, largely for ensuring regular flow of water into the canals already in existence. The Madhopur-Beas link was completed in two years by 1955. The Bhakra Dam scheme was taken up to be completed at a rapid pace. In 1957, more than 6½ million acres of land were under canal irrigation, adding more than 2½ millions to the irrigated acreage of 1947. From a deficit area in food in 1947, the Punjab became a surplus area in 1957. The *élan* imparted by the refugees as much as the policy of the government accounted for a rather rapid rehabilitation in terms of transportation and industry as well.[2] A new university, a new high court and eventually a new capital were established at Chandigarh.

Rehabilitation and resettlement after partition resulted in a significant change in the demographic pattern in the Punjab. In 1951 the Sikhs formed about 35 per cent of the total population of the state, while the Hindus represented the majority with over 62 per cent. The majority status of the Hindu population as well as the increase in the percentage of the Sikhs was a new thing. Furthermore, since the Sikh landowners settled mostly in the districts from which they had gone to the canal colonies, and both Sikhs and Hindus replaced the erstwhile Muslim population of the cities and towns, the bulk of the Sikh population came to be concentrated in the area between the Ravi and the Ghaggar. In fact, in the Sikh princely states and the districts of Gurdaspur, Amritsar, Jalandhar, Hoshiarpur, Ludhiana and Ferozepore, the Sikhs came to represent more than half of the total population. For the first time in their history they found themselves concentrated in a large contiguous territory.

Before the actual partition of the Punjab and the transfer of minority populations, Baldev Singh and Giani Kartar Singh had met Lord Mountbatten to suggest that either the Constituent Assembly should give weightage to the Sikhs in the new constitution or the Hindi-speaking areas of the East Punjab should be separated from its Punjabi-speaking areas. When Mountbatten broached the subject with Jawaharlal Nehru his reaction against the second proposition was rather strong; in his eyes it was 'a fundamentally wrong principle'.

---

[2] For the attitudes of the refugees, Stephen L. Keller, *Uprooting and Social Change*, Manohar Book Service, New Delhi, 1975.

However, weightage or reservation with joint electorates could be given 'with freedom to contest the general seats also'.[3]

Thinking in terms of weightage and reservations was not a new thing. All Indian politicians were familiar with this political idiom and practice. In October, 1948 the Shiromani Akali Dal passed a resolution in favour of continuing separate representation for the Sikhs because of an aggressive 'communal mentality' displayed by some Punjabi Hindus. Three weeks later the Minority Committee formed by the Punjab Chief Minister to represent the official viewpoint to the Constituent Assembly elaborated the terms of weightage and reservation for the Sikhs, adding significantly that if it were not possible to give weightage and reservation to the Sikhs a new province may be created with the districts of Gurdaspur, Amritsar, Jalandhar, Hoshiarpur, Ludhiana, Ferozepore and Ambala as its core.

The Constituent Assembly had been eager to consider the issue of statutory reservations for religious minorities before August, 1947, but after the creation of Pakistan it favoured the abolition of all such reservations. In May, 1949, the Advisory Committee of the Constituent Assembly was clearly of the view that there was no room for weightage to religious minorities in a federal republic with a parliamentary democracy based on adult suffrage, and with the fundamental rights of all its citizens enshrined in a written constitution. In any case, the Sikhs as 'a highly educated and virile community' needed no weightage.[4] It was feared in fact that even proportionate reservation with the right to contest additional seats would enable them to grab much more than what was their due share. The unsympathetic attitude of the Constituent Assembly was more clearly visible in its refusal to extend to the Sikh scheduled castes the concessions and reservations provided for the Hindu scheduled castes.[5] The last-minute efforts of the Sikh members of the Constituent Assembly to get at least reservation with the right to contest additional seats proved futile. They refused to sign the draft constitution to be adopted by the people of India on 26 January 1950. This was hardly an auspicious beginning.

[3] A. C. Kapur, *The Punjab Crisis*, S. Chand and Company, New Delhi, 1985, 131–32.

[4] Quoted, A. S. Narang, *Storm Over the Sutlej: The Akali Politics*, Gitanjali Publications, New Delhi, 1983, 91.

[5] Master Tara Singh and the other Akali leaders had to struggle for the inclusion of the Sikh scheduled castes in the general category until 1956.

II

On 15 July 1948, Sardar Patel referred to the Patiala and East Punjab States Union (Pepsu) as 'a Sikh homeland' when he inaugurated the new state. It had been formed two months earlier by merging the Sikh states of Patiala, Nabha, Jind, Faridkot, Kapurthala and Kalsia together with the states of Malerkotla and Nalagarh. The area of this new state was a little over 10,000 square miles and, in 1951, it had a population of nearly 3,500,000. Nearly half of this population was Sikh, which made the Sikhs a little more numerous than the Hindus. The number of Muslims in the new state was very small, only about 2 per cent. Before 1947 their number was nearly a million but the bulk of them had crossed over to Pakistan, and their place was taken by about 360,000 Sikhs and Hindus. The former chief of Patiala, Maharaja Yadvindra Singh, was made the Governor (Rajpramukh) for life, and the former chief of Kapurthala was made the Deputy Governor (Uprajpramukh) for life. A caretaker government was installed in August, 1948, under Sardar Gian Singh Rarewala. Thus, the top positions in the state, as much as the composition of its population, did appear to make Pepsu rather than the Punjab 'a Sikh homeland'.

The princely states of the Punjab had served the British as strong bastions of loyalty and support for more than a century and, though less 'modernized' and less 'progressive' than the British districts, neither the rulers nor their subjects had remained isolated from the developments in the British Punjab. The Akalis had taken interest in the affairs of the Sikh states and had considerable influence in their politics. In 1928, their leaders founded the Punjab States Praja Mandal, an organization that advocated constitutional and agrarian reform. For about a decade the Praja Mandal received support from the Congress and the Kisan leaders as well as the Akalis. The changing political situation of the Punjab in the 1940s found its reflection in the Sikh states. When the Akalis decided to support the British in their war effort, they came close to the Maharaja of Patiala. Emphasis was laid on Sikh interests and Sikh rights in the princely states. The Akalis began to leave the Praja Mandal while the number of educated Hindus from professional and business classes, who were coming under the influence of the Congress, began to increase within the Mandal.[6] As in the

[6] Ramesh Walia, *Praja Mandal Movement in East Punjab States*, Punjabi University, Patiala, 1972.

British Punjab so in the princely states, the dominant political parties among the non-Muslims on the eve of Independence were the Akalis and the Congress-oriented Praja Mandal. The first consisted entirely of Sikh leaders and the second very largely of Hindus, though it was to throw up leaders like Giani Zail Singh and the less-known Tirath Singh.

After Independence, the leaders of the Akalis and the Praja Mandal revealed their differences first on the question of merger. Whereas the Akali leaders favoured a union of Sikh states, or even the creation of two new states by keeping Patiala as a single unit, the Praja Mandal leaders advocated merger of the princely states with the East Punjab. The second important issue on which the two parties held divergent views was the formation of government in Pepsu. Because of their differences, Gian Singh Rarewala became the premier; he was neither an Akali nor a Praja Mandalist at that time. When he was sworn in at the beginning of 1949 he chose his colleagues from the Praja Mandal and the newly formed Lok Sewa Sabha led by Colonel Raghubir Singh. Before the middle of 1951, however, the leaders of the Praja Mandal and the Lok Sewa Sabha, Brish Bhan and Raghubir Singh, joined hands to oust Rarewala; Raghubir Singh became the Chief Minister and Brish Bhan agreed to be the Deputy Chief Minister.[7]

Before the first general elections in 1952 the Praja Mandal and the Lok Sewa Sabha merged together to form the Pepsu Pradesh Congress and captured twenty-six out of a total of sixty seats. The Akalis turned out to be the second largest party in the legislature with nineteen seats. The remaining seats were won by the Communists and other small parties and independent candidates. Without a clear majority the Congress was invited to form a ministry but only to be replaced by a United Front ministry under Gian Singh Rarewala on 21 April 1952. He was supported by the Akalis. This first non-Congress ministry in the country fell in March, 1953, when Gian Singh was unseated through an election petition. The assembly was dissolved and President's rule was promulgated in Pepsu, which again was the first instance of such a rule in the country.

The Akalis were resentful: Gian Singh could have been asked to get re-elected within six months, they argued; or, another leader of the

---

[7] For relevant information on the Sikh states, Barbara Ramusack, 'Punjab States: Maharajas and Gurdwaras: Patiala and the Sikh Community', *People, Princes and Paramount Power* (ed. Robin Jeffrey), Oxford University Press, 1978, 170–204. 'The Sikh States' and 'The Patiala and East Punjab States Union (Pepsu)', written for *The Encyclopaedia of Sikhism* by Barbara Ramusack, have been consulted in typescript through the author's courtesy.

United Front could have been invited to form a ministry. The Congress leaders at the centre appeared to be misusing the constitutional provisions to oust a non-Congress ministry. In any case, by the end of September, 1953, one of the demands of a Sikh convention held at Anandpur was early elections in Pepsu. In the mid-term polls in early 1954, the Akalis won only twelve seats (including two of the Rarewala group). In fact the Akalis were so hopelessly divided that they contested the elections on separate tickets. A Congress ministry was formed under Raghubir Singh. Upon his death in January, 1956, Brish Bhan became the Chief Minister of Pepsu. By now, the Akalis were asking for the merger of Pepsu with the Punjabi-speaking areas of the Punjab to form a new state on the basis of language.

III

For over a quarter of a century before 1947 the Indian National Congress had been harping on the reorganization of provinces on the basis of languages. After the partition of 1947, however, serious re-thinking started on the question of reorganization, more perhaps due to emotional than rational reaction. The Dar Commission recommended before the end of 1948 that contiguity, financial efficiency, administrative convenience, capacity for future development and a large measure of agreement among the people speaking a language should be the criteria for reorganization. In no case was the view of a majority to be imposed on a substantial minority. At the Congress session in December, 1948, a committee was formed to consider the recommendations of the Dar Commission; it consisted of Jawaharlal Nehru, Vallabbhai Patel and Pattabhi Sitarammaya. Its report was adopted by the Congress Working Committee in April, 1949. It made a distinction between the South and the North: 'We are clearly of the opinion that no question of rectification of the boundaries of the provinces of Northern India should be raised at the present moment whatever the merits of such a proposal might be.'[8] Jawaharlal Nehru, at one time the arch-advocate of linguistic states, now began to feel that a sense of the unity of India was to be given the top priority before linguistic states could be formed with the consent of all concerned.

The kind of 'consent' visualized by Jawaharlal was hard to find in the Punjab. Much before 1947 the languages had been 'communalized'. In

[8] Quoted, Ajit Singh Sarhadi, *Punjabi Suba*, U. C. Kapur and Sons, Delhi, 1970, 186–87.

June, 1948, the Punjab Government made Hindi and Punjabi the new media of instruction in schools in place of Urdu. In February, 1949, the Municipal Committee of Jalandhar, an old stronghold of the Arya Samaj, resolved to introduce Hindi in Devanagri script in all its schools. In June, 1949, the Senate of the Panjab University, virtually a bastion of the Arya Samaj, refused to have Punjabi in Gurmukhi or even Devanagri script as the medium of instruction in schools. The Sikhs in general and the Akalis in particular began to express their fears that Punjabi was likely to remain a secondary language even in free India.

In October, 1949, a formula was evolved by Giani Kartar Singh and the Chief Minister Bhim Sen Sachar to accommodate the Sikh concern for Punjabi. It created a zone in which Punjabi in Gurmukhi script was to be the medium of instruction up to matriculation and in which Hindi in Devanagri script was to be taught from the last year of the primary school. A parent could opt for Hindi as the medium if the number of such scholars was not less than ten at the primary stage; even so, a boy had to take up Punjabi as a compulsory language from the fourth class and a girl from the sixth. The districts of Gurdaspur, Amritsar, Jalandhar, Hoshiarpur, Ludhiana and Ferozepore constituted the Punjabi zone together with the Ropar and Kharar Tehsils of the Ambala district and the portions of Hissar district lying on the north of the Ghaggar. The rest of the Punjab formed the Hindi zone in which the position of Punjabi and Hindi was reversed.

Though the Akalis objected to the option given to parents, whether for Hindi or Punjabi, they welcomed the Sachar Formula. However, the Arya Samajists with their Urdu dailies in Jalandhar and Delhi were opposed to it. They were supported by the Jan Sangh and the Hindu Mahasabha. The Arya Samaj institutions refused to implement the formula; it was never to be implemented in the schools of the Arya Samajists. The language issue, a legacy of the pre-Independence days, had come to stay. The Arya Samaj attitude was in fact reinforced by the political implications of reorganization on a linguistic basis.

The denial of constitutional safeguards to the Sikhs in terms of reservation made the Akali leaders more eager about the creation of a Punjabi-speaking state. In the beginning of 1950, Hukam Singh was clarifying to the journalists in Bombay that the demand for a Punjabi-speaking state was not communal but secular and democratic. The Working Committee of the Akali Dal passed a formal resolution in May in favour of a state on the basis of Punjabi language and culture. It became the demand of a Panthic convention before the end of 1950. Early in 1951 the Arya Samajists, and others who shared their concerns and attitudes, persuaded many Hindus to return Hindi as their mother-tongue on the assumption that this would negate the argument for the formation of a Punjabi-speaking state.[9] Some of them chose to see an autonomous Sikh state behind the 'smoke screen' of a 'Punjabi Province'. In the elections of 1952 the Congress won with a more convincing majority in the Punjab than in Pepsu. The Akali aspiration to be 'free and equal partners in the destiny of the country', as they had said in their election manifesto in support of a Punjabi-speaking state, became stronger after their defeat.[10]

Moral support came to the Akalis from unexpected quarters. Towards the end of 1952, Potti Sriramulu died on fast for the creation of Andhra Pradesh; four days later the Prime Minister announced the separation of Andhra from Madras as a Telugu-speaking state. The movement for linguistic states gathered fresh momentum. In December, 1953, the Government of India announced the formation of States Reorganization Commission, which kindled hopes and fears in the Punjab. Its formation by itself was a sign of hope for the Akalis, who had been articulate on the issue throughout 1953, but Jawaharlal Nehru repeated his declaration against the Punjabi-speaking state during the Pepsu mid-term poll in early 1954. The Akalis prepared their case with care, strictly on the basis of language, using pre-1947 census figures, to argue that an area of over 35,000 square miles with a population of nearly 12 million was really Punjabi-speaking, though the Sikh population in this area was much less than half. The Communists and the Praja Socialists also supported the demand for the merger of the Punjab and Pepsu and the formation of a Punjabi-speaking state. The leaders of Himachal and Haryana too wanted separate states in their respective regions, complementing thus the demand for a Punjabi-speaking state.

There were many others, however, who advocated the merger not only of Pepsu but also of Himachal Pradesh, or even a few districts of Uttar Pradesh, with the Punjab to form a greater Punjab on economic, administrative, cultural, educational and patriotic arguments. They alleged that the demand for a linguistic state was only a ruse for

[9] Tempers rose so high on the issue that one person was killed in a Jalandhar village: Kailash Chander Gulati, *The Akalis Past and Present*, Ashajanak Publications, New Delhi, 1974, 157.
[10] *Ibid.*, 157.

creating a state with a Sikh majority; they feared that such a state would eventually lead to separation and logically to the disintegration of the country; they insisted that the language of the Punjab was actually Hindi, with several varieties of Punjabi as its dialects; and as the last resort they asserted paradoxically that every citizen of India had the right 'to choose' his 'mother-tongue'. The hard core of the protagonists of 'Maha-Punjab' consisted of the Arya Samajists and the Jan Sanghites.

Besides submitting their memoranda to the States Reorganization Commission, the protagonists of the 'Punjabi-Province' and the 'Maha-Punjab' used the press and addressed meetings to propagate their views. Very soon, however, anti-Sikh and anti-Hindu slogans became a common feature of such meetings. The government decided to impose a ban on slogans. The Akalis regarded this ban as essentially a ban on slogans in favour of the Punjabi Province. They decided to defy the ban. Master Tara Singh was arrested in May 1955. Sant Fateh Singh joined the *morchā* for the first time in his life. Within two months, thousands of volunteers courted arrest and the movement reached its peak in early July. The government began stopping the volunteers on their way to the Golden Temple. The arms licences of the SGPC were cancelled and on refusal to surrender arms the police entered the Golden Temple complex, stopped the *langar*, entered Guru Ram Das Sarai, arrested the head-priests, raided the Akali Dal Office and used tear gas shells on the volunteers gathered in the Temple complex. Troops were ordered to flag-march through the *bāzārs* and streets around the Golden Temple. But all this failed to overawe the Akalis. On July 12, the government withdrew the ban on slogans. The Chief Minister Sachar visited the Akāl Takht to offer a personal apology.[11]

The freedom gained by the Akalis to shout slogans in favour of the Punjabi Province did not impress the States Reorganization Commission. In its report submitted on 30 September 1955, the majority of the Punjabis were opposed to the demand for a Punjabi-speaking state. The most crucial part of this 'majority' was actually the articulate section of the Hindus of the Punjabi-speaking zone. The Commission confused the language issue with the issue of scripts on which 'sentiment was arrayed against sentiment'.[12] The 'sentiment' of the anti-Punjabi

---

[11] Sachar lost his Chief Ministership a few months later to Partap Singh Kairon.
[12] Quoted, Satya M. Rai, *Punjab Since Partition*, Durga Publications, Delhi, 1986, 292.

Map 7 Contemporary India

Hindus of the Punjabi-speaking zone won the battle. The Commission recommended the merger of Himachal Pradesh, Pepsu and the Punjab to form a new state. The criterion of language was totally set aside.[13] Giani Kartar Singh remarked that out of the fourteen languages regarded as 'national' in the Constitution of India, Punjabi alone was left without a state formed on its basis.

The report was rejected by the Akalis on the day following its release on 9 October 1955. They called a convention of all the parties and organizations of the Sikhs on October 16 and underlined the secular

[13] Satya M. Rai, *Punjab Since Partition*, 295–96. Master Tara Singh remarked that the Sikhs would have to fight now with their backs to the wall: quoted, A. S. Narang, *Storm Over the Sutlej*, 126.

and democratic character of the demand. The recommendation of the Commission appeared to be as partisan as the most rabid partisan could wish. Even the Sachar Formula, which the Commission recognized was not implemented, was whittled down. The convention authorized Master Tara Singh to approach the Government of India on behalf of the Sikh community.

Master Tara Singh met Jawaharlal Nehru on October 24 in the presence of Abul Kalam Azad and G. B. Pant. He was accompanied by Giani Kartar Singh, Hukam Singh, Gian Singh Rarewala and Bhai Jodh Singh. Their talks were inconclusive. Another deputation met the Prime Minister on behalf of the Punjab Government to suggest that the Pepsu formula could be extended to the Punjab for solving the language problem and the Punjabi language could be promoted in the whole state. Re-thinking of a sort had started before the annual session of the Congress was held at Amritsar in December. The Akalis also decided to hold their conference in Amritsar at the same time, and so did the protagonists of 'Maha-Punjab'. All took out processions as a demonstration of popular participation. The Akali procession was the most impressive. This popular demonstration appealed to the democratic instincts of Jawaharlal Nehru. He was now prepared to accommodate the Akalis as much as he could in the face of contending pressures.

Hukam Singh had formulated a scheme which essentially met some of the Akali demands without actually creating a Punjabi-speaking state. This became the basis of discussion in January 1956, and an agreement was reached before the end of February. In a general meeting of the Akali Dal on March 11 the majority of the leaders were in favour of accepting the scheme. Finalized afterwards, the scheme came to be known as the Regional Formula. From the viewpoint of the Akalis it was not a bad compromise. Not Himachal Pradesh but only Pepsu was to be merged with the Punjab. The new state was to be bi-lingual, but Punjabi in Gurmukhi script was to be the 'regional' and the official language in the Punjabi zone. The Punjab Government was to set up a separate department for the development of Punjabi as well as Hindi; the Union Government was to encourage Punjabi like any other 'regional' language in the country. All this appeared to take care of the language problem. On the political side, a regional committee was to be formed for each zone, with a certain degree of initiative and power to legislate on fourteen important subjects. Worked in the right

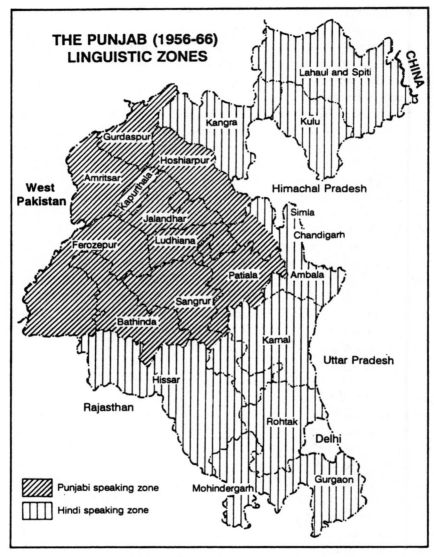

Map 8 The Punjab (1956–1966): linguistic zones

spirit, this provision promised a large measure of legislative autonomy.[14]

As a part of the understanding between the Akali and the Congress leaders, the Working Committee of the Akali Dal resolved on 30 September 1956, that the Dal would not have a separate political programme of its own. It would concentrate on the promotion of the religious, educational, cultural, social and economic interests of the Sikh Panth, and guard against any violation of 'fundamental rights' which might adversely affect Sikh interests; it would actively participate in the working out of the Regional Formula, and in the implementation of various plans for the development of the country.[15] Master Tara Singh declared that he would never forsake Jawaharlal Nehru, and Jawaharlal praised Master Tara Singh for his courage and honesty of purpose. The new Punjab state was inaugurated on 1 November 1956.

IV

The coalition ministry which had ended with Khizr Hayat's resignation in March, 1947 was revived after 15 August 1947, without the Unionists and those legislators whose constituencies were left in the West Punjab.[16] Dr Gopi Chand Bhargava headed the new ministry which included Swaran Singh and Ishar Singh Majhail. Recalling the promises of the Congress, particularly its resolution of 1929, and expressing their faith and trust in the great Congress leaders, the Akalis resolved in March, 1948 that all their legislators should join the Congress Assembly Party. This was done on March 18.

In June, 1948, Giani Kartar Singh was included in the cabinet in place of Ishar Singh Majhail as a concession to the Akalis. Giani Kartar Singh is believed to have cultivated Bhim Sen Sachar, the leader of the Congress Assembly Party before 1947, to work against Bhargava. In any case, Sachar replaced Bhargava as Chief Minister on 13 April 1949. It was at this time that Giani Kartar Singh worked on the new leader to evolve the language formula. Sachar lost his Chief Ministership within a few weeks and Bhargava was back in office in October, 1949.

---

[14] For the text of the 'regional plan', Satya M. Rai, *Partition of the Punjab*, Asia Publishing House, Bombay, 1965, 274–75.

[15] Quoted, Ajit Singh Sarhadi, *Punjabi Suba*, 284.

[16] Kailash Chander Gulati, *The Akalis Past and Present*, 149–50. That was why Dr Gopi Chand Bhargava became the leader of the Punjab Congress and not Bhim Sen Sachar.

By this time, the Akalis had failed to get any constitutional safe-guards.[17] In the Bhargava ministry they began to feel rather ineffective. In a meeting of the Working Committee of the Akali Dal on July 30 the merger was revoked on the grounds that the hopes of constructive sympathy and support from the great Congress leaders had been belied. However, the bulk of the erstwhile Akali legislators chose to remain in the Congress. At the end of 1950, the 'nationalist' Sikhs like Udham Singh Nagoke, Gurdial Singh Dhillon, Surjit Singh Majithia, Sohan Singh Jalal-Usman and Giani Zail Singh could hold a parallel Sikh convention at Amritsar to oppose the formation of a Punjabi-speaking state in the interest of 'the unity and strength of the country'.[18] The opponents of the Punjabi-Province, thus, were not only in Delhi, or among the 'communal' Hindus of the Punjab, but also among the Sikh leaders themselves, including some of the former members of the Akali Dal.

The Congress Party in the Punjab was no less divided by factions than the Akalis. Jawaharlal in 1951 was particularly unhappy about 'communalism' and 'factionalism' in the Punjab Congress.[19] Bhargava could not hold office for long, particularly after the death of his patron, Sardar Patel. When Bhargava resigned on 16 June 1951, the Congress High Command opted for President's rule in the Punjab rather than a new Congress ministry. Early in November, Giani Kartar Singh left the Congress and became General Secretary of the Shiromani Akali Dal. This could hardly improve the position of the Dal. The Akali Dal lost heavily in the elections of 1952, winning only thirteen seats in a house of 126. With a larger number of rural Sikh leaders in the Congress, the Akali Dal did not have much chance against the Congress even in the Punjabi-speaking zone dominated by the Sikhs. Furthermore, the Akalis fought the elections both in Pepsu and the Punjab on the issue of the Punjabi-speaking state, and this issue in the early years of Independence had no fascination for the Sikh peasantry.

The defeat of the Akalis did not mean a defeat of the Sikhs. In fact when Sachar was sworn in as the new Chief Minister he chose Swaran Singh, Partap Singh Kairon and Ujjal Singh as his cabinet colleagues from amongst the Sikh legislators. Not exactly through a convention

[17] In this context, Master Tara Singh made the statement that the Muslims got Pakistan and the scheduled castes got reservations but the Sikhs got kicks for seeking merely constitutional safeguards: Satya M. Rai, *Partition of the Punjab*, 203.

[18] Quoted, Kailash Chander Gulati, *The Akalis Past and Present*, 156.

[19] Quoted, Satya M. Rai, *Partition of the Punjab*, 212–13.

but because of the sheer exigency of the political situation, Sikh ministers had parity with the non-Sikh ministers in the Congress government. This lent plausibility to the contention of the Congressite Sikhs that even the interests of the community were better served by remaining in the Congress. When the Akalis decided towards the end of September, 1956, to have no separate political programme, they too were hopeful that they would serve themselves and the community better from within the Congress.

The tussle between the Akali and the Congressite Sikhs for the leadership of the Sikh community was not confined to the legislative assembly. The Akalis regarded the Shiromani Gurdwara Prabandhak Committee as their domain almost by right. With the changing political alignments of the early 1950s this prerogative was questioned. Mohan Singh Nagoke, who was the President of the SGPC on 15 August 1947, was replaced by Udham Singh Nagoke on 28 June 1948. At this time the Akalis were in the Congress. Gradually, however, Master Tara Singh realized that there was a possibility of the SGPC being captured by the Sikh leaders who were in the Congress or with the Congress. For about eight months in 1950 Udham Singh Nagoke remained out of office because Chanan Singh Orara, who had been asked to arbitrate between two rival claimants, chose himself to be the President. The Akali defeat in the elections of 1952 was attributed by them largely to the fact that the SGPC was not under their control. Even in June, 1952 Udham Singh Nagoke was able to get his own candidate elected. But within four months he was replaced by a nominee of Master Tara Singh. He remained in office for more than a year before he was replaced by Ishar Singh Majhail on 18 January 1954. Ishar Singh was replaced by Master Tara Singh himself in February 1955.

The importance of the SGPC for Sikh politics had been taken for granted before 1947. The tussle for its control in the first decade of Independence intensified the awareness of that importance. In fact certain amendments were deliberately made in the Gurdwara Act to enable the members of the General Body to oust the President if he did not enjoy its confidence. That was how Ishar Singh Majhail was brought in at the beginning of 1954. Not only the Congress Party but also the Communists entered the arena of SGPC elections in 1954, the former in the garb of the Khalsa Dal Front and the latter as the Desh Bhagat Board. But the Khalsa Dal won only three out of the 132 seats it contested. The Akalis won all the 110 seats they contested. They were nonetheless resentful of 'nationalist' interference in the affairs of the SGPC. They felt all the more sensitive about this 'religious' institution because it served as a strong base for their secular politics.

V

At the time of the inauguration of the new Punjab state on 1 November 1956, Partap Singh Kairon was the Chief Minister. The Akali legislators joined the Congress Party under his leadership. The Congress won 120 seats in a house of 164. There were fifty-eight Sikh legislators in the Congress Party, and nearly fifty of them represented the Punjabi 'region' which had seventy-one seats in all. However, the proportion of former Akalis among them was smaller than that of the Congressite Sikhs. In fact, Master Tara Singh had been rather unhappy about the number of tickets given to the 'Akalis'. He was not even consulted, and consequently he had encouraged independent candidates to contest the elections to demonstrate his resentment. It was not from the Akalis, however, that Kairon faced the first problem in his new tenure as Chief Minister. One of the provisions of the Regional Formula was to give no option to parents for Hindi in the Punjabi region. The Arya Samajists, who had earlier refused to implement the Sachar Formula in their schools, now opposed the Regional Formula as something much worse. Under the Hindi Raksha Samiti they started a 'save Hindi' movement in their opposition to Punjabi. This movement was supported by men like Suraj Bhan, Principal of D. A. V. College, Jalandhar, who later became Vice-Chancellor of the Panjab University, and the Arya Samajist politicians like Virendra, editor of the *Pratāp*. The language aspect of the Regional Formula was compromised by concessions to Hindi soon after the agitation started, though the agitation lasted for seven months.

Jawaharlal Nehru felt sorry in 1957 about the 'save Hindi' movement and feared that it would disintegrate the Punjab.[20] What he did not anticipate was that Partap Singh Kairon would not implement the Regional Formula. The Akali Dal daily *Jathedār* was to observe in October, 1961 that 'if the Regional Formula had been implemented in the spirit in which it had been conceived by the Central leadership under the guidance of Pandit Jawaharlal Nehru, then no further

[20] Quoted, Ajit Singh Sarhadi, *Punjabi Suba*, 301.

trouble would have arisen in the Punjab'. Till March, 1958 the foremost objective of the Akali Dal had been to get it implemented. In June, however, Master Tara Singh indicated that he would be compelled to reopen the demand for a Punjabi Province if the Regional Formula was not implemented. The first Punjabi-Province conference was held in October. Master Tara Singh was still prepared to accept an impartial arbitration on whether or not the Formula was being implemented.

Partap Singh Kairon made a successful move to dislodge Master Tara Singh from the Presidentship of the SGPC with the help of Giani Kartar Singh who was now a minister in his cabinet. On 16 November 1958 the Master lost the Presidentship by three votes. Kairon pressed the advantage by reviving an amendment bill apparently to accommodate the representatives of Pepsu on the SGPC but actually to change its constitution to dilute its democratic character. In the Act passed in January, 1959 however, his intention stood defeated because of a clearly articulated opposition from the Sikhs outside the Congress. Master Tara Singh decided to recover his lost position in the SGPC by fighting elections on the issue of the Punjabi Province. The Shiromani Akali Dal won 132 out of the total 139 seats, and all the Akali Dal members of the SGPC took a pledge at the Akāl Takht on 24 January 1960 to work for the achievement of a Punjabi Province with single-minded devotion and with all the resources at their command.

During 1960 the movement for a Punjabi-Province gained some momentum. Master Tara Singh, having failed to induce the majority of the erstwhile Akalis to resign as Congress legislators, called a Punjabi-Province conference in May, which was attended by some leaders of the Swatantra and Praja Socialist parties, and announced a demonstration march in Delhi in June. He was arrested; many other Akali leaders, including some legislators, were arrested; the Akali papers *Prabhāt* and *Akālī* were suppressed. Nearly 18,000 Akalis courted arrest at Amritsar before the end of July. Jawaharlal Nehru took notice of the demand in his Independence Day speech: 'every Punjabi should himself consider to learn both Hindi and Punjabi', but there could be no bifurcation of the Punjab.[21] Partap Singh Kairon started releasing Akali volunteers from jails to create the impression that they were recanting. The détenus at Bhatinda agitated over their release and four of them were killed in firing by the police. Sant Fateh Singh, who was the dictator of the *morchā* in the absence of Master Tara Singh,

[21] Quoted, Ajit Singh Sarhadi, *Punjabi Suba*, 331.

declared on the first of November that it had become necessary to lay down his life to save the country from 'dictatorial rule in the garb of democracy'.[22] On December 18 he went on fast unto death to move the Prime Minister to concede the legitimate demand for a Punjabi Province purely on linguistic basis.

Jawaharlal Nehru was now prepared to concede the claims for the Punjabi language. On December 23 he requested Sant Fateh Singh to give up the fast and come for talks. He was thinking in terms of making the entire Punjab unilingual.[23] Partap Singh Kairon released Master Tara Singh from detention in Dharamsala on 4 January 1961 apparently to enable Sant Fateh Singh to consult him but actually in the hope that he would diminish the possibility of an understanding between the Prime Minister and the Sant. Those who were advising Sant Fateh Singh that the proposal of the Punjab as a unilingual state should be accepted now felt weak, and Sant Fateh Singh declined to have talks with Jawaharlal Nehru.

Master Tara Singh met Jawaharlal Nehru at Bhavnagar on January 7 but failed to convince him about the formation of a Punjabi-speaking state. On the 8th, however, Nehru declared that no discrimination was deliberately made against the Punjabi language and the Sikh community. He underlined that Punjabi was the dominant language of the entire Punjab and deserved encouragement in every way. In his view this statement met the substance of the demand about Punjabi.[24] Master Tara Singh too insisted with Sant Fateh Singh that the demand had been essentially met and persuaded him to give up his fast. The Sant did so on 9 January 1961. All the Akali volunteers, officially stated to be 30,000, were released.

However, Sant Fateh Singh's talks with Jawaharlal in February and May, 1961 failed to produce any result. Apart from his own view of the situation there was pressure on Nehru from 'the other communities' against bifurcation of the Punjab. It was insinuated that the Akalis were in league with Pakistan. The Akali Dal expressed its resentment over the mendacious propaganda of their opponents and asserted that the

---

[22] This change in the method of agitation has been generally missed. Baldev Raj Nayyar, for instance, talks of Akali strategy in terms of constitutional, infiltrational and agitational methods without assigning much significance to individual fast unto death: *Minority Politics in the Punjab*, Princeton University Press, 1966, 325.
[23] Ajit Singh Sarhadi, *Punjabi Suba*, 338–39.
[24] Quoted, Kailash Chander Gulati, *The Akalis Past and Present*, 172.

Sikhs were a dynamic limb of the Indian nation.[25] Against the unrelenting attitude of the ruling party, the General Body of the Dal allowed Master Tara Singh to start his fast on 15 August 1961. Sant Fateh Singh met the Prime Minister ten days later but only to find that he was prepared to look into the grievances of the Sikhs but not to create a Punjabi-speaking state.

Master Tara Singh gave up his fast on the first of October when Hardit Singh Malik came to Amritsar professedly as an emissary of the Prime Minister. This was treated as a sign of impending settlement with the Akalis. There was a strong reaction from the anti-Punjabi lobbies. Jagat Narain, for example, who had resigned as a minister on the issue of the Regional Formula, warned the government on October 6 against any settlement with the Akalis: 'The Hindus of Punjab would not accept the settlement.'[26] Master Tara Singh met the Prime Minister on October 30. A Commission was formed a day later, with S. R. Das as its Chairman. Both the personnel of the Commission and its scope disappointed the Akali leaders and they decided to boycott the Das Commission. Its first meeting was held in December, 1961 and its report was submitted in February, 1962. Only a few representations were made to the Commission, including one by Virendra who argued that Punjabi was a dialect of Hindi and Gurmukhi merely a religious script. Balraj Madhok, a protagonist of the Jan Sangh, told the Commission that the real source of trouble was the Regional Formula and that the 'regional committees' should be scrapped. The Commission concluded that the implementation of the Regional Formula was only delayed but not stopped and therefore it involved no injustice. The government accepted the report promptly. The general elections were round the corner.

VI

The prestige of Master Tara Singh, like the morale of the Akali Dal, in early 1962 was rather low. Towards the end of November, 1961 Master Tara Singh and Sant Fateh Singh had been summoned by the Cherished-Five as the representatives of the Sikh Panth to explain why they had gone back on their decisions to fast unto death after a solemn prayer (ardās) in the presence of the Guru-Granth. They were found

---

[25] Resolution of the Shiromani Akali Dal, quoted, Ajit Singh Sarhadi, *Punjabi Suba*, 350.
[26] Quoted, Ajit Singh Sarhadi, *Punjabi Suba*, 365.

guilty, particularly Master Tara Singh who had not only broken his own fast but also persuaded Sant Fateh Singh earlier to break his fast without achieving its purpose. Master Tara Singh was 'punished' to perform an *akhand-pāṭh*, to read *bāṇī* in excess of the daily norm, to offer *kaṛāh parshād* worth 125 rupees, to clean utensils of the Guru's *langar* and to clean the shoes of the *sangat* visiting the Gurdwara. He did all this in atonement, and he was forgiven by the Cherished-Five. But his lapse was not forgotten by the Panth. For the first time in his life he had the sad experience of knowing that the Sikhs were no longer keen to listen to him; at places in fact they did not allow him to speak.

In the elections of 1962, the Congress won ninety seats out of 154, and Kairon entered the second term of his Chief Ministership. However, he himself won only by a margin of thirty-four votes, and that too was regarded by many as a result of rigging. There was a clear shift of Sikh votes in favour of the Akalis. They could win only nineteen seats but they got 20.7 per cent of the total votes. In the Punjabi-speaking region, they got over 1,500,000 of the Sikh votes while the Congress got less than 600,000. A little over 72 per cent of the Sikh voters, thus, supported the Akali candidates.

The defeat of the Akalis in the elections was followed by a division among them. Master Tara Singh was re-elected President of the SGPC but only seventy-four members participated in the election. Most of the remaining eighty-six members had stayed away in protest. In a convention held in the Ludhiana district in July, 1962 Master Tara Singh's failure to keep his solemn pledge was openly denounced as the cause of the failure of the Punjabi Province movement. It was resolved to take up the cause entirely on linguistic basis under the leadership of Sant Fateh Singh. On August 1 Sant Fateh Singh clarified to the press at Delhi that his concept of the Punjabi Province had been fundamentally different from that of the Master from the very beginning. Early in October, Master Tara Singh was dislodged from the Presidentship of the SGPC with a no-confidence vote of seventy-six against seventy-two. The Akali leaders of Delhi demonstrated their support for Master Tara Singh by severing all connections of the Delhi Gurdwara Prabandhak Committee with the SGPC at Amritsar. The Akali Dal was virtually divided into two.

During the Chinese incursion into Indian territory in October, 1962 both the Akali leaders demonstrated their patriotism by giving whole-hearted support to the government. All the Sikhs responded well, and the Punjab contributed more than 20 million rupees to the national defence fund, besides gold weighing double the weight of Jawaharlal Nehru. Sant Fateh Singh presented 50,000 rupees to him on behalf of the SGPC. In February, 1963 Sant Fateh Singh was still calling for a war effort to drive out the Chinese. In June, 1963 Master Tara Singh's effort to dislodge the Sant from the SGPC proved to be unsuccessful when a no-confidence motion was defeated by eighty-one votes to sixty-two. The support of Sant Fateh Singh had increased much in one year at the expense of Master Tara Singh's popularity.

Meanwhile, Kairon's leadership came to be openly criticized by a number of legislators.[27] They submitted a charge-sheet against him to the Congress President. A deputation of some opposition leaders had already met the President of India with over thirty charges of corruption, nepotism and favouritism against Kairon. Such charges in fact had been brought against him for the first time in 1958 but he was then strongly supported by Jawaharlal Nehru to ensure that the Punjab legislators did not pass a vote of no-confidence against him. Even in 1963 Jawaharlal Nehru was inclined to support him, but opposition was now stronger and more vocal. On 22 October 1963 Nehru recommended to the President that an enquiry may be made into the charges against Kairon. He added, however, that any change in the leadership of the Punjab might result in producing confusion and putting a stop to the progress the state was making under him. The Enquiry Commission started its work on 5 December 1963. Nehru's refusal to suspend Kairon led to the resignation of a few Congress legislators. The Commission's findings went against Kairon. He resigned on 14 June 1964, a week before the publication of the Commission's Report, carrying the verdict that he had connived at the exploitation of his influence by his sons and relatives, colleagues and government officials. Jawaharlal Nehru had died already in May, 1964. Kairon was assassinated in February, 1965.

At the time of Kairon's death, the Punjab was on the threshold of 'the green revolution'. His policies and measures for over eight years had contributed much towards that development. Jawaharlal Nehru was justified in saying that the Punjab had made great progress under his guiding care. His commitment to communal harmony and economic progress was in consonance with Nehru's thinking. Because

[27] For factionalism in the Punjab Congress and opposition to Kairon, Pandit Mohan Lal, *Disintegration of Punjab*, Sameer Prakashan, Chandigarh, 1984.

of his support, Kairon was able to withstand the popular movement of the Akalis. At the same time he tried to cater to the Punjab peasantry in general and the Sikh peasantry in particular, to create the impression that he could do more for the Jats than the Akalis could: acquisition of land for seed farms outside the plan, consolidation of landholdings, provision of electric power to villages, construction of metalled roads, loans for tube-wells, introduction of poultry farming and grape cultivation and establishment of the Punjab Agricultural University. He could do even more for the Punjabi language, he claimed, by establishing the Punjabi University at Patiala.[28]

The number of tenants in the Punjab decreased from hundreds of thousands to merely tens of thousands between 1955 and 1964. Agricultural production increased by 42 per cent. From the small beginnings made in the early years of Independence, nearly 22 million acres were brought under consolidation by 1964–1965, more than 5,000 villages were supplied with electric power and nearly 8,000 miles of metalled roads were under the wheels of buses and trucks. At the same time, more than 5,000 factories were registered. The growing prosperity of the Punjab and the policies of the government under Kairon won many voters for the Congress. The increasing alienation of the Akalis, however, was alienating the Sikh peasantry also from the Congress.

VII

On 18 January 1965, Sant Fateh Singh's group won ninety seats and Master Tara Singh's group got only forty-five seats in the SGPC elections. Master Tara Singh retired into the hills for six months. His supporters, however, remained active in the plains. In May, 1965 a conference was held at Ludhiana in which an important resolution was moved by 'Justice' Gurnam Singh, leader of the opposition in the Punjab Assembly, and seconded by the President of the Master Akali Dal, Giani Bhupinder Singh. It was stated in this resolution that the Sikh people were makers of history and conscious of their political destiny in a free India; the law, the judicial process and the executive action of the Indian Union were heavily weighted against the Sikhs;

---

[28] The Punjabi University was inaugurated by President S. Radhakrishnan in 1962 and Kairon underlined the importance of Punjabi as a great language. The institution was meant to fulfil a part of the objectives of the Regional Formula.

they had no other alternative left than the demand for a self-determined status within the Union. By the Urdu and Hindi press of the Punjabis it was interpreted as a demand for a sovereign Sikh state.[29]

Master Tara Singh returned to the plains in July and put forth his final thesis in August. He referred to the solemn promises of the Congress which, after the attainment of freedom, were forgotten; he referred to the new threat to all the minorities of India in the form of a resurgence of militant Hinduism, particularly to the Sikhs who shared much with the Hindus; he referred to the Sikh tradition of eschewing discrimination against others; he put forth the idea that Sikhism was against the concentration of wealth in individual hands and any abuse of the means of production; and he concluded that the Sikh demand for a space in the sun of free India to breathe the air of freedom was a legitimate demand. Indeed, what God and history had built could not be destroyed by the new rulers of India.[30] Clearly, then, Master Tara Singh was in favour of an autonomous state for the Sikhs within the Indian Union. Seriously put forward for the first time in free India, this idea of 'a Sikh homeland' was largely the result of Master Tara Singh's failure not only to get the Punjabi Province but also to retain his leadership of the Sikh Panth.

The Working Committee of the Sant Akali Dal passed a resolution that not to form a linguistic state in the Punjab was a clear discrimination against the people of the Punjab. Sant Fateh Singh was authorized to meet the new Prime Minister, Lal Bahadur Shastri, to press upon him the necessity of forming a Punjabi-speaking state. But his meeting with Shastri proved to be an unmitigated disappointment. He carried the impression that the leaders in Delhi did not trust the Sikhs. On August 16 he declared that he would go on fast on September 10 in the cause of the Punjabi Province and, if he survived the fast for fifteen days, he would immolate himself on the sixteenth day. However in view of the armed conflict with Pakistan, he decided on September 9 to postpone his fast. It was much appreciated by the President of India, Dr Sarvapalli Radhakrishnan. All sections of the Punjabis, once again, displayed great patriotic fervour during the three weeks of war till the cease-fire was declared on 26 September 1965. Soon afterwards, the Union Home Minister declared that the question of the Punjabi-Province would be examined all afresh and a Parliamentary Committee

[29] Ajit Singh Sarhadi, *Punjabi Suba*, 401–02.
[30] Quoted, Ajit Singh Sarhadi, *Punjabi Suba*, 402–06.

under the Chairmanship of Hukam Singh, the Speaker, would be set up. A cabinet subcommittee was also formed to advise the Parliamentary Committee from time to time. It consisted of Indira Gandhi, Y. B. Chavan and Mahavir Tyagi.

Lal Bahadur Shastri died at Tashkent on 11 January 1966 and Indira Gandhi became the Prime Minister on January 20. She thought of discussing the matter with a small committee appointed by Sant Fateh Singh but the Sant suspected further delay. He wrote back that he would wait for the decision of the government till the end of March. The delay resulted in the adoption of extreme postures; the Master Akali Dal reiterated its demand for a Sikh homeland and the Jan Sangh opposed the formation of even a Punjabi Province. On March 9 the Congress Working Committee recommended to the Union Government that a state with Punjabi as state language may be created out of the existing Punjab. In reaction, there were strikes, arson and murder, generally believed to have been orchestrated by the Jan Sangh. Three Congressmen were burnt alive in Panipat, including an old associate of Bhagat Singh.

The Union Home Minister, Gulzari Lal Nanda, announced the appointment of a Commission on 17 April. The falsified returns of 'mother-tongue' in the census of 1961 were made the basis of enumeration and the *tehsil*, instead of the village, was made the unit of bifurcation. These terms of reference minimized the relevance of 'other factors'. The Akalis sought all genuinely Punjabi-speaking areas for the reorganized Punjab in their memorandum to the Commission, headed by Justice Shah, a sitting judge of the Supreme Court, with two retired officials as its members. Two members of the Commission recommended exclusion of Tehsil Kharar from the Punjab, carrying the implication of the loss of its capital, Chandigarh, to the Punjab state. The report of the Commission was considered by the Congress Parliamentary Committee on 8 June, and accepted with some modifications. The Punjab Reorganization Bill provided not only for a linguistic state but also for the creation of Haryana and the Union Territory of Chandigarh. Introduced in the Lok Sabha on 3 September 1966, it was passed on 7 September. It received the President's assent on 18 September. Despite protests from the Akalis, the reorganized Punjab was inaugurated on 1 November 1966.

CHAPTER 10

IN THE NEW PUNJAB STATE (1966–1984)

I

The new Punjab state created new problems because of the way in which it was formed. Sant Fateh Singh expressed his dissatisfaction several months before the new state was inaugurated: genuinely Punjabi-speaking areas were being left out of the new state and given to Haryana or Himachal Pradesh; Chandigarh was unjustly being turned into a Union Territory; power and irrigation projects were being taken over by the Union Government. Opposing the Reorganization Bill in the Parliament, Kapur Singh referred to the promises made by the Congress and its leaders on various occasions; as late as July, 1946 Jawaharlal Nehru had told a press conference that the Sikhs were entitled to special consideration: 'I see no wrong in an area and a set-up in the North wherein the Sikhs can also experience a glow of freedom.' Kapur Singh too favoured a larger state irrespective of Sikh population, but a state standing in a special relationship to the Centre and having a special internal constitution, a Sikh homeland.[1]

Sant Fateh Singh demanded 'the same rights for the Suba administration as were allowed to other states, and the same status for the language as enjoyed in other areas'.[2] On 17 December 1966 he went on a fast with the declared intention of immolating himself ten days later. On the afternoon of December 27 Hukam Singh reached Amritsar to tell a large congregation in the Golden Temple that the Prime Minister Indira Gandhi had agreed to arbitrate on the issues involved and that Chandigarh belonged to the Punjab. Sant Fateh Singh was persuaded to break his fast. A few days later the Home Minister denied in the Parliament that any assurance had been given to the Sant. Indira Gandhi stated on 8 January 1967 that she had agreed to arbitrate but given no assurance to Sant Fateh Singh.

In the elections of 1967, Master Tara Singh's followers demanded a special status for the new Punjab, like Jammu and Kashmir. This idea

---

[1] Quoted, Ajit Singh Sarhadi, *Punjabi Suba*, U. C. Kapur and Sons, Delhi, 1970, 449–50.
[2] Quoted, Ajit Singh Sarhadi, *Punjabi Suba*, 457.

Map 9 Contemporary Punjab

of a Sikh homeland did not go well with the mass of the Sikhs, and the Master Akali Dal won only two seats, with about 4.5 per cent of the votes. The Sant Akali Dal, however, won twenty-four seats, with about 20.5 per cent of the votes. A sizeable section of the Sikh peasantry still supported the Congress which won forty-eight seats, with over 37.5 per cent of the votes. But the Congress failed for the first time after 1947 to have a majority in the Assembly. The Sant Akali Dal, under the leadership of 'Justice' Gurnam Singh, formed the first non-Congress,

United Front ministry in March with the support of the Jan Sangh, the Communist parties and others. The United Front ministry fell on 22 November 1967. Three days later, the defecting Akali leader Lachhman Singh Gill formed a new ministry with the support of the Congress. The leader of the Congress Assembly Party, Gian Singh Rarewala, tried to persuade the Congress High Command that the Punjab Congress may form a coalition ministry with the Akalis instead of merely supporting Lachhman Singh Gill. But the High Command did not even extend support to Gill for a long time. His ministry fell on 23 August 1968. President's rule was imposed in the new Punjab within two years of its formation.

The fall of two Akali ministries in less than nineteen months obliged the Akali leaders to review the political situation. Kapur Singh became Senior Vice-President of the combined Master and Sant Akali Dal. His ideas were reflected in the agreement reached and signed on 8 October 1968. The political objective of the Panth, it was stated, was well grounded in the commandments of Guru Gobind Singh and given concrete shape in Sikh history. The Khālsā were 'a sovereign people by birth-right'; all decision-making powers belonged to the Panth; and the goal of the Shiromani Akali Dal was to achieve an autonomous status in a well-demarcated territory within free India. More powers were demanded for the states because 'the Congress party in power has abused the Constitution to the detriment of the non-Congress Governments, and uses its power for its party interest'. The Shiromani Akali Dal demanded that the Constitution of India 'should be on a correct federal basis and that the states should have greater autonomy'.[3] The slogan of state autonomy was added to the earlier concern for getting Chandigarh included in the Punjab and regaining control of power and irrigation projects. In the mid-term elections of February 1969, which the Akalis fought in alliance with the Jan Sangh, they won forty-three seats, five more than the Congress. The percentage of the Sant Akali Dal votes too increased to 29.5 for the first time. Gurnam Singh headed the ministry again, in coalition with the Jan Sangh.

The issue of Chandigarh was now taken up by the advocates of Sikh homeland. Jathedar Darshan Singh Pheruman went on fast unto death on 15 August 1969 on this issue. He was determined to demonstrate that a true Sikh of the Guru did not go back on his vow (ardās) without attaining its objective. This did not reflect well on Sant Fateh Singh.

[3] Resolution of the Akali Dal, quoted, Ajit Singh Sarhadi, *Punjabi Suba*, 465–66.

Pheruman also declared that though the country was free, the Panth was still in bondage. And this was supposed not to reflect well on the Congress leadership. He wished to lay down his life for the ultimate objective of a Sikh homeland. The Working Committee of the Akali Dal resolved to struggle for all those objectives for which Sant Fateh Singh had kept his fast. Nearly all the political parties of the Punjab combined to take out a huge procession in Chandigarh, demanding its inclusion in the Punjab. Jathedar Darshan Singh Pheruman died on October 27.

On 24 November 1969 Sant Fateh Singh announced his decision to go on fast on the forthcoming Republic Day, 26 January 1970 and to immolate himself on February 1, if Chandigarh was not given to the Punjab. The Prime Minister Indira Gandhi announced her award on 29 January 1970 giving Chandigarh to the Punjab. But this was not all. A part of the Fazilka Tehsil in Ferozepur district was awarded to Haryana, with a corridor on the border with Rajasthan to bypass the Punjabi-speaking villages of the Muktsar Tehsil between Haryana and Fazilka. A commission was to be appointed to consider other territorial claims of the Punjab. The award was to be implemented five years later in 1975. The All-Parties Action Committee under the Chairmanship of the Jan Sangh leader Baldev Parkash denounced the award as unjust and illogical but asked Sant Fateh Singh to give up his fast because Chandigarh was awarded to the Punjab. Sant Fateh Singh broke his fast on 30 January 1970.

Within two months of the Prime Minister's award there occurred a rupture between the Akali Dal organization and its Assembly Party, more specifically between the President Sant Fateh Singh and the Chief Minister Gurnam Singh. The Chief Minister got Giani Bhupinder Singh elected to the Rajya Sabha against the candidate nominated by the Sant, and Sant Fateh Singh got them both expelled from the Akali Dal. On 27 March 1970 Parkash Singh Badal became the new Chief Minister of the Akali-Jan Sangh coalition. Before long, however, his supporters were asking him to get rid of their Jan Sangh partners who were becoming aggressive in demanding parity of Hindi with Punjabi and a change in the jurisdiction of Guru Nanak Dev University established by Gurnam Singh in November, 1969. The Jan Sangh members left the government on June 20. Dissension within the Akali Party synchronized with the increasing hold of Indira Gandhi over the ruling Congress. In the Parliamentary elections of March, 1971 the

Akalis won only one seat. Three months later, Badal advised the Governor to dissolve the Assembly, afraid of his removal from Chief Ministership due to defections. President's rule was imposed on the Punjab on 13 June 1971.

The general elections were held in the Punjab in March 1972 after the war with Pakistan resulted in the independence of Bangla Desh and the prestige of Indira Gandhi was at its highest. The Congress swept the elections in the Punjab, as in many other parts of the country, winning sixty-six out of the total 104 seats. Its communist allies won another ten. The Akalis had fought alone, and won only twenty-four seats. In terms of votes, however, the loss of the Akali Dal was rather marginal, falling from 29.5 per cent in 1969 to 27.7 per cent in 1972. The gain of the Congress was largely at the expense of the Jan Sangh which failed to win any seat and got only 5 per cent of the votes. The Sikh peasant base of the Akali Dal remained virtually intact. The Sikh scheduled and backward castes, however, like the urban Hindus and Hindu Harijans, largely supported the Congress. Thus, when Giani Zail Singh was elected as the leader of the Congress Assembly party on 15 March 1972, to become the Chief Minister of the Punjab, he did not enjoy the support of the Sikh landholders, even though nearly 60 per cent of the Congress legislators were Sikh.[4]

II

In spite of political instability, the first five years of the new Punjab state were marked by a spurt in economic growth. When the Akalis declared in 1967 that they would make the Punjab 'a model province', 'an object of envy' for the rest of the country, the green revolution had already begun. The consolidation of landholdings was completed in 1969. The rural share of electric power in 1970 rose to over 35 per cent. The percentage of irrigated area in the gross area under cultivation was increasing rather rapidly. Nearly 2,000 kms of link roads were constructed in 1969–1970, which was more than the total length of roads built during the First Five Year Plan. The majority of villages were linked with main roads and, therefore, with markets. The functioning of agricultural machinery was ensured by a certain degree

---

[4] For changes in the voting patterns, M. S. Dhami, 'Changing Support Base of the Congress Party in Punjab, 1952–80', *Punjab Journal of Politics*, Guru Nanak Dev University, Amritsar, 1984, Vol. 8, No. 1, 65–97.

of indigenization of technology. A high-yielding variety of dwarf wheat had been introduced in 1965 and within five years the farmers of the leading district of Ludhiana took entirely to this variety. The area under wheat doubled from 1960 to 1970, and the production of wheat increased five-fold.[5]

The Akali regime came to be associated with agrarian prosperity though the green revolution did not lose momentum afterwards. In the Punjab as a whole, wheat and rice production increased threefold from 1965–1966 to 1971–1972, wheat rising from 1.9 to 5.9 million tonnes and rice from 0.29 to 0.92 million tonnes. The rate of increase in the production of maize and cotton as well as wheat and rice became higher in the late 1970s. The output of cereals rose from less than 8 million tonnes in 1975 to nearly 12 million tonnes in 1980. In 1978–1979 the Punjab contributed over 6 million tonnes of foodgrains to the all India procurement of about 11 million tonnes. The production of sugarcane and cotton also increased steadily during the 1970s.

The economic development in the Punjab reduced the poverty ratio to the lowest in the country but industrial production lagged far behind the agricultural production. Small-scale industries came to be concentrated in Amritsar, Jalandhar and Ludhiana, engaged mainly in the production of cotton and woollen textiles, hosiery, cycles, machine tools, agricultural implements, sports goods, steel re-rolling and cotton ginning and pressing, accounting for over 78 per cent of the total value of small industrial production in 1973–1974, and for 90 per cent in 1978–1979. The large- and medium-scale units, about 200 in 1978–1979, accounted for about 48.5 per cent of the total production.[6] Nevertheless, the gap between the growth of agrarian economy and industrialization in the state became wider.

A considerable number of the Sikhs from the towns and villages of the Punjab were moving to other parts of the country in search of better opportunities. In 1971, when the Sikhs formed nearly 1.9 per cent of the total population of the country, more than 20 per cent of them were living outside the Punjab. Their largest number was in Haryana, well over 600,000, which was a part of the Punjab state only a few years before. The combined number of Sikhs in Uttar Pradesh and Rajasthan was larger than in Haryana, and most of them had gone there

[5] Partap C. Aggarwal, *The Green Revolution and Rural Labour*, Sri Ram Centre for Industrial Relations and Human Resources, New Delhi, 1973.

[6] Pramod Kumar and others, *Punjab Crisis: Context and Trends*, Centre for Research in Rural and Industrial Development, Chandigarh, 1984, 52–56.

to reclaim waste lands. Delhi came next with nearly 300,000 Sikhs. In Jammu and Kashmir and in Maharashtra the number of Sikhs was more than 100,000 each; in Madhya Pradesh, it was only a little less than 100,000. The percentage of increase in Sikh population in these states ranged from twenty-four to sixty-eight between 1961 and 1971, a clear index of their outmigration from the Punjab and their integration with national economy and polity.

Of over 8 million Sikhs in the Punjab in 1971, who formed a little over 60 per cent of the total population of the state, over 90 per cent were living in the countryside. Nearly 65 per cent of the Sikhs in the Punjab belonged to the cultivating castes, while Khatrī, Arora, Brahman and Rajput Sikhs formed only about 5 per cent. Even in cities and towns the artisan and scheduled castes among the Sikhs were as numerous as the Sikhs with a 'high caste' background. Altogether, the artisans and scheduled castes formed about a fifth of the total Sikh population, and lived mostly in the villages. The number and propor-tion of 'high castes' among the Sikhs was smaller than among the Hindus who lived mostly in cities and towns. The proportion of scheduled castes too was higher among the Hindus. The proportion of artisans and craftsmen as well as agriculturalists was much higher among the Sikhs.

The effects of agrarian growth in the Punjab on the landholders were not uniform. Amidst a decreasing number of tenants and an increasing number of labourers in the 1970s, the rich and middle-class farmers, owning more than ten acres of land (who formed about 23 per cent of the total landholders) came to operate nearly 65 per cent of the area under cultivation. The peasants owning five to ten acres of land constituted about 20 per cent of the landholders and cultivated about 20 per cent of the land. The poor peasants, who cultivated only about 15 per cent of the land, formed nearly 57 per cent of the landholders. A small class of rich peasants existed side by side with a large group of small and poor peasants. But they all felt concerned about higher prices and cheaper inputs. The Akali Chief Ministers from 1967 to 1971 catered largely to the countryside. Landholdings up to five acres were exempted from land-revenue. The abolition of betterment-fee levied on areas irrigated by the Bhakra canals was accepted in principle. Over 25 millions of dollars from a World Bank loan of 39 millions were earmarked to purchase tractors which could be 'hire-purchased' by farmers for 25 per cent of the price. Prices were 'guaranteed' for procurement. To appeal to the sentiments of landholders, the Akalis contemplated amendment in the Hindu Succession Act of 1956 to enable married women to get a share in the landed property of the father-in-law rather than the father to reduce fragmentation of land-holdings. To hammer the point that the ceiling of thirty acres was an anti-rural measure, the Akali leaders advocated a ceiling on urban property exceeding the value of thirty acres of agricultural land. To underline that middlemen and traders were substantial beneficiaries of the green revolution they proposed to take over the entire foodgrains trade.[7]

On the basis of their experience the Akali ministers became conscious of the areas of tension between the Centre and the State. One such area was funds for developmental purposes. They had a strong feeling that the Punjab was getting a much smaller share from the Centre than its due. No clearance was given by the Centre for the Thein Dam Project, and a thermal project had to be started without prior clearance. The Punjab was not getting its due share from the river waters. The prices of agricultural produce fixed by the Centre were rather low. 'At the political level also we faced interference in the very continuance of the Akali Ministry. These tactics of the Central Party were ultimately instrumental in the overthrowing of our Government.'[8] In the early 1970s, while a few of the Akali leaders were in favour of revising the Centre–State relations in financial matters and a few others were in favour of a separate constitution for the Punjab, the majority advocated the introduction of a genuinely federal system, with defence, foreign affairs, communications and currency as the great prerogatives of the Union Government. It was on the basis of such rethinking that a subcommittee was constituted by the Working Committee of the Akali Dal before the end of 1972 to chalk out a 'policy programme' of the Akali Dal for the future. The proposals of this sub-committee were accepted by the Working Committee in its meeting at Anandpur Sahib on the Baisākhī of 1973. Generally referred to as the Anandpur Sahib Resolution, it was to prove later to be the most controversial resolution passed by the Shiromani Akali Dal in its entire history.

---

[7] For the economic measures and ideas of the Akalis, A. S. Narang, *Storm Over the Sutlej: The Akalis Politics*, Gitanjali Publishing House, New Delhi, 1983, 194–99.

[8] M. S. Dhami, *Minority Leaders Image of the Indian Political System*, Sterling Publishers, Jullundur, 1975, 34–35.

III

During the ministry of Giani Zail Singh, the land ceiling was reduced from 30 to 17.5 standard acres and attempts were made to distribute surplus land among the tenants and the landless. The Akalis regarded this reform as a political stunt, and it did not endear Giani Zail Singh or the Congress to the Sikh landholders. From a 'socialistic' animosity towards large landholders to a thinly veiled antipathy towards the Jats was only a step. Before the end of his ministry in 1977, some of his admirers had begun to credit him with humbling the Jat leaders.

One of the major concerns of Giani Zail Singh, however, was to demonstrate that he was a better Sikh than the best of the Akalis. He was thoroughly familiar with the Sikh scriptures and knew how to use this asset with Sikh audiences. If the 300th anniversary of Guru Gobind Singh's birth was celebrated in 1967 and the 500th anniversary of Guru Nanak's birth in 1969, the Guru Gobind Singh and Guru Nanak Foundations were established during the tenure of Giani Zail Singh with substantial financial support from the government. On his initiative, *kīrtan darbārs* were organized, foundation stones of public buildings were laid with an *ardās* and state functions started with a Sikh ritual. A road was completed in the name of Guru Gobind Singh, to commemorate his march from Anandpur Sahib to Damdama Sahib, combining a large measure of fiction with convenience and utility. When it was inaugurated on 10 April 1973 the Akalis joined the procession. On April 13 Giani Zail Singh received a robe of honour (*saropā*) at Damdama Sahib, in recognition of his meritorious services to the Sikh Panth.

The events which led to the ouster of Giani Zail Singh and his ministry were taking place outside the Punjab. The Prime Minister Indira Gandhi was legally 'unseated' on 12 June 1974 and her popularity in the country was waning. The Akalis held a rally at Ludhiana in support of her arch opponent, Jaya Prakash Narayan. In 1975 they participated in his rally at Delhi in which a call was given for civil disobedience, and people were asked not to recognize Indira Gandhi as the legitimate Prime Minister of the country. On 25 June 1975 she declared that the country was under 'internal emergency'. In a special meeting of their executive on June 30 the Akalis resolved to oppose 'the fascist tendency of the Congress'.[9] On July 9 they launched a 'save

[9] Quoted A. S. Narang, *Storm Over the Sutlej*, 192.

democracy' *morchā*. They were unhappy with the Congress over the delay in starting work on the Thein Dam, discrimination in the allocation of heavy industry, and unremunerative prices for farm produce. The *morchā* continued throughout the period of the emergency, and nearly 40,000 Akalis courted arrest by the beginning of 1977 when the emergency was withdrawn.

In the Parliamentary elections of March, 1977 the Congress was routed. The Acting President of India, B. D. Jatti, dissolved assemblies in nine states in which the Congress was the ruling party and ordered fresh elections. The Akalis formed an alliance with the CPM and the Janata Party to contest the elections in June. Altogether they won ninety-one seats against the seventeen of the Congress. The Akalis alone won fifty-eight out of 117 seats. Parkash Singh Badal, who led the coalition ministry, declared after assuming office that the Punjab economy was largely rural and the countryside deserved great attention: 'The real Punjab lives in villages, and it is necessary that the benefits of our progress must percolate to the countryside and reach the needy people.'[10] The whole additional outlay of 480,000,000 rupees in 1977 was earmarked for increasing agricultural production through extension of irrigational facilities and improvement in infrastructure. An ambitious programme of integrated rural development was launched in November, 1978 in the shape of 'focal points' for groups of villages to provide health services, marketing centres, credit facilities and recreation. Interest rates on loans were reduced by 1 per cent and a new system of credit to farmers was introduced to make it more easily available. The measures and policies of the Akalis benefited the peasantry greatly, and the rich farmers even more.

Contrary to the general impression studiously spread by their self-interested opponents that the Akalis forget their demands when they come into power, in the All India Akali Conference held at Ludhiana in October, 1978 a dozen resolutions were passed in the light of the Anandpur Sahib Resolution endorsed by the Shiromani Akali Dal in 1977.[11] These resolutions represented their most important ideas on the long-term programme of the party, covering a wide range of political, economic, religious, cultural and social issues. A 'real federal shape' of the Indian constitution was demanded in the very first

---

[10] Quoted, A. S. Narang, *Storm Over the Sutlej*, 197.
[11] For the text of the resolution endorsed by Sant Longowal, Government of India, *White Paper on the Punjab Agitation*, Delhi, 1984, 67–90.

resolution 'to enable the states to play a useful role for the progress and prosperity of the Indian people in their respective areas by the meaningful exercise of their powers'. The merger of Chandigarh and other Punjabi-speaking areas in the Punjab, the control of all head-works, the just distribution of river waters, the maintenance of the 'present ratio' of the Sikhs in the army and protection to the Sikh settlers in the Terai areas of Uttar Pradesh were demanded in the second resolution. The third resolution asked among other things for a dry port at Amritsar and a stock exchange at Ludhiana. The fourth resolution asked for Punjabi to be the second language in the states which had a considerable number of Punjabi-speaking people. Some of the significant demands in the other resolutions were a broadcasting station at Amritsar to relay *gurbāṇī* to be erected at the expense of the Khālsā Panth but under the overall control of the Indian Government, and amendment in the Hindu Succession Act to enable a woman to inherit her share in the property of her father-in-law, exemption of farming land from wealth tax and estate duty and a special ministry for the economically backward classes, including the scheduled castes. On the whole, the resolutions of October, 1978 were more a manifesto of the politico-economic concerns of the Akalis than a demonstration of their religious or cultural preoccupations.[12]

IV

If the Akalis in power tended to become more secular, their opponents among the Sikhs tended to become more radical in the spheres of both religion and politics. In 1977 Sant Jarnail Singh succeeded to the headship of the Damdami Taksal at Chowk Mehta, near Amritsar, after the demise of Sant Kartar Singh Bhindranwale (spoken in the plural as a mark of reverence), an organization which had upheld Sikh 'orthodoxy' for several decades in free India. Running almost parallel with this mission was the 'heterodox' mission of the Sant Nirankārīs of Delhi who were much different from the successors of Baba Dayal, the founder of the Nirankārī movement. The Sant Nirankārīs based their teachings on the Sikh scriptures but their leader Baba Avtar Singh also composed his *Avtār Bāṇī* and *Yug Pursh*. Their decreasing reverence

---

[12] Anup Chand Kapur, *The Punjab Crisis*, S. Chand and Co., New Delhi, 1985, 202–05. The author sees a great difference between the resolutions passed at Ludhiana and the Anandpur Sahib Resolution without much justification.

for the Granth Sahib, coupled with their belief in the living *guru*, made the Sant Nirankārīs extremely unorthodox in the eyes of the Sikhs nurtured on the doctrines of the Singh Sabhas. The publication of a book on the nature, affluence and influence of the Sant Nirankārīs brought them into clearer focus.[13]

On the Baisāhī of 1978 the Nirankārī Guru Baba Gurbachan Singh held a congregation at Amritsar. Sant Jarnail Singh Bhindranwale, who subscribed to the twin doctrine of Guru-Granth and Guru-Panth, regarded Baba Gurbachan Singh's congregation in the holiest city of the Sikhs on the day when Guru Gobind Singh had instituted the Khālsā, as an affront to the entire Khālsā Panth. Encouraged by his open resentment over the Sant Nirankārī Congregation, a number of Sikhs went there with the idea of stopping its proceedings. The Sant Nirankārīs were ready. Their bullets proved to be more deadly than the traditional swords of the Khālsā who, consequently, lost many more lives than their opponents. The Akali government took legal action. In June, 1978 however, a *hukmnāma* was issued from the Akāl Takht to all the Sikhs that they should have no connection with the Sant Nirankārīs and they should discountenance their heterodoxy. The *hukmnāma* referred to the false claims of Baba Gurbachan Singh to be an *avtār* and to his turning away from the Shabad-Guru to preach the worship of a human being.[14] The Akalis and the Sikhs in general were content to invoke legal and social sanctions but there were others who wanted to avenge themselves on the Sant Nirankārīs by other means.

In August, 1978 a council of five was formed in Chandigarh to fight the 'Nirankārī onslaught on the Sikhs'. This small organization was called Dal Khālsā. It was believed to have been financed and encouraged by some Congress leaders opposed to the Akali Dal coalition. Another small organization which decided to take revenge upon those Nirankārīs and officials who were connected with the incident of the Baisākhī day of 1978 at Amritsar was a purely religious organization called the Akhand Kirtani Jatha headed by Bibi Amarjit Kaur, the widow of Fauja Singh, an Agricultural Inspector, who was one of the 'martyrs'. The hit squad created by Bibi Amarjit Kaur was headed by Talwinder Singh.

New political ideas and organizations were sprouting in the

[13] Balwant Gargi, *Nirankari Baba*, Thomson Press, Delhi, 1973.
[14] For the text of the *hukmnāma*, Harbans Singh, *Khālistān*, Pbi, Punjabi Writers Cooperative, New Delhi, 1982, 109–10.

1970s rather imperceptibly. The idea of Khalistan was thrown out by Dr Jagjit Singh Chauhan through a half-page advertisement in the *New York Times* in October, 1971 after his brief spell as a Finance Minister under Lachhman Singh Gill. Whatever the superficial historians or self-interested politicians and public men may say about its antècedents, the idea of Khalistan was altogether a new idea. In the 1970s it was treated as a hoax and Chauhan was treated well by some eminent Congress leaders during his visits to India. In the late 1970s the defunct Sikh Students Federation, originally founded in the 1940s, was revived as the All India Sikh Students' Federation (AISSF) by Bhai Amrik Singh, son of the deceased Sant Kartar Singh Bhindranwale, who was closely linked with Sant Jarnail Singh.[15]

Some of the new Sikh organizations were opposed to the Akalis. In the SGPC elections of 1979, for instance, the Dal Khālsā candidates fought against their candidates though without any success. Sant Jarnail Singh Bhindranwale also fielded about forty candidates who were backed by the Congress, but only four of them were elected. In the elections of 1980 Sant Jarnail Singh Bhindranwale supported some of the Congress candidates.[16]

Paradoxically, however, the Congress in the Punjab was becoming less and less representative of the Sikhs during the 1970s. It won sixty-three seats in the elections of 1980 when the Akalis and their Communist allies won only fifty-one. But this was no mean achievement during the 'Indira wave' of the 1980s. In any case, the main support to the Congress in the Punjab came from the Hindus living in urban and semi-urban areas and Harijans living in both villages and towns. Only a small section of the peasantry, and that too with growing interest in business and industry, voted for the Congress. The Akalis and their allies got the bulk of their votes from the agricultural castes, totalling only a little less than 38 per cent of the votes polled. The Akalis alone polled nearly 27 per cent of the votes. The increasing polarization between the country and the town was accompanied by an increasing polarization between the two major religious communities. This development affected the Congress Party in a significant way. The

[15] For 'extremist' organizations, Chand Joshi, *Bhindranwale: Myth and Reality*, Vikas Publishing House, New Delhi, 1984, 32–40.

[16] For the rise of Bhindranwale and the support he got from the Congress leaders, Mark Tully and Satish Jacob, *Amritsar: Mrs Gandhi's Last Battle*, Rupa and Co., Calcutta, 1985, 52–72.

number of Sikh legislators in the Congress was steadily decreasing, from about 65 per cent in 1967 to about 45 per cent in 1980.

V

The Congress Chief Minister Darbara Singh had to deal with a situation marked by increasing militancy and sectarian polarization.[17] Baba Gurbachan Singh, who had been acquitted along with his sixty-one followers by a court ouside the Punjab, was murdered in Delhi after the Punjab Government withdrew its appeal against him from the High Court on the fall of the Akali ministry. His son and successor, Baba Hardev Singh wrote a letter to the Jathedar of the Akāl Takht towards the end of 1981 that he and his followers had deep regard for the Sikh Gurus, that they were never disrespectful towards the traditions and practices of Sikhism, and that they regarded the Guru Granth Sahib as a revelation from God. Baba Hardev Singh also showed his willingness to expunge objectionable passages from the *Avtār Bāṇī* and the *Yug Pursh* by mutual agreement.[18] The Akalis were inclined to accept this apologetic gesture from the head of the Sant Nirankārīs, but there were others who were not.

Meanwhile, separatist ideas began to be aired. An announcement was made on 16 June 1980, about the formation of Khalistan by Balbir Singh Sandhu who put himself forth as the Secretary-General and Jagjit Singh Chauhan as the President of the National Council of Khalistan. Ganga Singh Dhillon, a US citizen, addressed the Sikh Education Conference at Chandigarh in March 1981 to expound the idea that the Sikhs are a distinct nation. His links with Jagjit Singh Chauhan and with the President of Pakistan were known to his Indian supporters, including Jathedar Jagdev Singh Talwandi and Jathedar Gurcharan Singh Tohra. The Chief Khalsa Diwan dissociated itself from the statement of Dhillon in a resolution of 16 April 1981 and asserted that the Sikhs were and would remain an inseparable part of Bharat. Obviously, the idea that the Sikhs are a distinct nation was taken to mean that it carried the implication of political separation. It was suggestive of Khalistan. Nevertheless, the SGPC did pass a resolution

[17] For major events from 1980 to 1984, Jagtar Singh, 'Chronology of Events', *The Punjab Crisis: Challenge and Response* (ed. Abida Samiuddin), Mittal Publications, Delhi, 1985, 702–10.
[18] For the text of his letter, Harbans Singh, *Khālistān*, 111–12.

in 1981 that the Sikhs are a nation. The National Council of Khalistan and the Dal Khālsā stood for an independent state for the Sikhs.

In May, 1981 the All India Sikh Students Federation demanded that tobacco and other intoxicants should be banned in the holy city of Amritsar before the end of the month. On May 28 the Arya Samaj and other 'Hindu' organizations led a huge procession in Amritsar to demand that not only tobacco but also alcohol and meat should be banned in the city of Amritsar. They did not relish the idea of lagging behind in expressing whipped-up religious concerns with political overtones. On May 31, Sant Jarnail Singh Bhindranwale led a procession which clashed with the police and nearly a dozen persons were killed. Tempers were rising.

Lala Jagat Narain, who was present in the Nirankārī congregation at Amritsar on April 13 in 1978 and who had given evidence in support of the Sant Nirankārīs before a special commission, was vociferous through a chain of papers he owned and edited against the protagonists of Khalistan whom he regarded as the enemies of the nation without making any subtle distinction between one group and another among the Sikhs. He was murdered on 9 September 1981. By his own press and by some others he was treated as a great martyr.

Sant Jarnail Singh Bhindranwale was a suspect now as he was after the murder of Baba Gurbachan Singh a year and a half earlier. Giani Zail Singh as the Home Minister had told the Parliament in 1980 that Sant Bhindranwale had no hand in the murder of the Nirankārī Baba. It was more difficult now to defend him openly. At his headquarters at Chowk Mehta, Sant Jarnail Singh chose to offer himself for arrest on 20 September 1981. Unfortunately, the police opened fire because of some misunderstanding and eleven persons were killed. Several incidents of random firing, sabotage and bomb explosions and the hijacking of an Indian Airlines plane took place before Sant Bhindranwale's release from police custody on October 15. Ironically, both Giani Zail Singh and the Akalis were keen for the release of Sant Jarnail Singh Bhindranwale. Two months later Jathedar Santokh Singh was shot dead and when Sant Bhindranwale went to Dehli for the *bhog* ceremony, Buta Singh, the Union Minister for Sports and Parliament Affairs as well as Giani Zail Singh greeted him with customary veneration.

Sant Harchand Singh Longowal presided over a World Sikh Convention in July, 1981 which directed the Akali Dal to plan *dharm yudh* (righteous war) to pursue the Anandpur Sahib Resolution. Early in September the Akali Dal mobilized support for its demands and gave a call for demonstration before the Parliament to present their memorandum of grievances to the Speaker of the Lok Sabha. Only a few of the volunteers were allowed to enter the capital. On September 21, however, the Akalis were able to present a list of forty-five grievances to the Prime Minister. They were asked to prepare a memorandum of their demands. A fresh memorandum of fifteen demands was presented to Indira Gandhi in October, 1981.[19]

The first meeting between the Prime Minister and the Akali leaders was held at New Delhi on October 16. It was meant primarily to identify issues, and the Foreign Minister Narasimha Rao was to take up the issues in detail later. But the Akali leaders who met Narasimha Rao found it 'a waste of time'. Their second meeting with the Prime Minister took place on November 26. One of the issues discussed was the circular issued by Indira Gandhi's government during the Emergency which laid down that recruitment to the defence services was to be made from the different states of the country on the basis of their population. Its implication for the Sikhs was obvious enough. The Akali leaders talked of merit as the main criterion of recruitment but the Prime Minister replied that she had to carry 'others' along, leaving the impression that it was a considered policy of her government to reduce the number of Sikhs in the Indian army.

The impression left on the Akali leaders regarding the more vital issue of river waters was even worse. According to the needs hurriedly estimated for the Indus Waters Treaty of 1955, the Punjab was supposed to require 7.20 million acre feet (maf) of water together with Pepsu, and Rajasthan was supposed to need 8.00 maf, while Jammu and Kashmir were supposed to require 0.65 maf of water. The Punjab Reorganization Act of 1966 stipulated that the waters of the Punjab rivers, but not of the Yamuna from which the Punjab till then had been drawing water for irrigation, were to be divided between the Punjab and Haryana on a basis mutually agreed. If they failed to agree, the Union Government was to decide their shares. Indira Gandhi had decided during the Emergency in 1976 that out of the 7.20 maf of the Punjab share, 0.20 be given to Delhi for drinking purposes and the round figure of 7.00 maf be equally divided between the Punjab and Haryana. Giani Zail Singh as the Chief Minister of the Punjab did not

[19] For these lists, *White Paper on the Punjab Agitation*, 61–65.

relish the patent injustice done to his state. He was given the choice to resign, which he was not inclined to exercise.

When the Akalis came into power they took up the issue with the Prime Minister, Morarji Desai. He could make the Rajasthanis see with their own eyes on the map that they had little to do with the Punjab rivers, but he was not prepared to reopen the decision of 1955. He was prepared to give his own verdict on the shares of the Punjab and Haryana but only on the condition that his verdict would be final. When the Akalis suggested that they could take the issue to the Supreme Court, Morarji Bhai had no objection. A suit was filed, and it was pending in the Supreme Court when Indira Gandhi met the Akalis on 26 November 1981. She gave assurances of much larger supplies of water and energy to the Punjab in the future on the basis of more scientific exploitation of sources but she was not in favour of revising earlier decisions.

Within five weeks, nevertheless, Indira Gandhi gave a unilateral decision. The available water was estimated at 17.17 maf, and out of the additional 1.32 maf 0.72 was given to the Punjab. But at the same time it was made clear to the Akalis that their talk about Rajasthan being a non-riparian state was a contemptible nonsense: even though it was not utilizing the water already allocated, Rajasthan was given the remaining 0.60 maf of the estimated additional waters. It was also decided that Satlej-Yamuna Link (SYL) canal should be completed in two years for Haryana. Of the three Congress Chief Ministers concerned two were eager to accept the decision in self-interest. The Punjab Government felt obliged to withdraw its case from the Supreme Court against its own interest.

After their third and last meeting with the Prime Minister on 5 April 1982 the Akali leaders returned from Delhi with the impression that Indira Gandhi had already made up her mind to let the issues wait. She had, but not on all issues. In view of the impending elections in Haryana she was keen on getting the SYL canal dug for Haryana.

The Shiromani Akali Dal organized a 'block the canal' (*nahar roko*) agitation on 24 April 1982 with the support of the Communist parties, at a village close to Kapuri from where the water of the Satlej was to be diverted to Haryana. Some of the volunteers were arrested. A month later another agitation was launched at Kapuri itself, which also failed to mobilize the peasantry. On July 26 the Akalis decided at last to launch their 'righteous war' (*dharm yudh*) with effect from August 4. It started with Parkash Singh Badal courting arrest with a large number of other volunteers.

Soon afterwards, Sant Jarnail Singh Bhindranwale joined the Akali *dharm yudh*. Two of his followers had been arrested on July 17. Bhai Amrik Singh offended the Punjab Governor Chenna Reddy during his visit to Amritsar by pleading the case of the arrested workers a little too vehemently, and he too was arrested on July 19. Thara Singh, another devoted follower of Sant Bhindranwale, was arrested on July 20. Sant Bhindranwale decided to leave Chowk Mehta to start a peaceful agitation from the Golden Temple complex against their arrest. His call failed to evoke much response. He approached the Akali leaders for support. They asked him to join the 'righteous war' under the leadership of Sant Harchand Singh Longowal. He accepted the suggestion. The two *morchās* became one.

The *dharm yudh* for the political, economic, cultural and religious demands of the Akalis gained increasing momentum in August and September. It became more and more difficult for the government to find room for the protesting volunteers in the existing jails. On September 11 a bus carrying arrested volunteers collided with a train near Tarn Taran and thirty-four of them died on the spot. An impressive procession in their honour was taken out in Delhi on October 10. Five days later Indira Gandhi decided to release all Akali volunteers on the auspicious day of the Diwālī of 1982. Before the end of October, Swaran Singh was negotiating settlement with the Akali leaders on behalf of the Prime Minister. He hammered out a mutually acceptable formula on several important issues, like Chandigarh and river waters, the relay of *kīrtan* from the All India Radio, the Centre-State relations. Indira Gandhi appointed a cabinet subcommittee consisting of Pranab Mukherjee, R. Venkatraman, Narasimha Rao and P. C. Sethi to consider the formula. They accepted it and Swaran Singh told the Akali leaders that the government had approved of the formula. However, the statement placed before the Parliament turned out to be materially different from what had been agreed upon. Indira Gandhi had changed her mind.

A despairing Sant Longowal announced in early November, 1982 that the Akali Dal would hold demonstrations in Delhi during the Asian games. An exhibition of 'Sikh grievances' in the capital on an occasion of international importance was better avoided. A Congress

Member of Parliament, Amrinder Singh, son of Maharaja Yadvindra Singh of Patiala, negotiated with the Akali leaders on behalf of the Prime Minister. An agreement was reached, but it was sabotaged by Bhajan Lal, the Chief Minister of Haryana. Among other things, he assured the Prime Minister that no Sikh demonstrators would be allowed to reach Delhi at the time of the Asiad. Bhajan Lal proved to be truer than his word. No Sikh, whether a Congress member of Parliament or a retired army general, was allowed to pass through Haryana without being humiliated in one way or the other. Many an ordinary Sikh lost not merely metaphorically his 'honour' but literally his turban. The veteran journalist Kuldip Nayyar observed that the Sikhs felt humiliated not as individuals but as members of a community. 'From that day their feeling of alienation has been increasing.'[20]

VI

The number of violent incidents had begun to increase steadily before the imposition of President's rule in October, 1983. In 1982 about sixty such incidents had taken place. In 1983, the number rose to nearly 140. The monthly average by September, 1983, rose to nine. In October the number of violent incidents rose suddenly to thirty-six and in May, 1984, shot up to over fifty. There were bank robberies, thefts of weapons, cutting of telegraph wires, setting fire to railway stations, attacks on policemen, bomb explosions, murders of Nirankārīs, murders of public men and attacks on ministers. There was also the breaking of idols, damage to temples, sacrilege of *gurdwāras*, firing on Hindu shopkeepers, killing of cigarette sellers, firing on *jagrātā* and Rām-Līlā crowds, indiscriminate firing and, finally, the killing of Hindu passengers taken out of buses.[21]

Some of the incidents were more significant than others. On 25 April 1983 for instance, a Deputy Inspector General of Police was shot dead when he was emerging from the Golden Temple. He was not quite an innocent worshipper as he was made out to be, but he was surely trying to perform his duties, risking his life in the process. On October 5–6, a number of innocent Hindu passengers were taken out of a Delhi-bound bus near Dhilwan on the river Beas and murdered in cold blood.

[20] Kuldip Nayyar and Khushwant Singh, *Tragedy of Punjab: Operation Bluestar and After*, Vision Books, New Delhi, 1984, 66.

[21] For a consolidated list of violent incidents, *White Paper on the Punjab Agitation*, 110–62.

It was decided to remove the Chief Minister Darbara Singh immediately to impose President's rule on October 6. Not without justification, he attributed his fall to the machinations of his opponents within the Congress. On the day following, the Punjab was declared to be a 'disturbed area'. The Bengal Governor B. D. Pande was sent to the Punjab as its Governor. His considered view that a political problem required a political solution went unheeded. He could not have a free hand even in the administration of law and order because of the 'backseat driving' of a Punjab Committee sitting in Delhi.

Within four weeks of the President's rule, on October 31, the Sealdah-Jammu Tawi Express was derailed and nineteen passengers lost their lives. The burning of a *gurdwāra* at Churu in Rajasthan on November 26–27 transformed the vicious circle into a spiral. On 14 February 1984 the Hindu Suraksha Samiti observed a *bandh* in which eleven persons died. 'Some members of extremist Hindu organizations committed the sacrilege of damaging the model of the Golden Temple and a picture of Guru Ram Das at the Amritsar Railway Station.'[22] From 15 to 20 February 1984, there was mob violence in Haryana against the Sikhs, generally believed to have been engineered by its Chief Minister on the insistence of the leader of a powerful lobby in Delhi. On February 19, eight Sikhs were killed on the Grand Trunk Road in Panipat within sight of the Haryana police. In retaliation, thirty-five 'Hindus' were killed in the five days following. Harbans Singh Manchanda, the pro-Congress President of the Delhi Gurdwara Prabandhak Committee, was assassinated in Delhi on March 28. On March 31 the examination branch of Guru Nanak Dev University at Amritsar was burnt to obviate the holding of its annual examinations involving nearly a lakh of students.[23] Harbans Lal Khanna, the Bharatiya Janata Party leader, was shot dead in Amritsar on April 2, and eight persons were killed during his funeral procession on the day following. On April 14 an attempt was made to burn down thirty-four railway stations. On May 12, Ramesh Chander, the son and successor of Lala Jagat Narain, was shot dead in Jalandhar. On 2 June 1984 the Janata leader Om Parkash Bagga was killed.

In this steadily worsening situation of escalating violence and

---

[22] *White Paper on the Punjab Agitation*, 30. In Amritsar, however, it was generally believed that this was the work of a Congress legislator.

[23] The *White Paper* is silent on the point but a non-Sikh official of the University was believed to have provided the information needed: such was the complexity of the pattern of violence.

communal polarization, the Akali leaders pursued their *dharm yudh*, looking for a way out of the impasse. Sant Harchand Singh Longowal asked the Akali legislators to resign their seats on 26 January 1983 but with effect from February 21. His call for a meeting of the Sikh ex-servicemen met a good response from nearly 5,000 persons. In the camp at Anandpur Sahib, held under the 'command' of Jathedar Gurcharan Singh Tohra for the training of 'non-violent self-sacrificing squads', the retired Generals J. S. Bhullar and Narinder Singh were present. On 4 April 1983 the Akali leaders organized a peaceful 'block the roads' (*rastā roko*) campaign but violence erupted in spite of their intentions, and twenty-six persons were killed. On June 17, the Akalis organized a 'stop the trains' (*rail roko*) campaign but the government decided not to run any trains, and yet there was some violence. The campaign of the Akalis to 'stop work' (*kām roko*) on August 29 was a great success.

However, the 'clean-hearted' Sikhs who responded to the call of Sant Jarnail Singh Bhindranwale on 3–4 September 1983 did not express much satisfaction with either the success or the methods of Sant Longowal. Tension in the Golden Temple complex was increasing. Sant Bhindranwale referred to the rooms of Sant Longowal as 'Gandhi Niwas' and Sant Longowal referred to his rooms as the 'Ravines of Chambal', known to have been the refuge of dacoits in Madhya Pradesh. Towards the end of 1983, the Bharatiya Janata Party and the Lok Dal demanded army action and the government gave the green signal for Sant Bhindranwale's arrest on December 16. He moved into the Akāl Takht on December 15. While the militants could engage even the security forces, the police felt demoralized; the judiciary was intimidated; Sant Bhindranwale started giving decisions on disputes between private persons, with the implication of a 'parallel government'.

On 8 February 1984 the Akalis organized a *bandh* to demonstrate their strength and their trust in non-violent agitation. It was a success. A tripartite meeting was held on February 14 and 15, which was attended by five cabinet ministers and five secretaries, five of the Akali leaders and fifteen leaders from the opposition parties.[24] It came close to a successful settlement. It was at this juncture that anti-Sikh violence

---

[24] For the tripartite as well as the secret meetings of the Akali leaders and their meetings with the Prime Minister and the cabinet ministers, *White Paper on the Punjab Agitation*, 91–97.

was orchestrated in Haryana to frustrate settlement. On February 27, the Akali leaders carried out their decision to burn the pages of the Constitution which contained Article 25(2) (b) in Delhi and Chandigarh, and they were arrested.[25] Others followed them to court arrest. Early in March Indira Gandhi unilaterally appointed the Sarkaria Commission to go into Centre–State relations.[26] On March 30, the Home Minister P. C. Sethi declared in Parliament that the government was willing to amend Article 25(2) (b). The Akali Dal withdrew the call given for observing the 'Panth Azad' week beginning with April 2. In the absence of any initiative from the Centre, Sant Longowal gave a call in May for non-cooperation with effect from June 3, the day on which Operation BlueStar was to start.

The question of army action in the Punjab was first discussed in December, 1983.[27] Indira Gandhi decided finally in favour of the army action in April, 1984. However, when Sant Longowal declared on May 23 that a *morchā* for non-cooperation would start on June 3, Indira Gandhi's emissaries met Parkash Singh Badal and Gurcharan Singh Tohra on May 27–28 to suggest that the Akali leaders should negotiate settlement instead of launching a *morchā*. The Akali leaders were prepared to pick up the old threads, but on June 2 it became clear that nothing short of the demands in the Anandpur Sahib Resolution was acceptable to Sant Jarnail Singh Bhindranwale.[28]

On June 3 the Punjab was cut off from the rest of the country and movement within the state was made impossible by the presence of troops everywhere. The supply of water and electricity to the Golden Temple complex was stopped. On June 4 the army opened exploratory fire. On June 5 the commandos and CS gas proved to be ineffective. On the morning of June 6 tanks were used against 'the enemy' in the Akāl Takht. Meanwhile, tanks and helicopters were used, among other things, to deter the thousands of agitated villagers from converging upon Amritsar, and several other *gurdwāras* in the state were taken

[25] The real issue, as Sant Longowal wrote to P. C. Sethi, was a separate personal law for the Sikhs, and therefore related to the question of the inheritance of landed property: Kuldip Nayyar and Khushwant Singh, *Tragedy of Punjab*, 85.
[26] Kuldip Nayyar and Khushwant Singh, *Tragedy of Punjab*, 71. The unilateral concessions did not help the Akali leaders to withdraw the *morchā*.
[27] Chand Joshi, *Bhindranwale: Myth and Reality*, 19. In this discussion the idea figured that army action would consolidate Hindu votes in favour of the Congress.
[28] The Prime Minister's broadcast to the nation on 2 June 1984, referred to settlement through negotiations but there was hardly any point in it by then. For the text of the broadcast, *White Paper on the Punjab Agitation*, 105–09.

over by the army. The crucial action in the Golden Temple complex was over before the nightfall of June 6. A large number of pilgrims, including women and children, died in cross-firing. The infuriated troops shot some young men dead with their hands tied at their backs with their own turbans. Some died of suffocation in the 'prisoners camp' set up in a room of Guru Nanak Niwas. According to one estimate, the total casualties of officers and men were about 700 and of civilians about 5,000.[29]

The officers and men of the Indian army commented on 'the courage and commitment' of the followers of Sant Jarnail Singh Bhindranwale who died in action. The Sikhs were outraged at the attack on the Golden Temple complex and the destruction of the Akāl Takht. All sections of Sikh opinion, from the urban sophisticates sipping Scotch in their bungalows in Delhi to the peasants in the fields, were horrified at what had happened. Two Congressite Sikhs resigned from the Parliament. The two best-known historians of the Sikhs returned 'honours' received from the President of India. Operation BlueStar revived the memories of Ahmad Shah Abdali in Sikh imagination. Action from Prime Minister Indira Gandhi came 'too late' and it proved to be 'too much'.[30]

[29] Chand Joshi, *Bhindranwale: Myth and Reality*, 161.
[30] Mark Tully and Satish Jacob, *Amritsar: Mrs Gandhi's Last Battle*, 13. According to Chand Joshi, the negotiations of the Pime Minister with the Akalis failed because they were not meant to succeed: *Bhindranwale: Myth and Reality*, 75.

EPILOGUE

The Akali leaders present in the Golden Temple complex during Operation BlueStar were taken into custody along with some 'extremists' and ordinary visitors, including women and children. The countryside was combed in search of arms and 'rebels', and about 5,000 young men were taken into custody. Quite a few innocent persons were killed in the process. Those who were supposed to have waged war against the state were to be tried by Special Courts. In reaction to the rumours of an attack on the Golden Temple, Sikh soldiers at several places in Bihar, Rajasthan, Assam and Jammu 'mutinied' to march towards Amritsar. Scores of them got killed in the attempt and a few thousand were marked for court martial. Some retired Sikh Generals who thought that these men had acted on the spur of the moment 'under a great emotional stress' wanted them not to be treated as 'ordinary deserters' but their appeal had no immediate effect on the trials.

Sikh reaction to BlueStar induced Prime Minister Indira Gandhi to rebuild the Akāl Takht. The octogenerian Baba Kharak Singh agreed to undertake this service (*kār sewā*) but only on the condition that the Golden Temple was cleared of troops. This was not acceptable to the Prime Minister. Her Minister Buta Singh persuaded Nihang Santa Singh to preside over the reconstruction undertaken essentially by the government. The speedily rebuilt Akāl Takht was handed back to the SGPC by October, 1984. This could hardly help; the building or rebuilding of the Akāl Takht had always been regarded as a prerogative of the Sikhs and their chosen representatives. Sikh resentment against the government was mounting. No computation in Delhi could gauge its intensity. On the morning of 31 October 1984 when the Prime Minister was traversing the short path from her residence to the adjoining office, one of her guards Beant Singh drew his revolver and shot at her; Satwant Singh emptied his sten gun into her frail body. She had returned from an election tour in Orissa; Beant Singh had returned from his home in the Punjab. Physically at one place, they were mentally and emotionally living in two different worlds.

The universality of Sikh resentment was reflected in a spontaneous celebration of the assassination of the Prime Minister in the towns and villages of the Punjab, in the capital of the country and in many parts of the world. An equally spontaneous anger over her assassination resulted in mob violence in Delhi and in some other cities of India. 'Sikhs were sought out and burned to death. Children were killed, shops looted, cars burnt, markets destroyed, houses gutted. Trains were stopped, and Sikhs were picked out and murdered.'[1] In the scenes of arson, looting and murder many policemen were seen in *khākī* and many Congressmen in *khaddar*. More brutal than the days of the partition, the Delhi happenings were a reminder of the historic massacres (*ghallūghārās*) of the eighteenth century. The psychological alienation of the Sikhs was almost complete.

Conversely, if Bluestar brought Indira Gandhi close to the electoral victory, her assassination ensured it for the Congress. To the slogan of unity and integrity of the country was added the charge of separatism in the Anandpur Sahib Resolution for the consumption of emotionally surcharged voters. The Congress scored a thumping victory in the parliamentary elections held towards the end of 1984. It gave the new Prime Minister Rajiv Gandhi great confidence. In March, 1985 the Akali leaders began to be released. The ban imposed on the All India Sikh Students' Federation was lifted. An inquiry into the Delhi massacres was ordered. Sant Harchand Singh Longowal asked the government to apologize to the Sikh community for storming the Golden Temple, demanded the release of Sikhs detained without trial and wanted the government to rehabilitate the Sikh 'deserters'. He declared himself to be against the idea of Khalistan. On invitation from the Prime Minister he went for a secret meeting to negotiate terms of settlement, so secret indeed that it was not known even to Parkash Singh Badal and Gurcharan Singh Tohra. On 24 July 1985 he signed a memorandum of settlement with Rajiv Gandhi, generally called the Rajiv-Longowal Accord.

There was nothing spectacular about the Accord. It provided for an *ex gratia* grant and compensation to sufferers of violence, rehabilitation of Sikh soldiers discharged from the army and extension of the inquiry into the violence against the Sikhs that happened in Kanpur and Bokaro. Some issues had been resolved before Bluestar, like merit as the criterion of selection for the army, an all India Gurdwara Act,

[1] M. J. Akbar, *India: The Siege Within*, Penguin Books, Harmondsworth, 1985, 109.

protection of minority interests and the promotion of Punjabi. The Anandpur Sahib Resolution, like other memoranda on the issue of Centre–State relations, could be submitted to the Sarkaria Commission already appointed. Regarding the two most important issues of territory and river waters, there were positive and rather concrete suggestions. The Accord was hailed as a great document by the bulk of the people in the country. Its spirit appeared to be more important than its letter. It was meant to bring to an end 'a period of confrontation' and to usher in 'an era of amity, goodwill and cooperation'.[2]

BlueStar had not put an end to militancy. The new spirit of protest and resentment it produced was reinforced by the Delhi massacres. There were incidents of violence in March and April, 1985. Nearly eighty persons were killed in transistor-bomb explosions in Delhi in the month of May. There was resentment against the Akali leaders too. Sant Bhindranwale's father Baba Joginder Singh formed the United Akali Dal, unilaterally dissolving the Longowal and Talwandi Akali Dals. Gurcharan Singh Tohra and Parkash Singh Badal retained their former positions only because the district Jathedars expressed their support for them. When the Accord was signed in this context it was denounced as a 'sellout' by Baba Joginder Singh as a spokesman of the militants. That was why Rajiv Gandhi appreciated the courage and guts of Sant Harchand Singh Longowal, and that was also why Sant Longowal was assassinated on 20 August 1985. His mantle fell on Surjit Singh Barnala who had been taken into confidence by Sant Harchand Singh Longowal for signing the Accord and who was more acceptable to the Congress High Command than the more senior leaders.

The polarization between Hindus and Sikhs of the Punjab which had been increasing gradually in the early 1980s and rather suddenly after BlueStar and the Delhi massacres was reflected in the elections held in the Punjab in September, 1985. The Akalis won seventy-three seats; the congress won only thirty-two. Among the Congress legislators there were only a few Sikhs, and many who had always voted for the Congress now voted for the Akalis. Just as the bulk of the Sikh support went to the Akalis, the bulk of the Hindu support went to the Congress. The consolation of the Congress leaders that there was only a slight margin in the votes polled in their favour and in favour of the Akalis was rather hollow. Never were the Punjabis split so clearly on

---

[2] Rajiv Gandhi-Longowal Accord, Satya M. Rai, *Punjab Since Partition*, Delhi, 1986, 405–08.

communal lines as in the elections of September 1985. Surjit Singh Barnala was sworn in as the Chief Minister on the 29th after nearly two years of President's rule in the Punjab. His hope was to see the Accord implemented. His problem was to contain the militants whose spokesmen had boycotted the elections.

The first jolt to the Accord came early, and it proved to be crucial. The capital project area of Chandigarh was to go to the Punjab and some Hindi-speaking territories in the Punjab were to go to Haryana in lieu of Chandigarh. A commission was to be appointed to determine the Hindi-speaking areas on the principle of contiguity and linguistic affinity with a village as a unit. The commission was to give its findings by 31 December 1985, and the transfer of these areas to Haryana and of Chandigarh to the Punjab was to take place simultaneously on 26 January 1986. However, the phrase 'other matters' was added to the terms of reference given to the Mathew Commission for this purpose. When the Akali leaders pointed out this departure from the letter of the Accord, the Prime Minister assured them that this phrase was included as a matter of routine. Nevertheless, though it was well known that a Punjabi-speaking village separated Haryana from the Abohar-Fazilka villages, the Commission identified Hindi-speaking areas in the Abohar-Fazilka region instead of looking elsewhere for Hindi-speaking villages contiguous to Haryana. The Commission, consequently, failed to give a verdict but suggested that another commission could be asked to identify Hindi-speaking areas. Mathew's successor Venkataramiah ruled rather arbitrarily that 70,000 acres should go to Haryana in lieu of Chandigarh, but he could identify only 45,000 acres as Hindi-speaking. It began to be argued now that the remaining 25,000 acres should somehow be given to Haryana. This was unacceptable to the Chief Minister Surjit Singh Barnala because such an area could only be a Punjabi-speaking area. The territorial issue was thus messed up, and Chandigarh was not transferred to the Punjab on 26 January 1986. B. G. Verghese of the *Indian Express* remarked about a year later that Chandigarh was 'a crucial test and posed the first deadline. The Centre must take major responsibility for derailing this part of the accord'.[3]

Militancy began to increase after January 26. By the end of 1986 more than 500 persons had been killed and violence spread from the districts of Amritsar and Gurdaspur to Jalandhar and Hoshiarpur

[3] *Indian Express*, 5 December 1986, editorial page.

across the Beas and to Ferozepur and Ludhiana across the Satlej, spilling into the Union Territory of Chandigarh. Batches of clean-shaven passengers were murdered in cold blood near Muktsar first and then in Hoshiarpur district on 30 November 1986. Early in October a nearly successful attempt was made on the life of Julio Francis Ribeiro, the Director General of Police. Killing of innocent villagers by the CRPF and the BSF personnel began to be reported, followed by 'fake encounters'. According to one report, over 500 crores of rupees were spent on Ribeiro's operations in 1986, inflating the police budget to five times the amount in 1983. The militants replenished their material resources with huge robberies to buy arms from Pakistan. They were partially successful in obliging Hindu families to leave the countyside for the towns and cities or to move out of the Punjab. Increasing militancy brought the question of law and order into focus to create a certain degree of confusion about priorities. A year after the Chandigarh fiasco, while the Chief Minister of the Punjab was complaining about 'the delay in the implementation of the Punjab accord by the Centre and the difficulties it had created for him within and without the party', the Centre in turn was complaining about 'the lack of adequate measures to check the deteriorating law and order situation in the state and the difficulties it had created for the Prime Minister in the rest of the country'.[4]

By now the Chief Minister of the Punjab was politically crippled. The United Akali Dal, which had been formed before the Accord, was sympathetic to the AISSF and the Damdami Taksal, both of which were believed to be the organizers of militancy. They had demolished the Akāl Takht and virtually taken over the *kār sewā* for its reconstruction after 26 January 1986. The police action in the Golden Temple on April 30 divided the Akali Dal into two groups. Though the larger number of Akali legislators were still supporting Surjit Singh Barnala, his opponents under the leadership of Parkash Singh Badal and Gurcharan Singh Tohra enjoyed more popular support. They had a more realistic assessment of the Sikh sentiments. Tohra won against the candidate of the ruling Akalis in the SGPC elections held on 30 November 1986. This was a clear indication of Barnala's fallen credit with the Sikh masses and his position as Chief Minister was further weakened. Parkash Singh Badal as well as Gurcharan Singh Tohra were placed under detention because of their soft attitude towards the

---

[4] *The Tribune*, 19 January 1987, 4.

militants. But this did not help the Chief Minister in handling the deteriorating situation.

Towards the end of 1986 there was an overwhelming media support for a political initiative by the Prime Minister in the form of talks with all segments of Sikhs including the Badal group, the extremists and the middle-roaders, and for implementation of the Accord. There was also a general feeling that the Jodhpur prisoners, barring those who were accused of waging war against the Indian Union, should be released and something should be done to heal the wounds of the riots of November, 1984. There was a near consensus that 'terrorism' could not be wiped out merely with 'superior state terrorism'.[5] Hard line could produce results only when combined with political initiative. Early in 1987 the Punjab appeared to be 'still manageable' to many like Kuldip Nayyar. In a seminar held at Delhi with spokesmen of nearly all Sikh groups there was a consensus that an informal dialogue could be started with the leaders of the Sikh youth in and outside the jails, besides the release of Jodhpur prisoners, the rehabilitation of the remaining 'deserters' and punishing the culprits of the Delhi massacres.[6]

In February 1987 came out the report of the Ranganath Misra Commission on the Delhi riots. The press treated it as 'a whitewash', 'flawed inquiry flawed report' and the 'best of a bad job'. The terms of reference for the inquiry had closed many legitimate angles because the Commission was to inquire into allegations of 'organized violence' and to recommend measures to obviate future recurrence of such violence. The report pointed out the participation of Congress leaders in the riots but absolved the Congress Party from the charge of organizing violence. Against the Congress leader H. K. L. Bhagat the Commission found no 'convincing material' that he had instigated the riots. The police and the Delhi administration were indicted but not the Home Ministry. The report appeared to be 'a great let-down'. The editor of *The Tribune* posed the question: 'should not the Congress(I) individuals who took part in the crimes be identified and punished'?[7] The veteran journalist S. Mulgaokar rightly observed that the report 'carried no conviction with the Sikh community. Instead of winning its trust in some measure it has made the community more distrustful of New Delhi's intentions'.[8] The Chief Minister Barnala, who had

[5] Bhabani Sen Gupta, *Indian Express*, 20 December 1986, 6.
[6] *The Tribune*, 22 January 1987, 3.
[7] *Ibid.*, 25 February 1987, editorial.
[8] *Indian Express*, 28 February 1987, editorial page.

insisted on the release of the report, could derive no consolation from it.

The Punjab Government and the Akali Dal (Longowal) submitted their memoranda to the Ranjit Singh Sarkaria Commission on the Centre–State relations, reiterating their political philosophy in favour of 'true federalism', with the balance of constitutional powers vested in the states and the centre exercising powers only in relation to national security, defence, foreign affairs, communications, railways, aviation and currency. The Constitution, in their view, should have checks and balances to ensure that the Governors of the States were not used by the ruling party at Delhi as rival centres of power to the State Governments. No Governor should have the right to dismiss a State Government until the loss of majority was established on the floor of the House. There should be more clearly laid down rules on when and how the President's rule could be imposed on the States. Ironically, Barnala's ministry was dismissed on 12 May and President's rule was imposed on the Punjab.

Many journalists like Khushwant Singh expected the Punjab Governor, Sidharatha Shankar Ray, to stamp out terrorism as the first priority of his administration. They also wanted the Governor to ensure that Chandigarh was transferred to the Punjab, the SYL canal was completed, and river waters were equitably distributed. The report of the Eradi Commission on river waters was released in June. It came as a great disappointment to the Punjab. According to the Accord, the farmers of the Punjab, Haryana and Rajasthan, were to continue getting water 'not less than what they were using from the Ravi-Beas system as on 1.7.1985'. The claims of the Punjab and Haryana over the remaining waters were to be adjudicated by a tribunal presided over by a judge of the Supreme Court. The SYL canal was to be completed by 15 August 1986. The tribunal presided over by Justice Balakrishna Eradi was to submit its report by 15 January 1987. In view of the elections in Haryana, however, he was asked to defer it to June. The Bhakra Beas Management Board had given the figures regarding usage of water on 1 July 1985, as 9.655 maf for the Punjab, 1.334 maf for Haryana and 4.500 maf for Rajasthan. The total water available was calculated to be 18.28 maf. Only less than 3.00 maf could be distributed between the Punjab and Haryana according to the terms of the Accord. The Punjab was therefore to get at least 10.00 maf. But it was awarded only 5.00 maf by the Commission, which was far less than even the actual usage. Haryana was awarded a much larger share than it actually used: 3.83 maf. The award clearly reflected the political interest of the ruling party in Delhi. The share of Rajasthan, as determined by the Prime Minister Indira Gandhi in 1981, was not touched at all: it remained 8.6 maf.

The editor of *The Tribune* felt constrained to observe that the Rajiv-Longowal memorandum of understanding was 'neither news nor is it any good. The spirit of accommodation and understanding it generated at the time has all but evaporated and the letter remains – a standing monument to the insincerity, waywardness and lack of commitment on the part of persons in authority.' Commitments went into cold storage; statements inundated the media and the society.[9] Another journalist observed a month later that the 'extremists' were gradually asserting their authority in the religio-political affairs of the Sikhs in the absence of any opposition from the Akali factions and the head priests.[10]

The militants were asserting themselves in politics. In the summer of 1987 there were more than a score of militant groups. Four of these were really important: the Khalistan Commando Force, the Khalistan Liberation Force, the Bhindranwale Tigers Force and the Babbar Khalsa. Early in August 1987, Professor Darshan Singh (Acting Jathedar of the Akal Takht since 1986) organized a World Sikh Convention. Its main resolution asked for an area in the north where the Sikhs could have 'a glow of freedom'. This ambiguous goal was actually a reminder of what Jawaharlal Nehru had said in 1946. It failed to impress the militants because it appeared to fall short of Khalistan. Jathedar Darshan Singh was obliged to leave the Golden Temple. In September the Panthic Committee (of the militants) got Khalistan declared as the goal of Sikh politics.

The report of the Sarkaria Commission came out in October 1987. No change in the Constitution was recommended but the Commission did hammer the point that its provisions had been misused by the ruling party at the Centre in its own interests. The report was shelved to gather dust. By this time Rajiv Gandhi had abandoned his political approach in favour of a law-and-order solution. Siddhartha Shankar Ray as the Punjab Governor and Julio F. Ribeiro as the Director General of Police adopted an aggressive policy of repression. Fully armed squads were let loose on the people in the form of

[9] *The Tribune*, 24 July 1987, editorial.   [10] *Indian Express*, 3 July 1987, 6

vigilante, consisting of dismissed policemen and militant approvers. This opened the door to misuse of police power. It was openly justified by Ribeiro and approved by Ray on the plea that the police all over the world used 'undercover people'. The militants were gaining ground nonetheless. In December 1987 they passed a resolution in support of Khalistan at Fatehgarh Sahib, not far from the state headquarters in Chandigarh.

Amidst a great spurt in militancy in early 1988, Bhai Jasbir Singh Rode was released from detention in March to work for a settlement short of Khalistan. He failed to persuade all the groups and there was a split among the militants. Arms were smuggled into the Golden Temple, giving the opportunity to K. P. S. Gill, the Director General of Police, to organize 'Operation Black Thunder'. The 'militants' who surrendered to the security forces were disowned by others and denounced as 'agents' of the government. K. P. S. Gill looked upon this operation as the high point of his career. But he was yet to struggle hard against the militants. Armed stalemate was to continue for a few years more. Even in 1991 a journalist observed that there was no government in the Punjab: there were either the militants or the police.

Meanwhile, V. P. Singh, as leader of the Janata Party, came into power at the Centre as Prime Minister of the National Front. He visited the Golden Temple in a gesture of goodwill towards the Sikhs and repealed the 59th Amendment to the Constitution which had provided for President's rule in the Punjab beyond three years and for declaring an 'emergency' if necessary. He announced speedy trial of the accused in the Delhi massacres, promised to rehabilitate the army deserters of 1984, and agreed to review the case of every Sikh detenu. Above all, he organized all-party meetings to evolve a reasonable political settlement.

The parliamentary elections of November 1989 had brought Simranjit Singh Mann to the fore in Sikh politics. Though still under detention, he was put up as a candidate by the United Akali Dal which won eight seats. The UAD victory was a reflection of the strength of the militants who looked upon Simranjit Singh Mann as a suitable leader. When he came out of jail, Sikhs thronged his meetings, journalists sought his views and politicians courted him. Knowing little about the political aspirations of the militants, he asked for autonomy within the Indian Union in terms of the

Anandpur Sahib Resolution. But the minority government of V. P. Singh was not in a position to concede any major concession. The militants stepped up their activities. By 13 April 1990, Mann was supporting plebiscite for self-determination as the only solution. Despite V. P. Singh's declaration and intentions, President's rule was extended for six months more and the elections due in May were postponed to October 1990. V. P. Singh's helplessness was demonstrated further by the postponement of elections due in October and the extension of President's rule in the Punjab by another six months. All the 'national' parties – the Congress, the BJP and the Communists – were opposed to the elections. They were afraid that the militants would win and resolve in favour of Khalistan in the Punjab Assembly.

Chandra Shekhar, who replaced V. P. Singh, was the leader of a splinter group of the Janata Party and, therefore, even more dependent on the Congress. He offered to discuss political settlement with all the Sikh leaders. Simranjit Singh Mann presented a memorandum, asking for the right of self-determination. The Prime Minister started secret negotiations with some of the militant groups to explore the possibilities of a solution within the framework of the Indian Constitution. The former Akali leaders were in favour of elections but the Congress threatened to revoke the elections if it came into power. Scheduled for 21 June 1991, the elections were postponed in the early hours of the polling day. The Union Home Minister said later that neither he nor Chandra Shekhar knew anything about it. The results of the Parliamentary elections were going in favour of the Congress and the Chief Election Commissioner 'bent backwards to please his new masters': on his own he stopped the polls. The Governor of the Punjab, General O. P. Malhotra, sincere in his commitment to hold elections, resigned on the same day.

The new Congress Prime Minister, P. V. Narsimha Rao, was in no hurry to introduce constitutional procedures. The elections in the Punjab were delayed and were held actually in February 1992. The Communist leader Satya Pal Dang remarked that there was heavy rigging in favour of the Congress. And yet, only about 22 per cent of the total votes were polled. In 70 (out of 117) constituencies, polling was extremely low. These were the constituencies where the Akalis had their roots and support. They had boycotted the elections and non-polling was virtually a referendum against the ruling party.

Nevertheless, the leader of the Punjab Congress, Sardar Beant Singh, claimed that he had got popular mandate.

Beant Singh pursued three interrelated objectives in his tenure of over three years: to suppress militancy, to prove his legitimacy, and to undermine the Akalis. The first three months of his Chief Ministership made no difference to the perilous phase through which the Punjab was passing. The media, the bureaucracy, the educational institutions, and the Panchayats felt obliged to follow the diktat of the militants. They evolved a five-point programme to subvert the banking system, to stop work on the SYL canal, to force intellectuals to sign support for Khalistan, to force Sarpanches to resign so that 'Khalsa Panchayats' were formed, and to target the media officials if they infringed the code imposed on them.

In the summer of 1992, the security forces succeeded in killing some important militant leaders: Rachhpal Singh and Surjit Singh Behla of the Bhindranwale Tigers Force, Amrik Singh Kauli and Sukhdev Singh of the Babbar Khalsa. The founder of the Babbar Khalsa, Talwinder Singh, was eliminated in October. At the end of the year, the editor of *The Tribune* was talking of an 'atmospheric change' in the Punjab. Gurbachan Singh Manochahal, one of the top leaders, was killed early in 1993. The area of Tarn Taran was 'recaptured' by the security forces. By the middle of 1993 the Punjab was relatively calm. Before the end of the year K. P. S. Gill could talk of the Punjab as 'the most peaceful state'. The return of normalcy brought the shocking surprise of 31 August 1995 into sharp relief: Beant Singh was killed by a human bomb which took more than a score of other lives. The Babbar Khalsa maintained that he had earned this punishment for betraying the Sikh community. The Congress Party honoured him as a 'martyr'.

Acutely conscious of a dubious mandate to the Congress, Beant Singh had ordered elections to municipalities in September 1992 with the first appearance of some relief from the militants. Victory of the Congress candidates in the cities and towns of the Punjab was a foregone conclusion: these were the traditional strongholds of the Congress. Elections to Panchayats in the villages were held in 1993 when the militants were 'retreating'. A massive rigging in favour of the Congress candidates was reported. Nevertheless, pro-Akali candidates formed the majority of over 2,400 candidates elected unopposed. In order to create the impression that all the elected

Sarpanches supported the government, a swearing-in ceremony was held at Fatehgarh Sahib. The media made much of Beant Singh's 'success'. But the people of the villages felt merely amused.

Fortunately for Beant Singh, the first by-election to a seat in Parliament took place in Jalandhar, a relatively strong constituency of the Congress. The seat was won by the Congress candidate, Sardar Umrao Singh. However, more than 80 per cent of the Sikh votes went to the Akali candidate, Sardar Kuldip Singh Wadala. In the by-election to the Punjab Assembly from Nakodar in 1994, despite rigging in favour of the ruling party, the Congress candidate won only by a narrow margin. The by-election from Ajnala was actually won by the Akali candidate. Beant Singh's credentials were at stake when he fought the last battle of his life in Gidderbaha, the home constituency of Sardar Parkash Singh Badal. All the Congress legislators and many bureaucrats worked in the field for weeks. Money flowed like water. The Akali candidate won by a narrow margin. But this was enough to indicate that Beant Singh did not rule on popular mandate.

Furthermore, the Gidderbaha battle demonstrated that Beant Singh had failed to undermine the Akalis. He had pursued this objective from day one. As a former editor of *The Tribune* recalled, Beant Singh's relentless campaign against the Akalis was buttressed by a 'ruthless use of government forces'. In 1993 he was actually talking in terms of abolishing the Sikh Gurdwaras Act of 1925. Towards the end of the year he addressed Sikh gatherings at Fatehgarh Sahib and Muktsar to convey his message to the audiences that the Akalis were responsible for all their ills. They were responsible for militancy in which innocent Sikhs lost their lives and suffered many other atrocities. Till he death in August 1995 Beant Singh lost no opportunity to assert that the Akalis were responsible for the decade-long turmoil in the state. However, this assertion did not carry much conviction with the people.

In his anxiety to curb and contain militancy, Beant Singh had not cared about the means and methods employed by the security forces. Along with the militants, innocent persons were killed. Human shields were used by the security forces and the innocent persons killed in the process were declared to be 'terrorists'. In the summer of 1992 it was reported that police excesses and high-handedness continued unabated. In September, some women were kicked to death, apparently to extort information. In transgressing all legal limits the security personnel found the easy way out in blaming all their acts on 'the terrorists'. The lure of rewards induced them to take the chance of killing innocent persons. The relatives of wanted militants were tortured to death. Persons were picked up by the police but in the police records they were neither wanted nor arrested. The 'undercover agents' of the security forces had no regard for life; they had great hunger for property. Early in 1993, villagers were discovering that among the men who plundered, raped or killed were actually policemen, including officers of the rank of Superintendent. It began to be aired that the 'super-cop' Gill was closing his eyes to police illegalities and atrocities. In retrospect this appears to have been an understatement. Such reports continued to pour in. The Chief Minister was either unable or unwilling to rein in the security forces. Peace returned but the people in the countryside remained frightened: they had to reckon with the police. Sad to say, but there were not many mourners in the Punjab at the news of Beant Singh's death.

The return of constitutional politics created some space for the political activity of the Akalis. Jathedar Gurcharan Singh Tohra was re-elected President of the SGPC in November 1992 and the SGPC paid tribute to a few militants as 'martyrs' in the cause of Sikhism. The House demanded the release of Bhai Ranjit Singh who was under detention due to his alleged involvement in the murder of the Nirankari Baba Gurbachan Singh and who had been made Jathedar of the Akal Takht by the SGPC. Resolutions were passed also with regard to the victims of the Delhi massacres of 1984, the second-language status for Punjabi in Haryana, Himachal Pradesh, Delhi and Rajasthan, and visas for Sikh pilgrims to Pakistan. Before the end of 1992, the SGPC asked for an investigation into the violation of human rights in the Punjab by a team from Amnesty International. The Akalis began to condemn the Congress government for its excesses and institutionalized corruption. A number of Akali leaders were arrested in December 1993. The police entered the Gurdwara at Gujjarwal and disrupted an *akhand pāṭh*. The Akalis launched a campaign of protest. In September 1994, Jaswant Singh Khalra was picked up by the police to vanish into thin air like thousands of others. But, unlike others, he had exposed violation of human rights in the Punjab as Secretary of the Human Rights Committee of the

Shiromani Akali Dal. The Akalis launched a *morchā* and many of them were put behind bars.

Gradually, but surely, the Akalis were picking up the old political threads. Before the end of 1993 Jathedar Jagdev Singh Talwandi declared that the aim of the Akalis was to get the demands of the Anandpur Sahib Resolution conceded and implemented, and not to establish Khalistan: the opponents of the Akalis were falsely bracketing them with the militants. In the summer of 1995, even Beant Singh felt impelled to declare that the Punjab could not spare a single drop of water for any other state. Sardar Parkash Singh Badal laid increasing emphasis on the Anandpur Sahib Resolution as the charter of Akali politics, and Jathedar Tohra laid increasing emphasis on Akali unity. The choice was between the political objectives formulated by the Akali leaders before 1984 and the post-BlueStar aspirations expressed by Simranjit Singh Mann. Eventually, the majority of the Akalis opted for their earlier moorings under the leadership of Parkash Singh Badal and Gurcharan Singh Tohra. They launched a sustained campaign of mobilization for elections early in 1996.

In the elections held in February 1997, the Shiromani Akali Dal won two-thirds of the total number of seats. Their unprecedented success can be taken as a measure of the alienation from the Congress of the people of the Punjab villages. The Sikhs of the Punjab feel gratified that they have survived the gravest crisis of their history since 1947. The Akalis are groping for solutions to the problems created for the Punjab since 1966. Many people in the country entertain the hope that the leaders of the so-called 'national' parties will learn to accommodate 'regional' aspirations and to move towards a genuinely federal system of polity. The future of the Sikhs of the Punjab is closely linked up with the nature and functioning of the Indian federation in the future.

THE SUCCESSORS OF GURU NANAK

1539–1552	Guru Angad (b.1504)
1552–1574	Guru Amar Das (b.1479)
1574–1581	Guru Ram Das (b.1534)
1581–1606	Guru Arjan (b.1563)
1606–1644	Guru Hargobind (b.1595)
1644–1661	Guru Har Rai (b.1630)
1661–1664	Guru Har Krishan (b.1656)
1664–1675	Guru Tegh Bahadur (b.1621)
1675–1708	Guru Gobind Singh (b.1666)

THE DESCENDANTS OF GURU RAM DAS

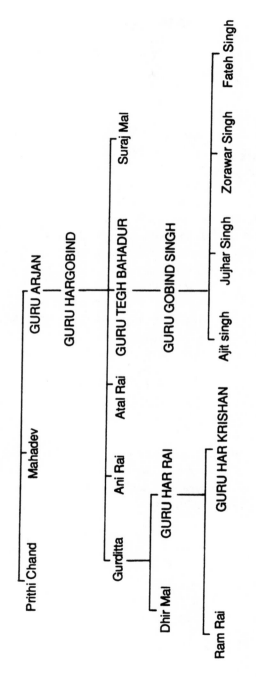

THE MUGHAL RULERS OF INDIA

1526–1530	Zahiruddin Muhammad Babur
1530–1556	Nasiruddin Muhammad Humayan*
1556–1605	Jalaluddin Muhammad Akbar
1605–1627	Nuruddin Jahangir
1627–1658	Shihabuddin Shah Jahan (dethroned)
1658–1707	Muhiyuddin Aurangzeb
1707–1712	Muhammad Mu'azzam Shah Alam Bahadur Shah
1712–1713	Muhammad Muizzuddin Jahandar Shah
1713–1719	Jalaluddin Muhammad Farrukh Siyar
1719–1719	Shamsuddin Muhammad Rafi ud-Darajat
1719–1719	Neko Siyar
1719–1748	Nasiruddin Muhammad Shah
1748–1754	Abu al-Nasir Muhammad Ahmad Shah
1754–1759	Muhammad Azizuddin Alamgir II
1759–1806	Jalaluddin Ali
	Gohar Shah Alam II (blinded in August 1788)
1806–1837	Muhiyuddin Akbar Shah II
1837–1858	Abul al-Zafar Muhammad
	Sirajuddin Bahadur Shah II (banished)

*After Humayun's defeat in May 1540 and his eventual expulsion from India, Sher Shah Suri and Islam Shah ruled over northern India till April 1554, and then their successors Muhammad Adil Shah, Ibrahim Shah and Sikandar Shah till July 1555.

CHRONOLOGY OF EVENTS
FROM 1708 TO 1997

1708	October 7 Guru Gobind Singh's death
1709	November 26 Samana sacked by Banda Bahadur
1710	May 14 Sarhind occupied by Banda Bahadur
1710	December 10–11 evacuation of Lohgarh by Banda Bahadur
1713	February 22 Abdus Samad Khan made governor of Lahore
1715	December 7 surrender of Banda Bahadur at Gurdas Nangal
1716	June 9 execution of Banda Bahadur at Delhi
1725	February occupation of Gujarat by the Marathas
1725	establishment of the Nizamat of Hyderabad
1726	Zakariya Khan made governor of Lahore
1733	February occupation of Malwa by the Marathas
1733	*jāgīr* given by Zakariya Khan to Kapur Singh with the title of Nawab to conciliate the Sikhs
1737	death of Abdus Samad Khan
1738	March the province of Qandahar taken over by Nadir Shah
1738	June the province of Kabul taken over by Nadir Shah
1738	November martyrdom of Bhai Mani Singh
1739	invasion of India by Nadir Shah: sack of Delhi; the four *parganas* of the province of Lahore and the Mughal territories west of the Indus ceded to Nadir Shah
1739	May Nadir Shah's baggage plundered by the Sikhs
1740	August Massa Ranghar murdered by Mahtab Singh and Sukha Singh
1740	foundation of the Nizamat of Bengal
1742	foundation of the kingdom of Awadh under Safdar Jang
1745	July 1 death of Zakariya Khan
1746	January 3 Yahiya Khan made governor of Lahore
1746	May 1 the first carnage (*chhotā ghallūghārā*)
1747	March Yahiya Khan ousted from Lahore by Shah Nawaz Khan
1748	January 12 Lahore occupied by Ahmad Shah Abdali
1748	March Ahmad Shah Abdali's defeat at Manupur near Sarhind
1748	April Ram Rauni built by the Sikhs at Amritsar

1748 April Muin-ul-Mulk, known as Mir Mannu, made governor of Lahore

1752 Mir Mannu defeated by Ahmad Shah Abdali but retained as the governor of Lahore; conquest of Kashmir by Ahmad Shah Abdali

1753 October death of 'Nawab' Kapur Singh

1753 November 4 death of Mir Mannu

1753 occupation of Fatehabad by Jassa Singh Ahluwalia

1757 Prince Timur Shah made the governor of Lahore by Ahmad Shah Abdali

1758 March Sarhind occupied by the Marathas

1758 April Lahore occupied by the Marathas

1761 January 14 the Marathas defeated by Ahmad Shah Abdali in the battle of Panipat

1761 March Ala Singh recognized as a vassal chief by Ahmad Shah Abdali

1761 September Khwaja Abed, the Afghan governor of Lahore, defeated by the Sikhs near Gujranwala

1762 February 5 the great carnage (*waddhā ghallūghārā*)

1762 April the Golden Temple destroyed by Ahmad Shah Abdali

1763 May Qasur sacked by the Sikhs under the leadership of Hari Singh Bhangi, Charhat Singh Sukarchakia, Jassa Singh Ramgarhia and Jai Singh Kanhiya

1764 January the Afghan governor Zain Khan killed and the territories of Sarhind occupied by the Sikhs.

1765 May Lahore captured by Gujjar Singh, Lehna Singh and Sobha Singh; Gobind Shahi coin struck at Lahore

1765 occupation of Gujrat by Gujjar Singh Bhangi; death of Hari Singh Bhangi

1765 death of Ala Singh of Patiala

1767 Rai Ahmad Manj, the Rajput chief of Nakodar, ousted by Tara Singh Dallewalia

1767 Pind Dadan Khan, Ahmadabad, Jehlam and Rohtas occupied by Charhat Singh Sukarchakia in concert with Gujjar Singh Bhangi

1767 the Gakkhar chief Muqarrab Khan ousted from Rawalpindi by Milkha Singh Thehpuria in association with Gujjar Singh Bhangi and Charhat Singh Sukarchakia

1771 occupation of Bhera by Dhanna Singh with the assistance of Jhanda Singh Bhangi

1772   October 23 death of Ahmad Shah Abdali
1772   occupation of Multan by Jhanda Singh Bhangi
1773   occupation of Sultanpur by Jassa Singh Ahluwalia
1774   death of Charhat Singh Sukarchakia and Jhanda Singh Bhangi
1775   Jassa Singh Ramgarhia dislodged from his territories by Jassa Singh Ahluwalia and Jai Singh Kanhiya
1780   November 13 birth of Ranjit Singh
1780   Rai Ibrahim Bhatti ousted from Kapurthala by Jassa Singh Ahluwalia
1780   Multan recovered by Timur Shah; Muzaffar Khan Saddozai appointed as its governor
1783   October 20 death of Jassa Singh Ahluwalia
1783   occupation of the Kangra fort by Jai Singh Kanhiya
1783   occupation of Alipur and Manchar by Mahan Singh Sukarchakia
1785   territory lost in 1775 recovered by Jassa Singh Ramgarhia
1786   recovery of the Kangra fort by Sansar Chand
1788   death of Gujjar Singh Bhangi
1790   occupation of Malka Hans by Bhagwan Singh Nakkai
1790   death of Mahan Singh Sukarchakia
1793   death of Jai Singh Kanhiya
1793   death of Timur Shah
1797   death of Lehna Singh Bhangi of Lahore
1798   November occupation of Lahore by Zaman Shah
1799   July 7 occupation of Lahore by Ranjit Singh
1803   tribute paid by Muzaffar Khan of Multan and Ahmad Khan Sial of Jhang to Ranjit Singh.
1804   tribute paid by Fateh Khan Baloch of Sahiwal and Jafar Khan Baloch of Khushab to Ranjit Singh
1805   occupation of Amritsar by Ranjit Singh
1806   January treaty of the East India Company with Ranjit Singh and Fateh Singh Ahluwalia
1807   occupation of Qasur, Dipalpur, Hujra Shah Muqim, Pathankot and Sialkot by Ranjit Singh
1808   occupation of the fort of Shaikhupura by Ranjit Singh
1809   April 25 the Treaty of Amritsar signed by Ranjit Singh alone with the East India Company
1809   August 24 occupation of the fort of Kangra by Ranjit Singh

1809   occupation of Philaur, Adina Nagar and Sujanpur by Ranjit Singh

1810   occupation of Sahiwal, Khushab, Kusak, Khari Khariali and Gujrat by Ranjit Singh

1811   October 7 occupation of Jalandhar by Ranjit Singh

1812   occupation of Akhnur by Ranjit Singh

1813   occupation of Shamsabad, Pindi Gheb and the fort of Attock by Ranjit Singh

1815   occupation of Jammu and Rawalpindi by Ranjit Singh

1816   occupation of Jhang and the territories of the Ramgarhias by Ranjit Singh

1817   occupation of Nurpur Tiwana by Ranjit Singh

1818   June 2 occupation of Multan by Ranjit Singh

1819   June 23 occupation of Rajauri by Ranjit Singh

1819   July conquest of Kashmir by Ranjit Singh

1821   December 14 occupation of Mankera by Ranjit Singh

1822   March Ventura and Allard employed by Ranjit Singh

1825   December Fateh Singh Ahluwalia seeks protection with the British across the Satlej

1826   return of Fateh Singh Ahluwalia to vassalage under Ranjit Singh

1828   March the title of Rajā-i-Rājgān conferred on Dhian Singh by Ranjit Singh

1831   the territory on the west of the Satlej allowed earlier to remain under Bahawal Khan now taken over by Ranjit Singh

1831   October 25 meeting between Ranjit Singh and William Bentinck at Ropar

1832   December 26 the Indus Navigation Treaty signed by Ranjit Singh with the East India Company

1834   occupation of Peshawar by Ranjit Singh

1836   occupation of Dera Ismail Khan by Ranjit Singh

1837   April 30 the battle of Jamrud

1837   October death of Fateh Singh Ahluwalia

1838   June 25 the Tripartite Treaty signed by Ranjit Singh with the British and Shah Shuja

1839   June 27 death of Ranjit Singh

1839   September 1 investiture of Kharak Singh as the ruler of Lahore

1840   occupation of Mandi, Suket and Kulu by Kharak Singh

1840   May Iskardu made tributary by Kharak Singh

1840   November 5 death of Kharak Singh and Prince Nau Nihal Singh

1840   December 2 Rani Chand Kaur proclaimed Regent of the Punjab

1841   January 17 Maharani Chand Kaur removed from the palace and given a *jāgīr*

1841   January 20 Prince Sher Singh invested as the Maharaja

1841   June 12 Maharani Chand Kaur murdered by her female attendants

1843   September 15 Maharaja Sher Singh and Raja Dhian Singh assassinated by the Sandhanwalias

1843   September Dalip Singh proclaimed Maharaja with Raja Hira Singh as the Prime Minister

1844   May 21 Raja Hira Singh and Pandit Jalla assassinated by the army Panchas

1845   September 21 Jawahar Singh, brother of Rani Jindan, murdered by the army Panchas

1845   December 11 the Satlej crossed by the Lahore army

1845   December 13 war declared by the British against the rulers of Lahore

1845   December 18 the battle of Mudki

1845   December 21–22 the battle of Pherushahr

1846   January 21 a skirmish near Baddowal

1846   January 28 the battle of Aliwal

1846   February 10 the battle of Sabraon

1846   March 9 the Treaty of Lahore

1846   March 16 a separate treaty signed by Raja Gulab Singh with the British by which he was made the ruler of Jammu and Kashmir in subordination to the British

1846   December 22 the Treaty of Bhayirowal

1848   April 20 murder of Vans Agnew and W. Anderson at Multan

1848   September 4 siege of Multan

1848   November 22 the battle of Ramnagar

1849   January 13 the battle of Chillianwala

1849   January 22 fall of Multan

1849   February 21 the battle of Gujrat

1849   March 11 Chattar Singh and Raja Sher Singh surrendered to Major Gilbert near Rawalpindi

1849   March 14 arms laid down by the supporters of Chattar Singh and Raja Sher Singh

1849   March 29 annexation of the Punjab

1857–58 uprisings in India and at a few places in the Punjab;
Muslims, Hindus and Sikhs of the Punjab support the British

1862 Baba Ram Singh institutes the Sant Khalsa

1863 Baba Ram Singh ordered not to leave his village

1872 Baba Ram Singh's Kūkās (Nāmdhārīs) strike at Malaud and
Malerkotla; sixty-five of them are blown from guns

1873 foundation of Sri Guru Singh Sabha at Amritsar

1877 the Brahmos start their monthly *Harī Hakīkat*; Swami
Dayanand visits the Punjab

1879 foundation of the Singh Sabha of Lahore

1880 publication of Giani Gian Singh's *Panth Parkash*

1882 the Punjab University is established at Lahore

1883 the Aryas of Lahore found a college in commemoration of
Swami Dayanand's death

1887 Sir Syed Ahmed Khan advises Muslims to remain aloof from
the Indian National Congress

1888 Arya 'fire-brands' of Lahore attack Sikh Gurus; Bhai Jawahar
Singh and Bhai Ditt Singh leave the Arya Samaj and join the
Singh Sabha; the Sikh leaders of Lahore submit to the
Governor General that the Sikhs should be treated as a
community separate from the Hindus

1892 the first Khalsa College is founded at Amritsar; the Kanya
Maha Vidyalaya is founded at Ferozepore; Giani Gian Singh's
Tawārīkh-i Gurū Khālsā is published

1893 Khalsa Diwan is founded at Amritsar; split in the Arya Samaj

1895 The Punjab National Bank is founded at Lahore

1896 Khalsa Diwan is founded at Lahore

1898 Bhai Kahn Singh Nabha's *Ham Hindū Nahīn* is published

1900 some Rehtia Sikhs are shaved by the Arya leaders of Lahore in
a ceremony of purification (*shuddhī*)

1902 Chief Khalsa Diwan is founded at Amritsar

1905 Sant Badan Singh's commentary on the *Ādi Granth* is published

1907 agitation over water tax and proprietary rights

1909 membership of the Punjab Council raised from nine to thirty
and election partially introduced; the first Hindu Conference is
held; the Anand Marriage Act is passed

1911 for the first time anyone claiming to be a Sikh is returned as
such in the census

1913 outer wall of Gurdwara Rakabganj is demolished; the *Sikh Re view* is launched as a part of Sikh agitation

1914 the Ghadarites resort to robberies for raising funds

1915 the Ghadarites approach army units for armed revolt; the Chief Khalsa Diwan publishes a comprehensive code of conduct as *Gurmat Parkāsh Bhāg Sanskār*

1917 a Sikh deputation meets the Punjab Governor for separate electorates

1918 representatives of the Sikh community impress upon the government the need to implement the principle of weightage and reservations enunciated in the Montford Report

1919 formation of Central Sikh League is announced at Lahore in March; it is inaugurated at Amritsar in December

1920 the Government reconstructs the wall of Gurdwara Rakab-ganj; Singh reformers take over the Golden Temple and the Akal Takht; Shiromani Gurdwara Prabandhak Committee and the Shiromani Akali Dal are formed

1921 Darbar Sahib at Tarn Taran is taken over by the Akalis; over a hundred Akalis are massacred at Nankana Sahib before its Gurdwaras are taken over by the SGPC; Sunder Singh Ram-garhia is asked to hand over the keys of the Golden Temple Complex to the SGPC President, Baba Kharak Singh

1922 keys of the Golden Temple are handed over to Baba Kharak Singh; Guru ka Bagh *morcha* begins; the Babbar Akali Jatha is formed and the *Babbar Akālī Doābā* is launched; Gurdwara Guru ka Bagh is handed over to the SGPC

1923 Maharaja Ripudaman Singh of Nabha is forced to abdicate; Akalis are arrested at Jaito and *akhand pāṭh* is interrupted; the SGPC and the Shiromani Akali Dal are declared to be un-lawful associations; the Babbar Akalis are declared to be unlawful

1924 21 February, a special *jathā* of 500 Akalis reaching Jaito is fired at; 300 are injured and 100 killed

1925 Sikh Gurdwaras Bill is introduced in the Punjab Legislative Council and passed, coming into force on 1 November; the *Kirtī* is launched

1926 six Babbar Akalis are hanged to death; Bhagat Singh founds the Naujawan Bharat Sabha

1928 Akali and Central Sikh League leaders attend the All-Parties Conference at Delhi; Mangal Singh Gill of the Central Sikh League is made a member of Moti Lal Nehru Committee; the Kirti Kisan Party is founded at Amritsar; protest against Simon Commission is made at Lahore; J. P. Saunders is murdered

1929 the Congress declares 'complete independence' as its goal and gives assurance to minorities that no constitution for India would be accepted without their consent

1930 the Central Sikh League, the Shiromani Akali Dal and the SGPC join the Civil Disobedience launched by Mahatma Gandhi

1931 Master Tara Singh presents a memorandum to Mahatma Gandhi as representative of the Sikhs at the Round Table Conference

1932 23 March, execution of Bhagat Singh, Sukhdev and Rajguru; formation of Khalsa Darbar to oppose the 'communal award'

1934 the Kirti Kisan Party is declared unlawful

1937 the Congress and the Shiromani Akali Dal contest the Sikh seats in the elections; Sikandar and Jinnah sign a pact

1938 All-India Akali Conference is held at Rawalpindi

1939 Outbreak of the Second World War

1940 Master Tara Singh resigns from the Congress Working Committee due to basic differences with Mahatma Gandhi on the issue of recruitment; All India Muslim League passes what is popularly known as the Pakistan resolution; V. S. Bhatti publishes his *Khālistān*

1941 formation of Khalsa Defence League under the Maharaja of Patiala

1942 Baldev Singh joins the ministry; Master Tara Singh presents a memorandum to Sir Stafford Cripps, asking for reorganization of the Punjab province; the Akalis put forward the Azad Punjab Scheme

1943 Sadhu Singh Hamdard publishes his *Āzād Punjab*

1944 Rajagopalachari's formula and Gandhi–Jinnah talks impel the Akalis to ask for a Sikh state as an alternative to Pakistan

1945 Failure of the Simla Conference

1946 the Akalis win twenty-three out of thirty-three Sikh seats in the elections; Khizr Hayat Khan forms a coalition ministry; the Cabinet Mission proposals are rejected by the Akalis;

Baldev Singh is allowed by the Panthic Pratinidhi Board to join the Interim Government as Defence Minister

1947 Khizr Hayat resigns; Lord Mountbatten replaces Lord Wavell; non-Muslim legislators of the Punjab resolve in favour of its partition; India is divided into two sovereign states, each having truncated Bengal and Punjab

1948 the Congress constitutes a committee to consider the recommendations of the Dar Commission; Akali legislators join the Congress Assembly Party and Giani Kartar Singh is inducted into the cabinet; Hindi and Punjabi replace Urdu as the medium of education in schools; PEPSU is inaugurated by Sardar Patel and a caretaker government is formed by Gian Singh Rarewala; the Shiromani Akali Dal resolves in favour of separate representation to the Sikhs; the Minority Committee formed by the Punjab Chief Minister recommends weightage for the Sikhs and formation of a new province of six districts as an alternative

1949 Jalandhar Municipal Committee makes Hindi in Devnagri script the medium of school education; the Senate of the Punjab University rejects Punjabi even in Devnagri script as the medium of school education; Bhim Sen Sachar evolves a language formula to give due recognition to Punjabi; he is replaced by Bhargava as Chief Minister; the Congress Working Committee adopts the report of the committee on the recommendations of the Dar Commission

1950 The Constitution of India remains unsigned by the Akali members of the Constituent Assembly; the Working Committee of the Akali Dal resolves in favour of a linguistic state in the Punjab, and revokes merger of the Akali legislators with the Congress Assembly Party

1951 Raghubir Singh becomes Chief Minister of PEPSU; the Arya leaders ask Hindus to return Hindi as their 'mother-tongue'; Bhargava resigns as Punjab Chief Minister and President's rule is imposed without any constitutional justification

1952 the Akalis win only thirteen seats; the Congress forms the ministry; the United Front ministry under Gian Singh Rarewala displaces the Congress ministry in PEPSU; a Telugu-speaking state is announced after fast unto death by Potti Sriramulu

1953 President's rule is imposed in PEPSU; the State Reorganization Commission is formed

1964 the Akalis win only twelve seats in the mid-term polls in PEPSU and the Congress forms ministry

1955 Master Tara Singh replaces Ishar Singh Majhail as the SGPC President; Sachar apologizes for police entry into the Golden Temple complex; the State Reorganization Commission recommends merger of PEPSU and Himachal Pradesh with the Punjab

1956 Hukam Singh works out a 'Regional Formula' which is acceptable to the Congress as well as to the Akalis; only PEPSU is merged with the Punjab and the new state is inaugurated on 1 November

1957 the 'save Hindi' agitation in the Punjab

1958 Master Tara Singh loses SGPC Presidentship to a candidate supported by Partap Singh Kairon

1960 all the 132 Akali members of the SGPC take pledge at the Akal Takht to work for the creation of a Punjabi-speaking state; Sant Fateh Singh goes on fast unto death

1961 Sant Fateh Singh is persuaded by Master Tara Singh to give up fast on the basis of his talks with Jawaharlal Nehru; Sant Fateh Singh's talks with Nehru fail; Master Tara Singh goes on fast; he is persuaded by Hardit Singh Malik to give it up; the S. R. Das Commission is appointed

1962 the Punjabi University is inaugurated at Patiala; report of the Das Commission finds no injustice in the delay to implement the Regional Formula; the Congress wins 90 out of 154 seats in the elections

1963 Jawaharlal Nehru recommends inquiry into charges against Kairon

1964 Nehru dies; Kairon resigns before he is indicted by the Enquiry Commission

1965 Sant Fateh Singh wins majority in the SGPC elections against Master Tara Singh; Kairon is assassinated; Sant Fateh Singh postpones fast unto death in view of the outbreak of war with Pakistan and gives support to the government; a Parliamentary Committee and a cabinet subcommittee are formed to create a Punjabi-speaking state

1966 Prime Minister Lal Bahadur Shastri dies and his place is taken by

Indira Gandhi; the Congress Working Committee recommends creation of a Punjabi-speaking state; a Commission is appointed (bypassing the Parliamentary Committee) with new terms of reference; the Punjabi-speaking state is created and inaugurated on 1 November despite protests from the Akalis; Sant Fateh Singh goes on fast to get Chandigarh included in the Punjab and Hukam Singh persuades him to give it up

1967 the Congress wins only forty-eight seats in the elections and the Akalis form a coalition government with 'Justice' Gurnam Singh as the Chief Minister; his ministry falls due to defection by Lachhman Singh Gill who is supported by the Congress

1968 the Congress withdraws support to Gill; the Akalis resolve in favour of a genuinely federal system

1969 Jathedar Darshan Singh Pheruman goes on fast and dies for getting Chandigarh included in the Punjab; Sant Fateh Singh announces his resolve to immolate himself on 1 February on the same issue; Guru Nanak University is inaugurated at Amritsar

1970 Indira Gandhi awards Chandigarh to the Punjab and a part of the Fazilka Tehsil to Haryana (with effect from 1975); Sant Fateh Singh is persuaded to give up his fast; Sardar Parkash Singh Badal becomes the Chief Minister in place of 'Justice' Gurnam Singh

1971 the Akalis win only one seat in the Parliamentary elections; President's rule is imposed on the Punjab after Badal's advice to the Governor to dissolve the Assembly

1972 the Congress wins 64 out of 104 seats of the Punjab Assembly and Giani Zail Singh becomes the Chief Minister

1973 the Working Committee of the Akali Dal passes a set of resolutions known collectively as the Anandpur Sahib Resolution

1974 Indira Gandhi is legally unseated

1975 Indira Gandhi declares 'internal emergency'; Akalis launch the 'save democracy' morchā

1976 Indira Gandhi awards only 3.5 maf of water to the Punjab

1977 the Akalis win 58 out of 117 seats in the Assembly elections and Parkash Singh Badal heads a coalition ministry

1978 the All-India Akali Conference at Ludhiana passes the

Anandpur Sahib Resolution as endorsed by the Akali Dal in 1977; a number of Sikhs are killed in a clash with the armed Sant Nirankaris in Amritsar; the Dal Khalsa is founded at Chandigarh to fight the Nirankari menace

1979 Candidates of the Dal Khalsa and Sant Jarnail Singh Bhindranwale contest elections to the SGPC

1981 Lala Jagat Narain is murdered; Sant Jarnail Singh Bhindranwale is arrested and released; Akalis meet the Prime Minister

1982 Indira Gandhi gives 0.72 maf more of water to the Punjab, 0.60 maf more to Rajasthan, and decides to complete the SYL canal for Haryana; the Akalis start the *nahar roko* agitation first and then *dharmyudh* for the Anandpur Sahib Resolution

1983 President's rule imposed on the Punjab; violence escalates

1984 violence escalates still further; the Akal Takht is destroyed in Operation BlueStar and Sant Jarnail Singh Bhindranwale is killed; Indira Gandhi is assassinated; the Sikhs are massacred in Delhi and some other cities

1985 Akali leaders are released from detention and Sant Longowal signs an agreement with Prime Minister Rajiv Gandhi; Sant Longowal is assassinated; Sardar Surjit Singh Barnala becomes Chief Minister after the September elections

1986 Police action in the Golden Temple; Jathedar Gurcharan Singh Tohra is re-elected as SGPC President against the candidate of the ruling Akalis

1987 Barnala ministry is dismissed and President's rule is imposed on the Punjab; a World Sikh Convention asks for an area of freedom for the Sikhs; resolution for Khalistan is passed at Fatehgarh Sahib

1988 Operation Black Thunder obliges some militants to surrender

1989 Simranjit Singh Mann is catapulted by the November elections as a militant leader; asks for autonomy in terms of the Anandpur Sahib Resolution

1990 Mann declares plebiscite for self-determination as the only solution

1992 February elections are boycotted by the Akalis; less than 22 per cent of the votes are polled; Beant Singh becomes the Congress Chief Minister; Jathedar Tohra is re-elected SGPC President

1993 Akali leaders are arrested

1994 by-elections in Nakodar and Ajnala take place; Jaswant Singh Khalra is picked up by the police and the Akalis launch an agitation

1995 by-election in Gidderbaha is won by the Akalis despite an all-out effort by Beant Singh; a human bomb blasts Beant Singh

1997 the Akalis win two-thirds of the seats in the February elections

HEADS OF BRITISH ADMINISTRATION IN THE PUNJAB

1849–1853	Board of Administration: Henry Lawrence, John Lawrence and Charles E. Mansel (replaced by Robert Montgomery in 1851)
1853–1858	John Lawrence as Chief Commissioner
1859	John Lawrence as Lieutenant Governor

LIEUTENANT GOVERNORS

1859–1865	Robert Montgomery
1865–1870	Donald McLeod
1870–1871	Henry Marion Durand
1871–1877	Robert Henry Davies
1877–1882	Robert Eyles Egerton
1882–1887	Charles Umphreston Aitchison
1887–1892	James Broadwood Lyall
1892–1897	Dennis Fitzpatrick
1897–1902	William MacWorth Young
1902–1907	Charles Montgomery Rivaz
1907–1908	E. J. Denzil Ibbetson (for a few months Thomas Gordon Walker acted in his place)
1908–1913	Louis William Dane
1913–1919	Michael O'Dwyer
1919–1921	E. D. Maclagan

GOVERNORS

1921–1924	E. D. Maclagan
1924–1928	Malcolm Hailey
1928–1933	Geoferrey Fitzbervey De Montmorency
1933–1938	H. W. Emerson
1938–1941	H. D. Craik
1941–1946	B. J. Glancy
1946–1947	E. M. Jenkins

BIBLIOGRAPHICAL ESSAY

This essay is by no means exhaustive. It is meant to serve as a guide to some of the best material on Sikh history, but the omission of a work is no reflection on its character. What is included is sufficiently representative of historical writing and major categories of source materials on the subject. The essay is divided into five parts. The first four cover the four distinct periods of Sikh history mentioned in the Preface. The last contains a few general observations.

I

After the classic work of Joseph Davey Cunningham, *A History of the Sikhs* (London, 1849), Gokal Chand Narang picked up the threads more than six decades later in his *Transformation of Sikhism* (4th edn, New Delhi, 1956) to be followed by J. C. Archer, *The Sikhs in Relation to Hindus, Moslems, Christians and Ahmadiyas: A Study in Comparative Religion* (Princeton, 1946); Teja Singh and Ganda Singh, *A Short History of the Sikhs* (Bombay, 1950); Indubhusan Banerjee, *Evolution of the Khalsa* (2nd edn, Calcutta, 1962); and Khushwant Singh, *A History of the Sikhs* (Oxford, 1963). More analytical than these general histories is Niharranjan Ray's *The Sikh Gurus and Sikh Society: A Study in Social Analysis* (Patiala, 1970). W. Owen Cole attempts to place the Sikh movement in a broad context in *Sikhism and its Indian Context 1469–1708* (New Delhi, 1984). For ideas and institutions, the trail was blazed by Teja Singh in *Sikhism: Its Ideals and Institutions* (Bombay, 1937), to be followed much later by W. H. McLeod, *The Evolution of the Sikh Community* (Oxford, 1975). A few critical essays on the period by J. S. Grewal, *From Guru Nanak to Maharaja Ranjit Singh* (2nd edn, Amritsar, 1982) provide some new insights.

Besides general histories, a number of scholars have written monographs on the Sikh Gurus, notably on the first and the last, and on Guru Tegh Bahadur: Teja Singh, *Guru Nanak and His Mission* (6th edn, SGPC, 1984); Harbans Singh, *Guru Nanak and Origins of the Sikh Faith* (Bombay, 1969); Gurbachan Singh Talib, *Guru Nanak: His Personality and Vision* (Delhi, 1969); and Surinder Singh Kohli, *Philosophy of Guru Nanak* (Chandigarh, 1969). The most critical in terms of Guru Nanak's biography and the most comprehensive in terms of the exposition of his ideas is W. H. McLeod, *Gurū Nānak and the Sikh Religion* (Oxford, 1968). In J. S. Grewal, *Guru Nanak in History* (2nd edn, Chandigarh, 1979) his mission is sought to be understood in terms of his response to his historical situation. A philosophic interpretation of Guru Gobind Singh's mission was given by Kapur Singh in his *Prashar-prasna Or the Baisakhi of Guru Gobind Singh* (Jullundur, 1959); a critical biography is presented by J. S. Grewal and S. S. Bal, *Guru Gobind Singh* (Chandigarh, 1967); and an interesting narrative by Harbans Singh, *Guru Gobind Singh* (New Delhi, 1979). A biography of Guru Tegh Bahadur was first attempted on an elaborate scale by Trilochan Singh, *Guru Tegh Bahadur: Prophet and Martyr* (Delhi, 1967), to be followed by Fauja Singh and Gurbachan Singh Talib, *Guru Tegh Bahadur: Martyr and Teacher* (Patiala, 1975), and Harbans Singh, *Guru Tegh Bahadur* (Delhi, 1982).

By far the most important source of early Sikh history is the *Ādi Srī Gurū Granth Sāhib Jī* (Sri Damdami Biṛ, various printed editions, standard pagination) which becomes easier to understand with the help of *Sabdārth Srī Guru Granth Sāhib Jī* (text and commentary, 1936–1941). An early English translation was attempted by Ernest Trumpp, *The Adi Granth* (London, 1887) to be replaced by Max Arthur Macauliffe's selected translations in *The Sikh Religion* (Oxford, 1909); a full translation by Gopal Singh, *Sri Guru Granth Sahib* (Delhi, 1962), has run into several editions. Next in importance to the Sikh scriptures is *Vārān Bhai Gurdas*, not yet translated into English. The *janamsākhi* literature has been thoroughly analysed by W. H. McLeod, *Early Sikh Tradition: A Study of the Janam-Sakhis* (Oxford, 1980). One of the earliest works in this genre has been translated into English by McLeod, *The B40 Janam-Sākhī* (Amritsar, 1981). *Srī Dasam Granth Sāhib*, edited by Bishan Singh, provides the major source for Guru Gobind Singh; it is discussed in C. H. Loehlin, *The Granth of Guru Gobind Singh and the Khalsa Brotherhood* (Lucknow, 1971). The extremely valuable letters of Guru Gobind Singh as well as Guru Tegh Bahadur are collected in Fauja Singh, *Hukamnamas of Shri Guru Tegh Bahadur Sahib* (Patiala, 1976) and Ganda Singh, *Hukamnamay* (Patiala, 1967). J. S. Grewal, *Guru Tegh Bahadur and the Persian Chroniclers* (Amritsar, 1976), reveals primarily the uselessness of this evidence on the times of Guru Tegh Bahadur. Senapat's *Sri Gur Sobha* (ed. Shamsher Singh – Amritsar, 1967) is the best evidence on the last decade of Guru Gobind Singh's life. Covering the entire period from Guru Nanak to Guru Gobind Singh, W. H. McLeod has given a good selection of texts in *Textual Sources for the Study of Sikhism* (Manchester, 1984). For a historical analysis of Sikh literature, Surjit Hans, *A Reconstruction of Sikh History from Sikh Literature* (Jalandhar, 1987).

There is some useful information in Persian works like the *Bāburnāma*, the *Akbarnāma*, the *Tuzk-i-Jahāngīrī*, the *Dabistān-i-Mazāhib*, the *Ma'āsir-i-Alamgīrī*, the *Khulāsat-ut-Tawārīkh* and other contemporary works, which have been put together by Ganda Singh, *Mākhiz-i-Tawārīkh Sikhān* (Amritsar, 1949). Much of the contemporary evidence makes better sense in the light of general studies like W. H. Moreland, *The Agrarian System of Moslem India* (2nd edn, Delhi, 1968), and *India at the Death of Akbar* (reprint, Delhi, 1962); Irfan Habib, *The Agrarian System of Mughal India* (Bombay, 1963); Nurul Hasan, *Thoughts on Agrarian Relations in Mughal India* (New Delhi, 1973); Tapan Raychaudhari and Irfan Habib, *Cambridge Economic History of India* (Hyderabad, 1984); Shireen Moosvi, *The Economy of the Mughal Empire* (Oxford, 1987); Ibn Hasan, *The Central Structure of the*

Mughal Empire (reprint, New Delhi, 1970); Ahsan Raza Khan, *Chieftains in the Mughal Empire During the Reign of Akbar* (Simla, 1977); Athar Ali, *The Mughal Nobility Under Aurangzeb* (reprint, Bombay, 1970); Athar Abbas Rizvi, *Muslim Revivalist Movements in Northern India in the Sixteenth and Seventeenth Centuries* (Agra, 1965); Chetan Singh's *Region and Empire: Punjab in the Seventeenth Century*, New Delhi, 1991.

II

Some of the general histories mentioned in the previous section cover partly or wholly the period from Guru Gobind Singh's death to the annexation of the Punjab by the British. N. K. Sinha's *Rise of the Sikh Power* (reprint, Calcutta, 1973), however, relates to the eighteenth century, followed by H. R. Gupta's three volumes of the *History of the Sikhs* (vol. 1 2nd edn Simla 1952 and vols. 2 and 3 Lahore, 1944) before 1947. Recently the ground has been covered more thoroughly by Veena Sachdeva's *Polity and Economy of the Punjab During the Late Eighteenth Century* (New Delhi, 1993). Individual leaders and rulers have been treated in Ganda Singh, *Life of Banda Singh Bahadur* (Amritsar, 1935) and *Ahmad Shah Durrani* (Bombay, 1959); Kirpal Singh, *A Short Life Sketch of Maharaja Ala Singh* (Amritsar, 1953); Henry T. Prinsep, *Life of Maharaja Ranjit Singh* (reprint, Patiala, 1970); N. K. Sinha, *Ranjit Singh* (Calcutta, 1968); Khushwant Singh, *Ranjit Singh: Maharaja of the Punjab* (London, 1962); Waheeduddin, *The Real Ranjit Singh* (4th edn, Karachi, 1965). The army of Maharaja Ranjit Singh and his successors is covered by Fauja Singh, *Military System of the Sikhs* (Delhi, 1964). For the early nineteenth century, Lepel Griffin, *Rajas of the Punjab* (reprint, Patiala, 1970); Gulshan Lal Chopra, *The Punjab As a Sovereign State* (Lahore, 1928); Indu Banga, *Agrarian System of the Sikhs* (New Delhi, 1978); J. S. Grewal, *The Reign of Maharaja Ranjit Singh: Structure of Power, Economy and Society* (Patiala, 1981).

The decade from the death of Ranjit Singh to the annexation of the Punjab is well covered by Sita Ram Kohli, *Sunset of the Sikh Empire* (New Delhi, 1967); Fauja Singh, *After Ranjit Singh* (New Delhi, 1982); Barkat Rai Chopra, *Kingdom of the Punjab, 1839–1845* (Hoshiarpur, 1969); S. S. Bal, *British Policy Towards the Punjab 1844–49* (Calcutta, 1971); N. M. Khilnani, *British Power in the Punjab 1839–1858* (New York, 1972); for the Anglo-Sikh Wars Charles Gough and Arthur D. Inns, *The Sikhs and the Sikh Wars* (reprint, Patiala, 1970). For some other aspects of the period see J. S. Grewal, *The City of the Golden Temple* (Amritsar, 1986); W. G. Archer, *Paintings of the Sikhs* (London, 1966); Sulakhan Singh, 'Udasis Under the Sikh Rule (1750–1850)' (doctoral thesis, Amritsar, 1985); Daljinder Singh Johal, 'Society and Culture As Reflected in Punjabi Literature (1750–1850)' (doctoral thesis, Amritsar, 1985); Indu Banga, 'State Formation Under Sikh Rule' *Journal of Regional History* (1980), and 'The Ruling Class in the Kingdom of Lahore', *ibid.* (1982); B. N. Goswamy, 'The Context of Painting in the Sikh Punjab', *ibid.* (1981); Reeta Grewal, 'Polity, Economy and Urbanization', *ibid.* (1983).

Important among the contemporary Persian works are, Tahmas Beg Khan's *Tahmās Nāmah*; Qazi Nur Muhammad's *Jang Nāmah*; Khushwaqt Rai, *Tawārīkh-i-Sikhān*; Ahmad Shah's *Tarīkh-i-Hind*; Ganash Das's, *Chār-Bagh-i-Panjab*; Sohan Lal Suri's *Umdat-ut-Tawārīkh*. For contemporary Persian documentary evidence and chronicles translated into English, B. N. Goswamy and J. S. Grewal, *The Mughals and the Jogis of Jakhbar* (Simla, 1967) and *The Mughal and the Sikh Rulers and the Vaishnavas of Pindori* (Simla, 1969); J. S. Grewal, *In the By-Lanes of History* (Simla, 1975); V. S. Suri, *Umdat-ut-Tawarikh* (New Delhi, 1961, 1972); J. S. Grewal and Indu Banga, *Early Nineteenth-Century Punjab* (Amritsar, 1975); H. L. O. Garrett and G. L. Chopra, *Events at the Court of Ranjit Singh 1810–1817* (reprint, Patiala, 1970); J. S. Grewal and Indu Banga, *The Civil and Military Affairs of Maharaja Ranjit Singh* (Amritsar, 1987). For information on the voluminous records of the government of Ranjit Singh and his successors now lodged in Maharaja Ranjit Singh Museum and Archives at Amritsar see Sita Ram Kohli, *Catalogue of Khalsa Darbar Records* (Lahore, 1919, 1927). There are some useful documents in J. Ph. Vogel, *Catalogue of Bhuri Singh Museum at Chamba* (Calcutta, 1909). For contemporary works in Punjabi see Kesar Singh Chhibber, *Bansāwalīnāmah* (Chandigarh, 1972); Sarup Das Bhalla, *Mahima Parkāsh* (Patiala, 1971); Ratan Singh Bhangu, *Prachīn Panth Parkāsh* (5th edn, Amritsar, 1972); Shah Muhamnmad, *Vār* (Ludhiana, 1972); Ram Sukh Rao, *Fateh Singh Partāp Parbhākar* (Patiala, 1980).

Some numismatic evidence and travel literature is available in C. J. Rodgers, 'On the Coins of the Sikhs', *Journal of the Asiatic Society of Benegal, vol. 1* (1881); Ganda Singh, *Early European Accounts of the Sikhs* (reprint, Calcutta, 1962); W. Moorcraft and G. Frebeck, *Travels in the Himalayan Provinces of Hindostan and the Punjab, in Ladak and Kashmir in Peshawar, Kabul and Kunduz and Bokhara from 1819 to 1825* (London, 1837); H. L. O. Garrett, *The Punjab a Hundred Years Ago, as Described by V. Jacquemont and A. Soltykoff* (reprint, Patiala, 1971); G. T. Vigne, *A Personal Narrative of a Visit to Ghazni, Cabul and Afghanistan and of a Residence at the Court of Dost Muhammad With Notices of Ranjit Singh, Khiva and Russian Expedition* (London, 1840); Baron Charles Hugel, *Travels in Cashmere and the Punjab* (London, 1845); W. G. Osborne, *The Court and Camp of Ranjeet Singh* (London, 1840); Alexander Burnes, *Travels in Bukhara* (London, 1834); Major Hugh Pearse, *Memories of Alexander Gardner Colonel of Artillery in the Service of Maharaja Ranjit Singh* (reprint, Patiala, 1970) and Sir Lepel Griffin, *The Punjab Chiefs: Historical and Biographical Notices of the Principal Families in the Lahore* (Lahore, 1865).

For some general developments during the period see Sir Jadu Nath Sarkar, *Fall of the Mughal Empire* in four volumes (Calcutta, 1932); Satish Chandra, *Parties and Politics at the Mughal Court (1707–1740)* (2nd edn, New Delhi, 1972), Zahir-ud-Din Malik, *The Reign of Muhammad Shah* (Bombay, 1977); Noman Ahmad Siddiqi, *Land Revenue Under the Mughals (1700–1750)* (Bombay, 1970); J. Hutchison and J. Ph. Vogel, *History of the Punjab Hill States* in two volumes (Lahore, 1933).

III

General histories by Khushwant Singh, Gopal Singh and Sangab Singh cover the period of colonial rule. There are several good monographs which add detail and depth, like Dolores Domin, *India: A Study in the Role of the Sikhs in 1857-59* (Berlin, 1977); John C. B. Webster, *The Nirankari Sikhs* (Delhi, 1979); Fauja Singh, *Kuka Movement: An Important Phase in Punjab's Role in India's Struggle for Freedom* (Delhi, 1965); Richard Fox, *Lions of the Punjab: Culture in the Making* (Berkeley, 1985); Mohinder Singh, *The Akali Movement* (Delhi, 1978); Sukhmani Bal, *Politics of the Central Sikh League* (New Delhi, 1991). Kailash Chander Gulati, *The Akalis: Past and Present* (New Delhi, 1974); K. L. Tuteja, *Sikh Politics (1920-1940)* (Kurukshetra, 1984); Ethne K. Marenco, *The Transformation of Sikh Society* (New Delhi, 1976); Tom G. Kessinger, *Vilyatpur 1848-1968: A Study of Social and Economic Change in a North Indian Village* (California, 1974). There are a few biographical studies like Durlab Singh, *The Valiant Fighter: A Biographical Study of Master Tara Singh* (Lahore, nd) and *Sikh Leadership* (Delhi, 1950); G. S. Deol, *Shahid Ajit Singh* (Patiala, 1973) and *Shahid Bhagat Singh* (Patiala, 1973); K. K. Khullar, *Shaheed Bhagat Singh* (New Delhi 1981); Gurcharan Singh, *Jiwani Sardar Sewa Singh Thikriwala* (2nd edn, Patiala 1974).

Quite a few studies, though not directly on Sikh history, have a close bearing on the subject, like Harish K. Puri, *Ghadar Movement: Ideology, Organization and Strategy* (Amritsar, 1983); Hugh Johnston, *The Voyage of the Komagata Maru* (Delhi, 1979); Ramesh Walia, *Praja Mandal Movement in East Punjab States* (Patiala, 1972); Kamlesh Mohan, *Militant Nationalism in the Punjab 1919-1935* (New Delhi, 1985); P. R. Uprety, *Religion and Politics in Punjab in the 1920s* (New Delhi, 1980); Bhagwan Josh, *Communist Movement in Punjab (1926-47)* (Delhi, 1979).

There are several works on the history of the Punjab which remain relevant for an understanding of Sikh history: P. H. M. van den Dungen, *The Punjab Tradition* (London, 1972); Norman Gerald Barrier, *Punjab History in Printed British Documents* (Missouri, 1969); N. Gerald Barrier and Paul Wallace, *The Punjab Press, 1880-1905* (Michigan, 1970); Himadri Banerjee, *Agrarian Society of the Punjab (1849-1901)* (New Delhi, 1982); Sukhwant Singh, 'Agricultural Development in the Punjab 1849-1947' (M.Phil. dissertation, Amritsar, 1980); Sukhdev Singh Sohal, 'The Middle Classes in The Punjab (1849-1947)' (doctoral thesis, Amritsar, 1987); Harish C. Sharma, *Artisans of the Punjab* (New Delhi, 1996). Sri Ram Sharma, *Punjab in Ferment* (Delhi, 1971); Kenneth W. Jones, *Arya Dharm: Hindu Consciousness in 19th Century Punjab* (London, 1976); Spencer Lavan, *The Ahmadiyah Movement: A History and Perspective* (New Delhi, 1974); Emmett Davis, *Press and Politics in British Western Punjab 1836-1947* (Delhi, 1983); Satya M. Rai, *Legislative Politics and the Freedom Struggle in the Punjab 1897-1947* (Delhi, 1984); Kirpal C. Yadav, *Elections in Punjab 1920-1947* (New Delhi, 1987).

The Jallianwala Bagh happenings are well covered in V. N. Datta, *Jallian-*

wala Bagh (Ludhiana, 1969); Raja Ram, *The Jallianwala Bagh Massacre: A Premeditated Plan* (2nd edn, Chandigarh, 1978); Alfred Draper, *Amritsar: The Massacre that Ended the Raj* (Delhi, 1981). On the partition, Penderal Moon, *Divide and Quit* (London, 1961); Kirpal Singh, *The Partition of the Punjab* (Patiala, 1972); Satya M. Rai, *Partition of the Punjab* (Bombay, 1965). There is a useful biographical study, *Fazl-i-Husain: A Political Biography* (Bombay, 1946), by Azim Husain.

The works of contemporary British administrators have their own merit in spite of their limitations: James Douie, *The Punjab, North Western Province and Kashmir* (Cambridge, 1916); S. S. Thorburn, *Musalmans and the Money-Lenders in the Punjab* (reprint, Delhi, 1983); S. S. Thorburn, *The Punjab in Peace and War* (reprint, Patiala 1970); H. K. Trevaskis, *Punjab of Today: An Economic Survey of the Punjab in Recent Years 1890–1925* in two volumes (Lahore, 1931) and *The Land of the Five Rivers: An Economic History of the Punjab from the Earliest Times to the Year of Grace 1890* (Oxford, 1926); H. Calvert, *The Wealth and Welfare of the Punjab: Being Some Studies in Punjab Rural Economics* (Lahore, 1922); Malcolm Lyall Darling, *The Punjab Peasant in Prosperity and Debt* (London, 1928).

There are some works on Indian history which provide a useful context for the Punjab and for Sikh history: Percival Spear, *India: A Modern History* (Michigan, 1972); A. R. Desai, *Social Background of Indian Nationalism* (Bombay, 1954); Sumit Sarkar, *Modern India 1885–1947* (Delhi, 1983); K. M. L. Saxena, *The Military System of India* (New Delhi, 1974); G. Macmunn, *The Armies of India* (reprint, Delhi, 1980); John C. B. Webster, *The Christian Community and Change in Nineteenth Century North India* (Delhi, 1976); J. N. Farquhar, *Modern Religious Movements in India* (London, 1924); Peter Hardy, *The Muslims of British India* (Cambridge, 1972); Ayesha Jalal, *The Sole Spokesman Jinnah: The Muslim League and the Demand for Pakistan* (Cambridge, 1985); V. P. Menon, *Transfer of Power in India* (reprint, New Delhi, 1979).

Some easily available contemporary evidence on Sikh history during this period is in Attar Singh, *Sakhee Book* (Benaras, 1873); Ganda Singh, *Kukiyān dī Vithya* (Amritsar, 1944 for the letters of Baba Ram Singh); N. Gerald Berrier, *The Sikhs and Their Literature* (Delhi, 1970); Bhagat Lakshman Singh, *An Autobiography* (Calcutta, 1965); *Some Confidential Papers on the Akali Movement* (SGPC, 1965), edited by Ganda Singh; Ruchi Ram Sahni, *Struggle for Freedom of Sikh Shrines* (SGPC, nd); G. R. Sethi, *Sikh Struggle for Gurdwara Reform* (Amritsar, 1927); Bhagat Singh, *Why I am an Atheist* (Delhi, 1979); J. S. Grewal and H. K. Puri, *Letters of Udham Singh* (Amritsar, 1974); Swarup Singh, *The Sikhs Demand Their Home Land* (London, 1946); Gurbachan Singh and L. S. Giani, *The Idea of the Sikh State* (Lahore, 1946); Sadhu Singh Hamdard, *Azad Punjab* (Amritsar, 1943).

Apart from gazetteers, reports and other government publications there is published official evidence having a direct bearing on Sikh history in *Gooroo Ram Singh and the Kuka Sikhs* (New Delhi, 1965) edited by Nahar Singh; *Maharaja Duleep Singh Correspondence* (Patiala, 1977) edited by Ganda

Singh; David Petrie's report of 1911, *Developments in Sikh Politics* (Amritsar, 1911); Confidential memorandum on the Akali Dal and the Shiromani Gurdwara Prabandhak Committee, 1921–22 (*The Punjab Past and Present 1967*, 252–311); John Maynard 'The Sikh Problem in the Punjab, 1920–23' (*The Punjab Past and Present 1977*, 129–141). There is some important contemporary evidence, though not exclusively on Sikh history, in Lepel Griffin and C. F. Massy, *Chiefs and Families of Note in the Punjab* (Lahore, 1891, 1909 and 1940); N. Gerald Barrier, *The Punjab in Nineteenth Century Tracts* (East Lansing, 1969) and *Banned Controversial Literature and Political Control in British India* (New Delhi, 1976); Larry Collins and Dominique Lapierre, *Mountbatten and the Partition of India March 22 – August 15, 1947* (Delhi, 1982).

There are some useful articles on the different aspects of Punjab and Sikh history during this period: Reeta Grewal 'The Pattern of Urbanization in the Punjab Under Colonial Rule', *Journal of Regional History* (1984) 69–81; J. S. Grewal, 'Business Communities of the Punjab', (*ibid.* 1984); Richard Fox, 'Urban Class and Communal Consciousness in Colonial Punjab: The Genesis of India's Intermediate Regime', *Modern Asian Studies* (1984), 459–89; Paul Wallace, 'Communalism, Factionalism and National Integration in the Pre-Independence Punjab', *Punjab Past and Present* (1975), 389–405; Ian J. Kerr, 'The British and the Administration of the Golden Temple in 1859', *Punjab Past and Present* (1976), 306–21; W. H. McLeod, 'The Kukas: A Millenarian Sect of the Punjab', *The Panjab Past and Present* (1979), 164–87; J. S. Grewal, 'The Emergence of the Punjabi Drama: A Cultural Response to Colonial Rule', *Journal of Regional History* (1984), 115–55; Fauja Singh, 'Akalis and the Indian National Congress (1920–1947)', *The Panjab Past and Present* (1981), 453–70; Barbara N. Ramusack, 'Punjab States: Maharajas and Gurdwaras: Patiala and the Sikh Community' (Oxford, 1978), 170–204; Harjot Singh Oberoi, 'From Gurdwara Rakabganj to the Viceregal Palace – A Study of Religious Protest', *The Panjab Past and Present* (1980), 182–98; Harbans Singh and N. Gerald Barreir, *Punjab Past and Present: Essays in Honour of Dr Ganda Singh* (Patiala, 1976).

IV

Satya M. Rai's *Partition of the Punjab* (Bombay, 1965) actually covers the history of the Indian Punjab up to 1956. Stephen L. Keller discusses the role of refugees in the development of the Punjab in his *Uprooting and Social Change* (Delhi, 1975). On the green revolution there are two books: Partap C. Aggarwal, *The Green Revolution and Rural Labour* (New Delhi, 1973) and M. S. Randhawa, *Green Revolution* (Ludhiana, 1974). In the *Political Dynamics of Punjab* (Amritsar, 1981), edited by Paul Wallace and Surendra Chopra, there are some good articles on the post-independence politics of the Punjab.

Baldev Raj Nayyar has studied Sikh politics before the creation of the Punjabi-speaking state in his *Minority Politics in the Punjab* (Princeton, 1966). Ajit Singh Sarhadi traces the background as well as the creation of the

Punjabi-speaking state in his *Punjabi Suba* (Delhi, 1970). Sikh politics in relation to language and religion finds good coverage in Paul Brass, *Language, Religion and Politics in North India* (London, 1974). The political system of the Sikh Jats is studied by Joyce Pettigrew in her *Robber Noblemen* (Boston, 1975). Pandit Mohan Lal's *Disintegration of Punjab* (Chandigarh, 1984) contains detailed information on the Politics of the Punjab, particularly during the 1960s. M. S. Dhami's *Minority Leaders Image of the Indian Political System* (New Delhi, 1975) is based on interviews with important Akali leaders. Some useful information is given by Gur Rattan Pal Singh in *The Illustrated History of the Sikhs (1947–78)* (Chandigarh, 1979). A. S. Narang discusses Akali politics after 1947 in his *Storm Over the Sutlej* (Delhi, 1983). The history of the SGPC after independence too is given by Gobinder Singh, *Religion and Politics in the Punjab* (New Delhi, 1986).

A considerable number of monographs and articles have been written on the crisis of the 1980s, particularly after Operation Bluestar: Parmod Kumar, Manmohan Sharma, Atul Sood and Ashwani Handa, *Punjab Crisis: Context and Trends* (Chandigarh, 1984); V. D. Chopra, R. K. Mishra and Nirmal Singh, *Agony of Punjab* (New Delhi, 1984); Kuldip Nayyar and Khushwant Singh, *Tragedy of Punjab: Operation Bluestar and After* (New Delhi, 1984); Chand Joshi, *Bhindranwale: Myth and Reality* (New Delhi, 1984); Mark Tully and Satish Jacob, *Amritsar: Mrs Gandhi's Last Battle* (London, 1985); Abida Samiuddin, *The Punjab Crisis: Challenge and Response* (Delhi, 1985). Satya M. Rai has extended her earlier work to the 1980s in *Punjab Since Partition* (Delhi, 1986). Rajiv A. Kapur's *Sikh Separatism: The Politics of Faith* (London, 1986) too, brings the narrative to the 1980s. *The Punjab in Prosperity and Violence*. Ed. J. S. Grewal and Indu Banga (New Delhi, 1998). There is useful information in Anup Chand Kapur, *The Punjab Crisis: An Analytical Study* (New Delhi, 1985), though the title hardly fulfils its promise.

v

There are some useful bibliographies: Ganda Singh, *A Bibliography of the Punjab* (Patiala, 1966); Ikram Ali Malik, *A Bibliography of the Punjab and its Dependencies (1849–1910)* (Lahore, 1968); W. Eric Gustafsan and Kenneth W. Jones, *Sources on Punjab History* (New Delhi, 1975). Useful for biographical references are: Fauja Singh's *Eminent Freedom Fighters of Punjab* (Patiala, 1972) and *Who is Who: Punjab Freedom Fighters* (Patiala, 1972); Jagdish Saran Sharma, *The National Biographical Dictionary of India* (Delhi, 1972); S. P. Sen, *Dictionary of National Biography*, four volumes (Calcutta, 1974). Equally useful for reference are: H. A. Rose, *A Glossary of the Tribes and Castes of the Punjab and North-West Frontier Province* (reprint, Patiala, 1970); H. H. Wilson, *A Glossary of Judicial and Revenue Terms*, (Delhi, 1968); B. H. Baden-Powell, *Handbook of the Economic Products of the Punjab, with a Combined Index and Glossary of Technical Vernacular Words* (Lahore, 1869 and 1872).

Articles on Sikh history appear from time to time in the *Proceedings of the Indian History Congress, Indian Economic and Social History Review, Modern Asian Studies, Journal of Asian Studies* and *Journal of the Asiatic Society of Bengal*. More important though recent, however, for articles on the Punjab and Sikh history are the *Proceedings of the Punjab History Conference* (Patiala), the *Journal of Regional History* (Amritsar), the *Punjab Journal of Politics* (Amritsar) and the *PSE Economic Analyst* (Amritsar). The most important periodical, particularly for the reprints of old and new articles, is *The Panjab Past and Present* (Patiala).

P.S.

The past decade was marked by controversies in Sikh studies, involving all major themes of the Sikh tradition. This protracted debate has been analyzed in J. S. Grewal, *Historical Perspectives on Sikh Identity* (Patiala, 1997) and in J. S. Grewal, *Contesting Interpretations of the Sikh Tradition* (New Delhi, 1998). Notable among the works which figure in these analyses are the recent publications of W. H. McLeod as well as his earlier works. With these stand bracketed the works of Piar Singh, Harjot Oberoi, Pashaura Singh and Gurinder Singh Mann. On the other side of the debate are mainly the works of Daljeet Singh, Jagjit Singh and G. S. Dhillon. There are other contestants, too numerous to be listed here.

INDEX

INDEX

INDEX

THE NEW CAMBRIDGE HISTORY OF INDIA

I The Mughals and Their Contemporaries

*M. N. PEARSON, *The Portuguese in India*
*BURTON STEIN, *Vijayanagara*
*MILO CLEVELAND BEACH, *Mughal and Rajput painting*
*CATHERINE ASHER, *Architecture of Mughal India*
†*JOHN F. RICHARDS, *The Mughal Empire*
*GEORGE MICHELL, *Architecture and art of Southern India*
RICHARD M. EATON, *Social history of the Deccan*
BRUCE R. LAWRENCE, *Indian Sufism and the Islamic world*
GEORGE MICHELL and MARK ZEBROWSKI, *Architecture and art of the Deccan Sultanates*

II Indian States and the Transition to Colonialism

†*C. A. BAYLY, *Indian society and the making of the British Empire*
*P. J. MARSHALL, *Bengal: the British bridgehead: eastern India 1740–1828*
†*J. S. GREWAL, *The Sikhs of the Punjab: revised edition*
*STEWART GORDON, *The Marathas 1600–1818*
*OM PRAKASH, *European Commercial Enterprise in Pre-Colonial India*
RICHARD B. BARNETT, *Muslim successor states*
DAVID WASHBROOK, *South India*

III The Indian Empire and the Beginnings of Modern Society

*KENNETH W. JONES, *Social and religious reform movements in British India*
*SUGATA BOSE, *Peasant labour and colonial capital: rural Bengal since 1770*
†*B. R. TOMLINSON, *The economy of modern India, 1860–1970*
†*THOMAS R. METCALF, *Ideologies of the Raj*
DAVID ARNOLD, *Science, technology and medicine, c. 1750–1947*
GORDON JOHNSON, *Government and politics in India*
DAVID LUDDEN, *Agriculture in Indian history*
B. N. RAMUSACK, *The Indian princes and their states*

IV The Evolution of Contemporary South Asia

†*PAUL R. BRASS, *The politics of India since Independence: second edition*
*GERALDINE FORBES, *Women in modern India*
*SUSAN BAYLY, *Caste, Society and politics in India from the eighteenth century to the modern age*
RAJNARAYAN CHANDAVARKAR, *The urban working classes*
NITA KUMAR, *Education and the rise of a new intelligentsia*
FRANCIS ROBINSON, *Islam in South Asia*
ANIL SEAL, *The transfer of power and the partition of India*

* Already published

CPSIA information can be obtained
at www.ICGtesting.com
Printed in the USA
LVOW10s2251010817

543429LV00002B/171/P